THE
UNIVERSITY
OF
COLORADO

1876–1976

THE
UNIVERSITY
OF
COLORADO

1876–1976

A Centennial Publication
of the University of Colorado

by

FREDERICK S. ALLEN   MARK S. FOSTER
ERNEST ANDRADE, JR.   PHILIP I. MITTERLING
H. LEE SCAMEHORN

HARCOURT BRACE JOVANOVICH, INC.
New York and London

Printed in the United States of America

Library of Congress Cataloging in Publication Data
Main entry under title:

The University of Colorado, 1876–1976.

Includes bibliographical references and index.
1. Colorado. University—History. I. Allen,
Frederick S.
LD1178.U54   378.788'63   76-20623
ISBN 0-15-193000-7

First edition
B C D E

for Louise McAllister
secretary to seven presidents of the University

semper parata et semper fidelis

CONTENTS

Preface
page ix

Prologue: The Promise of the State University
page 3

I   In the Beginning: 1870's to 1890's
page 14

II   Organizing a University: 1892–1919
page 52

III   Building a University: 1919–1939
page 83

IV   Change, Consolidation, and Conflict: 1939–1953
page 117

V   The Pursuit of Excellence: 1953–1963
page 166

vii

CONTENTS

VI   Developing a Multi-Campus University: 1960's to 1970's
page 205

Epilogue: The Future of a State University
page 257

Appendix One: Lectures on Research and Creative Work
page 263

Appendix Two: Chairmen of the Faculty Council
page 265

Notes to the Text
page 266

PREFACE

THE UNIVERSITY OF COLORADO today has a rather special character. Considering the roles of most state universities, this University is a cosmopolitan institution. The students and faculty come from all over the world. Its links with business and government span the nation. Its visibility in academic circles is clear and distinct. Reflecting on the origins of the University, its current stature is a considerable triumph. Starting in the 1870s on one of the country's last frontiers—amid the beauty of the Rocky Mountains—after many years of sporadic development, the University achieved national recognition in the 1960s. Until the 1920s, the University was constrained by the rustic conditions of frontier life and the isolation of the state from the mainstream of American society. These conditions, however, were rapidly changing in the 1940s. World War II stimulated economic development, brought many to Colorado for military training, and made airplane travel more common. The Denver metropolitan region was attractive to the federal government and major industries for offices and plants as well as to professional individuals. And the University was equally attractive to students and faculty outside of the state. The result is the existence, in the 1970s, of a University which serves the state and the nation.

This book is about the evolution and the shaping of the University of Colorado since its founding in 1876. A complex organization, a university engages many people in diverse activities, and over a century one institution can record several kinds of chronicles. A university's history thus depends on the perspective or interest of the historian. This history is essentially a study of the University as a whole with only periodic commentaries on certain of its activities or special concerns when these illuminate major developments. The purpose here, in addition to presenting an accurate record of events, is to analyze and interpret the succession of factors and decisions which have given the University its special character. To do this it has been necessary to take some account of both state and national history. Economic conditions, climates of political and social opinion, and trends in education undoubtedly set the course for the development of universities. But at each institution, local circumstances, individuals on the faculty or in the administration, and the interest of students in residence are fundamentally responsible for the histories of universities. So this history aims to understand the growth of the University of Colorado as an institution with a focus on its internal affairs but with some attention to its external relations.

Among annalists of institutions of higher education there is little agreement on the most expeditious way to organize the history of a university. Epochs, or major periods, in a particular history often lack distinct beginnings or clear terminal points. Themes and long-term trends have habits of submerging only to surface much later without ways for easy commentary or analysis. The selection of successive administrations of an institution does break up, sometimes arbitrarily, periods or trends, but such an organization can provide manageable units for comprehension as well as a useful perspective on the institution as a whole. Fortunately, a particular university's chronicle can provide a key to its own scheme for periodization. For the University of Colorado, a history organized by individual administrations, the Norlin years, or by combinations, the Sewall-Hale years, seems to fit the critical periods in the evolution of the University and to allow for a connected discussion of themes and trends.

There is always a problem in historical research with the availability of records, whether the subject is a nation, an institution, or an individual. The University of Colorado is no exception. Unfortunately, for the early periods, before the 1920s, the range of sources is narrow and those sources remaining are slim indeed. The minutes of a meeting of the Board of Regents in the 1880s appear in a single paragraph, written by hand, in a ledger. Two books, one by William E. Davis, *Glory Colorado! A History of the University of Colorado, 1858–1963* (1965), and the other by Michael McGiffert, *The Higher Learning in Colorado. An Historical Study, 1860–1940* (1964), are compendiums of information and provide useful bibliographical guides. But neither makes up for the shortage of University documents, individual letters or diaries, or public documents dealing with the early years of the University. However, for the more recent periods, the University Archives, various University office files, state documents, and newspaper files contain simply too much material to work over intelligently in a practical time span. Minutes of a Regents' meeting in the 1970s, with appendices, run to over one hundred printed pages. To cope with this problem, a number of individuals, including faculty and former presidents, were interviewed to assist in the selection of important topics and to gain their insight on events and developments. One such interview took place in New York City with former President Quigg Newton and several of his contemporaries in the administration. Further assistance for the most recent period came from the monograph, *The University of Colorado 1963–1973: A Review*, prepared by Professors Houston, Rainey, and Wilson for the Regents and the chronicle on University events prepared for the Associated Alumni Board by Edwin Banks.

The research and writing of a university history is a mammoth undertaking, one perhaps too time-consuming or too full of analytical pitfalls for a single author with less than two years of full-time responsibility for the project. The necessities of time and scholarship pressed for a collaborative venture for this book. In every sense, this book is the team effort of five authors, all historians with the University. As all were committed with regular responsibilities for teaching, administration, or scholarship and several with extra loads (such as the presidency of the local chapter of the American Association of University Professors), the early decision to share the work was fundamental to its completion. Particular responsibilities were as follows: Andrade, Chapters One and Two; Foster, Chapters Two and Three; Mitterling,

Chapter Four; Scamehorn, Chapter Five; and Allen, Prologue, Chapter Six, and Epilogue. In addition, Scamehorn made the selection of illustrations, Mitterling compiled the Index, and Allen served as editor.

The obligations incurred during sixteen months of work were numerous and extensive. For all who in one way or another helped this project along the way there is much appreciation and gratitude. Special mention, however, must go to the Executive Committee of the Centennial Commission of the University of Colorado, especially Geraldine Bean, H. H. Arnold, and Eugene H. Wilson, for their encouragement and support: to William Jovanovich, alumnus and publisher; and to the following individuals: Ruth Kinney, Erika Goedecke, Virginia Nelson, Lillian Pohorilak, Patricia Orton, Mark Meredith, Dorothy Greeno, John Brennan, Cassandra Tiberio, Doris Mitterling, Dorothy Greenman, Alvetta Knittel, Lucille Cliff, Mary Lou Eppelheimer, and Evelyn Eller.

The authors could not have written this book without this considerable assistance. In addition, the current administration of the University allowed for complete freedom of access to information and the formulation of judgments. But the responsibility for the presentation of information and the analysis of events and individuals remains solely with the authors.

Boulder
April 1976

FREDERICK S. ALLEN
ERNEST ANDRADE, JR.
MARK S. FOSTER
PHILIP I. MITTERLING
H. LEE SCAMEHORN

THE
UNIVERSITY
OF
COLORADO

1876–1976

THE PROMISE
OF THE
STATE UNIVERSITY

A REMARKABLE FEATURE of American higher education is its organizational variety. Across the country today one finds an array of private and public institutions—colleges and universities that vary considerably in size, educational philosophy, and academic standards. The long-standing unwillingness of the federal government to coordinate higher education, stemming from President Washington's failure to convince Congress to establish a national university, is partly responsible for this variety. Another explanation lies in the multitudinous reasons for founding colleges or universities, reasons which include goals that transcend education. This variety also results from changes imposed on institutions over time by the hard choices dictated by faltering income or shifts in sources of funding.

The evolution of the American college has passed through several stages. Nine colonial colleges, before 1770, provided for an educated ministry and a political and social elite. In 1770 the total living alumni of these colleges numbered about 3,000. Over the next century the new nation enthusiastically spawned more than 500 colleges, a number larger than in all of Europe. (Today only 182 of these survive.) This phenomenon not only reflected

3

the economic development and capacity of the country; it was also the consequence of the missionary zeal of various Protestant sects, as well as Catholics, to put at least one college of their own in each new state. And many frontier communities, sensitive to the impact on local business by the founding of a college, were as eager to build as the churches. The purpose of these new colleges was not very different from the colonial college except that a college education was seen by some as preparation for medical and legal training. Enrollments by 1870 topped 50,000.

After 1870 the university emerged in place of or alongside of the college. The university dedicated itself to reason rather than religion, engaged in research as well as education, and was a federation of various colleges or schools with different academic programs. The rise of the university paralleled the broadening of the purpose of higher education. In addition to training for the established professions, students now pursued a degree to assure themselves of opportunity in an America whose economy was becoming more industrial and urban. By 1970 there were over 2,500 colleges and universities and enrollments exceeded 7 million.[1] Of course, since colonial times, a perennial reason for parents to advocate higher education for their sons, if not their daughters, was to place their progeny in homes away from home where discipline might guide the stormy passage through adolescence to adulthood. Then, too, concern for the social status of a degree has always been a factor in college attendance.

Generally regarded as high points in the evolution of the college were the founding of five institutions: Harvard (1636), Virginia (1819), Cornell (1865), Johns Hopkins (1876), and Chicago (1890). Higher education in America began with Harvard. Puritan settlers in Massachusetts, graduates of Cambridge and Oxford in England, determined to build a new society, wanted a college to prepare both a learned clergy and lettered politicians. John Harvard, a young clergyman who died shortly after his arrival in Massachusetts, the first benefactor of this college with the legacy of his estate and books, earned lasting recognition of his name. Failing to broaden the classical curriculum of ancient languages at William and Mary, Thomas Jefferson promoted the University of Virginia to teach modern languages, mathematics, science, and applied subjects in commerce, manufacturing, and diplomacy. As the state legislature fell behind in its support, Jefferson's plan was not fulfilled in Virginia in the 1820s, but at Cornell in the 1870s. Cornell, founded as an institution where "any person can find instruction in any study,"[2] was the joint enterprise of Andrew White, a scientist and Cornell's first president, and Ezra Cornell, a major organizer and stockholder in Western Union. Perhaps the most ambitious foundation was that planned by the trustees of the estate of Johns Hopkins, an enterprising wholesale grocer of Baltimore and later a prime figure in the founding of the Baltimore and Ohio Railroad. Prodded by President James Angell of the University of Michigan, they determined to build a university for advanced studies, on the model of the University of Berlin, dedicated to research, human betterment, and material progress. Certainly the most rapid organization of a university occurred in Chicago in the 1890s as the American Baptist Education Society secured the eventual investment of $35 million by John D. Rockefeller and the leadership and management of its first president, William Rainey Harper, who left his professorship at Yale and went to Chicago to organize a model American university. The University of Chicago began to give instruction all year long, categorized study in the college into lower and upper, or advanced, divisions, and established a full array of professional schools. Harper emphasized that at Chicago ". . . the work of investigation was primary, the work of giving instruction secondary."[3]

The university had its origins in medieval Europe. It emerged in the twelfth century in Salerno, Bologna, and Paris. By the seventeenth century there were highly renowned universities in Italy, France, England, and Germany. These institutions enrolled only a few hundred students each. The curriculum, the academic organization, and the living modes, as they evolved over five hundred years, reflected the moral and intellectual preeminence of Christianity in medieval society. The curriculum was dominated by theology rather than law, medicine, or the arts. The titles of academic officers—chancellor, rector, warden, dean—were borrowed from the lay or monastic church hierarchy. Professors were called doctor, a Latin word used by the church, meaning "teacher." Faculties were organized either by schools (Theology at Paris), or by bequests (Trinity College at Cambridge). Students might live in town or on university property. University architecture, the prominence of the chapel, the commons for eating, the proximity of the library to the dormitories (particularly in England), resembled the typical cloister of the monastery. The universities served society by educating priests and officials for the church, lawyers and civil servants for the state, and medical doctors. During the Renaissance the aristocracy began sending their sons to the university to study the arts, primarily for cultural and social reasons—a development which added a certain prestige to the arts faculty. The arts curriculum, frequently called "the seven liberal arts," was essentially a study of language, speech, music, and mathematics; it varied in detail, but not in substance, from country to country and from generation to generation.

The arts curriculum developed at Cambridge and Oxford was the major influence on higher education in colonial America, and this influence persisted into the nineteenth century. The subjects studied in the colonial college were Latin, Greek, Hebrew, logic, rhetoric, mathematics, natural philosophy (science), and moral philosophy (ethics). Students registered for all these courses as they advanced toward a degree. Though concentrating on language and mathematics, the course of study also emphasized moral philosophy. This curriculum, which came to be called the "classical curriculum," received its most rigorous defense in a report by the Yale faculty in 1828. Selected passages reveal the key arguments, and distinguish between education and training:

> The two great points to be gained in intellectual culture are the discipline and the furniture of the mind, expanding its powers and storing it with knowledge. . . . Our prescribed course contains those subjects only which ought to be understood by everyone who aims at a thorough education. . . . The young merchant must be trained in the counting room, the mechanic in the workshop, the farmer in the field. . . ."[4]

These arguments, of course, were and remain sound justifications for higher education in general, but critics emerging in the 1820s wanted more modern and more practical subjects in the curriculum.

A reform movement associated with interest in science and engineering made progress in universities in Scotland, France, and Germany after 1780. The École Polytechnique, established in Paris in 1793, offered instruction in modern languages, chemistry, and civil engineering. It provided a model for the founding of the United States Military Academy, in West Point, in 1802. More significant, perhaps, was the opening of the University of Berlin in 1809. The curriculum evolving there bypassed the ancient languages and promoted science in all its existing branches. Furthermore, the faculty at Berlin was encouraged to work at advancing knowledge; research swiftly became the hallmark of German universities. Many Americans completed their advanced studies in Germany in the three decades before 1860 and brought home ideas about curriculum reform. In 1850, Francis Wayland, the president of Brown, presented a report to his corporation in which he spoke bluntly about the triviality of the classical curriculum. "What could Virgil and Horace and Homer and Demosthenes, with a little mathematics and natural philosophy, do towards developing the untold resources of this continent?" Wayland lamented.[5] He wanted Brown to offer new programs of courses in applied science, agriculture, law, and teaching. Though Wayland had little success in changing the curriculum at Brown, the country at large soon realized the importance of his attempt.

The exigencies of American life have continually shaped the development of its colleges and universities. The coordinate pressures of utility or pragmatism and the spirit of democracy have transformed the European models and have made discernibly American institutions. The necessity of taming a wilderness in colonial times and the challenge of developing resources early in the nineteenth century first promoted criticism of the classical curriculum and then ultimately made possible the acceptance of practical or applied studies. Benjamin Franklin's interest in experimental science helped place the study of science in the curriculum developed at the University of Pennsylvania after its founding in 1756. Stephen van Rensselaer's founding of the Polytechnic Institute in 1824 recognized the nation's need to instruct ". . . the sons and daughters of farmers and mechanics . . . in the application of experimental chemistry, philosophy, and natural history, to agriculture, domestic economy, the arts, and manufacture."[6] Even Yale and Harvard organized separate science schools, in the 1840s, in response to demands for practical studies. And more than thirty other institutions initiated or expanded science programs before 1870.

In the 1820s, America was moving toward both a more democratic process of government and a more open society. The promise of opportunity in a new country demanded not only economic but also political and legal freedom as well. The basis of the attack on privilege that is associated with the election of Andrew Jackson to the presidency, in 1828, was a profound belief in individual equality. Many social and political institutions had to confront and to resolve this belief over the following generations. Meanwhile the classical sectarian college became a major target for reform. Proponents of the democratic ideology sought to make colleges available to talent and ambition, to free them from control by class or tradition, and thus began to undercut the European elitist rationale for higher education. Where colleges could not be changed, new ones were organized.

Yet, even if access to higher education was philosophically open by the 1870s, other factors restricted attendance. Scholarship funds were small. Many colleges were distant from population centers. Furthermore the colleges were not perceived by prospective students as particularly helpful in preparing for careers other than the established professions. Also, colleges remained dependent on the organization of secondary schools, and the country did not really undertake to build high schools before the last decade of the century. An important legacy of building colleges before high schools were preparing students was to leave in doubt for our own day the precise educational roles of high schools and colleges.

One of the noteworthy features of American higher education is the opportunity that it has provided for women. Inspired by the climate for democracy, seminaries or high schools, for women, appeared in Troy, New York (1821), Hartford, Connecticut (1828), and South Hadley, Massachusetts (1836). Only one of these, Mt. Holyoke in South Hadley, developed into a college in the 1880s. Before that, however, coeducation had progressed. In 1837 Oberlin admitted four women to its freshman class. The University of Iowa followed in 1855 and the University of Wisconsin in 1863. A big thrust for coeducation came in 1872 when Cornell, the first institution in the east to do so, admitted women. But the most important event for women's education came when Matthew Vassar, a Poughkeepsie, New York, brewer, decided in 1861 to put a million dollars behind the opening of a college for women only. The curriculum for this college was to be patterned on the traditional college for men. Within thirty years independent colleges such as Smith, Wellesley, and Bryn Mawr had appeared, as had associate colleges of older institutions such as Radcliffe, Barnard, Pembroke, and Newcomb. By 1900, women were enrolled in all the major universities in the country.

A special note in the history of higher education in America is the evolution of the so-called extra-curriculum. Between the 1770s and the 1870s students seeking to avoid either the rigor or the boredom of their studies developed, in turn, debating clubs, literary societies, the Greek-letter fraternities, and organized athletics. The debating clubs owed their origin to the intense political situation in the country during the revolutionary and constitution-forming epochs. The literary societies, prominent in the 1820s and 1830s with their libraries and journals, were formed by students interested in modernizing the classical curriculum. The fraternities emerged in the 1840s, patterned on Freemasonry and other adult ritualistic clubs, to promote social activities fulfilling an emotional rather than an intellectual need. Previous to organized athletics young college men seem to have resorted frequently to riot, ostensibly in protest over some grievance but also as a way of releasing the tensions of youth. The histories of medieval universities record this as do the histories of several American colleges in the eighteenth century. The decades of the 1820s and 1830s witnessed college riots over the curriculum, food, living quarters, etc. However, organized collegiate athletics in the United States began during the 1840s and 1850s with the building of gymnasiums advocated by Germans living in America. In 1852, on Lake Winnipesaukee in New Hampshire, the first intercollegiate athletic contest took place with a crew race between Harvard and Yale. In 1859, Amherst and Williams played the first game of intercollegiate baseball and in 1869 Princeton and Rutgers were the first to meet on the football field.

The amalgam of American influences and the European models for higher education occurred most effectively in those institutions we call the state university. And it promises to become not only the most characteristic of American higher education institutions, but, considering the range of its responsibilities undertaken for society, the most important as well. The use of the term "state university" involves a definition of financing and control of the institution if not of a clientele. Today such a university is one subsidized by state tax dollars, in order to minimize the tuition, and its governing board is appointed or elected through the political process. This definition, however, has evolved.

The colonial colleges were subsidized by the state and controlled by the church. The Dartmouth College Case, in 1819, changed this. The case is not only a landmark in the history of the Supreme Court, it is also one in the history of American higher education. When the college president fell out with the trustees at Dartmouth, originally chartered by the state of New Hampshire, the issue of whether the college was a public or a private corporation arose. The state courts, siding with the president and the state legislature, determined that Dartmouth was a public corporation subject to legislative control. The trustees retained alumnus Daniel Webster as their attorney who took the case to the Supreme Court. Webster argued that Dartmouth was a private corporation serving the public. The Supreme Court agreed, adding that the college was an expression of private philanthropy and therefore subject only to the board of trustees responsible for its property and resources. This decision promoted an American concept of control residing in an external board rather than in the faculty as in England. It drew a sharp distinction between private and public colleges that did not exist before. As a consequence, legislatures in New England soon ceased to provide subsidies to the older colleges while elsewhere in the country legislatures were encouraged to develop public institutions of higher education.

State universities evolved in several waves. The first wave, inspired by independence, commenced with the University of Georgia, chartered in 1785, and generally spread across the South where there were no previous colleges. The second wave occurred with the movement west and was promoted by the North-west Ordinance of 1787, which authorized the federal government to grant two townships in each new state to support places of higher learning. Underwritten in this fashion, Ohio University and Miami University in Ohio were chartered by 1810. Before the 1860s another ten institutions were organized by the same process. Among these were Michigan (1817), Indiana (1820), Wisconsin (1848), and Minnesota (1851). After the Civil War, under the leadership of the University of Michigan, the state universities began to assume the preeminence in the Midwest and the West that they hold today. Here the small private colleges simply could not respond to all the various challenges of developing the country. Here, too, the spirit of democracy, reinforced by frontier conditions, demanded educational opportunity for all. As President Angell of Michigan observed in 1879, "We need all the intelligence, all the trained minds we can have."[7]

The state university has always been dependent to some extent on the resources of the federal government. The Morrill Federal Land-Grant Act of 1862 prompted a third wave of development for the state university. In 1857, Justin Morrill of Vermont wanted to ". . . promote the liberal and practical education of the industrial classes in the several pursuits and professions of life."[8] He believed the existing colleges did not do this and he was prepared to use federal land grants to bring curricular reform to higher education, to develop scientific agriculture, and to introduce, generally, culture to the frontier. With the secession of the South and its concern over the use of federal power, Congress seriously considered Morrill's proposal and passed the necessary legislation. The Morrill Act was in fact a federal endowment for higher education. It stipulated that each state could select 30,000 acres of public land for each legislator it sent to Washington. Proceeds from the sale of these lands could then be invested with the income used for endowing a college. The law provided for the support in every state of at least one college where ". . . the leading object shall be, without excluding other scientific or classical studies, to teach such branches of learning as are related to agriculture and the mechanic arts."[9]

Because the law left allocation of the land grants to the states, the Morrill Act and its 1890 successor were responsible

THE UNIVERSITY OF COLORADO

for a considerable variety of institutional patterns. Michigan, Pennsylvania, Maryland, and Iowa built agricultural and mechanical colleges on the foundations of earlier agricultural schools. Many other states, including Wisconsin, Minnesota, North Carolina, and Missouri, turned over the land grant to existing universities to serve the agricultural and mechanical interests. Some states, including Texas and Washington, set up entirely new colleges. California and Ohio founded new state universities and added agricultural and mechanical components. Still other states arranged for existing private colleges (including Yale, Brown, and even Dartmouth) to provide this kind of education. Massachusetts organized a new agricultural college with part of the land grant and donated the other part to the Massachusetts Institute of Technology. Both New York and Indiana joined the land grants with private benefactions to create, respectively, Cornell and Purdue.

Colorado, for important local reasons, determined to found an agricultural college in addition to a university. Three public higher education institutions opened in Colorado during the 1870s, the School of Mines at Golden (1874), the University of Colorado at Boulder (1877), and the Agricultural College at Fort Collins (1879); the Methodists reorganized their Colorado Seminary in Denver as the University of Denver in 1880. These towns had become population centers after the gold rush year of 1859 and are located on the plains east of, but close to, the Rocky Mountains. State pride and civic competition were the main reasons for this early proliferation; according to the rhetoric of the time, the early settlers believed the status of Colorado as a frontier civilization required the rapid advancement of learning. But the rivalry of communities seeking colleges predominated. The expectation was that the location of a college would develop a town's economy. Thus the public colleges and universities, along with the capital and the facilities for other public institutions, were plums of politics. Golden's claim to the School of Mines was secured not only by its proximity to productive mines in the Central City region, but also because it had lost the territorial capital to Denver. Denver, Golden, and Pueblo sought the location of the University, and Longmont, in Boulder County, almost received it. Tradition has it that Fort Collins gained the Agricultural College when Canon City opted for the penitentiary. A few doubted that the state, in its primitive condition, needed either an agricultural college or a university, let alone both. Still the various towns had their way. The consequent decentralization of higher education in Colorado, however, has been a problem ever since, especially for state finances.[10]

The twenty years after 1865 and the close of the Civil War were a turning point for public higher education in America. The older state universities progressed and many new ones opened, including Illinois (1867), California (1868), Ohio State (1870), and Texas (1881). The atmosphere was most congenial: rapid economic growth made available new sources of financial support; interest in science, as well as in agricultural and industrial education, was never stronger. If by the 1890s, these state universities had not come up to the standards of the established private colleges and universities of the East, they played an important role in stimulating educational change. The older, private institutions had accepted the challenge and embarked on reform, especially with the elective curriculum which permitted the teaching and study of science and other modern subjects according to individual student interests.

But full recognition of the state university still lay ahead. These institutions needed to develop distinctive characters both to make themselves useful to the citizens of their states and to earn academic reputations. However, the state university had effectively responded to the basic interests of American society by providing higher education, both liberal and practical, for all who aspired to the opportunities and privileges that education bestows. As Daniel Gilman, the new president of the University of California, put it in 1872, a state university is "a group of agencies organized to advance the arts and sciences of every sort and to train the young as scholars for all the intellectual callings of life."[11]

One

IN THE BEGINNING:
1870's to 1890's

H IGHER EDUCATION in Colorado originated in what appeared to be an unpromising environment. A sparsely populated community, separated by vast distances from economic and cultural support from the settled East, and dominated by the needs of survival in a rude frontier setting, did not seem to offer much to sustain the growth of a system of colleges and universities. The University of Colorado, founded in this environment, shared many of the problems of sister institutions established about the same time. A surge of dedication to support public higher education insured the founding of the University in a physical sense, but thereafter it suffered for many years from problems then common to most institutions of higher learning in Colorado: low enrollments, inadequate financial resources, and some uncertainty about the priorities within the University, as well as within the state educational system. During the University's difficult formative period, two presidents dealt with and, to a significant extent, overcame some of the problems, while the natural growth of the state solved or ameliorated others. By the time the University and the state entered the last decade of the nineteenth century, the University was an established institution; much remained to be done, but the foundations were set.

The earliest Anglo-American settlers in Colorado, who arrived between 1858 and 1861, would have been surprised had they been told that within twenty years they would be living in a state of the Union with a system of education that included all levels—from the primary grades up to and including state universities and private colleges. Attracted first by the lure of gold, then by the hope of a living based upon agriculture, merchant activities, and the professions (as well as mining), increasing numbers of people moved west to occupy a land which possessed a milder climate but a daunting number of negative physical features. High mountains and semi-arid basins and prairies posed many problems, as did the nomadic Indians scattered throughout the area. Furthermore, until the railroads could be pushed westward to link the new settlements with the East, the people in Colorado would have to live in a frontier environment largely isolated from the amenities of civilization.

Even though early Colorado was a rough place, most of those who lived there had no desire to see it remain so. In countless ways they dedicated at least part of their lives to creating a new state as quickly as possible—with towns and villages, farms, ranches, and mines—all bound together in an ordered society with institutions which they perceived as particularly American and peculiarly theirs. Perhaps foremost among these institutions was a system of education. Higher education, in particular, was seen as a major civilizing influence which would hasten the development of a stable community. While, ultimately, universities and colleges would help to shorten the duration of rude frontier ways, the condition of the frontier—with its scattered population, poor communications, and psychology of survival which involved hard work and disdain for what appeared to be unnecessary to daily living—was bound to have an inhibiting effect upon the growth of any education much beyond the elementary level. Thus, while James Baker, the third president of the University of Colorado, could proudly say at his inauguration in 1892 that the University had achieved in fifteen years what it took Harvard two hundred years to accomplish, he was overstating the case.[1] In 1878 the *Denver Times* expressed a widely held view when it said that although called a university, the institution at Boulder was far from being one.[2]

Naturally the development of higher education in Colorado would reflect the living conditions there. The objectives would look toward the economic advancement and social welfare of the state before efforts to extend culture. Devotion to community concerns was not simply a matter of philosophical choice reflecting the egalitarianism of the frontier; it was also a necessity, since support of higher learning in Colorado would need the active involvement of the people even more than was the case in the East.

Colorado still looked to the East for models. As the first settlements developed and the territory of Colorado was created, the settlers' communities, economic concerns, social mores, and political institutions came more and more to resemble those of the older society from which the settlers had come. One of the earliest concerns of the people of the Colorado Territory was to establish a school system, and the school law of 1861 was based on the one developed earlier by the Illinois Territory.[3] Later, when the University of Colorado was established, its elective curriculum was modeled upon that of the University of Michigan.[4] Thus the characteristics of Colorado's educational system would show a clear midwestern influence.

The legal and political foundations of the University of Colorado were laid in the fall of 1861. The territory of Colorado had just been established and the first Territorial Legislature was in session. On October 26, E. S. Wilhite, a representative from Denver, introduced a bill to establish a public university at Denver and, from that moment, the question of location of the University arose, only to be finally settled in 1874. After its introduction, the bill was elaborated upon and amended considerably, the major amendment being the elimination of a specific statement of location of the University. The members of the legislature evidently did not take too seriously the question of setting up a university at this early stage in Colorado's development, for when nominations for a board of trustees for the University were offered, the legislators enjoyed themselves by nominating several of their own members, as well as putting into nomination the names of Jefferson Davis, Abraham Lincoln, and Lewis Cass.[5] Although much of the discussion of the bill was frivolous, the debate became serious when the issue of the location of the University was again considered. On October 31, considerable wrangling and balloting took place, and, when it was over, Boulder had received a majority to be chosen as the official site.[6] The swing to Boulder, which eventually won on the third roll-call vote, was a tribute to the efforts of Charles F. Holly, Boulder County's representative, as well as to the jealousy of many of the legislators who did not wish to see Denver get the University for itself. After action by the council, the upper house of the legislature, the bill went to Governor William Gilpin and was signed by him on November 7.

The "Act to Establish the University of Colorado" was a landmark piece of legislation in the history of the University, of Boulder, and of Colorado. In addition to specifically locating the University in Boulder, the law also established a Board of Trustees, which was to govern the University in the name of the state, and which had broad powers to hold property, elect officers, and prescribe the curriculum. The act also stated the purpose of the University, which was "to promote and encourage the diffusion of knowledge, in all the branches of learning, including the scientific, literary, theological, legal, and medical departments of instruction."[7] Although subsequently modified, when the transition from territorial to state government occurred, the basic features of the legislation were retained—these included professional training as well as a liberal education, control by a supervisory board acting as agent of the people of the state, and location of the University at Boulder.

The passage of this legislation did not assure the instantaneous birth of a public university. Those first legislators probably doubted that a university was in the immediate future of the territory, and several factors further prevented serious consideration of a university for many years. The Civil War, which was already under way when the legislature met, caused problems: the slowing down of the movement of settlers into Colorado and the considerable decline of economic activity based on mining; the inflation caused by the war with the rest of the country; and, finally, the withdrawal of garrisons from the frontier posts during the earlier part of the war which left the Indians free to go on the warpath to redress their own grievances. The resulting Indian raids caused disruption along the whole frontier, Colorado suffering as much as, if not more than, other areas. By 1864 raids by Indians were causing so much fear that people in outlying areas were abandoning their homes to flee to nearby towns, and some smaller towns were temporarily evacuated.[8] Campaigns against the Indians, conducted mostly by Colorado militia forces and ending in the infamous Sand Creek Massacre, put an end to the Indian threat, but not before considerable havoc had been caused.

In the period after the war, little improvement in economic conditions occurred until the late 1860s, as a postwar depression gripped the nation. But factors emerged during this period which would soon bring Colorado more into the mainstream of national developments and which would lead to a resurgence of economic growth and the advancement of Colorado into statehood. The most important, all interrelated, were: the increased movement of people westward in the aftermath of the war, which led to an expansion of agricultural activity as new farms and ranches grew on the plains east of the Rockies; the pushing of the railroads into Colorado, connecting the towns along the front ranges with each other and with main lines to the east, north, and south; and new gold discoveries in the San Juan Mountains, the discovery of several silver lodes at Leadville, Aspen, and other places, and new methods of smelting to utilize previously unusable ores.[9] The impact of all this upon Colorado's growth and its future in the Union were remarkable. During the decade 1870–1880, the population of Colorado swelled from 40,000 to 194,000 people, and with this growth came a more diversified and stable economy, the establishment of important contacts with the rest of the country, and ultimately the crowning political achievement—the transition from territorial status to statehood—achieved in 1876 after previous premature statehood efforts had failed.[10] With statehood and the realization of a more mature economic, political, and social community, the people of Colorado could begin to give serious attention to developing a system of education to meet their needs. The decade of the 1870s was one of progress in this direction, especially for the University.

The town of Boulder, which became the site of the University of Colorado, developed as a result of the gold strikes made in the mountains nearby, notably at Gold Hill. The miners and prospectors who labored in the rapidly multiplying gold camps needed a base of supplies nearer than Denver, which had come into being only a year earlier to supply the gold seekers farther south. The natural route into the heart of the new prospecting area was the Canyon of Boulder Creek, and it was at the mouth of this canyon that Boulder developed. Founded as a town in February 1859 and originally named Boulder City, it was soon a mushrooming miner's supply camp extending about two miles along the north bank of Boulder Creek. In October of that year an early visitor to Boulder described the little community in these words: "Although Boulder City is but a few months old, there are sixty well-built houses with good stores and warehouses."[11]

Even as the year ended, however, Boulder was already beginning the transition from a mining camp to a more settled community. As disillusioned miners left for easier pickings, the remaining population turned gradually to agriculture, which increasingly displaced mining activities as the town's economic base. Boulder's population became more stable, with a higher proportion of businessmen and professionals who looked upon their community as a permanent home rather than a place of quick economic opportunity; they were interested in the needs of a permanent community, such as transportation, schools, and organized town government.[12] For a time after 1861, however, there was concern over Boulder's survival. Like the rest of Colorado the town suffered from the effects of the Civil War, and for a period after 1865 economic hardship persisted and growth practically ceased.[13]

When economic revival took place in Colorado after 1869, Boulder shared in the prosperity. The linking of Boulder to Denver by rail in 1873 sparked a rapid expansion of the community and nearby areas, as the cost of shipping goods was considerably lowered.[14] The beneficial effects were felt immediately. New businesses opened, and, as the population and economic bases expanded, demand for professional services of all kinds increased, bringing in doctors, lawyers, and teachers. Agriculture developed outside the town to meet the needs of the growing populace. By 1880, Boulder's population increased nearly tenfold to more than 3,000 people.[15]

As the doldrums of the 1860s gave way to the expanding prosperity of the 1870s, and as towns became more firmly established, the people of Colorado looked to the expansion of education. Primary and secondary schools, developed to a greater extent in some communities than in others, now were more highly regarded by all as necessities instead of expensive and perhaps irrelevant luxuries within the framework of survival. In the realm of higher education, the needs of the present and the shape of the future indicated the desirability of training doctors, engineers, and scientists for Colorado's economic development. In addition, the waning of frontier conditions which put a premium upon survival and practicality created a rising demand for the humanistic education which fostered civilization in its highest sense. It was deemed good for Colorado—and good for a city—if it had a college. Civic self-interest was also present, for many town leaders also saw growth and prosperity as a by-product of the location of a college within its precincts.[16]

As the Eighth Territorial Legislature was about to convene in early 1870, a meeting of leading Boulder citizens took place to develop local support for moves to obtain territorial action to begin a university, but it was not pursued. However, shortly after the legislature began its deliberations and a bill was introduced to reaffirm Boulder as the University site, Boulderites became intensely agitated by a rumor that the newly incorporated town of Burlington, east of Boulder and now absorbed into the town of Longmont, was trying to secure the University for itself. The rumor quickly proved true, for on January 11, John H. Wells, chairman of the House Committee on Incorporations (and, incidentally, Burlington's representative in the legislature), reported an amendment to the bill to change the location of the future university from Boulder to Burlington.[17] The citizens of Boulder united to fight the threat from Burlington. The attitude seemed to be that even if Boulder could not do anything at present to build a university, it would probably do so in the future; meantime Boulder would oppose any attempt to remove it. During the next week, agitated Boulderites met both formally and informally to register their indignation. The local newspaper, the *Boulder County News*, saw Burlington's scheme as no more than an attempt at robbery. "Boulder is the only place in this county that is entitled to it."[18] Thomas Graham, Boulder's representative in the house and also a member of the Committee on Incorporations, led a successful counterattack against Burlington's pretensions, and his recommendation that Boulder be reaffirmed as the site of the University was supported by the full house, which passed such reaffirmation later the same day.[19] A few days later the council likewise passed the bill[20] and on January 25, Governor Edward McCook signed it.

Thus the danger passed. But Burlington's threat stimulated interest in Boulder for development of a university as nothing else in nearly a decade had and, although events would show that the townspeople were not yet able to translate ideals and emotions into reality, the goal of building a university in Boulder was not again allowed to fade. In addition, the furor caused by Burlington brought the first concrete expression of financial support from Boulder's citizens, who offered several parcels of land for the University as well as pledges totaling more than $10,000 in cash.[21] A further important stimulation of Boulder's interest grew out of another feature of the 1870 act reaffirming Boulder's claim to the University. This was the section which reconstructed the University's Board of Trustees. The original bill of 1861 had established a Board of Trustees which, though composed of Colorado residents, included the name of only one Boulderite; the other Trustees lived in remote parts of the state. Under such conditions it is not surprising that the Board, though legally constituted, had not held a meeting since 1861. This impossible situation was corrected in the 1870 law which set up a new Board of nine members that included only one member who lived farther away than Denver, and no fewer than three members from Boulder.

The new Board of Trustees met at the Boulder Courthouse on January 29, 1870, only four days after the law creating it went into effect. The meeting was almost anticlimactic. Officers were chosen and Boulder was well represented since Granville Berkley, the chairman, and Thomas W. Graham, the secretary, were Boulderites.[22] The other Boulder member, Amos Widner, played a prominent role in the discussion which followed concerning a site for the University. Several offers of land were examined, but no decisions were reached. Bylaws were adopted which established regular meetings of the Board to be held four times a year: in January, April, July, and October. Then the meeting adjourned. It was not a dramatic beginning. At its next meeting, on April 4, only five members were present, just enough for a quorum, but at least one positive accomplishment resulted. The Board approved a site for the University east of town on 20 acres of land donated by Trustees Berkley and Widner, and made provisions for a survey of boundaries, clearing, and fencing of the land.[23]

Then plans for the University went into limbo for the next two years. The Trustees held no more meetings in 1870, and none in 1871. The major reason seems to have been lack of money. The Trustees had secured a site for the first buildings but nothing more; efforts in the summer of 1870 to affirm pledges made earlier and to raise more money appear to have been unsuccessful. In the spring of 1871, Graham tried to get subscribers to the original University fund in 1870 to advance some money, but with no success.[24] A further effort in October resulted in guarantees of about $3,000; evidently the economic problems of Boulder's townspeople were such that little more could be done. Under the circumstances, the Trustees decided to do nothing further until the next meeting of the territorial legislature, due to be held early the following year.

If the Boulder townspeople had hoped the legislature would relieve them of the need to sacrifice in order to begin the construction of a university, they were disappointed. Despite a determined effort by the Trustees and J. P. Maxwell, Boulder's representative in the house, to get an appropriation of $15,000, no funds were forthcoming.[25] Instead a move once more was launched in the legislature to relocate the University to Denver, to Colorado Springs, or to Greeley. Again Boulder was in an uproar and again influential citizens fought the proposal. The attempt was beaten and, as the legislature adjourned, Boulderites who wanted the University were more than ever convinced they might lose it to some other town if they did not begin construction of at least one building. Yet, in spite of the legislature's lack of interest in providing funds, the people of Boulder could not bestir themselves to raise the money. The Board of Trustees, which had reconstituted itself at the beginning of the year and had already been involved in the attempt to procure an appropriation, also launched a fund-raising drive.[26] They managed to get $1,135 in cash or pledges but then the drive lost its impetus. The primary reason for the drive's lack of success was that Boulder citizens at the same time were committing themselves to another fund-raising project which was of far greater importance to the town's future: the bond proposal to complete a railroad between Boulder and Denver. In these circumstances, it is doubtful that Boulder could have done more for the University. But the sense of anxiety remained.

Meanwhile the Trustees were compelled to deal with two unforeseen problems. When they met early in 1872 to reorganize themselves and to prepare their efforts to try to secure funds from the legislature, the Trustees found that the land which they thought had been secured actually had not been deeded to the University. Many questions concerning the suitability of the site had also arisen, especially in connection with its location directly athwart the area into which the town was most likely to expand in the near future. The Trustees decided to declare the site vacated, to examine other sites which had been offered earlier, and to consider the three most desirable offers. In addition to the original site, which still appealed to some members and was again offered by the owners, there was a site west of the town, near the mouth of Boulder Canyon, and one on heights to the south. After considerable debate and balloting the latter site was chosen, after its owners, Marinus Smith, George A. Andrews, and Anthony Arnett, agreed to add adjoining parcels to their original offer.[27] The warranty deeds transferred ownership to the University on January 8 and were recorded the next day.[28]

The site chosen for the future University of Colorado was an imposing one, and anyone who compares the possible sites offered to the Trustees would undoubtedly congratulate them on their choice. It consisted of three different connected parcels, forming a rough triangle of some 52 acres on the hill south of Boulder Creek, and it commanded an excellent view of the town to the north. At the same time, because of the steepness of the north side of the hill facing the creek, expansion of the city's boundaries in that direction would not likely take place for many years. Thus, although it was near Boulder, but not in Boulder, it would not obstruct the structural growth of the city.

At last a site had been chosen and confirmed, but the problem of finances still remained. In cash and pledges dating back to 1870, the Trustees had about $3,200—not nearly enough to carry out significant construction projects. Further efforts to raise money among the townspeople, during the rest of 1872, failed and, by the spring of 1873, enthusiasm began to flag. The *Boulder County News*, the town's leading newspaper, tried to revive interest by suggesting that citizens get together to beautify the University site by removing rocks and planting trees. This, it was claimed, would show that Boulder was interested in its University.[29] Evidently nothing came of the suggestion, and the imposing site remained rocky and treeless.

Events before 1874 showed that the decisive developments leading to a university at Boulder would arise in the legislature. Boulder people might play a supporting role, but clearly the initiative lay with the lawmakers. In 1861 they had created the University by giving it legal status and by providing for it a governing body. Now they would have to give it life by providing for its physical establishment in the form of buildings, faculty, and services.

The Tenth and last Territorial Legislature convened in Denver early in January 1874. On the sixth of January the University Trustees voted to ask the legislature for an appropriation of $30,000 to construct a building for the University.[30] They reaffirmed their position at another meeting on the thirteenth, and, the next day, Boulder's representative in the House, James P. Maxwell, introduced a bill.[31] As it happened, that session of the legislature had to deal with a number of bills with grave political implications, the most important of which was an attempt by anti-Denver interests to relocate the territorial capital from Denver to Pueblo. A considerable amount of intrigue developed, and several Colorado legislators and at least one Denver newspaper charged that the Boulder representatives "sold" their support for a relocation of the capital in exchange for support for the University appropriation.[32] Whether true or not, it is a fact that both Maxwell and Captain David M. Nichols, the other representative, considered to foster Boulder's interests, voted for the bill which duly passed the house. Such maneuvers, if they did occur, must have proved disappointing for both sides, for the relocation bill was defeated in the council,[33] while the bill to fund the University building was drastically changed by cutting the requested appropriation in half before it was finally passed by the house at the end of January. To complicate matters even further, Maxwell also introduced a bill providing for the funding, by the territory, of Boulder County's considerable debt, incurred mainly to finance railroad construction during the previous three years.[34] Referred to a special committee, this funding bill did not pass, but it probably caused even more difficulty for the supporters of a University appropriation than they otherwise would have faced. It may also have played a considerable role along with the capital-relocation scheme in cutting the appropriation.

The successful move by the University's opponents in the house to slash the appropriation before the bill's final passage may have actually been a move to kill the bill, for along with the cut from $30,000 to $15,000, there was a provision that the people of Boulder would not be able to use the appropriation until they had matched it. It was an astute move. Any faltering on the part of Boulder's citizens could be used as an excuse to defeat the bill, while even if it did pass, given Boulder's existing financial commitments and previous failures to raise funds for the University, it might prove impossible to raise $15,000. Either way, the University's chances appeared poor.

Obviously, the first problem to overcome was to secure commitments from Boulder that an amount would be raised to equal the proposed appropriation. According to a strong local tradition, Captain Nichols left his seat as Speaker of the House, rode to Boulder that same night, secured promises from leading citizens, and was back in his place the next morning in time to preside over the day's session with assurances to wavering legislators. Nichols' midnight ride may not actually have happened,[35] but it should have, because it was just the kind of dramatic move to prove Boulder's determination to support a university if the legislature would only provide the initial financial boost. The bill quickly passed both the house and the council, to be signed into law by Governor Samuel H. Elbert.[36]

When the news of the appropriation reached Boulder, expressions of joy and of triumph abounded. The *Boulder County News* commented that a university insured Boulder's growth. It wrote glowingly of how Boulder would gain, for "of the human tide that is sweeping westward year by year, the best will gravitate to us—those having means to expend in the education of their children, those especially interested in schools, and those who seek pleasant homes in the good society which a great university gathers."[37] But many realized the gain was not to be cultural alone. A few months later, the same newspaper made another point favoring establishing the University at Boulder: "so soon as the first of the University buildings is completed, there will not be an acre of land or a town lot in sight from its cupola, but will bear enhanced value by reason of its erection."[38] Clearly the public spirit and cultural pride felt by Boulder citizens were tempered by other considerations.

A revived spirit concerning the University's future swept through Boulder, and the Trustees decided to take advantage of the prevailing optimism by pushing further efforts to raise funds. It was recognized that the condition in the new law, requiring the raising of $15,000 by the townspeople, would be difficult to meet, since past efforts had succeeded only in raising much smaller sums. Accordingly the Trustees decided to enlist the aid of prominent Boulderites who were traveling east "to solicit and procure donations in the Eastern States and elsewhere for said University."[39] It is not known how much was raised by this effort, but it was probably insignificant. Local efforts did not do well either. By midsummer little support seems to have been realized, and, once more, the fear grew that failure to meet the conditions of the law would mean not only a further delay, but also perhaps the loss of the University to some town more willing and able to meet the requirements. In order to avoid such a crisis the Trustees decided to seek a loan, and George Corning, with his banking connections, was chosen for the task.[40] Ten days later he reported success in negotiating a loan for the required amount at 1½ percent interest per month for four months and, shortly thereafter, the Trustees approved the loan.[41] Again, an unexpected problem arose when the state auditor refused to release the legislative funds on the ground that the Trustees' loan was not valid.[42] Amid cries of outrage and threats of legal action by Boulderites and the Trustees, the latter mounted a vigorous effort to raise the matching funds by subscription, and by the spring of 1875 they succeeded in raising more than $16,000.[43] Thereafter the state funds were paid over to the Trustees.

Obtaining the appropriation was the last hurdle in the way

of constructing a building and thus concretely establishing the University. During the next year, the Trustees were almost exclusively occupied in the task of providing for and supervising the construction of the building which would ultimately be called "Old Main" but was first designated simply as the "University Building." The Trustees' work began when they appointed a committee to invite architects to present a plan, even before they had petitioned the territorial government for the University appropriation.[44] During the next few months, a plan by a Boulder architect, L. C. Dimick, was approved, a building committee was appointed to deal with actual construction, and a contract was released for construction bids. The contract was awarded in July to the Denver firm of McPhee and Keating.[45] Ground was broken for the laying of the foundation on July 27, 1875.

The Trustees then made plans for an impressive ceremony to commemorate the laying of the cornerstone. Special trains were provided to bring dignitaries from Denver, and Boulder organizations prepared their parts in the ceremony, which included a parade through the center of town and up the hill to the building site. All these plans, so meticulously laid, were set awry by the changeable Colorado weather, for on September 20, the day of the ceremony, a cold rain and snow began to fall. This dampened the ceremonies, figuratively and literally. The grand parade was called off, and instead of the large audience earlier anticipated at the building site, only a few notables and unusually interested or hardy citizens were on hand as the cornerstone was laid in its place. Thereafter everyone adjourned to more comfortable surroundings in Boulder's Union Hall to hear the laudatory speeches which were to have been delivered at the building site.[46] The *Boulder County News* remarked that the bad weather was a good thing since, according to the local weather prophets, early precipitation betokened a mild winter. A mild winter, in turn, meant no lengthy delays in finishing construction of the building.[47]

The local prophets were right, for, after the laying of the cornerstone, work on the University building proceeded rapidly. As its brick walls rose, it was estimated the building would be ready for spring, in time to open classes in the fall of 1876. On January 15, 1876, Governor John L. Routt and a party of state officials and members of the legislature came to Boulder to inspect the progress of the construction; by then the basement, walls, and roof were completed and work was starting on the building's main tower. It was a beautiful, sunny winter day, and the officials stayed all afternoon, enjoying their outing as well as learning about the building and the Trustees' plans for the future.[48]

The motives of the Trustees in inviting the legislators and other officials to see the progress of construction were clear. Another legislative session was under way, and it was evident that more money was going to be needed to provide plumbing, fixtures, and furniture for the new building. On February 11, the legislature passed an appropriation of $15,000 to install heating equipment, gas lighting fixtures, water pipes, sewage facilities, fencing, some furniture and equipment, and to provide for initial salaries for faculty.[49]

During the winter of 1875–76 and on into the spring, construction continued. Some difficulty was encountered with Boulder's notorious winds, which in mid-February blew down most of the recently completed main tower. The Trustees were kept busy changing the plans to strengthen the structure, while the local newspaper warded off thrusts from Denver which complained that the University never should have been located in Boulder in the first place. By April 18, the building was reported complete except for the front steps and exterior painting,[50] but further work proved necessary in the finishing of the interior, especially plastering and the floors, so the building was not finally accepted as finished by the Trustees until July 22. By then, it was too late to open classes for fall.

Meanwhile one of the most important developments in Colorado's history was taking place while the University building was being constructed. The economic growth of the early 1870s cleared away the last serious obstacles to statehood, and as early as 1872 the territorial legislature sensed the current trend when it asked Congress for statehood.[51] Political inertia delayed congressional action for a time but, in early 1875, action on Colorado's request was finally taken. Although it became entangled in last-ditch efforts of the Radical Republicans to keep Reconstruction in the South alive a while longer, the proposed Enabling Act was passed on March 3.[52] Thereafter Colorado moved rapidly to statehood. A constitutional convention met in December, and on

March 14, 1876, it adjourned. The constitution it produced was ratified by an overwhelming majority of Colorado's voters on July 1, and President Ulysses S. Grant proclaimed Colorado a state on August 1.

The provisions of the state constitution relating to the University should be noted. One major provision was the requirement that the state set apart 72 sections of land "for the use and support of a state university."[53] This was required by Congress's Enabling Act in statehood. Another major stipulation was the establishment of a six-member Board of Regents. Chosen by election, the members were to serve as the representatives of the people of Colorado to their University. The Board of Regents, acting as the main governing body of the University, would appoint a president of the University who would serve as an *ex-officio* member of the Board and would have control of the actual operation of the University under policies set by the Regents.

As far as the University was concerned, the creation of a Board of Regents was a significant improvement on the Board of Trustees which it succeeded. With a clear legal standing assuring permanence and with certainty of election assuring a full membership, the Regents had a stability from the beginning which the Trustees had lacked. The transition from Trustees to Regents began on October 30, 1876, when the Trustees held their last meeting. They dealt with matters pertaining to the new building and scheduled a meeting to be held in early November, but it never took place.[54] The Board of Regents held its first meeting on December 23, with four of its six members present. Frederick J. Elbert was chosen temporary chairman and Junius Berkley, a Boulderite and the sole member who previously had been a Trustee, was elected secretary.[55] The first full working meeting was convened on March 27, 1877. Levi Dolloff was elected chairman, Thomas Field treasurer, and Berkley was confirmed as secretary. At another meeting the next day, they decided to open the University in the fall with both a preparatory and a normal department as required by law. They also elected Joseph Addison Sewall the University's first President, and chose Justin E. Dow to serve as its first full-time faculty member.[56]

Now that the University was at last assured of opening in the near future, considerable discussion arose with respect to the nature of its curriculum and its educational objectives. The ferment of more than fifty years, which led to the demise of the older classical curriculum and the development of a more pragmatic one emphasizing science, was well under way by the 1870s. However, the old had not yet completely given way to the new, with the classical tradition strongest in private colleges and among the humanities faculties in public institutions. There seemed little doubt about the direction the new colleges in Colorado would take. Any system of higher education supported by a state like Colorado would have to emphasize the practical side of education if it were to survive. Yet the Jeffersonian ideal of a citizenry well educated in an understanding of the human condition was also widely respected, so the need was to introduce pragmatic and scientific education into the colleges without turning them into purely scientific institutes. The *Boulder County News* summed up the prevailing philosophy at the local level when it said that western colleges do not have to follow slavishly eastern examples. Men and women alike should have equal access to all state institutions of higher learning and a voice in determining the nature of the curriculum. At the same time a major purpose of the University would be to produce responsible citizens, and, to that end, some commonly accepted morality should also be taught, along with the social graces to enable University graduates to function as civilized people.[57]

Of more immediate concern was the question of assuring continuous financial support for the University. As statehood dawned, state and local pride generated an almost irresistible demand for a number of locally based colleges. This demand was rationalized by the argument that the new state should inaugurate a system of higher education, similar to other states, with a university and special-purpose schools. The School of Mines, whose importance to Colorado was recognized, had already opened in 1874 with the aid of state appropriations. Some questioned whether or not the population and financial condition of the state could support a number of institutions of higher learning. In 1876, the *Denver Tribune* was one of several newspapers which saw danger in the trend toward proliferation of colleges. A concentration of resources to produce one good state university, it wrote, was sounder than starting several weak institutions. If the decision was to concentrate the state's efforts in higher education, the best choice would be the University at Boulder, for "by every consideration of sound policy and the public good, the University at Boulder, the recognized University of the State of Colorado, is entitled to all the aid that the Legislature is able to grant to institutions of its class."[58] Nevertheless, the state, responding to local interests, opened an agricultural college at Fort Collins in 1879 and a teachers college at Greeley in 1890. In 1885 the legislature discussed a consolidation in Denver of all the state colleges, including the University. But no action was taken. By 1890, the state had thus established four different institutions of higher learning, committing itself to the support of each. This series of decisions played a major role in the subsequent history of all four institutions. It assured that during their formative years none would enjoy enough financial support to enable it to achieve its initial objectives.

The question of state financial support for the University was crucial, for it was assumed from the beginning that tuition, if charged at all, was to be merely nominal and would not be relied upon to finance University functions. Therefore, the state government had to provide a subsidy. The question of how best to provide it was settled for the next several years by the first state legislature, which agreed on a method for financing the University. Passed on March 15, 1877, the law set aside a one-fifth mill (a mill being a thousandth) of the total property tax in the state for the support of the University.[59] Since in other laws passed, at this time or soon after, additional mill levies were established to support the other state institutions of higher learning, it is clear the legislature intended that the state's property tax, rather than biennial appropriations, support higher education on a continuing basis. As will be seen, this decision proved to have both fortunate and unfortunate repercussions for the University.

With an income base established and with the selection of a president for the University, its supporters had gone some way toward assuring its development. Joseph Sewall, born in Maine, had earned both the M.D. and Ph.D. degrees at Harvard. He had practiced medicine for a time before becoming a professor of chemistry at Illinois Normal University. His health forced him to consider a move to a more congenial climate, and when he heard of the efforts to establish a university at Boulder he decided to try his future there. His ideas on education fit well with the objectives for the University which the Regents were trying to establish.[60] As a scientist he believed in the expansion of scientific subjects in the curriculum and a stress on practicality in higher education, but recognized the necessity of maintaining humanistic studies, which he considered as being also practical. He strongly advocated the expansion of the elective system, which was adopted at the University in the beginning, but also believed no graduate should be without a grounding in such subjects as history, economics, and international law. Basic agreement on educational objectives between the president and the Board of Regents provided an auspicious beginning.

The administration of President Sewall began with great hope for the future. Sewall's first practical concern was the opening of the University as scheduled in the fall of 1877. His immediate concern, however, was to bring his wife and children to Boulder and to see them comfortably established in the quarters set aside for their use on the third floor of the University Building.[61] During the rest of the summer he busied himself with setting up a curriculum, hiring faculty, and, finally, preparing the opening-day ceremonies which took place on September 5, 1877.[62]

There is no question that the University began operations in an atmosphere reflecting inadequacy in every major particular except its physical plant. Initial enrollment was small, with 44 students; only 10 of these were in University classes, the rest being enrolled in the Preparatory Department.[63] There was only one regular faculty member, Professor Justin E. Dow, formerly principal of Boulder's high school. President Sewall had to double as a faculty member, teaching classes in natural philosophy, biology, botany, physics, chemistry, political economy, astronomy, physiology, and logic.[64] Yet there were compensations. The dearth of students and restriction of the curriculum made the University Building, which had been planned for a much larger number, seem roomy. Shortly after the opening of classes, Regent Berkley and the editor of the *Boulder County News* visited the University and found much to acclaim. The *News* reported that the students appeared seriously interested in their studies, the faculty well prepared and dedicated. The paper further stated that the Regents and the legislature were aware of the University's needs, which would be provided for in due time.[65]

It was an optimistic statement. Sewall's administration was bedeviled from the beginning by a number of difficulties, but none was worse than the lack of money. It produced a chronic condition of poverty which caused great concern to the Regents and drove Sewall to despair. Many years later he recalled his presidency to an audience at the University in the following terms: "If you were to ask me what ten years of my life were most filled with sadness, disappointment and sorrow, it is the years I spent here on the grounds. . . . I tried to be hopeful, but it was bitter work."[66] In addition to difficulties normally associated with a new frontier state, there were serious disagreements over priorities; it was not so much a lack of financial resources as it was a lack of consensus concerning the question of the need for a comprehensive system of higher education, and an unwillingness to place the financial needs of such a system ahead of other needs considered more important. For example, in 1885, the state legislature was faced with urgent requests for funds, totaling about $35,000, from the University, the state Agricultural College at Fort Collins, and the School of Mines at Golden. But the legislature at that time was considering also the pressing demand for a state capitol building to house the state government. This demand was politically impossible to resist, and the need to make certain such a building would be as good as or better than the capitol of other states ensured it would be expensive. In the end, the legislature appropriated $400,000 in *initial* funds to construct a capitol building, while granting nothing to any of the state institutions of higher learning.[67]

There were several legally established sources of support to which the University could turn during its first forty years. The first was the sale of public lands granted by Congress and the state for the support of the University. By 1885, about 46,080 acres of federally owned land in Colorado had been set aside by the state for the needs of the University, most of it at the time that Colorado entered the Union. But much of the land was poor land which had not been taken by private interests; even as late as 1885 nearly a third remained unsold. The value of the lands involved may be gauged by those leased by the state, about 3,680 acres in all. These lands brought an annual rental of $239, hardly a princely sum to meet the University's needs.[68]

The second source of support for the University was in appropriations voted by the legislature. This was an important financial source in helping the University start its operations but, unfortunately, could not be counted upon on a continuing basis. While the lawmakers were willing, on occasion, to finance special University needs, particularly in building construction, they had made it clear when establishing the mill levy in 1877 that there was no intention of regularly voting appropriations in University operations.[69] After an initial period of seven years, during which the Regents' requests for funds were at least partially granted, the legislature refused further requests. From 1884 to 1890 three successive legislative sessions refused to appropriate so much as a penny for the University.

Clearly the University could not count on legislative largesse. That left the mill levy as the most important, almost the only, source of funds for day-to-day operations. Unfortunately the mill levy generally brought in only enough to cover such expenses if these were severely curtailed. In the years after 1885 the Regents established an auditing committee to keep a closer supervision of University accounts,[70] and figures brought up thereafter in meetings of the Regents show the pattern developed as a result of reliance upon the mill levy. Property taxes were collected by the state usually in April, and by the middle or the end of May the moneys due the University were deposited in its account by the state treasurer; after that, no additions to the account were recorded unless a windfall (such as a special donation) occurred—which was seldom. Early in the following year the account was often so depleted that the Regents and the president began worrying about which expenses ought to be cut in order to survive until the next deposit of property taxes. For example, in the spring of 1887 the amount in the general fund was down to $3,000, but by the end of May the annual levy deposit brought it to more than $15,700.[71] In May 1888, the account stood at $16,900; in December it was $5,540. The figures for May 1889 and April 1890 were $17,900 and $7,960, respectively.[72] So it went, year after year.

The mill levy, upon which everything depended, provided

between $16,000 and $20,000 annually, fluctuating with the economic climate in Colorado. Fortunately, until about 1891, the state's economy was quite prosperous. Continuing discoveries of gold and silver in the western and central mountains, a cycle of heavier precipitation which brought increased settlement in the eastern plains, the gradual expansion of agricultural and other settlements on the Western Slope, and continuing federal guarantees to purchase silver combined to produce increases in property tax income over the years. The University shared in this increase.[73] But the University's income was too dependent on good times.

In the first year or two, however, the financial support pattern had not yet developed. For a time it appeared the state legislature would provide for the University's needs in a way that would allow a creditable and wholly satisfying expansion. Once committed to providing the first building, the legislative leaders seemed impelled to continue some direct appropriations. In February 1879, the legislature distributed its blessings with a fairly free hand, giving $7,000 to the University to improve the grounds, to buy more furniture, and to make additional alterations to the University building. Leftover money, if any, could be used to purchase books for the library.[74] In 1881, the legislature gave its attention and its appropriations to the Agricultural College, but in 1883 the University, the Agricultural College, and the School of Mines received funds for further construction; the University's share was not by direct appropriation, but through the special allocation of an additional one-fifth mill property tax for the biennium only.[75] As it turned out, the year 1883 marked the high point of the state government's support of its institutions of higher learning. Nearly another decade was to pass before the University received any further direct funding, and during those years it had to survive almost solely from revenues provided by the mill levy. The difficulties arising from these circumstances would be largely responsible for the resignation of President Sewall and would be a major problem for the administration of his successor.

Sewall was ambitious to expand the University into a major institution as quickly as possible and saw a number of factors working in his favor. First, he had considerable general support from the Regents. Then, too, the Boulder community seemed willing and able to help. Boulder, like the rest of Colorado, was beginning to enjoy an increasing prosperity after 1875 and which continued through the decade of the 1880s. Between 1875 and 1880 the town's population and fortunes increased rapidly, but prosperity in the eighties was uneven, on balance not equaling the degree of growth in the rest of the state.[76] Sewall had good reason to hope for greater things. In 1878 he made plans for a College of Arts and Sciences to open that fall and to be the focal point of the University's program in the future.

The college as originally established had both a classical and a scientific curriculum. In each curriculum several elective courses were included, for Sewall's scientific background and philosophy of education made him a strong supporter of both scientific higher education and the elective principle as well. While science had by this time won a secure place for itself in American universities, the elective idea was only beginning to make headway in the East. Sewall's advancement of electives as part of the University of Colorado's curriculum at this early date marked one area at least where Colorado did not simply follow the older eastern schools, but instead shared in blazing a new trail. It was not all Sewall's doing, but reflects the strong underpinning of western support for such an idea as being in the best democratic and individualistic tradition. The college's classical course emphasized both modern languages and mathematics as required courses, but provided a high degree of selection through the number of courses offered. In languages, for example, a student could choose either French, German, or Italian, plus advanced courses in Latin or Greek, while in mathematics the choice ranged from geometry through trigonometry to calculus.[77] It was an ambitious program requiring more faculty, but lack of funds prohibited hiring more than one new member in 1878; that one, however, was Mary Rippon, destined to become one of the most respected members of the faculty. Because of the lack of faculty, the curriculum of the College of Arts and Sciences remained imposing on paper and largely unrealized in practice for many years. It was only the gargantuan efforts of the faculty, each one teaching four or five different courses each semester, that made the curriculum varied enough to meet even the minimum needs for a bachelor's degree.

As it turned out, the problems involving the curriculum went even deeper. The state's secondary school system, which would be the main source of university freshmen, was still primitive. The typical course of study did not necessarily prepare pupils adequately for college work; in addition, there were not enough public high schools to provide a significant number of college entrants.[78] There were no teacher-training institutions, with the result that in the territorial years the teachers in Colorado's few primary and secondary schools had received their training in other states. The framers of the University Law of 1877 sought to deal with these problems by requiring the Board of Regents to establish a Preparatory Department in the University as soon as it opened, and also a Normal course, which is to say, a teacher-training course, as soon as practicable. The Regents decided to open with both Preparatory and Normal departments thus assuring that, as soon as possible, the demand for trained teachers would be met and a reasonably steady flow of qualified students would enter the freshman program annually.[79]

Unfortunately, however, the development of these departments along with the regular University curriculum caused a considerable drain on the University's limited resources. In the case of the Preparatory Department the situation became even worse because of Boulder's inability to maintain its own high school. The Boulder school board at one point decided to close its school and send its students to the new high school at the University.[80] This decision was not satisfactory to many of the townspeople nor, presumably, to the University administration. The Boulder high school was soon functioning again, but the University felt compelled to lend support to Boulder in order to prevent the University from becoming predominantly a preparatory academy. Future presidents Hale and Baker eventually worked out an agreement with the Boulder school board which committed the University to partial support of the Boulder high schools. This, in turn, enabled the University to phase out its preparatory program gradually, as the Boulder schools expanded. Yet, as late as 1893, the Preparatory Department's courses enrolled more students than did liberal arts courses at the university level.[81] As for the Normal Department, its role at the University ended after the Normal School at Greeley opened in 1890. All in all, the responsibilities in preparatory work and teacher training probably brought more problems than benefits to the University and, for many years, kept it in the status of an academy rather than a true college or university. The situation also reveals clearly the tendency of Colorado, and various other western states as well, to have built educational systems from the top down.

Encumbered by the operation of the Preparatory and Normal departments, higher education at the University only grew slowly, but it did grow. Sewall gradually added faculty and increased course offerings over the years, but one suspects that, as far as students were concerned, the limitations may have been more noticeable than the opportunities. Certainly one cannot assume that the broad, impressive array of courses listed in the catalogues was ever offered in its entirety during the University's first twenty years. The array, at least, did show the intention of providing a course of study to make the bachelor's degree at the University a respectable one. As each succeeding class moved up the educational ladder, the University began to achieve a cohesive wholeness. The first graduating class was the Class of 1882. Nine men and one woman, had entered the University as freshmen in 1878. Attrition took its toll, however, and by 1882 the class consisted of six men. Several of them, such as Henry A. Drumm and Richard H. Whiteley, went on to become important contributors to the life of the state and their communities.[82] During the early years, the University continued to graduate small classes; two in 1883, only one in 1884, two in 1885, eight in 1886, and four in 1887.[83] By 1886, Sewall's last year as president, the College of Arts and Sciences still had only 28 students enrolled, while 85 were in the Preparatory Department.

The faculty which Sewall assembled during his administration was of high caliber. Justin Dow, the first full-time faculty member, stayed only two years, but the second member, Mary Rippon, remained until her retirement in 1910. Other faculty members who played major roles during long tenure with the University included: Isaac C. Dennett (Latin), Paul H. Hanus (mathematics), C. S. Palmer (chemistry), and J. Raymond Brackett (English). Considering faculty salaries, the University probably employed better professors than it deserved. In the beginning, when hopes were high, Sewall and Dow were hired at annual salaries of $3,000 and $2,000 respectively, Dow's salary being close to the norm farther east.[84] Within a short time, however, the Regents were compelled to reduce salaries. When, in 1878, a new faculty member was to be hired, the Regents specified "as low a salary as a competent teacher can be procured for."[85] As a result, Mary Rippon was hired at $1,200, a decidedly low figure. Thereafter salaries for all professors, except Rippon, varied somewhat with conditions. From an average of about $2,000 in 1883 they were reduced to $1,800 in 1885, rising gradually to reach about $2,000 again by the time President Baker took over in 1892.[86]

The slow growth in the student body was a nagging problem for Sewall and one which had not been anticipated. It was a problem because it was seized upon by Sewall's critics and became their primary point of attack on his administration. Since tuition was practically free, it could be evidence that something was wrong with the leadership of the University. In addition, this slowness of growth could be—and was—used as justification to refuse legislative appropriations and other aid. It was assumed that additional funds would be wasted until the University became larger. By the fall of 1884 the small graduating classes were causing some concern, and those who were never satisfied with the location of the University at Boulder used this concern as a springboard to mount an attack on Sewall. On January 16, 1885, the Regents dealt with the charges against Sewall and the University. Resolutions of support for the administration were read by several Boulder buisnessmen and other citizens, as well as from the University faculty, but no opponents appeared. The Regents then voted a resolution noting the absence of critics and concluding there were no grounds for the complaints.[87]

Sewall's troubles did not end with this incident, and the entire affair left many questions unanswered. In the absence of any clearly reasoned statement of facts, the Regents could only assume all was well, but the low enrollments still needed to be explained. The University at Boulder faced some special problems concerning students: principally, the financial burden to the student. Even though tuition was practically free, costs of room, board, and other expenses were considerable. Since no dormitories existed on the campus until 1884, students had to find lodgings in town, where housing was always a problem; unless they lived with relatives in Boulder it was, in many cases, an insurmountable problem. In these circumstances it is not surprising that during the mid-1880s between 75 and 80 percent of the student body were residents of Boulder County.[88] Another difficulty was the high turnover in the student body, largely caused by the attraction of well-paying jobs in the area. The sparse population in Colorado meant a labor shortage, and relatively high wages were paid for all kinds of jobs.[89] The job market had a seductive attractiveness for many students, who dropped out either temporarily to earn enough money to resume their studies later, or else permanently to make their way without what may have appeared to be the dubious benefits of a university education. Faculty also found the job market outside academia alluring and, as a result, faculty turnover was relatively high. In commenting on the resignation of mathematics Professor Paul H. Hanus to accept a good position in business, the student newspaper, *The Portfolio*, said,

> What else can one expect in a state characterized by western activity and a wonderfully rapid growth, where fresh opportunities for money-making daily appear to the energetic, where the prospects of sudden wealth continually allure."[90]

In 1881, Sewall seems to have recognized the lack of students as being related to the shortage of living facilities for students on campus, and he began to give thought to the matter.[91] By 1883, the Regents were persuaded to consider the problem, and the legislature's establishment of a special mill levy that year gave them the means to do something about it. The Regents decided in May to secure plans and prices for the construction of four cottages to be used as dormitories, and to construct a house for the president as well. By November, the bids had been examined, the funds from the mill levy secured, and the first two cottages and the president's house approved for construction.[92] Completed in 1884, these buildings were notable additions to the campus and made life much more secure for many students, especially the women. One of the cottages was set aside as a women's dorm and served as that for more than twenty years. It was hardly a luxurious place. Mrs. Fred G. Folsom ('02) recalled that the women residents had to bring their own furniture, and the only place to entertain guests was the small sitting room, so it was necessary for various groups to take turns in using it for social affairs.[93]

The construction of dormitory cottages was not the only remedy Sewall advocated to increase enrollment. Evidently he considered expansion of course offerings to meet the needs of as varied a student body as possible, for in 1883 he worked to establish new schools and departments. In April 1883, the Regents authorized a Music Department which offered courses that fall.[94] Called the Conservatory of Music by 1884, it was divided into instrumental and vocal units under the leadership of W. H. Mershon. It was associated with, but not actually a part of, the University until 1888, when it was reorganized as a regular department under Charles W. Farnsworth.[95] But the most ambitious undertaking along this line, as well as the most successful and controversial, was the establishment of a Medical School.

At their meeting of May 5, 1883, when they authorized the construction of student cottages, the Regents also agreed to establish a Medical Department at the University. Sewall, who had a degree in medicine, was particularly interested in a medical school as a means of attracting more students. In addition, it was believed the prestige attached to the operation of an institution to train doctors would reflect greater credit on the University. At the time Sewall urged his idea upon the Regents it seemed to make considerable sense, for only one medical school existed in the entire state. This was the University of Denver's Medical School, established in 1881, and the need for additional facilities to train doctors seemed evident. Unfortunately, Sewall was not the only person thinking along these lines. While Sewall and the Regents were considering a medical school at the University, preparations were being completed for the opening of another school in Denver, a private institution to be named the Gross Medical School. It is possible that neither Sewall nor the Regents were aware of this impending event, though it is not likely. In any case, it was arguable that a publicly operated medical school should be opened, and by the fall of 1883 the University's Medical Department was in operation. Then, in 1884, a Homeopathic College of Medicine was opened in Denver, so that within the short space of a year three medical schools were added to the first one established by the University of Denver, and all were soon competing vigorously for prospective students. This was at a time when the state's population was only approximately 135,000. The situation was to plague all four schools for a number of years.

Apparently none of the later difficulties was foreseen in 1883, and Sewall began the Medical Department with two students. He himself acted as head of the school and taught chemistry, while the full-time faculty member, Dr. W. R. Whitehead, taught anatomy and physiology.[96] Half the third floor of the University Building was given over to a dissection room and a chemistry laboratory.[97] In a circular the University sent to Colorado physicians, Sewall glowingly outlined the prospects of the Medical Department. The four-year curriculum provided a solid foundation for new doctors and entrance requirements were fairly rigorous. In addition to the regular faculty, doctors from Denver came to Boulder to give lectures on an honorarium basis. The Regents had already approved the construction of a hospital for the department and this was completed in 1885. Thus the prospects of the Medical Department appeared bright.

By 1885, the medical faculty had grown to eight, and that spring the school graduated its first two students, but difficulties already began to appear. At first, the major problem was too few students. After a promising expansion of the student body to sixteen, in 1884, growth practically stopped, and by the early part of the following year serious concern was expressed within the University about the department's future. The ambitious plans of Sewall and the Regents that had established a number of new departments since 1878 reached a point where the existing financial resources could not support them. The mill levy was practically the sole source of income, and it grew slowly from year to year; on the other hand, the proliferation of departments increased expenses faster year by year. By 1885, the University had added to its basic Preparatory, Normal, and Liberal Arts programs a Music Department, an Engineering Department, and, finally, the Medical Department and an associated School of Pharmacy. All this proved too much. The expense of operating the Medical Department and its newly opened hospital was especially high and thus a crisis arose, producing the first notable division within the faculty and misgivings on the part of the administration.

In the spring of 1885, the mill levy brought in about $21,000, a somewhat larger than average amount, but expenses were such that the Regents had to make some agonizing decisions concerning allocation of the funds. When they decided to provide only $2,600 for the operation of the Medical Department, the medical faculty was incensed. Led by Professor Whitehead, who resigned in protest, it remonstrated with the Regents. The stand of the medical faculty led to a reaction among several of the other members of the faculty, who claimed the Medical Department was not as vital a part of the University as other programs and feared it was using up resources needed elsewhere, particularly in liberal arts. The students soon joined in the argument, and just before the academic year ended they indulged in a demonstration which involved the hanging in effigy of Lieutenant W. F. C. Hasson, sole faculty member of the Engineering Department and a leader of the anti-Medical School faculty group.[98] The problem was temporarily solved when several members of the part-time medical faculty agreed to give their honorarium lectures without honorarium, but it was clear the difficulties were merely postponed.

For the rest of the decade, the Medical Department managed with its share of the Regents' allocation from the mill levy, plus the fees collected from operation of the hospital. The importance of the department was evidently recognized by the administration, which made sacrifices elsewhere in order to keep the medical program in existence. In 1887, the Regents provided funds from the mill levy to construct a small medical building to the south of the University Building, and, upon its completion the following year, the medical laboratories and offices were moved there. Taken in conjunction with the hospital, the medical facilities were an important part of the physical plant at that time and reflect the major role played by the Medical Department in the total life of the University. By that time, the medical course was a respectable one, covering three years of work taught by a faculty numbering about a dozen which included several prominent

---

Denver physicians and surgeons. Graduates totaled about twelve between 1887 and 1892 and represented nearly a third of all degrees granted by the University during that time.[99]

The difficulties concerning the Medical Department were but one aspect of the total discouraging situation facing Sewall and the Regents from 1884 to 1887. The problems were mainly financial and stemmed in part from the mill levy's failure to provide enough operating funds, but the legislature contributed to the difficulties by failing to appropriate money to make up for the mill levy's deficiencies. This left the University with the hard choice of cutting out important programs, thus seriously weakening the effort to expand and develop, or else continuing to operate everything on a shoestring while hoping that somehow the situation would improve. Sewall chose the latter course, evidently believing that cutbacks in the overall program would seriously hurt the University's ability to obtain funds from the legislature in the future. Yet it is clear that Sewall's choice had about as much to do with the critical developments of 1885–1886 as did the legislature's attitude. The charges of mismanagement leveled against Sewall in late 1884, though expressed in petty ways, were true expressions of concern over the financial situation. It is noteworthy that by mid-1885 the Regents decided to keep a close supervision over University accounts by appointing an Auditing Committee.[100] This could be interpreted as showing some lack of confidence in Sewall. In any event, the situation did not improve, nor could it as long as both the legislature and the University administration continued on their respective courses.

The 1885 financial crisis undermined morale not only among the medical faculty, but also among the rest of the faculty. Salaries were somewhat reduced, which did not improve tempers, and by 1886 Sewall was fast losing his grip on the situation. In Boulder, rumors and criticism grew again and, this time, the critics were better organized. At a Regents meeting on April 7, specific charges of mishandling of finances were made, but others attacked Sewall in vague terms, claiming that he should resign because of the growing lack of trust in him.[101] The pressure proved too much, and two months later Sewall tendered his resignation to the Regents, to take effect at the end of the year.[102] Sewall still had many staunch supporters. The *Boulder County*

Herald, which had defended him against all attacks, lamented Sewall's decision to give in.[103] On the other side, many believed they served the best interests of the University when they attacked Sewall, for they saw his policies as weakening the University and even endangering its future.

So Joseph Sewall stepped down as the first president of the University. He had had a difficult time, faced as he was by all the problems associated with bringing a university into being under such trying conditions. Sewall's decisions regarding continued growth, even at the risk of going beyond the bounds placed by severe financial restrictions, may be criticized. His failure to work harder to advertise the University to the people of Colorado, in order to assure a degree of grass-roots support, was probably unwise. Yet the Regents stood by him and must share whatever responsibility he bears. Overworked, ill-supported by the state and even, in the end, by much of the local community, he managed to open and keep the University going during its first decade in circumstances which might have driven a lesser man to early despair. When he resigned, however, he left an institution with an uncertain future and major problems to be faced.

Horace Morrison Hale, the second president of the University, came to his position without illusions. He was well aware of the difficulties ahead, for he had served as a Regent from 1878 to 1884. Like Sewall a New Englander by birth, Hale spent most of his boyhood and early adult life in New York. A graduate of Union College, he lived for a time in Tennessee and Michigan and came to Colorado in 1863, largely for reasons of health. An educator all his adult life, he served for a period as territorial superintendent of public schools before becoming a Regent and then president of the University.

A small man of great vigor, Hale immediately set about dealing with the problems confronting him. It was a critical time. In the wake of Sewall's resignation the counsels of despair had grown even louder. A legislative commission investigating the University in March 1887 found the University had overextended itself in terms of its economic base. A majority report of the commission recommended that the Medical Department, which they said produced less, relative to expenditure, than any other department, be discontinued and the hospital be "turned into some practical use." Somewhat illogically, the report also recommended a cut in the University's share of the mill levy from one-fifth mill to one-eighth. A minority report indicated financial support was the main difficulty, and proposed the mill levy be abolished and replaced by direct legislative appropriations, starting with $17,000 for 1887–88.[104] Nobody, it seems, was satisfied with the existing sources of income.

Not everyone saw the problem as being primarily financial. Politicians, reluctant to make commitments which might result in constantly increasing costs—and thus taxes—sought other explanations for the plight of the University. Governor Benjamin H. Eaton led the way, describing the problem as he saw it in a message to the legislature on January 12, 1887. He said there was a strong feeling throughout the state "that the institution is disappointing the expectations of its founders." In spite of a good foundation in the mill levy (which according to Eaton produced a sufficient income), an excellent faculty, a supportive community, and a fine climate, something was still lacking. The University had 120 students; Eaton maintained it should have 500 by now. He claimed the shortage of students was the consequence of insufficient concern shown by the administration in popularizing the University to the people of Colorado and other states. He hoped the new administration would change the situation and get better results.[105]

While many of Eaton's assertions were clearly exaggerations for effect and were quickly attacked by the University's supporters,[106] it was evident the University would have to show some effort to make itself better known before it could ask the legislature for financial support. Spurred by criticisms of Governor Eaton and others, plus the revelation of profound ignorance about the University in the state observed during a personal tour, President Hale set in motion plans to revitalize the University, and in this he was seconded by the Regents. Although the longer solution to the University's difficulties clearly lay in bringing a balance between expenditures and income, for the time being a vigorous advertising campaign was pushed. The *Colorado School Journal*, the most important publication for educators in the state, now began to carry advertisements of University programs, stressing the free tuition and low costs of room and board.[107]

Newspapers in other parts of the state began to carry similar advertisements. The faculty had already been enlisted in the project of selling the University, and during the summer vacation the travelers among them extolled the virtues of their school in other states as well as the more remote parts of Colorado.[108] In addition to this, the Regents authorized a major program in the summer of 1887 to improve the University's buildings and to beautify the grounds. New stone steps replaced the old ones at the entrances to the University Building, more trees were planted, and the University Lake was created by damming a small ravine on the campus.[109]

These efforts seem to have been effective because, within a short time, enrollments increased. In the fall of 1887, 131 students were in attendance as compared to approximately 110 at the close of the previous spring semester, and credit for the increase was given to Hale's efforts.[110] By the end of the following year, the improvement had come to the attention of people all over the state. In fact, the enrollment crisis had passed and, while various developments in the University came under considerable criticism in later years, enrollments were not generally an issue. By 1892, when Hale left office, enrollment had reached 170 students, 55 of whom were in the programs of higher education—not a spectacular increase but a definitely respectable one.[111]

Although advertising the University helped enrollments, it did nothing to solve financial problems. Eventually a healthy growth would inspire enough respect and assurance to persuade the legislature to be more generous; Hale and the Regents cultivated every opportunity to obtain more funds. For the time being, however, the best means of bringing costs and income into balance lay in drastic cost-cutting by curtailment of nonessential spending. Hale had already set the example by accepting, as president of the University, a salary of $2,500, about $1,000 less than Sewall was receiving when he resigned. Faculty salaries were not cut, but they were not increased either. By practicing strict economies elsewhere, the administration was able to increase the faculty with consequent improvements both in faculty morale and in the quality of education through a better variety of courses.[112]

The total effect of the new policies was considerable optimism. A legislative committee which investigated the condition of the University in early 1889 enthusiastically reported the achievements of the Hale administration: adequate, though not princely, faculty salaries; an increasing faculty and student body; and, above all, a better balance between income and expenses. The only need it saw was for another classroom building, since the increase in student body and course offerings indicated some crowding of facilities in the University Building within another year or two.[113]

As far as the students were concerned, the Hale years were a time when studies and survival were not the completely engrossing activities they had been earlier. When Sewall was president, students lived under such primitive conditions that long hours of study in the roomy University Building must have appeared a much better alternative to spending one's time in the generally cramped rooms available in town. The walk from town to the University was a tiring and often depressing experience in the early years. The sidewalk ended at the bridge over Boulder Creek and the way up the hill to the campus was dusty in the summer, a quagmire in wet times. Only after 1882, when a board sidewalk was finally constructed between the University grounds and the creek, and the dormitory cottages were built soon after, was it possible for most students to live and to attend classes in some degree of comfort.

Extracurricular activities were carried on from the beginning, but the students were certainly not overwhelmed by the variety of entertaining things to do. The early Music Department seems to have furnished considerable diversion both for the participants and their audiences. Literary societies were also popular, as were periodic lecture discussions on special topics by faculty members or by President Sewall himself. A student newspaper, *The Portfolio,* was begun in 1879 and every two months offered a four-page collection of student and faculty news, local news, information about activities in other universities, and articles by students on subjects such as "How to Succeed" and "Some Disadvantages of a Republican Form of Government."[114] If one may assume the newspaper reflected student interests, it is clear the early students were basically concerned with getting an education while enjoying themselves as conditions permitted. With the exception of woman suffrage, which appeared to be favored by most students, political discussion was infrequent. Local politics seemed to get close attention only when questions of legislative aid to the University arose. When aid was given, gratitude was expressed; when aid was withheld, adverse comments were common.[115] The Greenback and, later, the Free Silver questions did generate some debate but, on the other hand, the assassination of President Garfield in 1881 stirred no comment. In matters involving academic policy, however, there was considerable interest. Several student spokesmen favored the abolition of grades, while others favored the inclusion of more electives in the curriculum.[116]

The impression gained of students in the years before 1887 is of a group of people concerned mostly about their own education and aware of the need to develop the University in order to advance their own educational interests. Thus there was a strong attachment to the University as an academic rather than a social institution. During the years of Hale's presidency this attitude began to change. While concern for the University continued to be important, a strong interest began to appear which saw University life in terms of social activity and fulfillment as well as in terms of academic advancement. The change is probably most notably exemplified by the emergence of interscholastic football. Although impromptu football had been played on campus as a diversion as early as 1880, a football team, consisting of players with some expertise and developed specifically to compete against teams of other colleges, was organized in the fall of 1890. In addition to playing the Colorado School of Mines, which had the only other college team in the state, the University team played the local Boulder football association and those of other towns. It was not a winning team in its first two years, but it did attract considerable attention and support from the students and showed that athletics could be used to build a close identification between the University and outside interests as well as with students.[117]

Several developments increased student involvement and interest in expansion of both academic and nonacademic activities. By 1891 the Normal Department had been discontinued, and by 1892 negotiations between the University and the Boulder school board were on the verge of agreement to remove the Preparatory Department as well. The result was an increasingly homogeneous student body, no longer fragmented among high school students, teacher trainees, and regular University students seeking a degree. Also, it incidentally cleared the way for Hale, and more especially his successor James H. Baker, to devote exclusive attention to the needs of University students. Another development conducive to the growth of student self-awareness was the increasing proportion within the total student body of people from other parts of the state or from other states. When more than 75 percent of the students were from Boulder County, as was the case through the Sewall years, the student body was practically part of the town and interests were correspondingly narrow. By 1890, only 12 out of 53 new students were from Boulder, and no fewer than 9 were from outside the state.[118] A final factor which stimulated a greater attachment to the University was the growing pride in the physical appearance of the University. The trees planted in 1887 were now beginning to look like trees rather than saplings, while the two dormitory cottages, the president's house, the hospital, the new Medical Building, and sidewalks gave the campus a permanent look which contrasted strongly with the impressions of earlier students and visitors. During Hale's presidency the appearance was enhanced even more by the construction of two more large buildings. One was the men's dormitory, erected just east of the University Building, in 1890. Named after retiring Regent Roger W. Woodbury, it possessed a modern heating plant and was the first building on campus to be completely lighted by electricity. More important, it provided comfortable space for nearly all the men students who needed accommodations.[119] The other building grew out of the need for more classroom and laboratory space and reflected projections concerning future growth of both the student body and course offerings. Convincing the legislature of the need for such a building, Hale was able to obtain an appropriation of $30,000 from the 1891 session, the largest single sum yet voted by that body for the University, and in May the Regents authorized expenditure of the money on a large classroom building.[120] Subsequently, the Regents authorized more money from special funds on hand to enlarge it to provide more laboratory space. Begun in 1891 (and named in honor of President Hale), classes were first held in the building in 1894. After additions it was, for a time, the largest building on campus.

In May 1891, the University graduated its largest class up to that time: five M.D.s and nine bachelor's degrees, plus an honorary Doctorate of Laws and a Doctorate of Divinity. One of the M.D.s and five of the bachelor's degrees were awarded to women.[121] The 1891 graduating class symbolized probably better than anything else how far the University had developed under the guidance of President Hale. In only four years, Hale, working with the Regents, took the struggling institution left him by Sewall and set its financial situation in order. He added considerably to its facilities. He increased enrollments. He made the University better known among the people of the state. When Hale retired, the University of Colorado was not yet a real university, but it clearly was a college, and the larger goal was in sight.

Hale's resignation, unlike Sewall's, was not prompted by significant criticism of his administration. Hale had set himself the goal of reordering the University's finances and establishing the institution so firmly that its permanence was ensured. By mid-1891 he felt he had succeeded. He had taught school or had been an educational administrator most of his adult life and now concluded he had earned a rest. Never robust, he found the rigors of the past few years had weakened him physically. Finally, he may have been partly motivated by the need to leave a job which paid so poorly for, by 1891, he was perhaps the lowest-paid college president in the state.[122] His decision to retire at the end of the year was accepted by the Regents and the search for a successor begun. Because of Hale's work, the future held brighter prospects for the University.

Two

ORGANIZING A UNIVERSITY: 1892–1919

URING THE LENGTHY and distinguished presidency of James Hutchins Baker, the University of Colorado developed from what some critics labeled a glorified high school into an institution with many of the characteristics of a modern university. Important as was the growth of the student body and faculty, along with the campus itself, these advances were superseded by curriculum development. The Graduate School and most of the University's professional schools originated during the Baker administration. In a period of intensified competition among public and private colleges in Colorado, Baker managed to expand the University's influence in several new areas. Although the state's institutions of higher education failed to eliminate much wasteful duplication of programs and to develop a rational and efficient system, the Baker years witnessed marked improvement of relations between these schools. Despite what seemed at times to be almost reckless overexpansion of the University's functions, Baker managed to keep the University going during several years of severe financial stress. Baker turned over the presidency to Livingston Farrand in early 1914. During Farrand's brief tenure, the University proved its capacity to contribute handsomely to the national war effort in a variety of ways. By 1919, the University appeared to have established its place as the foremost institution of higher education in Colorado.

James H. Baker, third president of the University, held the presidency for 22 years, longer than any other president during the University's first century. Born in Maine in 1848, he received his B.A. and A.M. in Classics from Bates College in 1873 and 1876.[1] Venturing west to Denver in 1875, he served as principal of Denver High School for 17 years. In that capacity he demonstrated his administrative ability while he gained insights into the relationship between secondary schools and colleges which would serve him well in later years. Even before he was hired as the University's president in 1892, he served notice that he was strong willed. Offered a salary of $3,500 by the Regents, he demanded a salary of $4,500 plus $500 for moving expenses.[2] The Regents met his demands, and he was formally inaugurated as president on May 21, 1892.

Those present at his inaugural who were unfamiliar with his style might be excused for believing that Baker would assume the passive role of a caretaker-administrator. In his inaugural speech, he implied that his role would be modest. "The University has arrived at a new epoch in its history. The silent work of taking root and springing into the light has been done. It needs but the care of the fostering hand to insure a vigorous and rapid growth."[3] Insiders soon realized Baker's role would be anything but passive. Ten days after his initial meeting with the Regents in January 1892, he submitted a plan for the University to open a law school as soon as possible; he also requested a $150,000 appropriation from the state legislature for new buildings, additions, and repairs.[4] A few weeks later, he further outlined his goals for the University. He believed the University should rapidly increase the number of its schools and colleges, expand liberal arts, eliminate the Preparatory Department, cultivate its public image by more aggressively advertising its achievements and its services to Coloradans. During his first year, Baker stated that his ambition was to make the University the equal of Harvard, Yale, Columbia, and Michigan.[5]

Less optimistic visitors to the Boulder campus of 1892 probably perceived such visionary goals as unrealistic, if not downright ridiculous. The "University" was little more than an academy. Over 60 percent of its 169 students were enrolled in the Preparatory Department. All maintenance costs, plus the salaries of 32 faculty members, had to be met with an annual operating budget of roughly $61,000.[6] The entire campus consisted of no more than a dozen buildings, including maintenance sheds and stables. Few trees graced the barren, windswept "quadrangle"; in good weather, cows and pigs roamed the campus freely, the former even "maintaining" the front lawn of the president's house. The academic program appeared, if anything, even less advanced. The College of Liberal Arts was the only established school. Very little had been done to advance the sciences. The Medical Department had been founded in 1883 but, due in part to the inaccessibility of an adequate number of trained teachers, many of whom were practicing doctors in Denver, it was experiencing difficult times by 1892. Although the University had awarded several graduate degrees by 1892, no formal graduate school existed. The University would at least have to become a more mature institution before it challenged the Harvards and Michigans.

Baker believed that a modern university was a prerequisite for the state's continued social and economic development. In his mind, Colorado, not long previously a wild frontier territory, also needed the civilizing influence of a university. Thus, by expanding the institution at Boulder as rapidly as possible, Baker believed he would best serve the long-range needs of all of Colorado's citizens. His optimism and ambition for the University's future reflected that the state's population was growing and its economy was booming in the late 1880s. The mining industry was especially prosperous. Large silver ore discoveries at Creede, in 1890, and at Cripple Creek, in 1891, reinforced this trend. As mining thrived, so did transportation, commerce, and banking.[7]

During Baker's first year in office, however, the boom began to ebb. The collapse of the national market for silver in 1893 drastically affected Colorado's economy, since so many supporting industries and services depended upon the prosperity of mining. As silver mines closed, so did many banks. The real estate bubble burst, and ruined speculators and unemployed miners crowded Denver's streets. The agricultural prosperity of the

1880s had begun to falter, as a series of crop failures struck Colorado's eastern plains after 1890. By the fall of 1893, a major depression was under way. Not until 1897 did the state's economy begin to revive, and evidence of recovery was slight before 1900. However, the early years of the twentieth century were years of a return to prosperity. The development of several important mineral processing plants, the revival of agriculture, the rapid growth of the sugar beet industry, and the emergence of a variety of regional financial institutions all contributed to the economic revival.[8]

Regardless of whether Colorado's economy prospered or faltered, the University did expand rapidly. By any means of measurement, growth of the University during the Baker years was impressive. Although the state's economy collapsed during the years 1893 and 1894, the enrollments at the University doubled in the same period. By the time of Baker's departure in 1914, although the preparatory program was eliminated, the University's student body numbered more than 1,200 and was instructed by a faculty of over 200. Even more striking was the growth of the professional departments. In 1892, the entire professional enrollment consisted of 11 medical students; by 1914, some 456 students were distributed among six professional schools. Annual operating budgets, always marginal even in the best of times, had nevertheless increased to over $300,000 by 1914.[9]

The years after 1900 were also years of steady, if unspectacular, campus development. New building construction struggled to keep pace with expanding enrollments. Latter-day critics who lament the absence of a unified architectural style throughout the Baker years might be reminded that the harsh realities of the economy and the lack of an established building fund hampered comprehensive planning.[10] During a period when enrollments increased sevenfold, utility and low cost were more crucial determinants in choosing design than was architectural harmony. Major building projects during the Baker years included completion of the Hale Scientific Building (1894), a new engineering building and heating plant (1898), and the completion of a men's gymnasium and a chemistry building (also in 1898). Construction after the turn of the century included a new library (1903), the Guggenheim Law Building (1909), engineering shops and a new power plant (1910), and the Denison Memorial Laboratory (1911). Several additions and enlargements of existing buildings, and the completion of several smaller buildings, also marked the Baker years.

The greatest single building project was the construction of Macky Auditorium, for many years the largest structure on campus. This impressive new facility, which had a seating capacity of 2,600, was made possible when Andrew J. Macky, a Boulder banker, willed $300,000 to the University on his death in 1907. Groundbreaking occurred in September 1909, but construction was frequently interrupted because Mrs. George Oles, an adopted daughter, contested Macky's will. Construction could proceed in 1911 only after the legislature lent the University $90,000.[11] Although the auditorium was in use by 1912, the interior was not completed until 1922.

Significant as was the physical growth of the campus, curriculum development assumed even greater importance during Baker's administration. Like most nineteenth-century colleges, the University was founded with the primary purpose of perpetuating classical learning. It would not have been surprising if Baker, himself a classicist, carried on that tradition. Yet, in addition to his many other fine qualities, Baker was both practical and farsighted. Early in his tenure as president, he stressed the view that the University should be a service institution for the people of Colorado. He believed that in order to best serve the people, it must provide as complete and well-rounded a curriculum as funding would permit.[12]

When he assumed the presidency, there was a rather serious faculty conflict between two educational philosophies. The classicists were extremely wary of any effort to develop programs in the sciences. Baker refused to choose sides, suggesting that "Each tub must stand on its own bottom."[13] No single department would be favored at the expense of others. Instead, Baker planned to expand all departments and to add a number of new ones.

Baker was quite aware that by the 1890s the more successful state universities were following the lead of James B. Angell of the University of Michigan in promoting higher education not as a luxury, but as a necessity which should be made available to all who could benefit. If the University was to become the preeminent educational institution in Colorado, it would have to provide not only "generalists" and doctors, but also lawyers, teachers, scientists, engineers, and other professionals to the state's fledgling economy. To bear its name with pride, the University would have to develop a formal graduate program and drop its function as a preparatory school.

There were major changes in the University's curriculum almost from the moment of Baker's inauguration. The Law School opened in the fall of 1892, with 25 freshmen and one full-time faculty member. Baker was fortunate to hire Moses Hallett as Dean of the Law School. This distinguished barrister was the first U.S. District Court Judge in Colorado, appointed by President Grant in 1877. A specialist in mining law, he had intimate contacts throughout the state; he was thus able to induce a number of his associates to teach courses in their specialties on a part-time basis, with little or no compensation.[14] Originally a two-year course, the Law School curriculum was expanded to three years in 1898. Aspiring lawyers could apply their senior year's work toward the first year of Law School, thus winning both the B.A. and law degrees after six years. Ten years after its funding, the Law School enrolled 70 students, boasted a biweekly "practice" court, and was firmly rooted as a going concern.

Baker's second year in office, 1893, saw the start, on an informal basis, of a graduate program. The 1893 University catalog announced the availability of graduate courses leading to both the M.A. and the Ph.D. degrees. The University awarded its first earned M.A. degree the same year; in 1895 it awarded the first two earned Ph.D.s. Formal requirements for both higher degrees were rigorous from the beginning. The Ph.D. degree required three years in residence, written and oral examinations, and the presentation and defense of a thesis.[15] In 1900 there were 26 students formally engaged in advanced studies.

Despite the promising beginnings in graduate work at the University, no separate Graduate School existed until 1909, when the Regents officially established the school and appointed J. Raymond Brackett its first Dean. Until that date, the graduate faculty had included only professors who agreed to supervise graduate work on an overload basis, without compensation. Thus, for nearly twenty years, the University performed this vital new function at virtually no cost to the state's taxpayers.

The engineering program also dated from Baker's second year in office, when the Regents authorized the founding of the School of Technology. That fall, the school offered courses leading to the B.S. degree in both civil and electrical engineering. The next year an engineering building and heating plant on the site now occupied by Norlin Library was completed. Henry Fulton was appointed Dean of the new school in 1893, a post he occupied until his death in 1902. Dean Fulton experienced a good deal of frustration during his ten years in this position. Enrollments remained low, in part because of the hostility of many Liberal Arts faculty members, who perceived engineering as little more than vocational training. The school's name was changed to the School of Applied Science in 1895. A decade after its founding, the Department of Mechanical Engineering was added. With Baker's support, opposition from the faculty's classicists dwindled and enrollments grew. By 1903, some 123 students pursued engineering courses. With the appointment of the vigorous Milo Ketchum as Dean of Engineering in 1905, the school pushed hard for more facilities and an expanded organization. Thus in the early twentieth century, engineering was a firmly established and respected branch of the University's curriculum.

In his relentless drive to make the University an indispensable servant of the people, Baker stressed the importance of a liberal arts education for training quality teachers for Colorado's youth. Although the pedagogical curriculum offered by the newly opened State Normal School in Greeley (1890) might suffice for grade school teachers, the former high school principal believed that teachers at the higher level needed the more broadening intellectual experience provided by a liberal arts program. Baker organized the Department of Philosophy and Pedagogy the year of his arrival. The Regents fully supported Baker's ambition to influence the quality of Colorado's high school teachers. Noting that by 1906 over 80 percent of all high school teachers in the state were liberal arts graduates, the Regents stated: "It is natural and fit that school officials should look to the University for their high school teachers.[16] In 1908, the Regents expanded the department into the College of Education, though it remained a part of the College of Liberal Arts. The four-year program provided graduates with combined degrees in liberal arts and education. This attractive degree program grew rapidly. By 1911, there were 241 prospective teachers enrolled in the College of Education.

The first two years of Baker's presidency clearly saw an unprecedented flurry of significant curricular reform. But the Panic of 1893 and the national depression that shadowed most of the 1890s deeply affected the University; thus the middle years of the Baker presidency were marked by consolidation and retrenchment; the University struggled to maintain existing programs and had little opportunity to begin new ones.[17] Several programs which initially showed promise had to be either suspended or dropped altogether. A summer session, aimed primarily at providing refresher courses for school teachers, was founded in 1895. Although the student newspaper, *Silver and Gold*, reported general satisfaction with its operation,[18] the summer session was not offered the following year. Not until 1904 was the summer session reorganized on a lasting basis. In later years, the Summer School would become one of the University's most successful operations, as students and distinguished faculty from colleges across the land flocked to Boulder to learn from each other and enjoy the region's stimulating and beautiful environment.

While the interruptions or terminations of University programs were generally considered setbacks, in at least one case termination was a cause for cheer. Since the day he accepted the job as president, Baker viewed the existence of the preparatory school as an embarrassment to any institution with ambitions of being a university in fact as well as in name.[19] Under former President Hale, negotiation for takeover of the preparatory school by the Boulder school board had commenced; the board constructed Mapleton School in 1890 and by 1892 was building another high school. Thus Baker believed the time was propitious to push negotiations. In May 1893, the Regents reached agreement with the Boulder school board to remove preparatory classes from the University's facilities and to conduct them at Boulder's new Highland School. The University retained final authority over the Preparatory Department and paid most of the costs of operation. Over the next dozen years, the Boulder school board gradually assumed more administrative and financial responsibility, and in 1906 the University officially severed all remaining ties with the Preparatory Department.[20]

Another of Baker's fondest dreams was to initiate an extension program worthy of comparison with those at several of the most progressive midwestern state universities, particularly the University of Wisconsin. An ambitious attempt to coordinate the efforts of several educational institutions in Colorado along such lines began in 1892. But dreams turned to dust. Colorado's colleges and universities were too small, insecure, and protective of their individual interests to achieve genuine cooperation. And the times were bad too; 1892 was the year before a serious depression. As a result, although several colleges, including the University of Colorado, sent instructors to many towns throughout the state, their efforts were competitive, not cooperative. No firm evidence exists, but the University's formal extension service apparently folded in the mid 1890s.[21] Despite this early failure, Baker retained a keen interest in the concept. In 1911 the Regents endorsed the creation of the Extension Division, and it formally inaugurated its program the following year.[22] When Baker retired in 1914, over 300 students were enrolled in extension courses, and a number of professors gave lectures and courses in various towns across the state. Nevertheless, the full importance of the Extension Division remained for the future.

Despite temporary setbacks and the fact that some programs experienced slow growth, a second wave of important curricular developments occurred during the later years of the Baker presidency. In 1911 the Department of Pharmacy was founded as a branch of the Medical School, and it became a separate college in 1913, after the Medical School moved most of its operations to Denver. It is likely that no single achievement provided Baker more personal satisfaction than the culmination of a twenty-year fight to move the Medical School to Denver.[23] Although the University's Medical School was a going concern when Baker assumed the presidency, all of its operations were confined to Boulder. Baker and the Regents were acutely aware that the town's geographical isolation prevented most of the outstanding physicians in the state from contributing to the education of the

Medical School students. Also, a move to Denver would give the school access to better clinical facilities and a wider variety of patients. The Regents thus voted in April 1892 to conduct the last two years of the school's operation in Denver; the move was effected the following year.[24]

The Medical School thrived in its new central location. By 1895 its enrollment multiplied sixfold, and the course of study was lengthened from three to four years. Unfortunately, its very promise of success precipitated new problems. Denver Medical College, a branch of the University of Denver, opposed the University of Colorado's announced plans from the beginning. With good reason, University of Denver Chancellor William F. McDowell feared that the state university would raid his medical school's faculty and attract students with its lower fees.[25] The former institution took its case to court in 1892, noting that the state constitution enjoined the University of Colorado from conducting classes in Denver. In a fancy bit of hair-splitting, the latter insisted that since its administration of the Medical School was conducted wholly in Boulder, it was complying with the letter of the law.[26]

Although the case dragged on for several years, the Colorado Supreme Court eventually upheld the University of Denver's contention in 1897. Forced back into cramped quarters in Boulder, Medical School enrollments dwindled, faculty members lost enthusiasm, and the curriculum had to be temporarily shortened from four years to three. A less forceful president than Baker might have accepted this defeat gracefully and settled for a second-rate medical program. Determined to make the best of the situation, he marshaled much of the University's resources behind an effort to overcome the Medical School's handicap of isolation. A new forty-bed hospital facility was constructed in 1898, and a timely gift several years later from Mrs. Charles Denison permitted construction of the Henry S. Denison Research Laboratory, named in memory of her son, who had been an instructor in the Medical School. By 1900 the curriculum was expanded once again to four years; in 1910, the American Medical Association awarded the school an A rating, its highest rank.[27]

The year 1910 marked a critical turning point in the Medical School's progress. Dr. Abraham Flexner, a nationally renowned physician, published an influential survey of medical education in the United States.[28] His investigation of medical education in Colorado resulted in high marks for the University's Medical School and relatively low marks for the recently combined Denver and Gross Medical College, which was run under the auspices of the University of Denver. More important, Flexner's influential report recommended that all local medical institutions named be combined under the University's control in Denver. The report argued that "the state university alone . . . can hope to obtain the financial backing necessary to teach medicine in the proper way . . . and to it a monopoly should quickly fall."[29] The University of Denver's trustees, deeply worried over the institution's rapidly mounting financial difficulties, realized that they could not commit the funds necessary to raise Denver and Gross Medical College's AMA rating to match that of the University's Medical School. Conceding the logic of Flexner's report, they agreed to the recommended merger in June 1910.[30] Six months later, third- and fourth-year medical students from Boulder joined their new classmates from the former Denver and Gross Medical College in a large, converted residence at Thirteenth Avenue and Welton Street in downtown Denver. The makeshift "campus" would house the combined medical schools for the next thirteen years. In retirement, Baker lived to witness completion of the new Medical School and Colorado General Hospital facilities in 1924.

In one sense, Baker's expansion of the University's mission and the emergence of major new academic programs could not have come at a worse point. By the time University officials fully realized the impact of the national depression of the 1890s upon the state's economy, they were already committed to many new programs. Public support for the University would hardly be generous. The University might have been able to manage better had not enrollments increased rapidly between 1893 and 1900, jumping from 59 college-level students in the former year to 216 in the latter year.[31] Baker's aggressive expansion of the curriculum during the early 1890s unquestionably contributed to the University's financial difficulties later in the decade.

On the other hand, had Baker been a more cautious president and waited for "good times" to implement many of the more important curricular changes, the University's development might have been retarded for years. The fact that good times for University appropriations seemed distant throughout the Baker administration could have provided an excuse for maintaining the status quo for years. Baker's quick plunge into meaningful curricular reform was vindicated as the University emerged intact after two decades of his leadership. Even more important, he had developed a solid foundation for greater future growth.

Yet Baker was disappointed that one of his dreams, the active involvement of the University in Colorado's political affairs, was not realized. In the early years of the twentieth century, a new force, progressivism, influenced politics in many parts of the country. Baker realized that many of the leading state universities, particularly in the Midwest, were promoting themselves as "service institutions" to those who worked for a "progressive" reforming of American society.[32] Baker hoped that his institution might serve Colorado in a similar capacity. As Baker himself put it, "Educational centers can be strong allies in every beneficent crusade"; he envisioned the University's potential role as "the fourth estate in a democratic government."[33]

But, for a variety of reasons, the University failed to exert significant influence in Colorado's politics. One shrewd analyst of higher education in the state pointed out some of the causes: Progressive forces in Colorado never clearly established control of state politics for any extended period, thus politicians with progressive sympathies were not in a position to make use of the research and services which the University could potentially offer. They made few demands upon the University and, while Baker talked in general terms about the University's desire to serve, he offered few concrete proposals.[34] An important, if unstated reason, was that Baker probably anticipated future reprisals against the University when anti-Progressives regained control of the legislature.

Just as important, the University was not yet equipped to provide effective services to progressive interests. True, the University of Wisconsin provided extension courses for residents all over the state, as well as expert testimony to state regulatory commissions about how railroads should be controlled and banks reorganized—but this institution had an annual operating budget nearly six times as large as that of the University. By offering salaries at least half again as large as those at Colorado, older and more firmly established state universities could hire and retain faculty members who were primarily research oriented.

Another important reason for the University's relative lack of influence at the state level was that Colorado's system of higher education was extremely decentralized. Geographical distances, local pride, and political expediency had induced state legislators to create a comparatively large number of publicly financed colleges to serve the state's small population. By 1911, six public colleges and four private institutions competed to fulfill the educational needs of a population of only 800,000 people.[35]

This situation inevitably stimulated conflict between competing institutions. The University of Colorado and the University of Denver struggled for perhaps the highest stakes, as each had ambitions of being the most prominent university in the Rocky Mountain region. Baker's strong commitment to the doctrine of "manifest destiny" of public higher education aroused fear and hostility among officials at the University of Denver. They became particularly defensive when the University penetrated what they considered their own bailiwick, Denver itself. In addition to opposing the Boulder institution's Medical School, they objected to its efforts to establish extension courses in the capital city and recruit students from local high schools.

The University of Colorado was the storm center of many of the conflicts among institutions of higher learning, since it also competed with all of the public colleges for limited state appropriations.[36] With so many public colleges, duplication and overlapping of functions, to a certain degree, were inevitable. Baker's "imperialistic" concept of the University's mission alerted officials at other public institutions, who often believed the Boulder institution was attempting to usurp their functions. Thus, when the University upgraded the science and engineering programs in the early 1890s, it aroused the antagonism of officials at both the Colorado School of Mines and the Colorado Agricultural College in Fort Collins. Similarly, when the University expanded its Department of Philosophy and Pedagogy into the College of Education, the State Normal School at Greeley felt that its primary role of training secondary school teachers was threatened. When

Baker voiced support for a bill in 1911 which would enjoin any but liberal arts graduates from teaching in secondary schools, State Normal School President Zachariah X. Snyder challenged Baker: "What does your vaunted degree mean? It means nothing. My son attended the University. He received a degree after completing a course in liberal arts. What was he prepared for? Nothing."[37]

Yet the state university was not invariably the innocent victim of gibes of spokesmen from other institutions. The University jealously guarded its primacy in the liberal arts field. When the State Normal School and the Colorado Agricultural College attempted to develop their own liberal arts programs, the University ridiculed their ambitions to become "second-rate" universities.[38]

Despite sometimes bitter conflicts between public and private institutions of higher education in Colorado, the Baker years did witness a slow but general easing of hostile attitudes. Though feelings between the University of Denver and the University of Colorado were so tense that they suspended athletic relations for six years after 1908, they were able to agree on combining their medical schools in 1910. The fact that the state legislature in 1909 seriously debated a proposal to consolidate the public institutions of higher learning may have induced administrators to play down their hostilities and broaden their perspectives. By World War I, they were generally aware that their undignified public quarrels may have lost state support for all institutions. A milestone in cooperation between the public colleges in Colorado was a joint effort in 1917 to enact a ten-year mill levy for campus construction. Not only was the campaign successful, but the institutions even managed to reach agreement on a formula for dividing the proceeds. Although no educator in the early twentieth century articulated comprehensive statewide educational needs and objectives, the general trend was toward cooperation among Colorado's institutions of higher learning.

As in other frontier areas, education in Colorado had developed from the top downward.[39] The state's colleges and universities could hardly expect to survive unless they encouraged development of a strong state-supported secondary school system which would provide potential college students. The state's college and university officials naturally assumed leadership in Colorado's educational system. Secondary school officials, less influential and less organized, seldom questioned that leadership, at least before 1900. James E. Russell, professor of psychology and pedagogy at the University, exercised leadership in the effort to coordinate secondary and higher education in the state. In 1897 he informed the state's educational association that "It would be a serious mistake if we should accept the theory that the colleges must take whatever the schools choose to give."[40] In other words, the institutions of higher learning, since they controlled admissions, would continue to exert a voice in determining high school curricula in Colorado.

College officials realized that for their institutions to grow and thrive they had to sell their products to prospective students. The relatively few Colorado youths who planned to attend college after 1900 enjoyed the luxury of a "buyer's market." Recruiters and "field representatives" from several local colleges visited the high schools at frequent intervals. No institution was more aggressive in seeking students than the University, where President Baker inaugurated an annual High School Day in 1896. At this gala event, high school seniors were transported by special trains from Denver to the Boulder campus, where they were given campus tours, were entertained by debates and sporting events, and were feted by a variety of student service and social organizations. Commenting on the 1898 High School Day, which attracted over 200 prospective freshmen, the *Boulder Daily Camera* called it one of the most successful yet, which would "no doubt result in a number of accessions of students."[41]

After the turn of the century, several factors lessened the subservience of high school officials to the demands of college administrators. As the number of public high schools in Colorado multiplied rapidly, secondary school officials became more independent and developed better communication among themselves. As the general public pressured the high schools to offer more vocational courses, secondary school officials increasingly questioned not only the heavily "classical" curriculum, but also the concept that high schools should serve primarily as "feeders" to the state's colleges and universities. Increasingly, they demanded a greater voice in determining both high school curriculums and the admissions standards of the colleges.[42] A series of conferences between high school and college officials, sponsored by the University between 1896 and 1910, aired mutual grievances, but effected few solutions. The specific question of admissions standards was unsolved at that time, and it has remained a thorny problem since.[43]

Even in good economic times, state universities in the United States experience difficulty in securing adequate public support. Baker's ambitious development of the curriculum and the rapid expansion of student enrollments made the University particularly dependent upon the good graces of Colorado's legislators. Never before had the University been in greater need of expanded revenues. One observer noted the root of the University's financial dilemma when he stated that during the 1890s it "endeavored to do more and more on less and less."[44]

Unfortunately, the legislatures of the 1890s were not in a position to support expansion of the University. In a sense, the legislature's own overexpansion during the early 1890s paralleled that of the University. Confident of Colorado's economic prospects, the legislature approved a magnificent $3 million capitol building in 1890. The gold-leafed dome itself symbolized, at least to some, the distorted priorities of Colorado's lawmakers. When several legislators suggested, shortly after Baker's inauguration, that the state could save money by sending its students to out-of-state schools, former president Hale admonished that body:

> It may be true, but I do not believe it. We could farm out our legislation to Kansas and save money, and perhaps get wiser laws. But we are here . . . for a state in which we may take pride, for wise legislation, for progressive civilization. You talk about cost; the dome of the Capitol cost more than the whole University plant—and we ought to be ashamed.[45]

Even the appeal to state pride was insufficient to significantly increase public support for higher education.

Though University officials and other friends of the University frequently voiced dismay at the lack of revenue provided by the state, it would be unfair to suggest that the legislature was wholly lacking in sympathy for or understanding of the institution's needs. In fact, even during the depression of the 1890s, the legislators made several attempts to overcome the University's economic difficulties.

The base of the problem lay in the manner in which Colorado financed public education. Guaranteed University revenues were dependent upon a mill levy, which itself was directly dependent upon the valuation of real property in Colorado. Unfortunately, property valuation declined nearly 20 percent between 1893 and 1897. Thus, during a period in which the University was growing rapidly, guaranteed revenues from the mill levy were actually declining. Had Colorado boasted a progressive tax structure, residents might not have been so resolute in their opposition to tax increases for support of public institutions. Unfortunately, Colorado's regressive tax structure often placed the greatest burden on those least able to pay. Those with tangible assets, such as farmers and homeowners, paid taxes far in excess of their proportionate wealth. On the other hand, those with intangible property, such as income from stock shares, bank accounts, and bonds, paid almost no state taxes.[46] This unfair system of taxation had persisted for years. In 1899, the *Denver Republican* noted that the Colorado Equalization Board habitually placed a very low valuation on property held by large, powerful interests such as railroads and mining.[47] It is, therefore, hardly surprising that county tax assessors lowered real property valuations, especially during hard times.

Thus revenue to the University from the mill levy, insufficient even during periods of prosperity, proved woefully inadequate in times of economic stress. With its guaranteed source of revenue drying up in the 1890s, the University could do little, if any, long-range planning. At the same time, Baker was regularly forced to lobby directly for special appropriations, a responsibility which he loathed. Speaking for himself and other public college administrators, he recalled: "It may be fairly stated that one-third of [my] time and energy . . . was spent in a struggle to obtain what should have been fairly offered."[48]

To its credit, the legislature tried to meet the needs of public education. In 1893 it raised the mill levy by one-tenth of a mill, in the hope of increasing University revenue by $20,000.[49] Legislators voted special appropriations for the University several times during the 1890s: $34,000 in 1893; $40,000 in both 1895 and 1897; and a seemingly munificent $110,000 in 1899.[50] There were, however, two problems: First, because of declining property values, revenue from the increased mill levy failed to meet expectations; second, the legislature failed to provide the means to pay the special appropriations which it voted to the University. For example, Baker expected the 1893 mill levy to yield $20,000 additional revenue; in fact, it yielded only half of the anticipated amount. Of the $34,000 special appropriation the same year, the University received but $11,000. In 1897, Baker requested $60,000 in special appropriations, and the legislature cut his request to $40,000; only $17,000 eventually reached the University.[51] The *Boulder Daily Camera* expressed concern, stating that legislative support for the University had been "very discouraging and disheartening," concluding, "In despair, one is bound to ask 'when will it end?'"[52] The University received nothing from its $110,000 appropriation in 1899. The legislature had voted the funds as a third-class appropriation, and no funds remained after class-one and class-two priorities were met.[53]

Although Colorado's economy began to recover after 1897, University officials discovered by the late 1890s that they had drifted into deep financial trouble. Blessed with hindsight, one is tempted to blame University officials for operating in the red for several successive years. In 1895, the legislature gave the Regents exclusive control over all public lands which had been set aside for the University.[54] For the next several years, the Regents issued warrants on the University's land fund; in three years the fund declined by nearly 50 percent.[55] However, the Regents really had little choice but to dip into capital. As enrollments surged and state support lagged, immediate needs were critical. The building program was virtually suspended, as actual revenues had long since become inadequate to meet even day-to-day operational expenses.

By the summer of 1899, it became apparent that a financial crisis was imminent. For several months, the University was on the verge of closing. When the Regents learned that none of the anticipated $110,000 voted by the legislature could actually be paid, they concluded that they had no choice but to appeal to the general public for loans.[56] In the summer of 1899, they began to issue warrants against future revenues, at 6 percent interest, in the hope of raising $70,000. The money situation was so critical that the Regents decided they could not wait for the governor to authorize their action. Thus the warrants were not legal obligations, and those who purchased them had to accept on faith the Regents' word that the warrants would eventually be honored.[57]

The financial crisis of 1899 severely tested the courage of those who loved the University and wished it well. The *Boulder Daily Camera* warned that if the University closed permanently, the local economy would suffer grievous damage. Calling upon Boulder businessmen to subscribe between $25,000 and $30,000, the paper suggested that "if it closed even for a single semester, it [would] take a generation to regain its strength and prestige, in the face of the present competition for professors and students." Other state colleges, warned the *Camera*, would appropriate its university-level functions.[58] Asked to shore up the University, citizens of Boulder generously contributed $20,000, and another $50,000 was subscribed from individuals around the state. To be sure, some of the money took the form of bank loans, but much of it came in smaller amounts from concerned individuals. The faculty and administration also demonstrated their strong support. President Baker and Moses Hallett, Dean of the Law School, each subscribed $1,000. Librarian Mary Rippon and Dean of Liberal Arts Fred B. R. Hellems were among the faculty who subscribed smaller amounts.[59]

After January 1900, the crisis gradually receded. By spring, the Regents had sufficient cash on hand to meet the University's immediate debts, although building and other long-range commitments were still suspended. Over the next few years, as the state's economy recovered and expanded, the legislature was generally able to deliver the appropriations which it promised to the University. Since guaranteed revenue from the mill levy consistently failed to cover the University's needs, a new pattern of financing emerged, in which the state legislature covered University deficits with special biennial appropriations.[60] Although such arrangements proved adequate during prosperous times, special appropriations were wholly subject to the mood of legislatures, and University officials continued to press for a sounder system of financing.

Despite the failure to effect long-range financial solutions, the University struggled toward solvency. By 1903, the Regents were paying off some of the warrants issued four years earlier. They perhaps overstated the financial improvement when they passed a resolution that same year thanking the legislature for "providing an ample revenue for the present needs of the University."[61] Ten years later, the *Rocky Mountain News* pointed out that only three states spent less per capita to educate students at their state universities than did Colorado. Colorado's figure of $170 annual expense per student was in stark contrast to Michigan's $304, California's $383, and Missouri's $461. The *News* editorial praised Baker, stating that "no university in the country has done more with less money" and pleaded with the legislature to support the school "as far as the resources of the state will permit."[62] At the time of his retirement, President Baker stated that while the University's financial position was fairly sound, the mill levy should be increased to the point where the school would be independent of the caprice of legislators.[63] Though his immediate successors valiantly attempted to effect just such a goal, they failed to achieve it.

Baker fixed his stamp upon the Boulder campus in many areas. A sober, industrious man, he undoubtedly influenced many students to follow his hardworking example. Most students at the University realized that an opportunity to gain a college education was a privilege, if not a luxury. Some students were in college because they were unemployed; a few older students attended because they hoped to earn a degree and change careers. An example of the latter was Henry Fulton, who at the age of forty entered the University during the Hale years. A unique freshman, he was a Civil War veteran who had ridden in General Philip Sheridan's cavalry, had been wounded and captured by the Confederates, and had participated in many Indian campaigns. He must have fascinated classmates with his stories. Fulton graduated in 1881, was presented with a Master of Science degree from the University in 1893, and was immediately appointed Dean of the School of Applied Science.[64]

Life on campus was relatively austere for most students. Woodbury Hall, the new men's dormitory, contained a dozen two-bedroom suites and housed a total of 48 men. This facility was sufficiently large when constructed in 1890, but it was woefully inadequate by 1900. Most students made room-and-board arrangements off campus. While the accommodations were inexpensive, they were generally spartan. A few female students were housed on campus. Their cottage facilities, which cost $3 per month, were primitive. A small room with a chair and a bed were provided, but residents had to supply their own linen. They did have the privilege of cooking their own meals in small kitchens at the rear of the cottages. When Dean of Women Antoinette Bigelow suggested to Baker that the University should improve women's facilities, he replied that things were as they should be. Improvements, stated Baker, would "make the girls soft, and so useless."[65]

It is hardly surprising that administrative supervision of student activities was quite rigorous during the Baker years. There is little evidence that Baker's attitudes about what constituted proper student behavior mellowed in his later years. In a 1910 chapel speech to assembled students, he lectured on "the pleasures of grinding," advising them to avoid superficial distractions. Soon thereafter, he attempted, without success, to enforce a ban on smoking, after lecturing students on the evils of tobacco.[66] Classroom and chapel attendance was mandatory, with few exceptions. Women were carefully chaperoned at all social functions. One straitlaced Dean of Women insisted that all social functions be concluded by 11:30 P.M. The same guardian of youthful virtue suggested, too, that men should be chaperoned, as well as women.

Such strict discipline encouraged youthful rebellion, and several incidents which occurred were later greatly exaggerated. A man of other fine qualities, Baker was not blessed with an abundant sense of humor. In 1904, Law School students protested against their rigid, uncomfortable classroom benches by thrice removing the offending seats from the room surreptitiously and placing them on the lawn outside. After the third incident, Baker reacted by expelling the entire class from the University. Their threat to enroll en masse at the University of Denver quickly calmed him, and an amicable settlement was achieved.

Generally, it was students, not administrators, who overreacted. After an early snowstorm in October 1910, a number of upperclassmen forced eight freshmen to strip naked and "streak" two laps around Woodbury Hall. Hazing of freshmen was strictly against University rules, and Baker, after a brief inquiry, suspended seventeen students, most of them for only two weeks. Baker later suggested that the penalties were quite lenient, a view not shared by a number of student leaders at the time. Indignation meetings, followed by a protest parade, finally led to a vote by students to "strike" the University. Baker expressed unconcern and refused to reinstate the offenders, believing the strike would peter out, once students realized the folly of their protests. His strategy was sound. For two days, the strike succeeded, as few students crossed picket lines to attend classes. On the third day, however, the University's women, divided over the boycott from the start, began returning to classes in large numbers. Members of the football team who favored the strike at the beginning began to have second thoughts; they feared that campus unrest would force either cancellation or forfeiture of their important contest with Utah, scheduled the next weekend. As these disagreements among the students deepened, leaders acknowledged defeat and capitulated.[67] Baker took no reprisals against the instigators of the strike; he simply told them that they "had made great fools of themselves" and that they should get back to work.[68]

A number of student activities and organizations were initiated during the Baker years. In September 1892, the first issue of the student newspaper *Silver and Gold* was published, succeeding the older *Portfolio*. Initially a weekly paper, it was devoted almost entirely to athletics and social activities. Although the paper announced the intention of commenting on serious state and national concerns, it seldom did so. Not a word was said about national elections in 1896 and 1900, and state politics drew little comment, except for matters which directly affected the University. By the mid-1890s, no subject was of as consuming interest to students as athletics.

At the beginning of the Baker administration, it hardly seemed possible that football and baseball would someday become big-time sports. The University's football team played its first full season in 1890, when a ragtag collection of youths with little collective playing experience managed to score but a single touchdown all year. One of its more forgettable defeats was a

103–0 rout at the hands of the Colorado School of Mines. After that disastrous season, there was no way for the team's fortunes to go but up. President Hale, an ardent football fan, believed that organized athletics would stimulate student morale, enhance the University's public image, and stimulate financial support. President Baker, also an athletic enthusiast, shared Hale's view. During his later years, the football team became the scourge of the Rocky Mountain Athletic Conference. Under the able direction of its young coach, Fred G. Folsom, the 1909, 1910, and 1911 teams crushed all opposition, as they rang up 21 consecutive victories. During those glorious three seasons, the team's impenetrable defense did not yield a single touchdown.[69] Football was not yet "big-time" at the end of the Baker years. Crowds were limited to the few hundred who could squeeze into Gamble Field's small stands, and admissions fees were nominal. But the University band, formed in 1909, enlivened game-time festivities, and the sport began to acquire the trappings of its present-day pageantry. Football had come a long way in twenty years.

Baker also encouraged the emergence of other varsity sports. Under Coach Frank R. Castleman, the University's track team enjoyed seven consecutive undefeated seasons between 1906 and 1912. The baseball team, which had struggled against high school teams during its first season in 1889, was soon a power in the Rocky Mountain area. Basketball evolved more than a decade later than football and baseball, as the first University team began to play in 1901. Several nonvarsity, club-level sports also developed around 1900. Fred B. R. Hellems, Dean of Liberal Arts, and a Silver Medalist fencer in the 1896 Olympics, organized a fencing club. Boxing, tennis, and golf were also club sports in the early 1900s.

Nonathletically inclined students also found increasingly numerous outlets for their interests during Baker's years. The first yearbook, named the *Columbine*, appeared in 1893; in 1900 its name was changed to the *Coloradan*. One of the oldest campus activities, the debating club, held weekly meetings by 1900 and often participated in public debates with teams from other colleges. In sharp contrast to later years, debate champions were campus heroes who vied with athletic stars for the adulation of their peers. The dramatic club, founded in 1902, frequently pro-

74

vided good entertainment at campus celebrations. A dozen Greek-letter societies for both men and women developed and became popular; by the time of Baker's retirement, the pressures of rushing and pledging created problems which would frustrate later administrations. More seriously, a number of honorary Greek-letter societies also emerged. In 1904, the national honorary fraternity Phi Beta Kappa established a local chapter—testimony to the University's growing academic reputation.

Several campus traditions emanate from the Baker years. Senior classes, noting the absence of foliage on the campus, began planting a "senior tree" in 1894. In 1899, Dr. Arthur Allin, professor of psychology and education, presented a cane, to be carried by the outstanding student in each senior class at the graduation ceremony. Allin contributed a touch of international flavor to campus tradition since he had carried a similar cane as a leading member of the graduating class at Victoria College in Toronto, Canada. A gold ring listing the name of its bearer was added each year to the cane. Within three decades, the cane listed names of men who later became prominent (including governors and a Supreme Court judge).[70]

One of the most noteworthy of all of Baker's achievements during twenty-two years as president was his ability to attract first-rate faculty members. The same year he assumed the University's presidency, he was also elected president of the National Council of Education. This position enabled him to form valuable contacts, important aids in recruiting an able faculty, from all over the United States. Realizing that the relative obscurity of the University and the low salaries would not permit him to hire persons with outstanding reputations in their fields, he concentrated instead on hiring young men and women with character and academic promise. He hoped that the excitement of building a university and the joys of living in Colorado would persuade them to stay.

In the course of enlarging a faculty from 32 to over 200 regular and part-time members between 1892 and 1914, Baker eventually hired several hundred people. Some arrived, stayed briefly, and left without making any impact. But many of those Baker hired became distinguished, even nationally renowned figures, giving the University many years of dedicated service.

Fred B. R. Hellems, a Latin scholar, served as Dean of Liberal Arts until his death in 1928. George Norlin, a professor of Greek, joined the faculty in 1899 and stayed for forty years, the last twenty as the University's fifth president. Other distinguished faculty who came during the Baker years were Oliver C. Lester, a physicist, who served as Dean of the Graduate School for many years; James F. Willard (history); Frances Ramaley (biology); and T. D. A. Cockerell (zoology). A surprising number of those hired by Baker had earned doctoral degrees at some of the most prestigious European universities.[71]

Faculty members who stayed must have loved hard work. Certainly they did not join the faculty for the salaries; faculty salaries appear to have been fixed, with little or no merit differential. In 1904, new professors usually received $1,600 with annual raises of $100. After three years at a fixed salary of $2,000, one could progress to a ceiling of $2,500. Not until 1914 were top salaries for professors raised to $3,000.[72] None of the benefits many faculty take for granted today existed then: no health and life insurance, retirement pensions, or investment programs. Tenure was unknown. The 1898 Regents rules stipulated that "All appointments of Professors and Instructors are subject to revocation when in the judgment of the Regents the good of the University requires it."[73] Nor did the faculty exert a great deal of influence upon University policy; although a University Senate was formed in 1908, it was seldom involved in faculty matters. Throughout Baker's term, it focused largely on the regulation of student activities.[74]

While there were drawbacks to teaching at the University, there were also significant attractions. There were a few research-oriented professors, but there was little pressure to publish. The teaching load averaged twelve hours weekly in the classroom; thus it was not overly strenuous. There were excellent opportunities for advancement for ambitious faculty members. Departments and schools were small; capable men and women faced no danger of being buried in an impersonal hierarchy. Several were rapidly promoted to administrative positions. For example, Norlin, Hellems, Lester, and Willard all achieved positions of influence and responsibility as young men as department chairmen and deans. Under Baker, several individuals reached such positions while in their early thirties. Finally, although salaries were low, the Colorado life-style appealed to many. The state was some years away from being one of America's best promoted vacation areas, and that may have made the local fishing, hiking, riding, and hunting even more enjoyable for the athletically oriented faculty. Those who were more sedentary could draw inspiration from the beautiful mountain scenery.

As he neared the end of his twenty-second year in office, on December 3, 1913, Baker announced his decision to retire, effective New Year's Day, 1914. He probably believed that after twenty years he had made his mark upon the University, that it was time to turn the office over to a younger person, and that he had earned a rest.

After a brief search, the Regents selected Livingston Farrand as the University's fourth president. Farrand was in some ways the antithesis of his predecessor. Warm, friendly, and outgoing, where Baker was intimidating, gruff, and reserved, Farrand soon developed intimate relations with many of the faculty. After graduating from Princeton in 1888, Farrand received his medical degree from Columbia. Following several years of study in Europe, including one year each at both Cambridge and the University of Berlin, he joined the Psychology Department at Columbia in 1893. He remained in the Psychology Department for ten years before moving to a Chair in Columbia's Anthropology Department. He still occupied the latter position when appointed the University of Colorado's president in 1914.[75]

However different Baker and Farrand were in personality, their emphasis on the University's service mission in the state dovetailed perfectly. In his inaugural speech titled "The State University and Public Service," Farrand stated, "The University could play no finer part than to stand as the ready servant of the state which maintains it in surmounting the obstacles which block its progress."[76] This attitude was especially fitting as the country entered the period of World War I.

The five years after 1914 were stormy for the University. The principle of academic freedom was challenged; there were two changes in administration; and World War I prompted important curricular changes—and the rapid departures of many faculty members and students.

In a noted academic freedom case, James H. Brewster, an instructor at the Law School, was given a one-year appointment for the 1914–1915 academic year. In the spring of 1915, according to Brewster's later testimony, he was led to believe his appointment would be extended at least another year by John D. Fleming, Dean of the Law School. Some months earlier, however, in December 1914, Brewster had testified before a congressional committee investigating the Ludlow Strike and subsequent "massacre" of several miners' families by the Colorado militia. During a period in which there was mounting national hysteria against any suspected "labor radicalism," Brewster had testified on behalf of the United Mine Workers.

According to Brewster, sometime after his conversations with Dean Fleming about his future at the University, he requested permission from Dr. Farrand to go to Washington to testify once again on behalf of the miners. Farrand allegedly warned him that in the event he absented himself from the classroom, his connection with the University would be terminated. Even though Brewster did not make the trip to Washington, he was informed in May 1915 that his appointment would not be renewed.[77] Shortly thereafter, Brewster publicized his charges that he was fired for political reasons. In response to newspaper stories, Farrand admitted that he had received a phone call from Governor Ammons urging him to fire Brewster. He insisted, however, that he had refused to yield to the governor's pressure. Farrand also denied having pressured Brewster not to testify.[78]

In response to the uproar, the American Association of University Professors (AAUP), founded in 1915, launched its first formal investigation on behalf of academic freedom at the University of Colorado. The AAUP investigating committee eventually exonerated the University administration. Its final report stated that the University had never intended to renew Brewster's one-year contract. Labeling the whole affair a "misunderstanding," it blamed the University only for notifying Brewster of his termination late in the academic year.[79] However, it is difficult to accept the AAUP's final report completely. There may indeed have been no hard evidence that the University was pressured into abandoning any thought of extending Brewster's contract. Nevertheless, it is difficult to accept the view that the administration's decision to terminate Brewster was unaffected by its fear of future economic reprisals by legislatures strongly influenced by conservative business interests. Brewster was, after all, associated with a radical cause at a time when such causes were increasingly unpopular with both the press and the general public.

Although Farrand's administration was marred by an investigation of academic freedom, it would be a serious error to assume that it was an unfortunate interlude in the history of the University. The Farrand years were a period of transition rather than a new era—they were distinguished by important decisions, many of which reached fruition later. In particular, Farrand was a strong force behind the successful effort of Colorado's public institutions of higher learning to win a ten-year mill levy for capital construction from the legislature. The new levy reinforced the successful effort of later administrations to develop a unified architectural style at the Boulder campus. Perhaps his most important contribution to the University's future was the leading role he played in opening negotiations with the Rockefeller Foundation for a grant to develop a new Denver campus for the Medical School.

There is no evidence that Farrand planned to make his stay at the University brief. But the University, like other institutions of higher learning, had to make sacrifices when the United States entered World War I. President Farrand was one of those called to "higher duty" when he requested a leave of absence to head the Rockefeller Foundation's medical mission in Paris in July 1917. As the shadow of war lengthened over the University in 1917 and 1918, one-third of the faculty and 15 percent of the students interrupted careers and studies to enlist in the "war to end all wars."[80] When he departed, Farrand planned to return. George Norlin, professor of Greek, was named acting president. Few at the time anticipated that Norlin's temporary elevation would stretch into a career which would almost equal Baker's in length.[81]

Under Acting President Norlin, the University enthusiastically committed itself to the war effort. A few days after Congress declared war, Farrand sent a telegram which was read to the students urging them to "indicate [their] willingness to serve."[82]

However, the *Silver and Gold* cautioned students against a precipitous rush to enlist in the armed services. ". . . We must not forget to consider where our services can be of most value. Three great armies of men will be required if this country is to be a factor of consequence in this war—a military, an industrial, and an agricultural army."[83] Women, as well as men, were called, joining the Red Cross and a Conservation Committee. They joined faculty wives in knitting sweaters, wrapping surgical dressings, and making bandages. They worked as farm laborers and also gave instructions on the best methods of canning food.[84]

The campus itself soon resembled an armed camp. The faculty voted for establishment of a Reserve Officer Training Corps (ROTC), though it refused to make military training compulsory. The student response was spirited and, soon after establishment of a unit in October 1917, some 400 men were enrolled. The military presence was even more pronounced when the War Department set up a Student Army Training Corps (SATC) program. Army draftees were sent to college campuses across the country for the special training they would need as officers. Future second lieutenants studied mathematics, mechanics, engineering, and the sciences. By May 1918, about 250 men were studying special military skills courses at the University, mostly in engineering. Khaki dominated the campus scene as hundreds of uniformed men drilled. Navy blue also appeared, after a 60-man naval training unit was created in September 1918.[85]

World War I was a period in which the public generally demanded expressions of patriotism from their employees. The public servant who did not stand "foursquare" behind the flag and, more important, the war effort, was subject to severe censure. Academic freedom was a casualty all over the country, as few administrators braved the rage of legislators and the press by defending faculty who expressed unorthodox views. Acting President Norlin, whether because of his inexperience at the job or personal inclination, succumbed to political pressure. When Governor Elias Ammons inquired into the allegedly unpatriotic statements of a professor, Norlin cautiously replied,

> I should perhaps say emphatically that should it be clear to me that Mr. Chadwick [the professor] has continued [since the declaration of war] or is continuing to make remarks re-

flecting upon this country's part in the war, we should have to face the problem squarely and take action. That the University has not been overly conservative on this question is indicated by the fact that since the beginning of the year two members of our Faculty have been dropped because of expressed pro-German sympathies.[86]

Norlin also acquiesced to the governor's request that he serve as chairman of the state's Commission on Americanization. The committee coordinated the statewide effort to teach the English language and "patriotism" to "aliens." Although the Regents voted 3–2 against eliminating German from the curriculum, the vote was based not upon any principle of academic freedom, but that students were ignoring the subject by their own choice.[87] Despite the emphasis on forced patriotism in Boulder during the war years, there appears to have been at least as much tolerance for freedom of expression at the University of Colorado as there was at other institutions of higher learning in the state and nation.[88]

At Boulder, during the war, it seemed that everyone wished to join the war effort. Though their "sacrifice" was somewhat delayed, the Inter-Fraternity Council voted in September 1918 to suspend all activities: that fall there would be no rushing, pledging, or other social activities.[89] For a time there was discussion of abolishing all athletics for the duration of the war. Although nothing came of that proposal, "unnecessary frivolities" such as dances and other innocent social gatherings were sharply curtailed. At one point it appeared that everyone would sacrifice for the war effort, voluntarily or otherwise. In September 1918, a serious influenza epidemic began among one of the military units. Efforts to isolate the disease failed. By November 1918, the epidemic forced the closing of campus for a month. Several fraternity houses were converted to hospitals, and the whole military program was thrown into a turmoil. The war probably seemed very close to Boulderites at the time of the armistice, as the epidemic eventually took the lives of nineteen young men.[90]

Shortly after the armistice there were a number of signs that the University was entering a new era. President Farrand announced his resignation in 1919 in order to accept the presidency of Cornell University, and George Norlin was appointed to the presidency on a permanent basis. The University divested itself of its military activities in a pell-mell rush to "return to normalcy." Although Norlin and the Regents attempted to continue the ROTC program, students generally opposed it, and the administration dropped the idea.[91] Special military courses were rapidly weeded out of the curriculum, and the "tent city" and temporary barracks which had housed the military units east of the railway tracks were quickly dismantled. World War I had little lasting effect upon the University. As it entered the Roaring Twenties, the war seemed a distant memory.

The changes wrought at the University during the period from 1892 to 1919 were enormous. The Baker years in particular were critical for the organization of a real, public university. Baker's willingness to take risks at times seemed reckless, yet his force-feeding of curriculum change developed the framework of a comprehensive university with a variety of educational programs long before such an institution could have emerged under a more cautious president. Physical expansion of the Boulder campus and numerical growth of both faculty and the student body were important accomplishments. Baker was quite successful in hiring a faculty with sound credentials and scholarly promise. Yet Baker's great achievement was his success in articulating to the public the University's service role and in taking important steps toward implementing that role. In subsequent years the University would in fact become the multipurpose service institution that Baker envisioned in the 1890s.

Three

BUILDING
A UNIVERSITY:
1919—1939

W HEN GEORGE NORLIN became president early in 1919, few
doubted that the University had established its role as a
leader among institutions of higher education in Colorado. Since
the 1890s, the University experienced steady—and sometimes rapid
—growth. While its size and academic reputation hardly matched
those of the larger state universities or the prestigious eastern colleges, it did surpass most of the small liberal arts colleges west of
the Mississippi. The challenge now was to build quality into the
University's many educational programs and to establish a reputation for training students at the graduate level. In short, the challenge for Norlin was to build a mature university while rein-
forcing the leadership of the University of Colorado in the state.

The most obvious changes during the Norlin years were
physical. Graduates returning to the campus in 1939 for the first
time in twenty years hardly recognized the University. Alumni
were impressed by the array of new buildings. Between 1920 and
1939, the famed "Colorado Style" of campus architecture emerged,
dominating construction on the Boulder campus until the 1960s.
Enrollments had more than tripled, from 1,300 to over 4,400.[1]
Perhaps the greatest single achievement during the Norlin years

was the creation of a new campus for the University's Medical School in Denver.

Despite these advances, the development of the University during the Norlin administration was, at best, very uneven. In part reflecting national trends, there was relatively little intellectual experimentation and curriculum expansion at the University during the 1920s and 1930s. By 1939, the University was still not comparable with the older, more established state universities. The main reason was that the institution's administration was, of necessity, concerned primarily with survival. Between 1919 and 1939, the University experienced a seemingly interminable series of crises, mostly as a result of inadequate funding. Unfortunately, the state's economy failed to reflect the national prosperity during the 1920s; it suffered sharp reverses during the Depression, and it recovered very slowly in the late 1930s. State legislators were swamped by demands for state support by increasing numbers of vigorously competing interest groups, and they put a low priority on the needs of the University, particularly during the 1930s. Norlin thus had the unenviable task of providing quality education for continually growing numbers of students with decreasing per capita resources.

Ironically, however, the legislature's parsimonious support during the Norlin years may have worked to the University's long-range advantage. Forced to seek support beyond the borders of Colorado, the University went to the boardrooms of eastern foundations and to the federal bureaucracy. The practical lessons learned through efforts to secure external funding in the 1920s and 1930s prepared University officials to react quickly and imaginatively to the outpouring of federal grants beginning with World War II.

During nearly a quarter century of leadership at the University, George Norlin not only effected many concrete achievements, but also became a symbol, a link between the past and the future. He was born on the western frontier; as a graduate student and scholar, he had immersed himself in the task of translating major Greek classics. Yet, as a twentieth-century university president, he was able to absorb the extraordinary pressures of academic administration and articulate long-range objectives for his institution. Equally impressive, he developed critical insights into the nature of contemporary society and the drift of world events. As Visiting Roosevelt Professor at the University of Berlin in 1933, he witnessed firsthand Hitler's rise to power. His repeated warnings about the nature and the objects of German fascism provided a dimension to the intellectual life of the campus during his later years which it might not otherwise have obtained.[2]

Norlin arrived in Boulder in the fall of 1899, after earning a Ph.D. from the University of Chicago. To succeed as a member of the faculty at a relatively obscure, fledgling western university, one needed a pioneering instinct, a capacity for working long hours, and a passionate dedication to teaching. He promptly established a reputation as a first-rate scholar and teacher. One of his former students later recalled, "His clear, farseeing mind was a lens bringing to us the rays from other minds and ages. It was a purely intellectual process." A colleague noted that his classes "never seemed to hurry over their texts, yet there was a satisfying sense of accomplishment."[3]

Promotions came rapidly and he was entrusted with several administrative assignments; yet nobody was more surprised than Norlin when he was asked by the Regents to serve as acting president to replace Livingston Farrand in the spring of 1917.[4] Two years later, when Farrand resigned, the Regents offered Norlin the presidency on a permanent basis. He was confronted with a crucial career decision. His natural instinct was to continue primarily as a teacher and scholar. Translating Greek classics matched his love of fishing, gardening, long hikes—and poker. Accepting the presidency would mean the sharp curtailment of these pleasurable activities. To complicate matters further, his former mentor, Paul Shorey, offered him the prospect of a Chair in Classics at the University of Chicago, one of the preeminent institutions of higher education in America.

On the other hand, he was flattered by the pressure exerted upon him to accept the presidency of the University on a permanent basis. In an uncharacteristically revealing letter to Farrand dated February 19, 1919, Norlin discussed the situation and voiced his apparent indecision:

There seems to be a general expectation . . . that I shall continue in this office to stabilize conditions. It is a question which I shall probably have to decide for my own future as things now look, and I have been going through no little distress of mind regarding it. My aspirations have, as I think you know, looked in another direction and it is by no means easy to put them aside once and for all. Nor is it easy, on the other hand, to refuse responsibilities which circumstances threaten to put upon you.[5]

It is difficult to determine whether Norlin in fact viewed his acceptance as a temporary commitment, solely to "stabilize conditions," or as a "once and for all" change in the direction of his career. His uncertainty apparently resolved, he accepted the position a week later.[6]

At the outset of Norlin's presidency, some of his colleagues may have doubted that he had a personality suitable for the demands of his office. When Norlin was concluding his career as president twenty years later, a young colleague labeled as "paradoxical" the fact "that a shy and slender professor of Greek . . . should become the head of a large state university, in a milieu where education often has to fight for its life in the hurlyburly of politics."[7] Averse to publicity, and loathing the role of supplicant, Norlin refused to lobby personally for funds at the state capitol, except in the direst emergencies.[8] Although he occasionally dramatized the University's needs through public speeches, either to small groups or over radio, he preferred to work behind the scenes, coordinating the efforts of others. For example, in 1920 a constitutional amendment to increase the mill levy for the benefit of Colorado's institutions of higher learning was presented to the voters. Norlin was chosen to supervise overall campaign strategy, while the presidents of several other publicly supported colleges embarked on extensive speaking tours on behalf of the amendment.[9] Quiet and aloof to strangers, and formal with even his closest associates, he was unwilling to stump the state as a handshaking politician.[10]

Norlin generally disliked the ceremonial duties attached to the presidency; he preferred to devote his energy to more intellectual matters. During his tenure as president, he somehow found the time to write and publish essays on a wide range of important topics. One of his major concerns was defining the mission of a modern university. Clearly, different colleges and universities should perform different tasks. Having come to Colorado straight from the University of Chicago, which offered one of the most ambitious experimental graduate programs in America, Norlin might have been expected to attempt to duplicate the Chicago model in Boulder. Norlin quickly realized that geography, lack of facilities, and lack of public interest in such a direction dimmed the prospects of placing the primary emphasis on graduate work. As a classicist, he stressed the idea that the University should turn out liberally educated generalists. He was fearful lest the American university succumb to the demands of commerce and produce a plethora of what he termed "uneducated specialists." In the mid-1920s, at a time when the University of Colorado and other American universities were rapidly expanding their professional schools, Norlin was concerned that they might graduate

> . . . too many specialists of our industrial order, of our factory system, mere bolts and rivets in a vastly complicated machine . . . condemned to see life in fragments and live it in fragments, with little comprehension of the whole, with no integrating vision to give zest or meaning to their isolated tasks.

Insisting that "the first business of public education [was] to keep civilization alive," Norlin believed that the University should

> . . . organize and integrate . . . a common body of knowledge which would serve to make us feel at home in [both] . . . the world of human relationships and the physical universe—a curriculum of training in the fundamentals of a common, cultivated life.[11]

Economic rewards and professional advancement, suggested Norlin, naturally followed the student who conscientiously pursued a broadly based humanistic curriculum. Since the Colorado Agricultural College and the Colorado School of Mines specialized in providing programs for argiculture, mining, and engineering, Norlin perceived that the University's essential mission was to offer the finest publicly funded liberal arts program available in

---

87

the Rocky Mountain region.[12] While the University competed with other public colleges in Colorado for state funds and, to a degree, for students, their primary missions did not seriously overlap.

Norlin was acutely aware that it was one thing to discuss University goals in intellectually abstract terms, but quite another matter to overcome the practical obstacles to these goals. Even before his promotion to the presidency, Norlin realized that the University's physical plant was woefully inadequate to meet even the basic demands of a rapidly growing student body, let alone provide a harmonious social and intellectual setting. Fortunately for the University, the Colorado General Assembly had passed a ten-year mill levy in 1917 to provide funds for much needed buildings. Thus one of Norlin's first tasks was to formulate a long-range campus building plan.

Devising a campus plan was a formidable challenge. The campus of 1917 consisted of two dozen buildings; almost half were maintenance sheds and other service structures. There were but three or four prominent buildings, including Old Main and Macky Auditorium. No particular architectural style predominated. Prior to 1919, styles were chosen primarily on the basis of function and economy, with little concept of architectural harmony. The campus was divided into two parts by the Colorado and Southern Railway and the Denver and Interurban Railway tracks. Trains frequently interfered with the peace and solitude of life on campus. Some years later, one staff member recalled that "recitations and lectures in the Engineering Building ceased whenever a struggling, whistling freight began lurching up the hill."[13] Writing in 1937, Norlin later described the campus of 1917 as being "bleak, barren, and forbidding"; in a less charitable passage, he recalled the campus as basically resembling a "third-rate farm."[14]

Norlin and the Board of Regents decided that some symmetry in architectural style was desirable; the problem was to reach agreement on which one. A number of campus styles were suggested, including the popular Gothic and Georgian. After several indecisive meetings, the Regents hired the Philadelphia firm of Day and Klauder to guide future building at the Boulder campus. The choice was most fortunate. Charles Klauder visited the campus for several days and eventually concluded that none of the popular contemporary styles was wholly appropriate to the University's special natural setting. Uncovering some old photographs he had taken of buildings in the mountains of northern Italy, Klauder rediscovered an unpretentious but picturesque style of architecture which he believed would blend magnificently into Boulder's mountain setting. The buildings featured rough, untrimmed stone walls, varying in color from a pale yellow to a reddish purple. The architect believed that the "Colorado Style" which he proposed would not be widely copied on other campuses; it would give the University a uniqueness of its own. Klauder carefully considered costs; most of the stonemasonry was available in local quarries and thus would be relatively inexpensive.[15] The plans he presented in 1918 comprised a plausible layout of how the campus would appear two decades later.

Convinced by Klauder's vision and his detailed proposals, the Regents approved the plans in 1918.[16] The next step was to determine the priority of the specific building projects. By early 1920, the Regents had endorsed a ten-year building plan, to cost nearly $1,000,000. Equally pleased with the prospect of a thoroughly modern campus and sensing the importance of the commitment, the student newspaper, the Silver and Gold, editorialized:

> The University has entered a new era of building. . . . [It] is past the formative period, but . . . is still in the youth of her life. Colorado has never lacked visioners [sic] and her students are glad that she still has high servants who are willing to dare for her. The new building program is one of the greatest ventures that any similar institution has attempted.[17]

The first major project in the Colorado Style was a new building for the College of Arts and Sciences, constructed in 1921. Among the other large projects completed during the 1920s were a men's gymnasium (1924); a football stadium (1924); two new wings in the chemistry building (1926); and a women's gymnasium (1928).[18]

However impressive the new building program appeared, it barely kept pace with even the most critical physical needs of a rapidly growing university. Inadequate facilities were a chronic problem during the Norlin years. Unfortunately, the 1927 legislature refused to renew the ten-year mill levy passed in 1917. There were several reasons for the legislature's intransigence. Though its influence was waning by 1927, the Ku Klux Klan dominated state government briefly and apparently contemplated the dismissal of Catholic and Jewish faculty from the state university and colleges. The state's junior colleges, which had been excluded from the new mill-levy bill, actively opposed it. In addition, the legislature was in the process of investigating charges that the state colleges were maintaining lobbyists for their interests who were paid out of public funds.[19] When one adds to these considerations that the state's economy was less healthy in 1927 than it was in 1917, legislators may have felt more than justified in refusing to approve ten more years of guaranteed building funds for state colleges. The state-supported colleges thus lost a source of revenue which had been yielding nearly $200,000 annually.[20]

University officials were stunned by the unexpected reversal. Despite the construction activity, financed by the mill levy since 1920, there was actually less floor space per student in 1927 than in 1917.[21] Hoping to induce the legislators to change their minds and to restore the levy, Norlin predicted that the decision would force the University to admit fewer students and simultaneously raise tuition fees.[22] The warning was totally ignored. In 1930, Norlin tried a different tack of appealing to the legislators' state pride. He suggested that their failure to provide building funds in 1927 had placed the University at a competitive disadvantage with other state universities. "We do not want conditions at home to be such that our Colorado boys and girls may find it to their advantage to go out of state to pursue their education at better equipped universities."[23]

Along with the excitement and uncertainties of the building program at the Boulder campus during the 1920s, the greatest "brick-and-mortar-achievement" during the decade was unquestionably the construction of a new Medical School facility in Denver. The consolidation of the University's Medical School and the Denver and Gross Medical Colleges had occurred in 1911. Expanding enrollments during World War I convinced all concerned that larger facilities were needed. Medical education in Colorado would best be served if facilities and a large hospital were built in Denver for the Medical School.[24]

It was equally apparent that the University could not finance the buildings alone. Norlin realized that state aid would be unlikely unless the University generated the bulk of necessary funding from outside sources.[25] The University was fortunate in that before his resignation from the presidency, Livingston Farrand had pleaded for a major grant for medical education from the Rockefeller Foundation.[26] Norlin then assumed control of the negotiations with the foundation after his elevation to the presidency. His persistent efforts succeeded. In November 1920, the University received the heartening news that it had been awarded a substantial grant of $700,000 for construction of a new medical school, plus a $50,000 annual appropriation for the first three years of operation to help cover maintenance costs.[27]

Securing the Rockefeller Foundation grant was only the first step in the University's quest for its new medical facility. The award stipulated that matching funds must be generated from other sources. Norlin believed that the legislature would be uncooperative unless the University assumed responsibility for raising at least part of the funds. He therefore proposed to Governor Oliver Shoup that the University would raise $200,000 if the legislature would appropriate $600,000.[28] To his delight, the legislature accepted the arrangement. The University's fund drive went smoothly, and when Frederick G. Bonfils, owner of the *Denver Post*, offered a 17-acre site at Colorado Boulevard and Ninth Avenue as a gift to the University in 1922, the last serious obstacle was overcome.

Construction commenced in the fall of 1922 and was completed two years later, in time for the opening of the 1924–25 academic year. Initial construction included, in addition to the University's Medical School, the original 150-bed Colorado General Hospital, the 80-bed Colorado Psychopathic Hospital, and a residence hall for ninety nurses. The final cost came to nearly $2,000,000 including equipment and supplies.[29] When the Colorado General Hospital began admitting patients in January 1925, the University sponsored a three-day dedication ceremony at which local, state, and University officials were eloquent regard-

ing the exciting future in store for both Colorado medical education and medical care.[30]

Completion of the impressive new facility brought both
prestige and headaches to the University. New buildings did not
automatically attract a qualified student body. Two years after
the Denver campus opened, Dean Maurice H. Rees admitted that
while there were two applications for every freshman class position, "even with this large number of applicants we had to admit
about eight with very low premedical standing."[31] Finances,
however, threatened to present still greater problems. Before the
new school opened, Norlin feared that the added cost of maintaining and operating the facility would exert a financial drain
upon the other parts of the University's operation. Late in 1922,
Norlin suggested that the legislature enact a permanent mill levy
for maintenance, which he estimated would yield about $80,000
annually.[32] Noting that present University revenues were inadequate to maintain both the new Medical School and other existing
departments, he justified his separate request on the grounds that
the Medical School, "being in a sense a distinct institution, should
be handled by the State as a special financial problem."[33] Norlin's
statement presaged a growing tension between the Medical
School and the University in Boulder which degenerated into
barely concealed hostility during the financial crunch of the Depression years. Although the legislature eventually passed a one-
tenth mill levy in the late 1920s, the Medical School operated in
the red throughout the Norlin years.[34]

Nevertheless, the University's commitment to develop a first-
rate medical school clearly brought it a high degree of local
visibility. University officials hoped it would also create greater
prestige for the University at the national level. Many faculty
and administrators felt ambivalent toward the better known eastern universities. They were delighted to hire new faculty with
Ph.D.s from Harvard, Johns Hopkins, and Chicago. They were
grateful for the quality of professors attracted, and they were
generally content to follow the lead of the eastern colleges in
academic experimentation. On the other hand, many in the University resented its "colonial" dependency upon the eastern institutions. They were anxious, nevertheless, that the University gain

full-fledged acceptance and recognition by the national academic establishment.[35]

This last hope was forcefully stated in Norlin's reaction to the 1924 announcement that the University had been denied admission to the Association of American Universities, an organization which included virtually all of the elite eastern colleges and a number of established western and midwestern state universities. An association official informed Norlin that his institution "has felt benefit from its small size," but that Colorado could not be admitted because "graduate study and research in no more than a few departments seem to be, at best, beyond the experimental stage."[36] Exasperated by the former comment and sensitive to the latter point, Norlin drew from his classical training and responded with more than a touch of sarcasm:

> . . . we must possess ourselves in humility and patience, consoling ourselves with the philosophy of Cato who, when asked why his stature did not stand with others in the Forum, replied that he preferred to have people ask the question why it was not there rather than why it was there.[37]

Clearly, the Graduate School was a fledgling operation; it is likely that it detracted from the University's national image. While the University granted its first graduate degree in 1885 and formally organized the Graduate School in 1893, graduate work remained a small part of the University's total academic programs. When Norlin assumed the presidency, the Graduate School had not awarded a single Ph.D. in four years. The school was so poorly funded that its dean, Oliver C. Lester, did all of the necessary clerical work himself. He had no secretary, and his office was not even equipped with a typewriter.[38]

Nevertheless, under Norlin, the Graduate School commenced a period of steady enrollment growth. From a post–World War I low of 53 students in the 1919–20 academic year, the school grew to 141 full-time students in 1922–23. A 1924 report of its operations noted that: "As yet it has no glorious record of which we might be prone to boast, but in its accomplishments we may take a quiet pride and upon them rest our confidence for the future."[39] By 1938–39, the total graduate student body reached nearly 400 during the regular academic year, plus another 1,525 during the summer quarter.[40] Several new graduate programs were introduced during the Norlin years: they included masters degrees in science, music, education, and fine arts.

Enrollment growth and new degree programs did not, however, signify the emergence of a first-rate graduate school; much to their credit, University officials pointed out its shortcomings during the Norlin years. To a young man inquiring into the possibility of pursuing a Ph.D. in political science in 1929, Jacob Van Ek, Dean of Arts and Sciences, candidly replied, "I wonder if it would not be worth your while to consider going to a university where they have had more time and resources to develop research facilities."[41] Eight years later, in a forthright plea to the Rockefeller Foundation for a grant for a proposed new library building, Norlin stated that the University's poorly stocked and equipped library was a primary obstacle to building a strong graduate school. Near the close of his presidency, Norlin pointed out that the Graduate School was still one of the University's problems:

> The Graduate School should be put on a par with its undergraduate and professional divisions. It's not there now, I am sorry to say. The University has reached the point, in our opinion, that it is no longer justified in generally advising its graduate students to go to the larger universities to complete their work for the doctorate.

Even in this candid statement of the University's shortcomings, he was unable to resist criticism of the eastern educational establishment, as he concluded, "we should be able to do better by [our students] here than by consigning them to the mass production of the 'Ph.D. Mills.' "[42]

While the Graduate School was struggling to achieve maturity, the undergraduate program developed at a satisfying rate and several professional schools evolved. In the 1920s the departments of home economics, journalism, and art, and a School of Business Administration were organized. The Summer School, which reopened in 1904 with 60 students, also grew quickly.

In 1918, its single six-week schedule was expanded into two six-week sessions. That summer it served 1,327 young men and women. The new program proved extremely popular with out-of-state students, as they were able to combine a vacation period with earning academic credits. By 1920, the Summer School ranked among the country's top ten in terms of number of students attending. However, there were those who questioned the rigor of its demands. One out-of-town newspaper dubbed it "Education's Country Club," and wondered how anyone could get much done amid the splendid scenery and variety of recreational diversions which Boulder offered. In all likelihood, such negative publicity attracted even more students. Even during the Depression, the Summer School continued to grow; by 1940 it served 4,330 students, a number roughly equal to enrollment during the regular academic year.[43]

Despite the growth of the University in physical and numerical terms, and the emergence of new schools and departments, there was relatively little substantive academic innovation or experimentation under Norlin. The University experienced a period of relatively quiet growth and consolidation in contrast to considerable curriculum change in colleges and universities across the country. Course offerings and degree requirements changed remarkably little between 1919 and 1939. Nevertheless, the Norlin years produced at least one significant innovation in the curriculum in Arts and Sciences: the Honors program.

The Honors program was introduced in 1930; it clearly derived much of its inspiration from the pioneering work done by President Frank Aydelotte at Swarthmore during the early 1920s.[44] Prior to 1930, Honors at the University were determined solely on the basis of grades. The primary object of the new plan for Honors, according to Dean Van Ek, was to encourage superior students to go beyond regular undergraduate course work by undertaking additional readings from bibliographies carefully selected by the various academic departments. Students committing themselves to the additional work would benefit from the tutorial supervision provided by the faculty members who agreed to monitor the program. The plan was designed to free Honors students from the routine of standard courses, but they were required to put in at least 200 hours of reading from the selected bibliography during a given academic year. Van Ek hoped that under the plan Honors candidates would

> . . . give evidence of an intellectual interest in the world they live in, of an educated person's appreciation . . . of the spirit and method of science, an awareness of social institutions, a sense of the world as one of history, of development, of change. . . .[45]

The optional program was available only to the top 30 percent of all students registered in Arts and Sciences.

Though announced with considerable fanfare, the program experienced slow going at first. From the outset, the number of students enrolled remained small. The *Silver and Gold* noted in 1932 that of some 60 members of the class of 1932 who entered the program in 1930, only about 20 remained.[46] Several departments complained that professors who agreed to undertake tutorials with students received no recognition in the form of reduced teaching loads.[47] They insisted that the program was "too elaborate" in that it made excessive personal demands upon staffs which were "too small and already overworked."[48] Generally, Honors programs also appeared, in the opinion of one scholar, to be moving against common trends of public education during the Depression years:

> In the public universities during [the 1930s] the trend was away from a direct concern for the needs of the most gifted segment of the undergraduate body and toward "democratizing" education, which meant in part placing major emphasis upon enabling weaker students to survive."[49]

Nevertheless, the same individual labeled the University's program as one of the "outstanding Honors programs" at any state university in the United States.[50]

Two other changes in Arts and Sciences were significant. In 1934 the College dropped the old numerical system of grading and converted to the letter system. Of more importance, Arts and Sciences divided its curriculum into upper and lower "divisions" in 1937. The faculty had become concerned that there seemed to be little coherence in the curriculum offerings of the freshman and sophomore years. Also, many students determined their majors as early as their freshman year; then they switched majors once or more, often during their sophomore and junior years. The new system was designed to achieve two goals. By emphasizing a broadly based, general curriculum in the first two years, students who left school without degrees would at least be exposed systematically to the rudiments of a liberal education instead of a potpourri of electives. In addition, by preventing students from selecting majors until the end of their sophomore year, it was hoped that the new system would eliminate a number of false starts toward hastily chosen degree programs.[51]

According to a number of popular views, the 1920s produced a generation of college students which was extraordinarily immune to the appeals of even the most imaginative and stimulating curriculum developments. In some respects, students of the University of Colorado fit the stereotype of the college student popularized by F. Scott Fitzgerald, H. L. Mencken, and others. Denver newspapers periodically charged fraternities with sponsoring sex orgies, where inordinate amounts of "bathtub booze" were consumed.[52] Students definitely followed national styles with enthusiasm. "Sheiks" and "flappers" appeared on the campus, with their raccoon coats, roadsters, and hip flasks. Football began to reach "big time" importance. Folsom Stadium was constructed in 1924, replacing Gamble Field. The new facility regularly hosted crowds over 10,000. By the early 1920s, the University began to schedule name teams throughout the United States, and even beyond the borders. In 1924 the University team traveled to Hawaii for two scheduled games.[53] Student interest soared as Coach Myron Witham led the team to impressive seasons, particularly during the mid-1920s; ardent fans thronged to distant contests, transported by "student special" railroad cars.[54]

Perusal of the student newspaper, the *Silver and Gold*, during the 1920s suggests at times an almost total lack of concern among students about matters of the mind. A member of the class of 1928, when asked what he got out of four years at the University, replied:

> A gymnasium towel with "Colorado" in block letters printed across the top, thirty pieces of silver collected from various nunneries on the hill, a habit of wearing sloppy clothes, two

97

hundred signs representing various firms in Boulder, and a sweet, lissome maiden with smoldering eyes.[55]

On the other hand 1927 Arts and Sciences survey suggests that the distinction between the supposedly frivolous college generation of the 1920s and the sober, industrious collegians of the 1930s has been over-done. The stereotypes are too facile. At the University of Colorado, a number of students were attracted by serious pursuits during the 1920s. While the popularity vis-à-vis athletics declined at the University, the debate team frequently competed against other colleges in Macky Auditorium before large audiences. As late as 1927, an international debate against a Cambridge University team attracted 400 spectators, who witnessed a Colorado victory.[56] A number of students were interested enough to become actively involved in promoting University interests outside of Boulder. When the administration decided to campaign for additional mill-levy support for University maintenance in the fall of 1920, hundreds of students organized to publicize the cause. The Associated Students of the University of Colorado helped plan a parade in downtown Denver preceding a football game with Denver University. Denied permission for the march by city authorities, students instead staged an impressive demonstration for the mill levy at halftime of the football game.[57]

In contrast to the image of the empty-headed Jazz Age college student, many observers have portrayed the student of the Depression era as sober, industrious, and inclined to indulge himself in fewer, simpler pleasures. Certainly there is some validity to this characterization. The Depression brought marked changes in student life-styles at colleges across the country, including Colorado. At times, the dominant concern among students in Boulder appeared to be staying in college to avoid the uncertainties of the marketplace. A Silver and Gold editorial in December 1930 titled "More Unemployed?" captured some of the urgency of the situation:

> Economists tell us that a good many of the students in colleges are there because they have no other place to go. . . . Should they be dismissed from college, their livelihood would be cut off. . . . Students must exert themselves, must give special and intensive effort to passing their courses. Professors must be lenient. . . .[58]

The student paper also contained frequent columns suggesting ways to save money. The Dean of Men, Harry Carlson, reported that when groups of students "batched it" by sharing an apartment, and cooking and cleaning chores, room and board costs could drop to as little as $15 per month. He also cited the case of one student who went out to a local road in the evening to scavenge for coal which dropped off loaded trucks; he thus avoided large fuel bills for his apartment.[59] An editorial in the spring of 1932 suggested closing the University several weeks earlier than planned; Colorado's late closing would permit students from other colleges to get the jump on University students searching for precious summer jobs. A large proportion of students worked at least on a part-time basis to help pay their expenses. The *Silver and Gold* reported in 1931 that about 25 percent of all students worked during the school year as "hashers," maintenance men, maids, housecleaners, etc.[60] Without question, more students would have worked had they been able to find jobs. When the Federal Emergency Relief Administration (FERA) granted funds for 315 part-time student jobs at the Boulder campus in the fall of 1934, over 1,200 students applied.[61]

The Depression, interestingly, had the salutary effect of drawing students, faculty, and the administration closer together. At the height of the economic crisis the Boulder faculty, already saddled with wage cuts averaging 10 percent, voted to set aside 1 percent of their salaries for the purpose of creating student employment. Research assistantships, clerical and secretarial positions paying 30¢ per hour were funded.[62] Despite declining budgets, the administration increased the money available for loans to needy students. In 1932, over 1,000 students received direct loans from the University. The administration also provided other, less formal types of assistance to students. For example, Dean Carlson set aside a closet in his office for storing contributions of clothing by more affluent students and faculty; needy students were thus able to secure overcoats and galoshes at no expense.[63]

Yet student life on campus during the Depression was not all work and hardship. Many, if not all, students immersed themselves in athletics and other extracurricular activities, and in the excitement of fraternity and sorority life. Under Coach Bernard "Bunny" Oakes, the football team experienced marked success in

99

the late 1930s. The 1937 team, sparked by All-American halfback and future Rhodes Scholar and Supreme Court Justice Byron "Whizzer" White, gained national stature by defeating Missouri, going undefeated and untied in Big Seven Conference play, and winning an invitation to the Cotton Bowl. On occasion, student government elections were marred by egg-throwing brawls between competing factions. The administration, fearful of the impression such spectacles had on the minds of tightfisted legislators, felt compelled to suspend student government elections for a time in the spring of 1931.[64]

Fraternity and sorority activities continued to cause headaches for University officials. Investigation revealed that in the fall of 1932 sororities spent almost three times the amount allowed by the Dean of Women for rushing functions. In 1938 and 1939, the excessive demands of fraternity Hell Weeks on pledges became serious enough for the Denver newspapers to have a field day exposing allegedly "barbaric tortures." The resulting publicity induced the University's Board of Regents to formally outlaw Hell Weeks in the spring of 1939.[65]

Largely, life for the majority of students in Boulder was not radically altered by the Depression. Students were geographically isolated from much of the Depression turmoil witnessed by students on urban campuses such as City College of New York or the University of Chicago. The daily experiences of passing bread lines and Hooverville shacks and witnessing communist or socialist marches were foreign to them. No trainloads of Bonus Expeditionary Force veterans passed through Boulder. For most students, real poverty seemed remote. A 1932 *Silver and Gold* editorial noted:

> College men and women, we believe, are conservative because they do not think as much as they should. Conditions seem all right as they are to students because they have not felt the press of the financial situation. They simply do not care.[66]

Intellectual fervor seemed to be in low key on the campus even during the 1930s. Radical and pacifist student organizations periodically appeared on campus, but they attracted small followings. A "peace" strike on April 22, 1936, induced no more than

200 students to boycott classes. In the fall of 1938, Allen E. Merrick, a former University student, was killed in Spain while fighting for the Loyalists in the Spanish Civil War. Some months later, his mother enlisted the aid of the Pueblo branch of the American Legion to prove that her son had come under the influence of "communistic" professors while attending the University. Although the *Silver and Gold* and the legionnaires traded insults, no probe ever materialized.[67] Such incidents of student activism, involvement in "great causes," were the exception, not the rule, in Boulder during the 1930s.

Changes in student concerns and roles since the Norlin years are obvious, but changes in those of the faculty are even more profound. Professors were expected to be teachers first, and to have a strong interest in providing individual counseling to students. Research was incidental, a fact lamented by a few professors. In 1919, biologist Theodore D. A. Cockerell, a prolific writer himself, expressed his frustration at the lack of recognition accorded to those on the faculty with research interests:

> To put the thing bluntly, with regard to research—I consider the status of the University as something to be ashamed of. . . . No serious effort to recognize or encourage research has been made. . . . The result is that very little is being done, and the faculty cares very little about it. For me to start a movement in the faculty to secure support of research would, I fear, be inopportune; the faculty as a whole does not consist of research men, and will not with any zeal support a plan for the greater recognition of research functions as normal to University departments.[68]

The Regents voted early in 1920 to provide a sabbatical leave "for men of professorial rank to enable them to engage in special study and research to enhance their value to the University."[69] This action did not, however, stimulate a significant upswing in research activity during the Norlin years. Few sabbaticals were granted during a time of economic troubles. A random sampling of 100 "position description" forms submitted by faculty members during 1938, Norlin's last full year, revealed that only a bare majority of faculty members reported *any* research or writing effort during the year.[70]

During the Norlin years, far more emphasis was placed on

teaching than on research which led directly to publication. Dean Jacob Van Ek of Arts and Sciences labeled the period as one of "quiet scholarship," in which research and reading for purposes of enlivening classroom lectures were valued as highly as was research for publication. Faculty members were also required to supervise student activities more closely than now. An assistant professor of English stated in 1938 that 25 percent of his week was spent proctoring the men's dormitory, "maintaining order, arranging and conducting social functions, advising students on various points, answering foolish questions." Another professor noted that she spent at least half of her time "grading themes and quizzes" and reviewing the results with students.[71]

Nor did administrators shirk counseling duties. According to one admirer, President Norlin took the time to visit with any student who requested an individual conference.[72] Dean Van Ek estimated that he spent at least fifteen hours each week in counseling individual students. Significantly, parents of students expected close attention by administrators to the needs and problems of their sons and daughters. One parent, distraught over the indication that emotional disturbances might cause her son to flunk out, requested the dean to seek out the boy and provide counseling.[73]

Presumably, such efforts by administrators and faculty members brought them deep personal satisfaction; certainly they resulted in little monetary compensation. Salaries for all employees were at a low level throughout the Norlin years. In fact, the University's low salaries may have been the primary reason for failure to attract, or retain, well-published faculty. In 1917, Dr. Charles N. Meador, Dean of the Medical School, complained to Norlin that a national advertisement of an instructorship in pharmacology, paying $1,200 per year, attracted "only two applications, both from third-year medical students, who would have been wholly unsatisfactory for our purposes."[74] Throughout the Norlin period, professors at other schools frequently turned down job offers from the University because they received considerably higher salary offers elsewhere.[75]

The alarmingly rapid rate of inflation in the United States between 1914 and 1919 (nearly 100 percent) was crushing for the University's faculty—their salaries increased only about 20 percent during that period.[76] When Norlin assumed the presidency, he established the goal of increasing faculty salaries as his first priority. In a letter to Governor Oliver Shoup, he stated that while past years' budgets were "inadequate," the 1919–1920 state appropriation for faculty salaries was "hopelessly insufficient." He further stated that the University was in a "critical situation," and he warned the governor:

> Other universities have increased salaries to meet new conditions while our salaries remain largely where they have been. These institutions are taking the pick of our men. . . . I could name to you a couple of dozen of our men who could double, in some cases treble, their present salaries. . . . We can, of course, keep the faculty filled up with such men as our present salaries will command, but surely this solution is unworthy of a progressive state at a critical time in its history.[77]

Even after the legislature appropriated funds sufficient to raise salaries for professors and instructors an average of a further 20 percent, the situation remained critical.[78] In 1924, Norlin voiced concern that low salaries had forced "a general exodus" of experienced and established faculty from the areas of economics, political science, and business. "We have this year largely a new and untried faculty in these lines of work, and we have not been able, I fear, to replace the old men with a staff equally as good."[79] A 1921 survey of faculty salaries, which Norlin initiated, revealed that most other state universities maintained pay scales far superior to Colorado's. The University's minimum salary of $1,200 for beginning instructors was fairly competitive with minimums at other state universities. However, significant differentials emerged when comparing salaries for more experienced faculty and those at the professorial level. Colorado's top salary of $1,800 for instructors in 1921 compared poorly with maximum salaries for Texas and Minnesota, $2,200; and Iowa, $2,750. Full professors at Colorado fared even worse; the University's maximum salary of $3,500 in 1921 was in sharp contrast to top salaries of $4,350 at Arkansas; $5,000 at Minnesota and Texas; and $5,700 at Iowa.[80] Five years later, Norlin expressed the fear that the University's salaries had made it a "training ground for other universities that pay higher salaries."[81]

However, the University boasted a number of attractions which permitted it to compete effectively at least for young faculty with high potential, if not for those with national reputations in their fields. Some new faculty members were drawn to Boulder by the challenge of building a good university in a "frontier setting," where rigid tradition was not thwarting experimentation.[82] Quality of life in Boulder also exerted a strong pull. One young instructor rejected a $2,000 salary offer elsewhere in favor of a $1,700 per year appointment at Colorado because friends had described Boulder in such glowing terms.[83] While most faculty members did not receive large salary increases once they had arrived, they often received rapid promotions, especially during the 1920s. Colin B. Goodykoontz joined the History Department as an assistant professor in 1921, having just earned his Ph.D. The very next year, he was promoted to associate professor, and just two years later, was advanced to professor. Jacob Van Ek earned his Ph.D. in political science at the University of Iowa in 1924. That fall he came to Boulder as an assistant professor. In 1926, he was promoted to associate professor. The following year, he was appointed acting dean of the College of Arts and Sciences; and two years later he was named professor and permanent Dean of the College.[84]

There were still other benefits to faculty members at Boulder during Norlin's administration. The Depression forced severe budgetary retrenchments at other colleges and universities during the 1930s; at Colorado, faculty members were forced to accept salary cuts which averaged 16 percent between 1932 and 1935.[85] However, at a time when other universities were drastically cutting back faculty personnel, Norlin could proudly point out that "not a single instructor was dismissed in the name of economy."[86] Dean Van Ek believed that the administration's strong support for a faculty which had truly committed itself to the University in those trying times further intensified an already strong sense of community among students, faculty, and the administration.[87]

High morale was extremely important, since a succession of crises marked the Norlin years. The cause of most of the University's problems was insufficient operating and capital budgets. In 1919 the University depended on the state property tax for most of its income. By 1939 the state supplied less than half of the

University's budget. At first glance, it would seem appropriate to blame the University's financial difficulties upon provincial, mean-spirited, or anti-intellectual state legislators. To be sure, the University had a few enemies in the state legislature. The 1920s and the 1930s were, however, extremely difficult for the Colorado legislature as the state experienced hard times.

During the generally prosperous 1920s, Colorado's economy largely failed to share the good times. Agriculture and mining both declined in output between 1919 and 1929; farm output dropped from $180 million to $120 million; mineral production from $70 mlilion to $50 million.[88] In the depths of the Depression in 1934, farm production was but one-third what it had been fifteen years earlier. The federal government's abandonment of the gold standard in 1934 drove up the price of gold—from under $21 to $35 per ounce; Coloradans reopened a number of gold mines in response.[89] Nevertheless, the state's total mineral output in 1934 was just over half what it had been in 1919.[90]

Legislators might be forgiven for placing the University's interests at a low priority. In the 1930s, particularly, as unemployment mounted and as dust storms blew away most of eastern Colorado farmers' topsoil, local relief funds dried up. State officials had little choice but to focus their primary efforts on reviving the flagging economy and caring for people's physical needs. Publicly supported educational institutions contributed little of immediate benefit to the state's economy. It was hoped that an ambitious highway building program would attract tourists to Colorado's cities and national parks. By 1939, state highway construction absorbed 34.4 percent of all state expenditures; in 1930, they had taken only 28.9 percent. The impact of old-age pensions was even more dramatic. Unfunded in 1930, they consumed 22.2 percent of all state expenditures in 1938. In contrast, state output for all educational institutions declined from 18.3 percent of the budget in 1930 to a mere 6.1 percent in 1939.[91]

One of the chief reasons why state funding for higher education declined, both proportionally and in actual dollars spent, was that funding was directly tied to property valuation. The one-fifth mill levy for maintenance of state colleges and universities provided the only fixed source of revenue throughout the Norlin years. Real property assessments rose gradually in the 1920s. Unfortunately for the state's public colleges, the valuation of real property declined by approximately one-third between 1930 and 1934.[92] The University's share of the mill revenue declined from $850,000 in 1930 to a low of $513,000 in 1934. By 1937, as University enrollments continued to grow, the estimated yield from the mill levy was still below $600,000.[93]

There were other potential sources of revenue for the University: grants from private sources; tuition increases; and special appropriations from the legislature. While the University had experienced some success in securing additional funds from the state in the early 1920s, its luck soon ran out. The mid-1920s were lean years for the state's colleges and universities, especially after Ku Klux Klan-backed Clarence J. Morley was elected governor in 1924.[94] By 1939, the state was actually spending $142 per student—$58 less per student than it had spent twenty years earlier.[95]

During the Depression years, when state support for the University was declining, Norlin continually stated his case for special appropriations to all who would listen. In a 1932 address to the Boulder Chamber of Commerce, he presented his plea in the most practical terms:

> I venture to suggest . . . that the best "dole," the only "dole" which is intelligent and not demoralizing is a "dole" for education. . . . We solve in a large measure the problem of unemployment by occupying not less but more of our youth in the business of education, and for a longer time than we do now.[96]

University officials were most concerned that inadequate revenue from the state or other sources left them with no choice but to raise tuition fees. Between 1919 and 1932, tuition charges increased roughly 300 percent. In 1933, Acting President Oliver C. Lester noted:

> While [the University's] fees are not as high as those in many private institutions, they are among the highest paid in any state university. They cannot be increased without depriving many students of the advantages which the University was designed to give them. . . .[97]

By the mid-1930s student fees and tuition constituted one-third of the University's total income, a proportion which continued to increase in subsequent years. In 1938, faced with the necessity of authorizing yet another tuition increase, Norlin stated:

> It is a desperate situation in which we must choose between running a first-class University or a third-class University. We will keep faith with the students by raising tuition fees to enable us to continue to conduct a first-class University.[98]

Despite Norlin's promise that the University would continue to offer a first-class education, the consequences of continued inadequate funding may have convinced some students that the University provided something less than a challenging learning environment. As early as 1927 many departments were suffering from a severe shortage of funds to hire appropriate teaching personnel. For example, the Psychology Department was not able to hire graduate students to run large sections of its freshman and sophomore courses; instead, it was forced to hire seniors to conduct classes of 30 or more students.[99] By the late 1930s, demands on the University's limited physical facilities were so great that occasionally two classes had to meet simultaneously in the same room.[100]

The decline in state funding was accompanied by deterioration of the physical plant. In 1936 Norlin observed that the University had been able to survive the Depression only by eliminating many of the expenditures that "sooner or later must be made by a progressive university."[101] According to Dean Maurice H. Rees, the Medical School had suffered by 1939. In a long letter to Norlin, Rees complained that low budgets forced him to practice false economy in purchasing cheaply made equipment. Galvanized metal steam tables were corroded by rust; rugs were threadbare; tables and chairs were beyond repair because of heavy and constant use.[102]

Years of fiscal austerity also had adverse effects upon the University which were less obvious. Low budgets had forced repeated cutbacks of both the library staff and in acquisition of new books and journals. By 1936 affairs at the library were, according to one independent consultant, in a shambles. Returned books often stood in unsorted stacks for weeks due to lack of clerical personnel for reshelving. Insufficiently trained supervisory personnel resulted in "countless small errors and failures which in the aggregate [had] rendered the catalogs and the classification of the library highly inefficient."[103] Fortunately for the University, with the hiring of Ralph Ellsworth as director in 1937, the library turned toward recovery. Ellsworth immediately applied a newer and more efficient cataloging system. He was assisted by dozens of clerical workers, hired with newly available Works Progress Administration (WPA) funds.[104] A spacious new library, under construction in 1938, was also a major decision for improvement in an area vital to the life of a modern university.

By the late 1930s, the University's financial situation was so critical that the administrators were deeply worried over the possibility that they would literally have to close their doors. The specter of insolvency was very real, and it surfaced first at the Medical School's Denver campus. Actually, the Medical School drained University funds for years, and it was threatened with closure as early as 1933.[105] In 1936, when the Rockefeller Foundation refused to continue its supplemental grants to the school to cover a large percentage of its maintenance costs, the crisis deepened.[106] By January 1938, it was apparent that the Medical School would run out of funds from its biennial appropriation from the state legislature some three months before the end of the fiscal year. Dean Rees informed Norlin that without a supplemental appropriation, the Medical School would be forced to suspend operations.[107] The state legislature circumvented the immediate crisis by raising the debt ceiling under which the Medical School might operate. By the spring of 1939, however, its financial troubles surfaced again, when employees of the Medical School were not paid for two weeks.[108]

University officials realized that the Medical School's crisis portended a similar crisis at the Boulder campus. What they failed to foresee was how quickly it would occur. By early 1939, rumors circulated that the Boulder campus would shut down.[109] Because of financial problems caused by the old-age pension plan, the state treasurer had impounded all funds intended for the

University. While Norlin denied rumors of closing, he angrily informed Governor Ralph Carr:

> We can cut no further without cutting a vein. The state schools have been in outer darkness while the state has been prodigal in its expenditures for other functions.[110]

Although the funds were released, the University came within a few days of having to close.

Considering the University's difficulties with the state legislature during the 1930s, its survival alone seems miraculous. Ironically, the "hard times" caused by the termination of the mill levy for building in 1927 and lower proceeds from the maintenance levy after 1929 may have worked to the University's long-range benefit. In response, University officials began the search for new sources of income and support. When they became aware of the grants and loans available through several New Deal agencies, they envisioned a revival of the University's building program, largely dormant since 1928. Working closely with building engineer Waldo E. Brockway, Norlin made sure that the University stood at the front of the line in requesting New Deal funding for its building projects.[111] Late in the decade, one federal official complimented the Norlin administration for "being alert in taking advantage of the opportunity for Federal Grants." He also praised "the fine showing the institution . . . made during the Public Works program."[112] This praise was well deserved. Direct grants from the PWA, exceeding $900,000, helped finance fifteen separate building projects on the Boulder and Medical School campuses between 1933 and 1939. In Boulder, they included a new Field House (1935); the Natural History Museum (1937); the Women's Club building (1937); new wings for the College of Arts and Sciences building (1938); the administration building for engineering (1938); the Faculty Club (1939); and a new library (1939). The PWA grant of $243,000, almost half of the total cost of construction and furnishings, made the building of the library possible. On the Medical School campus, a PWA grant of $122,600 went toward the completion of a new wing on the Colorado General Hospital.[113] Grants from the federal government were the largest single source

109

of funding for University building projects during the New Deal period. The federal government provided, in addition, large loans to the University. The decision in 1933 to build a complex of women's dormitories was facilitated by a $550,000 loan from the Reconstruction Finance Corporation (RFC). Brockway underscored the importance of the New Deal's impact upon campus development when he stated that

> very little, if any, of the work . . . could have been done had it not been for federal grants and loans.[114]

While the Norlin administration demonstrated its ability to develop a special relationship with the federal government, it proved less successful in communicating with a variety of state and local interest groups, including the other state colleges and their promoters. Relations among the various state colleges had improved markedly since their colorful squabbles of the late nineteenth and early twentieth centuries.[115] Nevertheless, on important occasions during the 1920s and 1930s, they continued to bicker among themselves. These family quarrels often disgusted state legislators and led them to collectively punish the colleges when reviewing budget requests.

Conflict between Colorado's colleges and universities was inevitable. The state's vast geographical spread would create hardships for many students if higher education were consolidated into one or two institutions. But small population and low population density worked against efficient and economical administration at any single campus. By the early 1930s, there were already seven state-supported four-year colleges and two junior colleges. There were, in addition, nine private colleges and seminaries.[116] It was natural that there would be severe competition for limited funds. Thus, when the University of Colorado asked the state legislature in 1921 for a special appropriation of $600,000 to help match the Rockefeller Foundation grant for the Medical School, leaders at Colorado Agricultural College felt threatened. A year earlier, during the constitutional amendment fight to raise the mill levy on property for increased maintenance funds in higher education, the heads of six colleges informally agreed to divide proceeds from the new tax on a specific pro rata basis. Dr. Charles A. Lory of the Agricultural College insisted that the pro rata formula prevail for all appropriations. He thus perceived in Norlin's special request for the Medical School a violation of a gentlemen's agreement, and he publicly charged him with "breaking faith with the people of the state."[117] Try as he might, Norlin could not convince Lory that the benefits to the people of Colorado from acquiring a first-rate medical facility superseded those achieved by a pro rata distribution of state funds.

Occasionally, however, University administrators found themselves in a situation where they had to fight to hold their share of state funding. In 1927 the citizens of Grand Junction initiated a campaign to win state support for a proposed junior college. While leaders at the University insisted that they had "always been friendly to Grand Junction" and sympathetic to the special needs of students on the Western Slope, they argued that junior colleges should be funded locally. They feared that once they conceded the principle of state support for a junior college, those institutions would gradually absorb increasing proportions of state funding, which was already inadequate to meet the needs of existing colleges.[118] University officials pointed out that the overwhelming majority of junior colleges in the United States in 1927 were wholly supported by local funding. Should Colorado begin providing state funds for new junior colleges, the state would inevitably be diluting the quality of public education by spreading its limited resources too thinly.[119] Whether or not such a stand was sound from an academic and financial viewpoint, it undoubtedly cost the University public support from Western Slope citizens and legislators. Nor is it likely that the University won any new friends when Norlin labeled the legislature's funding of two new junior colleges as porkbarrel politics. In a 1932 speech on KOA radio, Norlin stated:

> While this has been gratifying to local pride and interest, it has been done against the judgment of educational leaders, and has not been in the interest of either education or economy.[120]

This distinctly elitist view of higher education probably alienated scores of those who were sympathetic to the objectives of local junior colleges.

The University also lost public support by opposing Colorado's old-age pension amendment, which had been approved by voters in the 1936 election.[121] Two days before the election, the *Denver Post* editorialized that even the modest-appearing $45 per month maximum pension for those over sixty would stretch the state budget to the point where "it will be financially impossible for Colorado to adequately finance [its] schools. . . ."[122] Even with such warnings, the pension bill was approved by nearly a 2-to-1 vote, and by a margin of nearly 105,000 votes.

University officials were apprehensive over the potential impact of the pension upon Colorado's finances, but in the absence of organized opposition they decided they would not bear the standard against it by themselves. Had they, or anyone else, realized the havoc which the pension was to create in the state's finances, they would almost certainly have opposed it in 1936. Within weeks after state lawmakers passed legislation to implement the pension plan in 1937, it was clear to many that they had created a monster. Between September and December of 1937, the average monthly cost to the state was $1.2 million; worse, hundreds of potential pensioners were flocking to Colorado to cash in on the bonanza.[123]

As the cost of the old-age pension program continued to mount in 1938, a variety of interest groups organized a campaign for repeal. Included were numerous business, professional, and taxpayer organizations. In February 1938, the Regents agreed that it would be against the best interest of the University to overtly side with the forces opposing the pension plan.[124] They did not, however, prevent individual administrators and faculty from working against the pension plan on an unofficial basis. One of the more active opponents was Don C. Sowers, director of government and business research at the University. His probe into the financial ramifications of pensions yielded valuable evidence for other opponents to circulate in their anti-pension drive.[125]

Pension supporters reacted angrily to this publication of university-sponsored research. Leaders of the National Annuity League, the pensioners' powerful political arm, responded by launching an all-out offensive against the University. By mid-1938, the league's official publication, a weekly newspaper called *The Bulletin*, had leveled an incredible series of charges against the University and its president. Norlin was portrayed as a financially corrupt despot, with a taste for luxurious entertainment at taxpayers' expense. *The Bulletin* charged that Norlin was intolerant of dissent from his viewpoint, and that he controlled the University's "propaganda mill."[126] One typical editorial attack charged that

> now the powerful educational bloc, headed by Dr. George Norlin, president of Colorado University, joins the chorus seeking repeal. Why? . . . Dr. Norlin's educational dynasty never has done anything without an ulterior motive; generally for educational funds; always selfish.[127]

In more normal times, University officials might have been amused by such wild charges. Unfortunately, the National Annuity League was an exceptionally powerful organization, and its scathing attacks landed upon the University when it was extremely vulnerable to unfavorable publicity of any kind.[128]

Though many of the University's public relations imbroglios were rooted in money matters, it did confront other dilemmas. In some situations where the University generated a degree of ill will among Colorado residents, it was a victim of circumstances. Nowhere was this more apparent than in the related issues of admissions, high academic standards, and failures. Colorado residents demanded a fairly loose admissions policy (loose enough, at least, to admit their offspring), yet at the same time they demanded high academic standards and a low failure rate. University officials viewed these goals as viable in theory, but contradictory in practice. With the University growing rapidly due to natural causes in the 1920s and 1930s, they perceived their basic task to be the tightening of admissions requirements rather than relaxing them. In the early 1920s, the University accepted any graduate from an accredited high school in Colorado. When University officials suggested that the failure rate could be improved markedly if students in the bottom quarter of graduating classes were denied admission, they encountered stiff opposition. Dean Van Ek noted charges that the University was becoming elitist when he commented in 1928, "It is open to question whether the people of Colorado are ready for any more rigorous demands than we make at the present."[129]

The pressures created by the problems of admissions policy also created tension in the relationship between the University and the state's high schools. High school officials resented the University's practice of unilaterally and arbitrarily changing entrance requirements. Each change at the University required significant alteration of high school curricula across the state.[130] University officials, on the other hand, complained that relatively high failure rates at the University were largely due to the failure of high schools to adequately prepare students for college. At times such feelings received rather unfortunate publicity. For example, a *Silver and Gold* headline in late 1932 publicized charges by Professor of Psychology and Regent Lawrence Cole that "High Schools Fail to Teach, Prep Institutions Only Entertain."[131] One high school administrator admonished Van Ek that such attitudes hurt the University because they "aroused old hatreds" among high school officials and state legislators.[132]

Almost two decades of managing a university increasingly beset by problems had taken their toll, and George Norlin began thinking about retirement. Any hopes he might have had of tranquilly closing his administration were dashed by a series of events which shook the entire University community during Norlin's last two years in office. The old-age pension fight and the threatened closing of the University were but two of the problems he confronted in 1938 and 1939.

Even as University officials struggled to keep the University open in the spring of 1939, the University suffered still other financial blows. In early June, the *Rocky Mountain News* published a story charging Comptroller Frank H. Wolcott with mismanagement of University funds.[133] Mr. Wolcott had been given the responsibility of investing certain University funds in stocks and bonds for a number of years. At the June meeting of the Regents, Mr. Wolcott informed them that "solely for the sake of convenience," he had recorded many of the securities transactions in his own name. Not until several weeks after Norlin's resignation from the presidency in September 1939 was it determined that certain of Wolcott's investments had lost nearly $165,000 in University funds. Mr. Wolcott was eventually cleared completely of personal guilt, and an out-of-court settlement with the investment firm of Otis and Company, in 1941, resulted in recovery of the entire amount lost by the University. Nevertheless, the suspicion of a stock scandal created the very worst kind of publicity for the University at a time when it was struggling to secure its appropriation from the state.

Two other incidents clouded Norlin's last weeks as president. Early in 1939, Regent Cole charged that Norlin received double compensation for a trip he took to New York in November 1938. Norlin made the trip for the dual purpose of scouting for a president to succeed him and to attend a trustee's meeting of the Carnegie Foundation for the Advancement of Teaching. The March 1939 meeting of the Regents, in which Regent Valentine Fisher supported Regent Cole's effort to investigate Norlin's expense vouchers, was indeed stormy. The investigation eventually resulted in Norlin's vindication, and the faculty voted unanimously its complete confidence in Norlin's integrity. Regent Fisher, however was not satisfied; in a subsequent meeting of the Regents, he charged:

> The truth is that the University has been a one-man operation for 22 years under Dr. Norlin, and a majority of the Regents have let him get away with it. . . . Dr. Norlin himself has been increasingly out of touch with all except his favorites.[134]

Unfortunately, the developing animosity between Norlin and Regents Cole and Fisher did not end even after Norlin retired. In the weeks following his resignation, the Regents considered the question of what constituted a proper monthly pension for the ex-president. According to Norlin, Cole and Fisher circulated the "fantastic rumor" that he was receiving $750 a month. In extremely bitter and uncharacteristic prose, Norlin informed the new president, Robert Stearns:

> Certainly, I do not expect that any facts will shut the mouths of Cole and Fisher, but I should find some satisfaction in their being placed in positions where, when they lie they know they lie.[135]

Norlin could not forgive easily. When he learned that Regent Fisher would be on the platform in June 1940 during the dedication ceremony of the new library which would bear Norlin's name, he at first declined an invitation to attend. Only the personal appeals of numerous friends finally induced him to change his mind.

In retrospect, the crises and chaos of Norlin's last two years in office may have minimized some of the solid achievements of the University during his administration. The Norlin years were marked most noticeably by the growth of the physical plant. Not only did the University develop a distinctive and cohesive architectural style, but the value of its property increased from $1.9 million to nearly $11 million.[136] The largest and the most important single project was construction of the new Medical School facilities in Denver. Under his leadership, regular academic year enrollment tripled, and registration in summer school multiplied more than sixfold.

Important as these tangible achievements were, perhaps Norlin's greatest accomplishment was in continuing to publicize the role of a university as a place of learning and research when it was difficult, and at times impossible, to obtain the necessary funding. During two decades when economic conditions were dominated first by inflation and then by the Great Depression, the state legislature was especially tight with money for higher education. The Norlin administration, however, was sufficiently resourceful to develop alternative means of support from sources as different as private foundations and the federal government. Given the circumstances, it is hardly surprising that development of the University during the Norlin years fell below the aspirations of the faculty and the administration. But as the scholar-president, Norlin stood for educational quality and academic integrity and his essential legacy remains his years of dedication trying to build the stature of the University.

CHANGE, CONSOLIDATION, AND CONFLICT:

1939–1953

T HE LEADERSHIP of the University during the turbulent years of World War II and of the Cold War was vigorous, dedicated, and, for the most part, effective. President Robert L. Stearns was an administrator who inspired the loyalty and devotion of students, faculty, and alumni. A lawyer rather than an academician, he concentrated on the here and now rather than the future. To solve the problem of declining enrollment during the war, he converted the institution into a naval installation without sacrificing liberal education for civilians. Later, the deluge of returning veterans was met expeditiously. The faculty was enlarged and permanent dormitories were constructed in a remarkably short time. Science was accorded appropriate attention. Curricular change, innovation, and improvement were given dramatic focus in the Medical School. The University survived the tensions of the McCarthy era—but not without rancor, bitterness, and dissension. Stearns' resignation from the presidency in 1953 was clouded by recriminations.

Robert Stearns displayed refreshing openness, candor, and humility, as well as a reassuring grasp of the University's needs in his initial address to the faculty. "Many of you don't know me very well," he stated. "I may not know myself in a new position but I can assure you . . . that I am not given to personal prejudices or animosities and so far as is humanly possible they will not weigh with me in my relations with the faculty." If he ever proved unreasonable or arbitrary, he urged faculty to come to him individually or collectively, "but please adopt the philosophy of the planked shad and be open and above board." He was not given to pride of office save that in which its essential dignity and decorum required. Relationships between the faculty and administration should not be formalized. They should proceed "naturally and spontaneously."

But, clearly, the University's image and external relations were uppermost in Stearns' mind. He came out unabashedly in favor of improved public relations and lobbying. "If you should look toward the President's box next Saturday afternoon and see a lot of brass hats, don't think for a moment that the President and his wife are losing their sense of proportion and are trying to cut a dash." They would be making contacts to bring "the University and its accomplishments and its needs to the attention of representative and official persons." State officials and legislatures were constantly changing, but the University went on forever. "If I can help it, there will be no skeletons in the closet to cause us embarrassment at critical times."[1]

Stearns was a son of the University—the first alumnus named president. He had earned a wide reputation as a legal researcher, educator, and reformer. After graduation from the Univerity in 1914, completion of law studies at Columbia University two years later, and service in World War I, he combined an extensive courtroom practice with teaching in the Denver University School of Law. When he headed the Colorado Bar Association in 1936–37, Stearns campaigned for improvements in the system of selecting judges and in reform of the Colorado parole system. He received national attention when he devised a system of law school classification and chaired the investigation of the Louisiana State University Law School in 1934 which led to the removal of that institution from the American Bar Association's approved list. This school was proved guilty of granting degrees for political reasons under Huey Long's influence. Stearns had been Dean of the University of Colorado School of Law since 1935. The *Denver Post* said the new president could "with equal facility, chum with the nobbies at the Denver or Cactus club or with bar association executives, and get down to cases with stubborn legislators."[2]

A major problem after Stearns entered the presidency was one of the "nobbies," Rex P. Arthur, whose business relationships with the University had been under question for some months. Arthur, reputedly the highest salaried Coloradan in 1937, was president of Otis and Company, a Denver investment firm. With the approval of Comptroller Frank Wolcott he had been buying and selling securities for University endowment funds since 1932. Many of these transactions were made without the knowledge and supervision of the Board of Regents. An audit of student loan, prize, scholarship, endowment, and other nonexpendable funds, as well as an investigation by a Regents committee, disclosed serious discrepancies between the market and carrying values of these investments, many of which were illegal under Colorado law. Wolcott was absolved of wrongdoing, but not of serious errors in investment judgment.

During the December 1939 Regents meeting, proposals to reform business policies and practices were presented. A plan was adopted reorganizing the business office under Waldo Brockway, supervising engineer, who was appointed treasurer, and placing endowment and other funds under the direct supervision and control of the Board. A committee on investments made up of the president, treasurer, and one Regent would submit recommendations for investment and reinvestment of these funds to the whole Board for approval. Claims later were advanced against Otis, and Charles Bromley, a former Regent, was hired as attorney. Negotiations proceeded satisfactorily until Otis' parent organization in Cleveland refused to help the local company or to buy back the disputed securities at the net cash investment.[3] The Regents filed a fraud suit in Denver District Court against the brokers in an effort to recover the funds.

In a complaint of 135 charges set forth in 253 pages, Rex Arthur and the Otis companies were accused of a breach of trust obligations and fraud in the purchase of securities for the University. Arthur, it was alleged, had gained the full confidence of Wolcott, and on his own initiative purchased whatever stocks and bonds he saw fit for the University's accounts. All of these securities were of a highly speculative character. Many were unlisted and were in companies underwritten by the brokerage house in which Otis officials were directors. The University's suit was followed by the announcement that the Securities and Exchange Commission was launching an investigation of the brokers.[4]

The case against Arthur and the companies was concluded in an out-of-court settlement on November 1, 1941. President Stearns proclaimed that the University would be repaid the total amount invested with the brokerage house between 1931 and 1939 plus accrued interest on these funds of 3 percent compounded annually. This sum was $164,914.47. A contract guaranteeing payment was substituted for "uncertain and costly litigation."[5]

During the time this embarrassing and expensive problem was being solved, the administration of the University was gearing for war. A Coordinating Committee on National Defense was named with Professor W. F. Dyde (education) as chairman. By December 1940, this group not only had formulated a position concerning the place of the University in relation to national defense, but also had made preparations for war as well. While the University's applications for naval and military ROTC were being considered in Washington, young men on the Boulder campus were being instructed in a voluntary military training unit. A Committee on Selective Service was advising prospective draftees. The Department of Mechanical Engineering was preparing pilots for the Civil Aeronautics Authority. The School of Engineering and the Departments of Chemistry and Physics were broadcasting a series of weekly radio programs, entitled, "We Defend America," that covered phases of military mobilization. The University's older radio series, "History in the Making," had been aired on ten stations in Colorado and Wyoming for six months. This news commentator program was unusually popular. Broadcasting assignments were rotated among Dean Jacob Van

Ek (Arts and Sciences), and Professors James Allen (history), Frederick Bramhall (political science), and Earl Crockett (economics). Physicians, dentists, and nurses were being recruited for a military hospital unit at the Medical School, and students were contributing to the Red Cross effort.[6]

The defense committee recognized a need for "intellectual and moral preparedness" through study and discussion with students. Most undergraduates were afraid the United States would become involved in war. In May 1940, a peace group sought signatures on a petition proclaiming the futility of 1917–18. According to the petitioners, American intervention in World War I proved the folly of attempting to settle Europe's feuds: "From the old battlefields of Europe came the old slogans, the old cries for American sympathy, while on the battlefields Europe's young lives are squandered to pay for the incompetence of Europe's statesmen." Americans had attempted to "make the world safe for democracy" but had only burdened their nation with Europe's agony: "1917 WAS FUTILE, 1917 REPEATED WOULD BE A DISASTER. Not the affairs of the Bloody Continent, but the problems of America are our concern." Similar attitudes also were expressed by the Youth Committee against the War in handbills distributed when men registered in the first peacetime draft in October.[7]

Instilling intellectual and moral preparedness took form in convocations, credit courses, and group meetings. Even public functions were organized around defense themes. Convocations on national defense presented conflicting points of view. Student organizations held meetings on topics such as "Shall We Feed the Hungry of Europe?" and "Race, Religion, and Democracy in War." When the 1941 Homecoming was organized on the theme "The University and National Defense," some students thought this was going too far. Homecoming should be an opportunity to forget worries. "The alumni are interested in coming here to get pie-eyed, shoot craps, and imagine once again that they are college boys." Centering this celebration on defense was similar to "inviting the local pastor along for the annual beer bust of the lodge."[8]

Although 55 percent of the students polled opposed the

Lend-Lease Act in the fall of 1941, Pearl Harbor and the declaration of war were met with equanimity. In an emergency convocation, President Stearns called for calm and deliberate judgment. Show the effects of educated intelligence, he counseled. "We are approaching the period of final examinations and the end of the fall quarter. Finish the immediate task first. Stand ready. Complete the quarter's work and take examinations." The editor of the *Silver and Gold* entreated his peers to heed the advice of the "older boys," such as the prexy. "Just do the best possible and mutter a prayer and trust to good luck." Entertainments were canceled and flags were flown, but there was virtually no hysteria. Examinations were taken, the quarter was completed, and students went home for Christmas vacation.[9]

The war effort brought change to the campus. Fort Warren and Lowry Field were on the football schedule, but basketball was given up for the duration. Senior Week also was a casualty. Faculty who did not enlist or who were not drafted were called by the state Council of Defense to conduct victory rallies in various towns and cities. The administration and Board of Regents, anxious over the effect of the draft, quickly approved the use of all facilities for V-5 (Navy Aviation) and V-7 (Navy Reserve), established a V-1 Program (pre-induction training), and signed a contract with the Navy to teach 400 radiomen, who eventually were billeted in the Field House. When the federal government began evacuating citizens of Japanese ancestry from the West Coast, the University admitted the sons and daughters of these people.[10]

One of the most significant developments of the war years was the transfer of the Navy's Japanese Language School from Berkeley, California, to the University. This unit, which prepared intelligence officers, took over the men's residence hall for housing and most of the main floor of the Memorial Building for instruction. It also raised the intellectual level of the community. Under the direction of Florence Walne, who had lived in Japan for many years, a faculty was recruited among relocated Japanese-Americans. Students were enlisted from across the nation. To qualify as a yeoman second class in this 14-month program, it was necessary to have been elected to Phi Beta Kappa or to have graduated either *magna* or *summa cum laude* from an institution of higher learning. It was a common sight on campus and in town to see these young men drawing Japanese characters on their Magic Slates or writing them in the air. The Regents' actions concerning the Japanese-American students and the Language School were approved by the Boulder city government and Chamber of Commerce. They were met with consternation by elements in the citizenry, but without overt opposition.[11]

With the entrance of a V-12 unit in 1943, the Navy had arrived en masse. More than 6,000 students were being instructed in an accelerated three-term system. The presence of the military helped to keep dormitories and classrooms occupied and to pay faculty salaries. The University also leased fraternity houses for freshman women. In spite of these changes, Stearns and the faculty attempted to maintain an "all-round structure of university education" and a relatively normal college life.[12]

But the president was trying to do two jobs. In the fall of 1942, he was given the first of several short leaves of absence to serve as a civilian consultant to the Air Force School of Applied Tactics in Orlando, Florida. This institution was a precursor of the Air University. During his time away from the campus, the president's functions were carried on by a trio of administrators. Except for Waldo Brockway, who had been treasurer for almost three years, these leaders were comparatively inexperienced. W. F. Dyde had been recently appointed administrative assistant to the president, while Reuben G. Gustavson (chemistry) was Dean of the Graduate School. Brockway and Gustavson did their own jobs, and Dyde minded the president's office. They wrestled with housing for an expanding Language School and other pressing matters.

This administrative arrangement was not completely satisfactory. Some Regents were annoyed by Stearns' absences from the campus. When viewing administrative problems, the president himself lamented to Dyde that the last three years should have been put on paper. He had run a virtual one-man band, and now this was regrettable. In the late summer of 1943, the Air Force requested an indefinite leave for Stearns to serve in the southwest Pacific, and the Regents reluctantly accepted. He worked in the Pacific for one year and then became Chief of the Operations Analysis Division of the 20th Air Force in Washington.[13] Reuben Gustavson became Stearns' replacement. A noted biochemist, he had been head of the Chemistry Department since 1937.

With Gustavson's accession to the presidency, Walters Farrell Dyde, who had been elevated to Dean of the Faculties shortly before Stearns' departure, predicted that the University would be in a period of quiet until postwar problems arose. On March 14, 1944, however, quiet was shattered when it was announced that Harry Bridges, leader of the International Longshoremen's Association in San Francisco, had been invited by the Convocations Committee to deliver a public address. The labor leader's deportation for alleged membership in the Communist party was under appeal before the Supreme Court. The committee had scheduled lectures from other labor leaders, but they were forced to decline because of the pressure of work. When the CIO offered to supply Bridges free of charge, the committee accepted even though they knew his appearance would arouse public reaction. They reasoned, however, that since the labor leader had lectured at Harvard and Yale his appearance at Colorado could be defended.

The American Legion vehemently protested the University's action and demanded that Bridges' speech be canceled. In a telegram to Gustavson, Trevor P. Thomas, commander of the organization's Colorado department, specified that Bridges was known for his un-American activities and was under deportation orders. He should not be permitted to speak before a group of young Americans, especially in an institution where a Navy unit was located. The president declined to answer the Legionnaires' wire. He responded publicly, however, that "it is part of the function of a university to allow every shade of opinion to be heard. . . ." Thomas also would be issued an invitation to speak.[14]

Macky Auditorium was jammed with 2,400 students, faculty, and townspeople. Fifty seats had been reserved for Legion members but only two attended. In introducing Bridges, Gustavson expressed his gratitude to the veterans' organization for the publicity. The audience heard the labor leader urge "unity and understanding among ourselves and with other nations if we are to win the war and secure the peace." Some interpreted this as a call for the reelection of President Roosevelt and a rubber-stamp Congress, but altogether it was a tepid speech.[15]

Benjamin C. Hilliard, Legion national committeeman, took his organization's objections to the Regents. Freedom of speech was not the issue, he argued. The issue was whether or not Bridges should be allowed a public building and be paid with public funds to lecture students. He questioned Gustavson's fitness for office when he assumed that he had the authority to determine policies and contemptuously reject citizens' protests. Regent Lawrence Cole, a former University psychology professor, bluntly charged that the institution had lost considerable prestige during the past twenty years because of teaching communism. He was convinced that the Regents violated their oath of office by allowing Bridges to speak. His colleagues did not share this opinion. The Regents supported Gustavson, but they indicated that a mistake had been made and that they might have to be consulted in the future before speaking invitations were extended. A final decision was put off until their April meeting so they could study Bridges' remarks.[16]

A spontaneous reaction to the threat of Regent-censored convocations and lectures spread across the campus. Students circulated petitions and in a few days signatures of 568 civilians were collected. The Convocations Committee prepared a lengthy defense of its activities. They pointed out that Regent-censorship of public lectures not only would be impractical but also would violate the fundamental principle that University personnel should be free to carry out educational functions. Censorship of lectures was the first step in a process that would lead to the complete elimination of academic freedom. The governing board, they counseled, should not sacrifice what is true and of educational value for what is expedient.[17]

By a 3-to-2 margin, the Regents upheld the authority of University officials to invite speakers to the campus without receiving approval by the Board. They said they had examined Bridges' speech and found nothing unlawful; neither had they discovered any contributions to learning nor anything that would justify the time of faculty or students. A serious error of judgment had been made when Bridges was invited. The editor of the *Silver and Gold* did not agree. He thought students had learned more from the Bridges affair than from any other single incident.

They had learned about the University. "We learned that it is an institution of higher learning which cannot be dictated to by pressure groups."[18]

Academic freedom and the role of the Regents in the governance of the University continued to be a volatile issue. During the May 25, 1945, meeting of the Board, in what was to have been a routine consideration of the budget, newly elected Regents Roy Chapman (Boulder) and Merritt Perkins (Denver) presented a motion denying merit salary increases to Professors Joseph Cohen (philosophy), Clay Malick (political science), Morris Garnsey (economics), and Edwin Walker (philosophy). These men, they said, were guilty of making public and classroom statements on subjects not approved by the people of the state, and these utterances had resulted in damage to the University. Chapman was convinced that his and Perkins' election by a large majority represented a mandate to do something about this situation.[19]

In the discussion of the motion, Cohen was attacked because of attitudes expressed by George F. Whicher, of Amherst College, in an Honors Convocation address. Malick was denied additional remuneration because "Pearl Street" (local businessmen) did not like him, and Garnsey was condemned for advocating the establishment of the Missouri Valley Authority. While no specific charges were brought against Walker, it was evident that he had been included for chairing the Convocations Committee that brought Harry Bridges to the campus. Perkins later told Stearns that the Whicher address had precipitated the action. In a convocation which, by the Laws of the Regents, should be devoted to public emphasis on the significance of scholastic honors, Whicher had advocated a collective society in the United States, the nationalization of major industries, "a ceiling to the zone of free enterprise," and more government in business. Cohen, who was chairman of the Honors Council,

> either knew what might be expected from Dr. Whicher's address, in which event he was guilty of prostituting his position, or he did not use due care to make certain that the speaker's assignment was properly carried out, in which event he was negligent.[20]

Gustavson and Dyde tried to convince the Regents that the increases had been recommended for the professors either as a reward for their contributions to the creative life of the University or to bring their remuneration in line with the salaries of other men in their rank. The motion represented "poor administration." It was the function of the Board to "look over the policies of the University as a whole," but they had to depend on administrative officers for details of administration. These entreaties were useless. The Regents not only passed the motion unanimously, but also raised the wages of Professors Carl Borgmann, Warren Raeder, and Norman Parker of the Engineering School. They further introduced a resolution prescribing that in the future every new faculty appointment and every recommendation for an advance in rank should be presented to the Board thirty days before action was to be taken. Dyde, who was responsible for faculty evaluations, regarded the Regents' action as serious criticism of his performance. He was so upset he insisted on retiring from the meeting room while the Regents considered his place in the institution. They gave him a strong vote of confidence.[21]

The administration moved quickly to correct what they regarded as "one of the most serious situations that has ever risen in the history of the University." Stearns, who was preparing to return to the University as president in July, since Gustavson had accepted a vice presidency at the University of Chicago, made plans to attend the June meeting of the Regents. In this meeting, he told the Regents that presidential leadership was at stake. He described the problems he had solved successfully in the past and requested reconsideration of the Regents' action on salary increases. The Regents only agreed to place the matter on the agenda for the July meeting. Chances of maintaining open-mindedness were seriously diminished, however, by several events. The three engineers, Borgmann, Raeder, and Parker, who had been granted increases by the Regents, refused these rewards because they were not recommended by their dean and departments. Details of the salary squabble were leaked to the *Rocky Mountain News*. The newspaper charged that Cohen, Malick, Garnsey, and Walker had been denied salary increases for political reasons. The controversy resulted from the appearance of Harry Bridges and the Regents' objections to speeches in support of the Missouri Valley Authority. The Associated Students of the University of Colorado sent a letter to the Board protesting the "infringement upon academic freedom."[22]

The Regents vehemently denied the charge that they had been motivated by political considerations. Speaking for the Board, Merritt Perkins said that Edwin Walker's connection with the committee that sponsored Bridges had not been considered. Respecting the Missouri Valley Authority, the Regents asked only that both sides of the question be elucidated. Perkins and his colleagues agreed to allow President Stearns to study the entire salary question and make recommendations.[23]

On July 27, 1945, the Board supported the president's recommendation of salary increases for Cohen, Malick, Garnsey, and Walker. They also unanimously approved the establishment of an annual University Convocation at which public emphasis would be on the "history and significance of constitutional government in the United States." In a radio broadcast, Stearns let it be known how the University should be run. University governance was a cooperative endeavor. Governing boards were the chief determiners and arbiters of policy, he said, but they had to depend on the administrative officers. The president had major responsibility for the final determination of policy. His considered judgment and recommendations should be respected and should be a guide to administrative action. The Regents, he concluded, undoubtedly would accept these principles.[24]

To make certain the Regents understood the nature of academic freedom and the relationship between the governing board, administration, and faculty in the management of the institution, the local chapter of the American Association of University Professors called a meeting which was attended by 100 faculty and formed a Committee of Five. This group, which was chaired by Ralph Crosman (journalism) and included Dean Van Ek, Dean of Business Elmore Petersen, Frederick Bramhall, and Carl Borgmann, began extensive deliberations on a statement governing the relationships between the Regents, administration, and faculty. At about the time, in June 1946, when this document, which called for shared governance and defined the responsibility of faculty concerning extramural utterances, was ready for transmittal to the Board, the Regents rejected a recommendation of the administration and a faculty-search committee that Borgmann, head of Chemical Engineering and director of the Engineering Research Station, be named permanent Dean of the Graduate School. They gave P. G. Worcester (geology), who had been acting dean, a three-year contract. The search committee passed over Worcester because they believed the school needed a younger, research-oriented leader to direct and supervise expanding enrollments and burgeoning research demands.[25]

Many faculty believed the Regents' action was retributive. Borgmann, a liberal with eclectic interests, had been a member of the committee that had issued the invitation to Bridges and had embarrassed the Board when he convinced his colleagues to refuse their proffered salary increases. The AAUP chapter and the American Federation of Teachers local, acting in concert, sent a strongly worded resolution to the Board. They asked the Regents to reconsider their decision, and Stearns assigned the Committee of Five to meet with a Regents committee. But the Board remained unyielding. As compensation, Borgmann was named Director of Research. Thus research and graduate study were separated at a time when both operations were being consolidated in other institutions. Dean Van Ek later reported that relationships between faculty and Regents had been improved, but an understanding on academic freedom and the authority of the Board had not been reached. At any rate, the Regents did not act capriciously again during the Stearns administration.[26]

At the time Stearns departed from the University to serve the Air Force, a controversy involving the School of Medicine and the Colorado State Medical Society came to a head. For some years, there had been grumblings by members of the society concerning the appointment of full-time faculty in the Medical School's clinical departments, i.e., medicine, psychiatry, and surgery, and, more particularly, a provision that would permit full-time professors to engage in private practice as a supplement to their salaries. Dean of Medicine Maurice Rees regarded these objections and the society's activities surrounding them as an effort to exert control over the policies of the institution. "Contacting certain disgruntled physicians to get their opinions as to whether we should employ full-time clinical teachers," he said, "does not appear to be conducive of any progress along any line in the School of Medicine." Such doctors had not kept abreast of developments and changing problems in medical education. Some even had difficulty understanding and appreciating the extent to which an up-to-date medical school improved medical practice in the community.[27]

It was important, Dean Rees proposed, to recruit two or three more faculty in each of the major medical departments as well as to devise a salary scale that included practice or consultation privileges. The departments no longer could depend on non-salaried, volunteer teachers whose practices often prevented them from meeting scheduled classes and precluded bedside teaching in the hospital wards. Providing full-time salaries plus consultation privileges had distinct advantages. It would be less expensive for the school as well as more attractive to qualified and stimulating teachers. Consultations would keep the professor cognizant of problems in the practice of medicine and would militate against his becoming too "theoretical and institutionalized." Furthermore, this was a service the school should provide to private physicians and the people of the state.[28]

After interviewing a number of members, the Medical Society's Public Policy Committee brought the private practitioners' concern to President Gustavson in August 1943. Gustavson did not respond immediately to the committee's letter. His office and the University's Privilege and Tenure Committee were conducting studies of comparative living costs in Denver and Boulder as well as the practice concerning consultations in other state universities with a view toward establishing a uniform University policy. Dean Rees, in proposing a salary schedule for medical faculty, had said, "it is possible that one can live as cheaply in Denver as in Boulder, but it is also certain that one can retain his self-respect in Boulder on a smaller income than is necessary in Denver." His faculty associated with physicians who had comfortable incomes and fine homes. This made "a low paid teacher very conscious of his lower station in life." Gustavson, for his part, believed that salary scales on the Boulder and Denver campuses should be brought into line. "After all we are a group of scholars engaged in a common project, namely that of education.

. . ." Meanwhile, the Board of Regents began selectively raising the salaries of clinical professors and denying them extramural work.[29]

Gustavson's position and the Regents' actions precipitated something of a crisis in the School of Medicine. The head of pathology, whose consultation privileges had not been altered, resigned to direct the pathology service at a private hospital because he was convinced that his freedom of action was threatened. Dean Rees complained bitterly that the Regents were being unfair and discriminatory. For criticisms of policy, he received a stern lecture from Gustavson. "If you have lost faith in our School of Medicine," the president admonished, "how can we expect the faculty and students to maintain their faith? It is very evident to me that you are not giving the School the type of leadership that it must have and I think you should give serious thought to your attitude." Unable to inaugurate a consistent policy concerning outside work for the entire institution, the Regents adopted a ruling permitting "reasonable consultation privileges" until the beginning of the first fiscal year following the termination of the war.[30]

When members of the Medical Society's Public Policy Committee were informed of this decision, they replied to Gustavson with indignation. Public confidence in the University and Regents could not be developed and must inevitably be impaired by using the war as justification for continuing abuses.

> This is a particularly surprising position for the University to take in view of the fact that the issue of abuse of official position on the part of certain full-time faculty members of the Medical School has been a constant source of friction and ill-will for the past ten or fifteen years.

The competition of full-time teachers with private practitioners was "vicious." These faculty used state property for their private offices and also employed telephone service, secretarial help, psychological and social work assistance, laboratory, X-ray diagnosis, and treatment aids free of charge. It was "sheer evasion and subterfuge to speak of 'reasonable consultation privileges' for the full-time teaching staff at the Medical School. . . ." The head of psychiatry, for instance, reserved a whole section of a private facility for his patients. This was the number one point of disagreement, and other clinical professors were being subjected to criticisms because of it. The committee reminded the president that the School of Medicine had come into existence largely through the "sacrifice and support and loyalty" of Colorado's medical profession. It could not operate even for a single day without the volunteer services of private physicians.[31]

In response to these charges and also to soothe the feelings of colleagues in the basic science departments, such as anatomy, physiology, biochemistry, and bacteriology, whose salaries were considerably lower than those of the clinical faculty, the executive faculty of the Medical School took action to regulate themselves with respect to consultations. This was an effort to attain peace and harmony in the institution. They proposed limits on the amount of income that could be earned from extramural professional work, which was rejected by the Regents, and emphasized that they only wanted to maintain a "reasonable measure of security and personal independence." A special committee of all six faculty enjoying consultation privileges formulated a definition of consultation. All private practice activities should be discontinued when they involved referred practice and the routine performance of laboratory work. When the Regents approved this recommendation it was with the understanding that full-time professors would consult only on the invitation of a private doctor. This quieted the Medical Society.[32]

The next year when consultantships with the Veterans Administration, Army, Navy, U.S. Public Health Service, and other organizations were opening, the Regents approved a resolution from the executive faculty limiting consultantships to one-sixth of a faculty member's time. This corresponded to one day per week. Months of time could not be accumulated under this rule. A limit of six or seven days was established. Thus medical faculty could establish offices in Denver, open one day or two half-days per week and carry on their consultations. In the long run, however, this provision enabled them to earn very little extra income, because they could not render any type of definitive or continuing care for the referred patient. The one-sixth rule was made University policy in December 1947 and has remained policy for faculty except, ironically, those in medicine.[33]

Attaining a resolution of the practice problem with the Medical Society was an imperative for those members of the faculty who realized that postwar demands concerning medical practice and service would require a transformation in the quality, outlook, and objectives of medical education. Prior to World War II, the School of Medicine was an undergraduate institution devoted almost solely to the training of M.D.s. It had a creditable record. More than half the physicians practicing in Colorado had gained their degrees from the University. The teaching of these men and women had been accomplished by members of the medical profession in Denver. Only in psychiatry, where the Commonwealth Fund had been providing graduate fellowships and an adequate full-time faculty existed, were a significant number of physicians being prepared for specialty board examinations. But following the war, the Medical School would need to become a medical center. This concept implied certain activities and abilities. These were teaching young men and women to become physicians, training interns, nurses, and technicians, offering graduate and postgraduate opportunities to general physicians, specialists, and basic scientists, providing the best in medical care to patients in the hospitals and clinics, and performing biological and medical research.[34]

Leadership for much of the postwar planning and change was provided by Dr. Ward Darley. A volunteer faculty member since 1931, he was recruited as the second full-time professor in the Department of Medicine in 1944. Darley was graduated from the school in 1929, and was also one of the few internal medicine specialists who took their residencies in the institution. When Maurice Rees died suddenly during the summer of 1945, Darley was appointed Dean. In 1949, when the school became a medical center and the administration required reorganization, Darley was named Vice President for Health Services.

As the chairman of a faculty committee soon after his appointment to the full-time faculty, Darley urged departments to review their teaching programs and develop the most practical and inspirational methods of presenting their subjects. Only through a reform of pedagogical methods could undergraduate and graduate study be prosecuted successfully. More immediately, he recommended affiliations with public and private hospitals in Denver to increase the number of teaching beds, staffing the Out-Patient Department with full-time men so that this facility could be used more effectively for instruction, and constructing laboratories for clinical departments. The Medical School and Colorado General Hospital had been completed in 1925 without laboratories for research.[35]

At the center of postwar reform in both undergraduate and graduate education was the preparation of general practitioners. In assessing the needs of the state with its predominantly rural population and large geographical areas with a lack or paucity of doctors and medical facilities, Darley and the medical faculty determined that organizing the undergraduate curriculum around general practice and developing residencies in this field were prime needs. General practice was the most neglected field in medicine, although the family physician was and always would be the backbone of medical practice. They also reasoned that a graduate prepared for general medicine would be in a better position to decide on additional training in this field or on work in a specialty.[36] Training general physicians was fighting the trend toward specialization in the medical profession generally, but it made the School of Medicine unique and brought it national recognition.

The new undergraduate curriculum, instituted in 1947 after more than a year of planning, was based on the assumption that it was impossible for an individual to become familiar with the vast range of medical knowledge. Instead of emphasizing factual knowledge, as in the past, the medical student had to be taught to think, to evaluate knowledge, and to put it to effective use. Every patient was a research problem and students were required to appraise the merit of information and interpret its significance. Knowledge of most value to people in general practice was emphasized. Since, for example, 50 to 70 percent of all patients entering hospitals and clinics had an emotional component in their illness, psychiatry was presented as psychosomatic medicine, mental hygiene, and as a clinical subject throughout the four years.[37]

It was recognized further that the sick patient with advanced and complicated pathology was overemphasized in most medical schools with an accompanying underemphasis on preventive medicine and the continuing care of the patient as a human being.

One of the most impressive innovations in the curriculum was a course in human biology emphasizing the organic growth of individuals, development of personality and behavior, and the problems presented by life as a social animal. This offering was given by the recently organized Department of Human Growth, a unit of members of the Child Research Council which, since the 1920s, had been studying healthy growth throughout the life cycle. This organization had achieved national eminence and was the Medical School's most distinguished research institute. Finally, the junior and senior years were entirely clinical. Students received their training in the wards and the Out-Patient Department.[38] After affiliation with Denver General Hospital in 1947, approximately 50 percent of the time of senior students was spent in this facility.

Much of the success of the curricular innovation, both undergraduate and graduate, resulted from the contract with the City of Denver whereby staff appointments in Denver General Hospital were limited to School of Medicine faculty. This arrangement was inspired by Ward Darley, Mayor J. Quigg Newton, Dr. Solomon Kauvar, director of the Bureau of Health and Hospitals, and Dr. Florence Sabin, retired from the Rockefeller Institute for Medical Research, in New York, where she had performed monumental research in immunology. Dr. Sabin had stumped the state for improvement in public health as chairman of the governor's postwar commission and was serving as an advisor to the mayor. Newton, Kauvar, and Sabin were dissatisfied with the medical care Denver was providing and determined to find ways of improving it. Through Darley, success was achieved.

The affiliation of Denver General Hospital with the Medical School was productive for both. The University furnished expert care and the 600-bed hospital was integrated into the educational program. Denver General complemented the 325-bed Colorado General Hospital. It was a hospital with extremely active clinical services that treated patients with types of ailments seen in the average medical practice, whereas Colorado General was populated by patients with complicated, medically interesting afflictions. Eventually, a comprehensive general medical clinic, financed by the Commonwealth Fund, was established in the public hospital. This was a family medical service with nursing care and social work that functioned in the patient's home, in the clinic, and in the wards of the hospital. All-inclusive training in general medicine for undergraduates, interns, and residents thus was furnished an ideal setting.[39]

The affiliation with Denver General Hospital was one of a number of relationships the Medical School established with public and private hospitals. These arrangements enabled the school to fulfill its commitment to increase residencies and, at the same time, to institute proper training programs. About half the candidates for specialty board certification in the country were failing their examinations mainly because the hospitals in which they were being trained did not have effective programs with university affiliations. The University's residency programs were under the jurisdiction of Dr. Frode Jensen, director of graduate and postgraduate medical education, whose office was funded by a grant from the W. I. Kellogg Foundation, and residents were registered for graduate study in the Clinical Division of the Graduate School.[40]

As the Medical Center developed, teaching and service to communities and the state became a central activity. Following a disastrous polio epidemic in 1946, the Infantile Paralysis Center was inaugurated through a five-year, $100,000 grant from the National Foundation for Infantile Paralysis. The Premature Infant Center rendered consultation to any hospital that wished to set up such a department. Students in the Medical School saw every variety of heart disease peculiar to children in the Rheumatic Fever Diagnostic Service, and also learned to appreciate the wide range of normality in the hearts of growing children. This organization was founded in 1944 when it was discovered that rheumatic heart disease was the third leading cause of death in Denver children, five to fifteen years old. Total care for the victims of epilepsy was supplied by the Epilepsy Clinic which was under the direction of the Division of Psychosomatic Medicine of the Department of Psychiatry. This department and the Psychopathic Hospital, through the Mental Hygiene Clinic established in 1928, extended their operations to mental health clinics and other organizations throughout the state. Finally, statewide services affording the best in whole blood and plasma were provided by the Belle Bonfils Memorial Blood Bank.

The Bonfils family also furnished financial support for the Frederic B. Bonfils Tumor Clinic. An annual $25,000 grant from the National Cancer Institute permitted a reorganization of this clinic and led to the establishment of the Division of Oncology (specialty of cancer) in the Department of General Surgery. This division symbolized two significant aspects of medical research in the late forties and early fifties. First, research in the School of Medicine had to be a cooperative enterprise. The physical plant did not permit any one department to be self-sufficient in the research field. Remodeling the Medical School and hospitals provided needed laboratories but, until the Florence Sabin Institute for Cellular Biology was opened in 1951, space remained a problem. This four-story edifice mainly housed facilities for research on cancer, but research on other matters, such as enzymes and hormones, also was undertaken there.[41]

Second, emphasis in medical science shifted from contagious and infectious diseases to interest in abnormalities of growth and development, as well as the investigation of the factors involved in degenerative conditions.

> Just as the most exciting advances in the physical sciences are coming from the exploration of the atom, so one can expect the future progress in the medical sciences to come from the exploration of the chemical structure and electrical activity of the living cell.

To understand cancer, wound healing, congenital malformation, and the so-called degenerative ailments, such as hardening of the arteries, many mental diseases, and certain types of heart disease, knowledge of the basic physical, physiological, and chemical reactions in cellular tissue, as well as organ growth and differentiation, was required. It was believed that two of the most baffling infectious diseases, rheumatic fever and infantile paralysis, had their secrets locked in these basic processes.[42]

Representative of this change in medical research was the formation of the Department of Biophysics, in 1948, under the leadership of Dr. Theodore Puck. Through financial grants from the Boettcher Foundation, Atomic Energy Commission, and the National Cancer Institute, this new department, the first of its kind in the nation, pioneered in the training of physicians and

Ph.D.s in the biological application of atomic energy. Radioisotopes were used as diagnostic and therapeutic agents.[43]

The federal grants and foundation support indicate the Medical Center was achieving national recognition in its work but, throughout this period of impressive accomplishment, money was a constant problem. Medical education was expensive and, to exacerbate matters, the late forties and early fifties were a time of inflation. Employing full-time teachers and keeping their remuneration abreast of advances in the cost of living and competitive with salaries paid in other universities, pharmaceutical companies, government, and private practice was a costly undertaking. Salaries in the School of Medicine always ranked low in comparison to those in other institutions and organizations. In addition, the activities of medical professors had to be supported by nurses, technical personnel such as X-ray technicians, medical technologists, and physical therapists, as well as other workers.

The Medical School was financed by the mill levy, biennial appropriations from the legislature, tuition and fees, and miscellaneous charges for laboratory service and supplies. Only once during the period of transformation to a medical center did the state provide an adequate appropriation. In the 1947–1949 biennium, the willingness of the legislature to increase support from $70,000 to $400,000 permitted the expansion of the programs and curricula that were demanded. Even then, almost $521,000 had been requested. The Medical School's growing operations were financed largely through increases in undergraduate tuition and tuition from the Clinical Division of the Graduate School.[44]

Ward Darley's strategy for the financial situation was to make the Medical Center a regional institution and charge cost tuition for all students. Since Colorado and Utah were the only two medical schools in the Rocky Mountain region, they could serve students from Wyoming, Montana, Arizona, New Mexico, Idaho, and other states. State appropriations should be viewed as covering the cost of tuition for a certain number of resident students. If this number was 50 and the school could effectively teach 70 students in each class, then the remaining 20 students should be recruited from other states. He did not believe that charging cost tuition, which amounted to more than $2,600 per year at Colorado, was excessive, since medical education guaranteed a better-than-average income. Scholarships should support less-affluent students. Besides, making such a fiscal arrangement would, in time, put medical education on a self-sustaining basis. Darley presented these proposals to the Regents and Colorado's governor, Lee Knous. The Regents decided not to charge Colorado residents cost tuition but they did approve a plan whereby contracts for cost tuition could be made with universities of those Rocky Mountain states without medical schools. This led to the formation, in 1953, of the Western Interstate Commission of Higher Education, an organization that provided for many kinds of cooperation in the field of higher education, including student exchanges upon a cost basis.[45]

If financing the Medical School remained tenuous during Darley's stewardship, support for the two hospitals was a source of tribulation. Colorado General and the Psychopathic Hospital, which was funded by charges to patients and state appropriations, suffered deficits almost every year. Credit managers in business would not have accepted as credit risks most of the patients admitted to the hospitals. By law, the University was limited to admitting only people who were unable to pay the full cost of hospital and medical care. In the case of Colorado General, counties were required to pay part of the hospitalization for patients the commissioners sent to the hospital. As for the Psychopathic Hospital, after 1949, when the state attorney general ruled that counties did not have to pay for services in that institution, the only way payments could be collected was by filing claims against the estates of patients.[46]

The state treasurer withheld appropriations from the hospitals in that same year, because Attorney General John W. Metzger decreed that the hospitals and their staff employees were under the jurisdiction of the state rather than the Board of Regents. It was Metzger's opinion that the constitutional provisions giving the Regents control over all University funds and appropriations did not extend to the hospitals because they were agencies founded by statute and employees should be under civil service. He made this ruling, he said, in response to a petition from workers in the two institutions for salaries equal to those paid civil service employees. The University was forced to take the unusual step of filing a lawsuit against the state treasurer to compel payment of the appropriations. The case was not settled until the election of Duke Dunbar as attorney general in 1950. Then the suit was dismissed with prejudice. This was the last time a state official attempted to place University funds and employees under state control until changes were made in the constitution in 1972.[47]

The 1947–1949 budget years, when the Medical School began its takeoff period, were also critical for the University in Boulder. All of the state's institutions—educational, penal, correctional— were experiencing financial difficulties. Public schools badly needed funds to pay teachers who were leaving the state in considerable numbers for higher salaries. Enrollment on the Boulder campus, with the return of veterans on the G.I. Bill, leaped from 4,500 in 1945 to more than 7,700 in 1946. For the first time, salary and wage scales were instituted for faculty and staff. Faculty, who labored through the accelerated program of the war years, were to be accorded a quarter's leave of absence every eighth quarter for research, study, and rejuvenation. Over $350,000 was appropriated for the University in the 1945–1947 period, and now a total of $844,700 was being requested. This sum would keep essential services in operation, but would not permit any expansion or new developments.

The University, and other state institutions, embarked on a program to influence favorably the legislature and public leaders. They were not only asking for increased funding. They were explaining to leaders that taxes must be raised. The tradition in Colorado that said the state was poor and could not afford to maintain adequately elementary, secondary, and higher schools had to be broken. The task college and university presidents and other officials set for themselves was a difficult one. They were seeking to alter the thinking of political, commercial, industrial, and journalistic leaders who had systematically developed the notion that taxes must be kept down, regardless of the effect on education. Many state legislators were amenable to some increases in appropriations, but they asked the standard question, "Where will the money come from?"

The University tried to provide some answers concerning taxes and the state's responsibility. Economics Professor Earl Crockett prepared studies of the state taxation system that were mailed to every legislator. He concluded that the income tax, enacted in 1937, would be the most effective source of revenue to solve the state's financial crisis. It was emphasized over and over again by President Stearns and other spokesmen that the state was not fulfilling its obligations to its major institution of higher learning or to its young people. Students from Colorado, through tuition, were furnishing 61 percent of the cost of their education. Tuition was paying more than half of the operating costs of the University. Another significant source of revenue came from the federal government, which was paying the actual instructional costs, plus 15 percent administrative overhead, for all veterans under the G.I. Bill.

What was the state doing? In 1935, when enrollment was 3,357 the mill levy provided $723,902. Now, in 1946, when registrations peaked at 7,700, estimated state support, including the mill levy and special appropriation, was only $840,000. Put another way, Colorado taxpayers paid $215.63 to support each student in 1935, while in 1947 they were contributing only $190.09. And 1935 was a Depression year when costs were low. It was estimated that the cost of instruction had advanced 246 percent.[48]

President Stearns determined to broadcast these facts to the people. Thirteen alumni clubs were founded in Colorado. The *Alumnus Magazine*, which won a prize for editorial excellence in national competition, kept graduates informed of progress. Bulletins were sent to important people. A convocation, where students were requested to write to their parents, was held on campus. Stearns was careful to emphasize that he was not proposing a student lobby. After efforts such as these, the legislature appropriated $750,000 to the University. Wealthy interests, however, operating through the state Chamber of Commerce, Association of Manufacturers, Mining Association, and the Colorado Retailers Association lobbied successfully against a sizable increase in the income tax.[49]

Although the public relations organization established in 1947 served the University well in future campaigns for appropriations and funds, sufficient income remained a problem. The school did not ask for extras or even for the sums needed to put faculty salaries on a par with those in competing institutions. Budgets usually were increased at a rate of 5 to 10 percent. And enrollment hit a postwar high of about 9,300 in 1948. It was estimated that 15,000 hammered at the door for entrance.

Throughout Stearns' presidency, the University remained a student-financed institution. In 1949, the state appropriation comprised only 29 percent of revenue with the remaining 71 percent coming from tuition, fees, and other charges. At this time, the University was not receiving its fair share of funds appropriated in Colorado for higher education. It was educating about 46 percent of Colorado students, and was receiving only 36 percent of total state support to higher education institutions. The Colorado School of Mines, by contrast, enrolled slightly more than 3 percent of state students and gained 12 percent of state appropriations. The state rarely provided more than 75 percent of the University's budget requests. When the total budget reached $4,696,000 in 1952, the legislature grated $1,485,000 plus $953,000 from the mill levy and motor vehicle tax. The University never had enough funding to improve the student-teacher ratio beyond 19 to 1, build a first-class research collection in the library, support graduate education sufficiently, or launch the new general education program in the College of Arts and Sciences effectively. This important innovation, appearing in many other universities, was designed to reduce specialization and increase interdisciplinary understanding.[50]

Additional housing to accommodate the thousands of veterans and nonveterans who entered the University was necessary. Officials saw that living space would become critical by 1946. Shortly after V-J Day, the first of several temporary expedients was introduced. The Regents leased 200 house trailers from an army air base and installed them near the baseball diamond north of Folsom Stadium. Thus Vetsville was founded. These structures, which rented for as little as $20 per month, represented substandard housing to say the least. Students endured harsh winds that swept through the floors and heavy rains that leaked through the roofs. Water had to be carried from central spigots and only public toilet facilities were available. But most of the residents welcomed any housing as long as they could gain an education, and they resented being referred to as "pioneers." One veteran wrote to Stearns:

My service was with the Infantry and at times very difficult. It was during those more exacting moments when seeds of bitterness were planted, but they have found very little nourishment upon which to grow since I've been back and here at the University.

The trailer camp was soon followed by the installation of Quonset huts and barracks-type apartment buildings.[51]

The great difficulty encountered by the University with prefabricated housing was the cost. Adequate, nonslum dwellings, unless financed with federal funds, were expensive. If they were purchased and constructed with borrowed money, they would have to be amortized over a fairly long period to keep rents low. The problem that faced the institution very soon after large numbers of veterans began matriculating was whether to invest in temporary buildings or to erect permanent structures. It was decided to build six permanent dormitories. To expedite matters, the firm of Platt Rogers, Inc., from Pueblo, was employed on a construction-management contract. The idea was to begin building in 1946 under the construction manager while specifications were being completed and building materials purchased. It was critical for the University to buy materials when they were available at sizable discounts. If a general contract for these buildings were offered for open bids, it would be necessary to have all the plans completed before the bids could be submitted. This would delay completing the structures for at least four to six months. The construction-management arrangement was new in the 1940s and it enabled the University to erect housing for 840 students in a relatively short time. In 1947 and 1948, Farrand, Aden, Cockerell, Crosman, Reed, and Brackett Halls were opened. These dormitories cost more than $2,800,000.[52]

The most audacious construction project was the University Memorial Center, dedicated in September 1953 as the official state memorial for those who died in World Wars I and II. This student center has exterior dimensions of 280 by 170 feet, roughly the size of a standard football gridiron, and is five stories high. It meets the needs for recreation space, meeting rooms, entertainment facilities, and offices for student government. When the fund drive for this building was initiated at Homecoming in 1947, there was not a dance floor on the campus large enough to accommodate even half the student body and alumni. Described as one of the finest student union buildings in the nation when it opened, the UMC cost $2,500,000 and was financed by donations of alumni and friends, student assessment, and bonds to be paid by student fees.[53]

Academic construction also proceeded. To meet the need for classrooms and laboratories quickly, six hospital buildings were moved to the campus from Buckley Field in Denver. Several of these "temporary" structures served faculty and students until the 1960s. Meanwhile, a faculty-administrative committee, chaired by Dean Edward King (law), was charged with making recommendations concerning the "immediate and urgent" permanent construction requirements. Approximately $1,000,000 was available from the mill levy, an inadequate sum according to the committee. In a policy decision, King's group determined that the first obligation of the University was to meet the requirements of undergraduate education rather than those of graduate study and research. The departments most needing space were physics, chemistry, and biology, as well as the College of Engineering. The committee recommended construction of additional wings on the Engineering Laboratories and the Chemistry Building, and a new Physics building. After physics was moved from Hale, the basement could be remodeled to meet partially the demands of biology. The wing on the Engineering Building was completed in 1948, and the chemistry addition in 1950. The $609,000 Physics Building was opened in 1952. Plans for this structure were so scaled down to meet available funds that it was obsolete in terms of the Physics Department's programs from the very beginning. It provided, however, a necessary additional 50,000 feet of floor space. Also in 1952, an addition to the Geology Building, partially financed by gifts from alumni, was completed.[54]

President Stearns heralded the advent of a new era in research and graduate study in the summer of 1946. This was "not only inevitable in view of the growth of the institution and the trend of modern times but is vitally necessary if the institution is to discharge its function toward graduate students, toward faculty members, and toward the country as a whole." Demands for scientific knowledge were at the forefront of intellectual consideration, and opportunities for research, financed by federal agencies and private sources, were growing rapidly. Financial assistance would support graduate study. But the president also uttered a word of caution.

. . . in undertaking this expanded field of research development we must bear in mind that our coordinate if not our major responsibility is in the field of undergraduate training and education, particularly with the demands made upon us for the education of returning veterans.

Each research project approved had to be weighed carefully in terms of advantages and disadvantages. Would it distract the faculty from their normal teaching duties?[55]

Manpower for research was a problem, because faculty were overloaded. Most were teaching twelve or more hours per week and serving on an inordinate number of senate, college, and departmental committees, many with overlapping responsibilities. Some relief from committee assignments came when the Senate of the University was reorganized, but not until 1951. This desirable reform consolidated standing committees into functional areas such as privilege and tenure, student affairs, educational policy and university standards, budget, faculty personnel, and the development and utilization of University resources. Altogether, nine committees were designated, responsibilities defined, and membership specified.[56]

Graduate study grew as enrollment expanded. But the graduate program was never carefully planned, budgeted, or given the recognition it deserved. Graduate Dean Philip Worcester, expostulating for his school, said the University was spending more money and devoting more time and attention to lower division students, half of whom dropped out before the end of the sophomore year. Adjustments were not made in the teaching loads of instructors who directed research and theses. Professor John Lacher (chemistry) was supervising the work of seven Ph.D. candidates in 1949 and also chairing the committee that arranged doctoral and postdoctoral fellowships under the same Atomic Energy Commission grant that funded the Department of Biophysics in the Medical Center. Chemistry was outdistancing other science departments in the number of graduate degree candidates and the amount of sponsored research. Of the departments outside the sciences, members of history were heavily engaged in the training of graduates and writing. This work received little financial support. The total amount budgeted for research in the Graduate School was increased from $3,000 in 1939 to only $7,200 in 1952.[57]

By the late 1940s, budgets began reflecting the fact that sponsored research grants were paying portions of some professors' salaries. For example, Lacher, Stanley Cristol, Karl Dittmer, Joseph Park, John Meek, Orville Sweeting, and Irving Goodman (in chemistry), and William Rense, Frank Walz, and James Broxon (in physics) were awarded funds by the Office of Naval Research, Air Force, Atomic Energy Commission, Research Corporation, and other agencies. Working as a team, the chemists were studying the chemistry and physiology of nucleic acids and their derivatives. They were synthesizing nucleic acid derivatives "tagged" with radioactive elements, examining their biochemical, crystallographic, and physical properties, and measuring the effect of radiation on the biological properties of these compounds. A small isotopes laboratory was built northeast of Folsom Stadium for some of this work. Goodman was awarded a Guggenheim Fellowship to further his studies. In addition, Cristol became a leader in the study of organic reactions and was later designated as a Fellow in the National Academy of Sciences for his research.[58]

The most important research enterprise in physics was the Upper Air Project. Rense and others became expert in building devices that could be pointed at astronomical objects such as the sun, moon, or even the stars to make spectrographic photography of what was there. These devices or controls were extremely sophisticated. They had to be light in weight and durable. To photograph the sun in ultraviolet light, an ultraviolet spectrometer was flown in a rocket. The controls built in the Physics Department aimed these optical instruments. This work led to the establishment of the Laboratory for Atmospheric and Space Physics on the campus. In time, graduate students in the program organized the research arm of Ball Brothers Corporation in Boulder.[59]

Front view of Norlin Library. Inscription above the entrance reads: "Who knows only his own generation remains a child." (CU Photographic Department)

Mary Rippon came to the University in 1878 to teach French and German. The first woman on the school's faculty, she taught modern languages until her retirement in 1910. An outdoor theater, enclosed on three sides by Hellems building, is named in honor of Mary Rippon. (CU Photographic Department)

Old Main as it appeared in 1889. (Western History Collection)

Students on walk leading to the anatomy building, spring 1898. The women are Misses Dreck, Ricketts, and Richardson. The man is unidentified. The anatomy building was erected in 1888 for medical classes and later used by the School of Pharmacy before being torn down in 1921. (Brackett Collection, Norlin Library)

In this 1902 football game with Nebraska, as seen from the roof of Old Main, Colorado lost by a score of 10 to 0. The building in the left foreground is the old chemistry classroom structure (Ekeley), which was torn down in 1972. Two oil well derricks are visible in the background, one in the center, the other to the left of center. (Brackett Collection, Norlin Library)

University of Colorado Hospital on the Boulder campus, 1903. Dr. Lyman Griffin is one of the two men on the front steps. The women are unidentified. (Brackett Collection, Norlin Library)

May Day exercises, ca. 1912. The engineering building, on the site now occupied by Norlin Library, is in the background. Spectators at the right are standing on the steps of what was then the University Library and is now the University Theater. (Brackett Collection, Norlin Library)

The Grand March at the Junior Prom, 1919. (Snow Photograph, Western History Collection)

Macky Auditorium was constructed with a gift from Andrew J. Macky. Completed in 1922, the building contained, in addition to a 2,500-seat auditorium, the University's principal administrative offices. (CU Photographic Department)

Student processional entering Macky Auditorium for graduation exercises, 1924. (Snow Photograph, Western History Collection)

Basketball game between the University of Colorado and Brigham Young University, 1937. (Snow Photograph, Western History Collection)

Byron (Whizzer) White with University of Colorado football coach Bernard (Bunny) Oakes. White, who earned his B.A. in 1938, was named an Associate Justice of the United States Supreme Court on March 30, 1962. (CU Photographic Department)

The University Faculty Club, later called Regent Hall for a time, opened in September 1939. The structure housed the Navy's Japanese language school during World War II, and afterwards served as a women's residence until 1956, when it reverted to a faculty club. (CU Photographic Department)

Navy units on review, Folsom Stadium, 1944. During World War II, several naval training programs were conducted at the University of Colorado, including the Navy College Training Program (V-2), Naval Aviation Program (V-5), and Naval Medical Training Program (V-12), the latter at the Denver medical campus. (CU Photographic Department)

The formal surrender of Japan on September 2, 1945, prompted students to join with Boulder's permanent residents in staging a VJ parade. Participants are shown marching along Pearl Street. (CU Photographic Department)

Sewall Hall, named in honor of the University's first president, was completed in 1934 and served for many years as a residence for women. This picture, taken shortly after the close of World War II, reveals the trailers of Vetsville in the background. (CU Photographic Department)

A Pi Beta Phi sorority formal dance, Boulder campus, 1947. (CU Photographic Department)

Play action during University of Colorado and University of Oklahoma baseball game, 1949. (CU Photographic Department)

Aerial view of the Boulder campus in the early 1950s, prior to construction of the south and

east stands of Folsom Stadium and of Libby Hall. (CU Photographic Department)

University of Colorado Medical Center. The building in the center is Colorado General Hospital, with a research bridge spanning Ninth Avenue, connecting the new structure (completed in 1965) with the Medical School. In the left foreground is Dennison Memorial Library. (CU Medical Center Information Service)

The downtown Denver campus of the University of Colorado. The buildings, constructed in 1910 by the Denver Tramway Corporation, were purchased by the University in 1956. (CU Photographic Department)

The 1961 football team was undefeated in regular season play, winning for the University of Colorado its first Big Eight championship. On New Year's Day, 1962, the team was defeated by Louisiana State University in the Orange Bowl. (CU Photographic Department)

Teddy Woods, University of Colorado track star, performing during an indoor meet, 1960. Woods, a freshman sensation, recorded a sizzling 0:48.9 in the 440 in his first appearance with the school's track team. He was undefeated in the quarter-mile in 1960, capping the winter schedule with a victory in the Big Eight Meet in Kansas City. (CU Photographic Department)

Students registering for classes at Regent Hall, 1965. (CU Photographic Department)

The Engineering Center, dedicated in May, 1966, provides in a single complex some ten acres of classroom, office, and research space. A major event during the dedication was "Dean Hutchinson Day," in honor of the retirement of Charles A. Hutchinson after 48 years on the College of Engineering faculty. (CU Photographic Department)

Aerial view of the Boulder campus, 1969. (CU Photographic Department)

Fountain area on the north side of the University Memorial Center. The fourteen-foot bronze statue was presented to the University in 1971 as a memorial by the parents of Daniel Louis Touff (1941-1963), a chemistry major who died while mountain-climbing near Boulder. The sculptor was Edgar Britton, a Denver artist. (CU Photographic Department)

Mass meeting of students on quadrangle in front of Norlin Library on May 8, 1970, as part of the protest against the war in Southeast Asia. President Richard M. Nixon's announcement that American forces in Vietnam were intervening in Cambodia triggered a three-day demonstration, the largest in the history of the University of Colorado. (CU Photographic Department)

The Black Student Program held its second annual Career Day Fair in April 1971, during which numerous black men and women discussed with students opportunities for careers in a variety of fields. (CU Photographic Department)

Play action during the University of Colorado and University of Oklahoma football game, October 21, 1972. (CU Photographic Department)

Ralphie, the furry mascot of the University, with handlers, September 1974. The bison was given to the school in 1957 by the father of a member of the freshman class. (CU Photographic Department)

The 1973 University cheerleaders. (CU Photographic Department)

Gallery of Presidents, 1877–1976

Joseph A. Sewall
1877–1887

Horace M. Hale
1887–1892

Joseph Hutchins Baker
1892–1914

Livingston Farrand
1914–1919

George Norlin
1919–1939

Robert L. Stearns
1939–1953

Ward Darley
1953–1956

Quigg Newton
1957–1963

Joseph R. Smiley
1963–1969

Eugene H. Wilson
1969

Frederick P. Thieme
1969–1974

Roland Rautentraus
1974–

The formation of a corporation, in 1945, that included both the University and Harvard in the control and operation of the High Altitude Observatory at Climax, Colorado, had great significance for the future of Boulder and the state. Harvard had been operating a pilot solar observatory on the property of the Climax Molybdenum Company, 11,500 feet above sea level, since 1940. During the war, observations concerning the prediction of radio communication disturbances were telegraphed daily to Washington and London. Research proved that solar observations made at high altitudes had great potentiality for the study of the sun, particularly in its direct effect on the earth. The sun's changeability is of vital significance. Weather, plant growth, rainfall, fuel, and light—indeed all human life—depend on it. Harvard wanted to move the project to another site on the mining company's property where visibility would not be obscured by dust from the mining operation, and to install a larger and more sophisticated coronagraph, an instrument for observing and photographing the sun. The cost of this project was estimated at $225,000.

Even before Stearns' return from war service, negotiations concerning an affiliation with the University were opened by Harvard astronomer Harlow Shapley. To expand the operation, funds were needed. Since a Colorado site was decided on, Colorado foundations were the most likely source. A definite connection with a Colorado institution was needed. Shapley visualized the formation of a public corporation called the High Altitude Observatory of Harvard University and the University of Colorado which would raise funds, hold and disburse money, and delegate to Harvard the task of constructing the observatory, managing it, and planning its research program. Scientists and students from both schools would participate. At a specified time in the future the property and instruments of the corporation would be turned over to the University of Colorado.[60]

Although the Regents were shocked at the magnitude of the enterprise and concerned that a fund-raising effort could compete with other projects, they resolved to move ahead with negotiations, because Harvard could raise money in Colorado without the collaboration of the University. Stearns, for his part, was enthusiastic. By the fall of 1945, an agreement for incorporation was drawn along the lines suggested by Shapley. Local interest was great, he said, and he wanted to set the stage for the fund drive. Stearns, Donald Menzel, of the Harvard Observatory, and Walter Orr Roberts, superintendent of the High Altitude Observatory, visited national and Colorado foundations and industry, but money-raising lagged. It was some years before plans at Climax were completed. Eventually, an observatory was built on a promontory of land on the campus southeast of the new dormitories to house the Boulder offices and operations of the observatory. The building was provided by a gift from the estate of Mrs. William Sommers, and Harvard induced the Bausch and Lomb Optical Company to donate the telescope. The National Bureau of Standards later located their Radio Propagation Laboratory in Boulder to be near the Harvard-CU corporation.[61]

Of future significance also, although in an entirely different realm, was the University's admission to the Big Six Athletic Conference (later the Big Eight) in March 1947. The school thus gained the opportunity to play football, basketball, and other sports in a league with universities such as Kansas, Nebraska, Missouri, and Oklahoma against whom it was competing academically. This was recognized by the *Silver and Gold.* "Association in one of the nation's 'big-time' athletic conferences takes CU out of the hinterland of sport and places it in close association with other state universities who have shown equally high standards off and on the field." The editor of the paper wrote that the name of Athletics Director Harry Carlson should be "emblazoned in large letters" across the pages of the history of the University. He had maintained athletic standards comparable to any university in the country and had built the top athletic department in the Rocky Mountain region. After admission to the Big Six was announced, as a sign of the changing outlook, athletic scholarships were increased from 40 to 100, with 60 going to football.[62]

The history of the postwar period in higher education, as in the nation, was one of great activity and substantial change. It was also one of great commotion. From the late 1940s an irrational fear of communism, Communist subversion, and even Communist tendencies that approached national paranoia was expressed by leaders and citizenry alike. In universities and colleges around the country, the "Red scare" threatened the foundations of academic freedom, menaced the careers of faculty members, and tried the mettle of administrators. This represented a monumental failure on the part of many individuals to understand the mission of the university. Administration became an excruciating business. The first instance in the University occurred early in 1947 when President Stearns revoked the charter of the 50-member Tom Paine Chapter of the American Youth for Democracy.

After strong criticisms of this organization by Professors Walter Franklin (business) and Carl McGuire (economics), and some students, the president asked Edward King, James Broxon, and Earl Crockett to find out if the AYD was controlled by regularly enrolled students and whether the organization was progressive or a front for some undisclosed ideology. This committee probed extensively and reached the conclusion that the Tom Paine Chapter had autonomy and was controlled by regularly enrolled students. At the same time, however, they learned, mainly from the pages of the Communist newspaper, the *Daily Worker*, that the AYD was the successor of the Young Communist League. It was a Communist front, being Communist in origin, sponsorship, and objectives.[63]

Stearns regarded this as circumstantially conclusive evidence and revoked the charter of the AYD chapter. He explained that "in taking this action I want to make clear that this institution does not intend to interfere with free discussion which is a vital part of the educational process nor is it opposed in any way to liberal or progressive student organizations." At the same time, the chapter of a national organization that was a front for a foreign ideology would not be sanctioned on "this" campus. The president's decision was popular, but some students and student groups disagreed. The Young Democrats, for example, believed the "action sets a precedent whereby one man as an arbitrator of morals can exclude any organization by the vague and fuzzy accusation that it is not what it purports to be. . . ."[64]

The expeditious manner with which Stearns handled the AYD case was quickly forgotten when the *Denver Post* broadcast on Sunday, December 28, 1950, in a front-page, banner headline, "C.U. Prof Reveals Red Link." The testimony of David Hawkins, professor of philosophy, before the Un-American Activities Committee of the House of Representatives had been made public. Thus began a fateful debate that was to have immense implications for the University, its president, and faculty.

Hawkins was personally recruited and hired by Stearns in 1947 to direct the physical science course in the College of Arts and Sciences' new general education program. He served as an administrative assistant to J. Robert Oppenheimer, and as project historian, at the Los Alamos, New Mexico, atomic laboratory during the war. His clearance for work on the atomic bomb and access to classified information was carried out by Military Intelligence with the Manhattan Engineer District. They had certified his loyalty to his country.

Hawkins was one of a significant number of college students in the 1930s who had joined the Communist party, a legal entity in those days, out of disillusionment with capitalism and fear of war. The party was only slightly more to the "left" than the New Deal domestically, and its demand for sanctions and collective security arrangements against the fascist powers, particularly Nazi Germany, appealed to many idealistic young Americans. It became more attractive with evidence that the Nazis would not be stopped by appeasement.

In his testimony before the Un-American Activities Committee, Hawkins admitted that he had joined the Communist party as a 25-year-old graduate student at the University of California in 1938, but had given up membership and stopped paying dues in 1943. Concerning his resignation, the philosopher explained:

> . . . I felt increasingly, as a member of a University community, as a political, I hoped, professor in philosophy, and as a person who wanted to live in the fuller sense of the word among colleagues and students, that continued membership in the Communist Party would create a gap, and almost necessarily a duplicity.

The professor had been caught in the Un-American Activities Committee's dragnet presumably because its members wanted to tie Robert Oppenheimer and Hawkins' brother-in-law, publisher William Sloane, to communism. Sloane had published a book highly critical of the FBI and J. Edgar Hoover. In his testimony, Hawkins refused to become an informer. He talked freely about himself, but declined to testify against former associates whom he knew were loyal citizens and had performed no illegal acts. To inform would be to create injustices which followed from the activities of the committee and the atmosphere of the time. While his position had flimsy, if any, legal basis, he was not cited for contempt by the committee.[65]

Stearns was pressed hard by forces outside the University from the time of the announcement of Hawkins' former Communist affiliation. It is ironic that only a few days earlier, the distinguished humanist, Howard Mumford Jones, speaking at the University's seventy-fifth anniversary convocation, called for a national outlook that permitted and encouraged "the individual to think and then say and write what he thinks, regardless of what interests might be embarrassed." These words were forgotten when the influential *Denver Post*, in a sharply worded editorial, argued that the University was confronted with two grave problems. Hawkins' loyalty to "American standards of life and to the American ideal of free and honest education," as well as his fitness to teach in the state University, had to be determined. The professor had been dishonest because he had not informed the University of his former affiliation and, moreover, he was unstable because he had been a member of the Communist party for five years. It was incumbent on Stearns to make clear that he would not tolerate totalitarianism. He had been an effective leader, "but if he is not willing to take strong action, the regents should get a new president. . . ."[66]

Early in 1951 there were demands in the legislature for a sweeping investigation of Communist influences in state-supported schools, and it was evident that this suggestion would be enthusiastically embraced. Representative A. W. (Woody) Hewett, Republican, of Boulder, introduced legislation severing Communists from any source of state money. He said there were "all shades of Reds" at the University. Others in the state urged that a loyalty oath enacted during the "Red scare" of 1921 when the Ku Klux Klan had been politically powerful in the state be instituted for college and university teachers. Attorney General Duke Dunbar ruled that professors in all higher education institutions, both public and private, were subject to this affirmation of loyalty.[67]

The president and Regents moved rapidly. Following the attorney general's ruling, the oath of allegiance was required. They obviously did not fear a repetition of the situation at the University of California, where several hundred faculty members refused to sign a loyalty oath. After all, the Colorado oath was a simple statement of loyalty to the constitutions of the United States and Colorado and an expression of intent to teach "reverence for law and order and undivided allegiance to the government of one country. . . ." The California pledge, on the other hand, forced faculty to swear, as a condition of employment, that they did not believe in or support any organization that taught the overthrow of the government of the United States by force or violence. In a month's time, every professor subscribed to the oath without open protest.[68]

To forestall an investigation of the University by members of the state legislature, the Regents announced that they would conduct a fair and complete investigation of Communist activities on the campus "with full regard for the values of the University as a teaching institution." They employed two "experienced and qualified investigative counsel," Dudley Hutchinson, of Boulder, and Harold Hafer, of Fort Collins, both attorneys who formerly were agents of the FBI. This decision undoubtedly was regarded as good strategy, but it proved to be the opposite. Inquiries of this type have lives of their own. Results have to be forthcoming.

The two former FBI agents began their investigation apparently without specific instructions, criteria for loyalty, or an implicit request from the administration that the faculty should cooperate. A group of senior professors inquired of the president about procedures, but they were not enlightened. Stearns reviewed his career at the University and asked for their confidence. The investigators never were a presence on the campus; few teachers were interviewed. Hutchinson and Hafer moved into the community and the state developing a system of informers among students, former students, and citizens. Many faculty feared the outcome of the inquiry. They immersed themselves in their disciplines and hoped for the best.[69]

As for Hawkins, Stearns stated that his admission of former membership in the Communist party was not sufficient grounds for summary dismissal. Under the Laws of the Regents, a faculty member could be ousted for cause, but only after consultation with appropriate faculty committees. The Committee on Privilege and Tenure had responsibility for determining the qualifications of faculty. This body would investigate Hawkins and report to the Regents. Stearns prescribed the scope of the investigation by drawing up a list of charges, all of which originated outside the University, for the committee to examine. These were that Hawkins admitted former membership in the Communist party; that he failed to divulge this information when hired at Los Alamos and the University; that he refused to answer some questions and was evasive concerning others before the Un-American Activities Committee; that the Marxist Study Group on the campus, which he had served as an advisor, became an action organization; and that his resignation from the Communist party was more nominal than real.[70]

Faculty at the University were apprehensive, but most maintained confidence in Stearns and the Regents. Only a few were critical of the decision concerning Hawkins. They felt he should be fired, if for no other reason than the impact of his disclosure on the legislature at a time it was considering appropriations. The actions of the president and Regents quieted even the most outspoken critics in the state. Republican Governor Dan Thornton, who exerted a moderating influence, announced that he would not order a legislative investigation until the University completed its efforts to ascertain facts. The governor's position was attributable to his respect for Stearns, who was a leading Republican. The president also was commended by the *Denver Post* "for the forthright manner in which he . . . handled a difficult matter."[71]

The Privilege and Tenure Committee, composed of Clay Malick, chairman, Wayne Beattie (mechanical engineering), Paul Dean (chemistry), Bernard Longwell (biochemistry in the Medical School), Frederick Storke (law), and Eugene Wilson (Director of the Libraries), held hearings throughout March and April 1951. An ad hoc faculty group led by the mathematician, Aubrey Kempner, raised $700 to provide Hawkins with legal counsel. The committee proceedings were prosecuted impeccably. Both the committee and the "defendant" called witnesses; administrators, faculty, and students testified. A great deal of time was

devoted to examining the charge that Hawkins allowed the Marxist Study Group to become an action organization. This body
brought speakers to the campus, some of whom were Communists, and had announced these meetings in a handbill, lightheart-
edly called, *The Pink Buffalo*. In the end, to prevent charges of a
whitewash, Chairman Malick issued an invitation to the public
for testimony. Not a person who might have wished to testify
adversely stepped forward.[72]

In examining the charges, the committee found that Hawkins' previous membership in the Communist party was not sufficient reason for his dismissal, particularly since his resignation
from the organization was sincere. He did not disclose his former
Communist membership when employed at Los Alamos and the
University because he was not required to do so. The intelligence
unit at the atomic project knew about his former associations
and, nevertheless, he was given increasingly responsible positions.
The University did not have any political tests for employment.
Indeed, there had long been a policy not to enquire concerning
political and religious beliefs. As for his performance before the
Un-American Activities Committee, the members of Privilege
and Tenure did not completely approve, but they understood his
reluctance to identify individuals whom he knew had not engaged in subversive activities. As for being evasive, this simply
was forgetfulness. Hawkins did not encourage political activity
on the part of the Marxist Study Group. He cooperated fully
with the Dean of Students in keeping the group within the limits
of its charter. All in all, the committee found no evidence that
the professor was sympathetic to any subversive ideology. He
was an objective and stimulating teacher, who did not attempt to
influence students, slant his lectures, or follow the party line. It
was Privilege and Tenure's unanimous decision that Hawkins
should be retained without any change of status on the faculty of
the University.[73]

After studying this report, the Regents decided that a final
decision would be made after an open hearing on May 11. This
meeting would be conducted along judicial lines with the Regents questioning invited individuals. Only two witnesses appeared. One was Representative Hewett, who introduced two
reports prepared by the Un-American Activities Committee as

well as an article condemning Hawkins and William Sloane, written by the right-wing columnist, Fulton Lewis, Jr. One report was of Hawkins' testimony before the committee while the other identified him as one of 500 sponsors of a Scientific and Cultural Conference for World Peace held in New York City in March 1949. This conference was linked to the Communist peace offensive. The party was calling for an end to the Cold War. The other witness, Robert Donner, of Colorado Springs, identified himself as a member of the Colorado Protective Association. Others reported that he had been denounced by the Anti-Defamation League for supporting anti-Semitic causes. He managed to get into the record his assumption that Hawkins was really a secret member of the Communist party working on a conspiracy in education. After hearing his testimony, the Regents voted 4–1 to keep the professor on the faculty. Only Charles Bromley voted negatively. The *Denver Post* protested that the Privilege and Tenure Committee and the Regents had served the University badly. Hawkins had been evasive before the Un-American Activities Committee. He had taken upon himself the right to be "judge, jury and sole determiner of the honesty and integrity of friends." This was not serving our government or freedom responsibly. Hawkins had not been above reproach and he should not have been retained.[74]

During February 1951, when action was being taken concerning David Hawkins, Chemistry Head Paul Dean initiated a series of communications with assistant professor Irving Goodman, who was studying on a Guggenheim Fellowship in Paris, regarding the biochemist's prospects in the department. He said that many faculty were upset over recent charges of Communist activity on the campus and there were threats of investigations. He was not suggesting, however, that Goodman would be investigated, although the assistant professor had admitted membership in the Communist party from 1942 to 1944 when the Navy objected to his participation in a research project in 1947. Dean emphasized that he was proposing a change of employment for Goodman because biochemistry was being de-emphasized on the Boulder campus. The Medical School had a large department and an active graduate program. Altogether, Goodman's future in the University was not "rosy."[75]

In April, Stearns met with Dean Van Ek, Vice President Dyde, and Dean to decide Goodman's future. Although specific charges were not expressed in this meeting, it was evident that the Communist issue was prominent in the president's mind when he argued that the biochemist's appointment should be terminated. By this time, the former FBI agents had reported. The Chemistry Department and Dean Van Ek recommended that Goodman be given a terminal year. Stearns refused this proposal. The chemist had been given adequate notice and his appointment would be concluded by July, even though his leave of absence already had been extended until September. If Goodman accepted this action, reasons would not be given. If he protested, however, an explanation of the decision would be advanced, and he would have to suffer the consequences.[76]

Goodman expressed a willingness to seek employment elsewhere, but he "protested" his "summary dismissal" to the president. "I cannot believe," he argued, "that all of my work for the past years can be so lightly dismissed without even so much as an explanation of the basis for this action." His future was in jeopardy, because his economic status would not permit a long period of unemployment. Would it be possible for the administration to give him assurances concerning the extension of his leave until September and also a letter of recommendation, he asked. Stearns informed the biochemist that his service with the University would end on June 30, 1951. This judgment was in the interests of the institution.[77]

In their meeting of June 29, the Regents decided three significant matters. They met in executive session to study the Hutchinson-Hafer report. The president had prepared a summary of the document that was never released to the press. The investigators found that three assistant professors and instructors "almost certainly" had been active Communists and these individuals had left the University. It was obvious that Stearns had made a decision on this important matter. Several other faculty, the report indicated, had participated in Communist-front organizations under the mistaken belief that they were aiding liberal causes. Between 1946 and 1950, about 30 students, in a student body that ranged from 7,000 to 9,300, were Communist party members or sympathizers. The press was told that the investigation would be continued. Less than 1 percent of a faculty of 500 were still under examination.

Second, the Regents denied Irving Goodman's protest and presented, in publication, the following reasons for his dismissal. Although not a Communist then, the chemist had been an active member of the party during part of his service with the University. More important, he had been untruthful with President Stearns in 1947 when he explained that he had given up party membership in 1944. He had actually continued his affiliation.

The final action taken by the Regents was an "implementation" of the oath of allegiance. It became the policy of the University not to employ any person, in any capacity, who was

> a member of or otherwise affiliated with any organization, group, society or other association which advocates, encourages, abets or teaches, by written or spoken word, the duty, necessity or propriety of or has among its objects or purposes changing the form of government of the United States or of the State of Colorado by any means other than those prescribed by the respective laws and constitutions thereof.[78]

Goodman learned the reasons for his firing when he read the newspapers and he responded in a letter to the *Boulder Daily Camera* published on July 29. The president had resorted to "calumny," he said, to discredit a colleague. During a private conversation concerning his politics in 1947, Goodman had answered all questions frankly and in a straightforward manner. He never deliberately gave false information. Stearns probably had reached erroneous conclusions.

> One cannot avoid concluding that President Stearns has been driven by an irrational and panic-stricken national mentality into an action which he was not prepared to take in 1947, although all of the relevant facts were known to him at the time.[79]

On the campus, Dean Van Ek and the Faculty Group for Study of Academic Freedom requested that Goodman be accorded a hearing. The faculty group, chaired by Dudley Wynn (English), reminded Stearns that he had told the Regents in April that dismissal for cause would include a hearing for the accused. They regarded the presidents' publicizing of the reasons for

Goodman's dismissal as "an action unbecoming the dignity and prestige of the institution." This body was a small minority of never more than twenty faculty who tried to keep in touch with Stearns and the Regents. They avoided all publicity because they did not wish to appear as being in opposition to the administration. They were chastized frequently, however, by many faculty for being radical and anti-administration. The faculty generally abided by the slogan, "Let the administration handle it." This was evidence of their confidence in Stearns, but it was also testimony to their demoralization.[80]

Demoralization was never more apparent than in the response to the implementation of the loyalty oath. The Regents converted a relatively innocuous affirmation into a requirement that faculty demonstrate their loyalty by nonmembership in groups that were neither named nor defined. Furthermore, the implementation contained the implication that any individual who advocated, encouraged, abetted, or taught the duty, necessity, or propriety of changing the form of government of the nation and state by other than lawful means would be in violation of his oath. This proscription represented a danger to academic freedom and the scientific presentation of information, since it did not distinguish between teaching facts and agitating action. This change in the oath, after its promulgation, certainly was the basis for strong protest, but only Dean Van Ek and the Faculty Group for the Study of Academic Freedom raised their voices against the resolution and urged its revocation.

In December 1951, the *Silver and Gold* informed the University community that the contract of Morris Judd, instructor in philosophy, had not been renewed for reasons of incompetence. This action, the paper reported, seemingly was taken by the president without consultation with the department. Judd was a member of Phi Beta Kappa and a *summa cum laude* graduate of the University in 1938. His graduate study, where he completed all the requirements for the Ph.D. except the dissertation, was at Columbia University. His teaching began in 1949 when he was appointed instructor in American philosophy. The Philosophy Department was required to cut its staff in 1951 because of declining enrollments, and he was the only instructor recommended for retention.[81]

Judd was the first faculty member to admit to his colleagues that he had been interrogated by Hutchinson and Hafer. The two former FBI agents interviewed him on May 1, and he refused to answer their questions on the ground that this was a political test, a violation of academic principles, and an invasion of constitutional rights. Judd wrote to Stearns and explained his motivation in refusing the investigators. In a meeting with the president, he reiterated his stand. Stearns requested answers to two questions: Was he a member of the Communist party? Had he ever been a party member? He answered the first in the negative, but refused to respond to the second.[82]

During the summer, when the philosopher did not receive a letter of reappointment for the 1951–52 academic year, the Philosophy Department learned that it was being held up because Judd refused to answer the questions. When the Regents met on August 10, they approved a recommendation from the administration that the instructor's appointment for the next year would be terminal. Only Regent Vance Austin voted negatively. He argued that if Judd were unqualified, he should be dropped immediately and not retained for another academic year. If guilty of conduct that made him unfit for the faculty, this should be shown. Only "suspicions and innuendos" from anonymous sources had been brought forward. No evidence had been presented that Judd was unfit. In a democratic society, Austin concluded, a man should be innocent until proved guilty, and should be held in his position until such took place. Proof should be presented and "not merely a repetition of the accusations of anonymous accusers."[83] The Regents' animadversions were not made public until the Judd case was being adjudicated.

Judd was informed by the administration that his reappointment was for "two semesters only," but nothing was said that his service with the University would be terminated after that time. It was not until November that he learned he was in his last year of employment. When this information was reported to Edward Machle, chairman of philosophy, the department reacted strongly. If Judd was being terminated for incompetence—the word "pedestrian" was bandied about—then the department should have been consulted. Machle was later informed verbally by the president that the reasons for Judd's nonreappointment were incompetence, failure to make satisfactory progress toward the Ph.D., a lack of intellectual honesty based on his refusal to answer the questions concerning past political affiliations, and noncooperation with the administration's efforts to implement the oath of allegiance.[84] This last reason was difficult to comprehend, because the implementation took place more than a month after the philosopher's conversation with the president.

Judd appealed to the Privilege and Tenure Committee and the American Association of University Professors that his privileges as an instructor had been violated. The Philosophy Department, in his behalf, argued before the committee that departmental autonomy had been abridged. The committee decided to hold hearings. Judd was in a difficult position. The reasons for his non-reappointment were common knowledge, but they had never been stated in writing. He not only had to prove reasons had been advanced, but also had to answer them at the same time.[85]

In the hearings, President Stearns refused to testify on the basis that the committee did not have jurisdiction in the case. Judd was not dismissed for cause. He was not reappointed. Concerning short-term appointments of instructors, there was no obligation on the part of the administration to make reappointments nor to give reasons for refusing to do so. Administrations must have the freedom to determine whether or not a probationary teacher was to be accorded continuous tenure. This position was supported by the AAUP. The president argued that the Senate of the University should determine the jurisdiction of Privilege and Tenure in the Judd case, and the Committee on Faculty Personnel should conduct a study toward changes in policy.[86]

A Senate meeting was held on April 1, 1952. Henry Ehrmann, chairman of Privilege and Tenure, moved that the Senate confirm the decision of the committee to take jurisdiction in all cases where there was evidence of an infringement of academic freedom. This was defeated by a close 112 to 109 vote. It was then moved that the rules of the University regarding academic freedom and tenure be referred to the Personnel Committee for a thorough study and possible revision. This motion carried easily. At the conclusion of the Personnel Committee's study in June 1953, the Regents approved the establishment of a Grievance

Committee which would hear cases of faculty on limited appointments who believed their nonrenewal was unjustified and represented an abrogation of their rights. It became the responsibility of the aggrieved faculty member, however, to establish a *prima facie* case. Proceedings in the Judd case also were confirmed when a resolution was passed that all cases pending before Privilege and Tenure should be heard during the period the Personnel Committee was studying the rules.[87]

Following the Senate meeting, Stearns agreed to testify. Many believed the close vote on Privilege and Tenure's original motion influenced his decision. In his meeting with the committee, however, he refused to express reasons for Judd's nonreappointment that could be construed as charges. When the president finished his testimony, members of Privilege and Tenure unanimously agreed that "the procedure followed in the matter of Judd's nonreappointment was not in the best interests of all concerned." Nonrenewal for incompetence should result only after "close consultation" between the department and the administration. Faculty members being terminated should be told specifically that their appointments were terminal.

But on the important matter of academic freedom, the committee divided 4 to 2. The majority, composed of Archibald Buchanan (assistant dean of the Medical School), William DeSouchet (law), Leo Novak (civil engineering), and Benjamin Spurlock (mechanical engineering), were convinced that Judd's prerogatives were not violated. The administration had every right not to supply reasons, and evidence concerning them before the committee was hearsay. Such evidence would be excluded in any court of law because of its unreliability, and a finding in favor of Judd should not be based on it. The minority, Ehrmann and Morris Garnsey, on the other hand, emphasized that Judd had been subjected to political questioning by the president. It was also a fact that Regent Vance Austin had pointed to "anonymous accusers" rather than professional evaluation of the instructor, and this was evidence of a transgression of academic freedom. To describe the evidence in the case as hearsay, they concluded, was unfair and unjust to the participants and also contrary to the procedures of an informal hearing.[88]

The Colorado Federation of Teachers, which had provided Judd with $300 for legal counsel, petitioned the Regents to examine the evidence and to reconsider the decision of the committee. This petition was denied. The AAUP chapter pursued the case. At the chapter's instigation, a special meeting of the Senate was called on June 2 to discuss the majority and minority reports of the Privilege and Tenure Committee. Discussion, however, did not take place. After the meeting was called to order, Dean Elmore Peterson was recognized and he immediately moved adoption of the majority statement. A letter from Dean Edward King was read in which he maintained that Judd had been given "full and fair opportunity" to present his case. The Privilege and Tenure Committee made its decision and the case was closed. The Senate approved the Peterson motion. Stearns held the meeting after adjournment. He told the faculty he would happily resign if the conduct of the administration was unsatisfactory. In approving the majority report, he argued, the Senate did not support the administration. It sustained an orderly procedure under which a community of scholars could work. The Judd case had resulted from a failure to understand ideas that had been communicated, he explained.[89]

Following the Senate's action, a number of professors requested intervention in the case by the AAUP. The AAUP General Secretary, Ralph Himstead, appealed to Eugene Wilson, a member of the association's national council, for advice. In telling Himstead how to proceed, it was Wilson's conclusion that events did not support intervention. He had discussed the Judd case with Stearns, members of the Privilege and Tenure Committee, as well as faculty colleagues. Due process was strictly followed. Judd had his day in court. When the association finally reported on the Hawkins, Goodman, and Judd cases in 1956, it did not recommend censure of the administration of the University. The administration deserved credit for refusing, under pressure, to dismiss Hawkins. It also acted commendably in allowing the Senate to judge its action in the Judd case.[90]

On September 2, 1952, Robert Stearns resigned, effective July 1, 1953, to accept the presidency of the Boettcher Foundation. He said the University had reached a point of equilibrium and would move steadily forward. It would soon be faced by new pressures, however, from the young people crowding the public schools. "Bold plans" would have to be made soon to meet the needs of these students. The institution required "a vigorous and forward-looking administration." Stearns estimated that peak activity would come in 1960 which would be the year of his compulsory retirement. Instead of an older president facing retirement in that year, there should be an "active man" at the head of the school. For this reason, it was time for him to leave.[91]

During the last months of his administration, he faced criticisms from Republican State Senator Morton Wyatt, of Lamar, as well as pressures resulting from the Hutchinson-Hafer report. Senator Wyatt apparently had aspirations of becoming the "little Joe McCarthy" of Colorado. Frustrated by the legislature in launching a wide-ranging investigation of communism in the schools, he demanded that the former FBI agents' report on the University be made public. The people deserved to know that at least eleven professors were past or present members of Communist-front organizations, he declared. In his actions, he attacked the Republican governor, Republican president of the University, and three members of the faculty.

After the Lamar Republican began making his demands, Republican Regents Charles Bromley, Erskine Meyer, and Virginia Blue caucused with Republican legislators to discuss the report's contents and to quiet the storm. They said eight faculty had left the University as a result of the inquiry, that a total of fifteen had been investigated. Four were cleared for lack of evidence, while three were absolved by the Regents. This description was an exaggeration. Evidence suggests that only three faculty "left" the University—Irving Goodman, Morris Judd, and Robert Albright (speech), who had been subjected to "the intimidating process of a special loyalty test," and accepted positions elsewhere.[92]

The Regents' disclosure quieted Wyatt momentarily, but soon he was demanding release of the names of the eight professors who resigned or were fired, accusing Stearns of laxity and suggesting he was dismissed by the Board, claiming that Governor Dan Thornton had not cooperated in pursuing Communists, and attacking Harl Douglass (education), Morris Garnsey, and

John Livingston (economics) on the floor of the state senate as subversives. The president, who enjoyed communicating with limericks, summed up his thoughts in this manner:

> Comes now one Senator Wyatt
> Whom no one seems to keep quiet
> Though without any facts
> He says I am lax
> While he feeds me a laxative diet.

Many of the senator's colleagues thought he had gone too far. He was condemned by the newspapers. In the senate, his remarks were described as "nauseating" and the *Rocky Mountain News* plainly said, "Now Shut Up!" The University had investigated and communism was a "dead issue."[93]

In Boulder, an ad hoc committee reflected the view of many troubled faculty when they proposed that all copies of the Hutchinson-Hafer report be destroyed save one which would be sent to the FBI as a record. Dean Van Ek expressed the opinion that the investigation had been a mistake. The University should have fought on the first line when the attackers showed up. President Stearns and the Regents opposed the report's destruction. They placed it in a safety deposit box at the First National Bank where it has remained, and they assured the faculty that the investigation was over. Every present faculty member, they emphasized, had been cleared completely of any subversive activities.[94]

While the furor over the investigation diminished, fear and trepidation lingered. The erosion of freedom that took place after 1950 was never more evident than when Governor Dan Thornton sent a communication from the FBI to Stearns listing faculty who should be fired for subversive activities and when the annual lecture named in honor of retired English Professor George Reynolds was canceled in 1953. The FBI letter was ignored, but not before Stearns brought it to the Regents. The respected composer, Aaron Copland, had been invited as Reynolds lecturer. At the instigation of five faculty members, the president launched an investigation of the musician. He wrote to Senator Eugene Milliken and asked that he procure information concerning Copland from the House Un-American Activities Committee. Stearns received a report listing the Communist-front groups the composer had supported. Rather than risk renewal of public clamor over communism, the Reynolds lecture was called off.[95]

Robert Stearns' administration of the University began and ended in controversy. He solved the problem of the endowment funds and many more quite successfully, but the stultifying effects of his decisions during the McCarthy era continued beyond his presidency. A growing number of professors believed he should have stood up to critics outside the institution thus preventing the eclipse of academic freedom and imagination that took place. But throughout his thirteen years in office, for the most part, he enjoyed the support and confidence of faculty and students. Except for the Communist hunt, Stearns capably guided the school during a period marked by disruption and change. The varied challenges of the war and postwar periods were met with considerable verve and resourcefulness. The Boulder campus gained new buildings, mostly dormitories to house the expanding student population, and reorganization in Denver produced a new Medical Center and earned it national recognition. The University, with the exception of the Medical School, remained essentially an undergraduate institution. Its mission continued to be the education of undergraduates, and research and graduate study were not expanded substantially. Yet Stearns made few plans for the future. He was cognizant of the future, as his letter of resignation indicated, but when he departed in 1953, the University was not a significantly different enterprise than it had been in 1939.

Five

THE PURSUIT OF
EXCELLENCE:
1953–1963

URING THE FIFTIES, most American colleges and universities
underwent striking transformations brought about by their
response to several interrelated events. They accepted students
in unprecedented numbers, adapted to changing intellectual currents, and became involved in the concerns of society. Even well
into the sixties, these institutions remained caught in the clash of
ideas resulting from continued growth, shifting academic empha-
ses, preoccupation with graduate training and research, and an
increasingly intimate relationship with—and dependence on—the
federal government.

In the decade before 1963, the University of Colorado experienced dramatic change. It more than doubled in size, emerging from geographical isolation to become a leader among its
sister institutions in the Rocky Mountain region. During the administrations of Ward Darley and Quigg Newton, the University deliberately pursued excellence to enhance the quality and
quantity of its services to Colorado and the West. Teachers and
scholars with established reputations were attracted to the campus, admission standards were raised for undergraduate and graduate students, and programs were initiated, particularly at

advanced levels in the applied and theoretical sciences. Simultaneously, the University won enlarged financial support from the state of Colorado and competed successfully for a larger share of federal dollars to fund new activities and research.

The expansion and reorientation of the University of Colorado reflected changes that occurred within the nation, state, and region. The fifties were a time of general economic prosperity. Colorado's population increased by about one-third, ranking it eighth among the fastest growing states in the country. For the most part, growth was restricted to a narrow corridor along the Eastern Slope of the Rockies from Fort Collins to Pueblo. Denver, the focal point of commercial, financial, and industrial activities in the mountain states, grew more than 50 percent in population; the inhabitants of the five-county Denver Metropolitan Area increased about one-fifth.[1]

During the fifties, Boulder emerged from semi-isolation to experience almost unrestricted growth. In 1952, the opening of the Denver-Boulder Turnpike and the establishment of the laboratories of the National Bureau of Standards attracted new residents and created new jobs on a large scale.[2] Subsequently, the appearance of several large industries—Dow Chemical, Beech Aircraft, and Ball Brothers Research corporations—also had enormous impact on the community.[3]

The transformation was startling. Boulder's physical area more than doubled as its population jumped from approximately 20,000 to 45,000 during the years 1950–1963. There was an unprecedented demand for construction as residential areas spread beyond the city's expanding boundaries; five major shopping centers yielded a threefold increase in retail sales. In addition, the community's economic base continued to broaden as more research and industrial enterprises were attracted to the Boulder Valley.[4]

Growth was interacting. Advances in higher education stimulated development within the region and the community, in turn inducing expanded activities within the state's colleges and universities. Like other public-supported institutions of higher learning in the area, the University's enrollment shot upward. The size of the student body had descended to a post-World War II low in 1951 before turning up again in the years 1953–

1956, a trend that continued for more than a decade. In the period 1951–1963, all public and private colleges and universities in Colorado recorded a 51 percent rise in enrollments, while the number of students on the Boulder campus jumped from 8,059 to 12,538, a 56 percent growth.[5]

The campus population explosion absorbed the attention of the Darley and Newton administrations. Both, although committed to improving the quality as well as the size of educational programs, had first to respond to the challenge of sheer numbers as more and more prospective students clamored for admission to the University.

Assuming executive leadership of the University in mid-1953, just as the potential of the student influx became apparent, Dr. Ward Darley was able to draw upon his thirty-year association with the institution in seeking solutions to the problems of growth. A native of Colorado and trained as a physician, Darley served from 1945–1949 as Dean of the Medical School, and from 1949–1953 as vice president for Health Services. When President Stearns accepted an invitation to head the Denver-based Boettcher Foundation, the Board of Regents asked Darley to serve as the University's seventh president.[6] His 3½ years in that post coincided with the initial thrust of the second postwar surge of students and rising enrollments that threatened to overwhelm the state's preeminent University.

Commencing in 1953, enrollment climbed rapidly on the Boulder campus. A record freshman class matriculated that fall despite the closing of admission for out-of-state women on May 1 because of lack of housing.[7] The size of the student body advanced from 7,262 in 1953 to 9,844 in 1956, and was projected to reach 13,000 within ten years.[8] That inpouring of students, what Darley and others called the "rising tide," placed a severe strain on the University's physical facilities.

In order to cope with these numbers, the most urgent need was buildings: classrooms had to be added rapidly to keep pace with the rising tide. The formal dedication of the University Memorial Center in the fall of 1953 allowed officials to acquire and remodel the old student union for the School of Business.[9] At the same time, the basement of Hellems, in part occupied by the bookstore, was transformed into classrooms and offices for the College of Arts and Sciences. Also, a third floor was added to the Service Building to provide space for the Department of Architecture and Architectural Engineering.[10]

Additional construction provided facilities for expanding programs. The College of Music building, completed in 1955, combined functions that had been housed in five different structures on the campus.[11] That same year, work began on Hellems Annex, erected between Hellems and the geology building on what was the site of temporary office and classroom units. The new three-story "wing" to Hellems was eventually occupied by the College of Education, the Division of General Education, and the Department of Psychology.[12] Expansion of Folsom Stadium, raising the capacity by almost one-third, to 44,000 seats, allowed the space beneath the new east and south stands to be enclosed and converted to the needs of three ROTC units, the Audio-Visual Department, the University's mailroom, and physical-plant service shops.[13] A four-story chemistry building, authorized in 1956 and scheduled for completion within three years, was to fill the parking lot located directly north of the University Memorial Center.[14]

The relentless pressure of the rising tide also prompted a large student housing construction program. In August 1953, in an appeal to Boulder residents to make rooms available to students, Darley noted that since World War II the University had built living accommodations for about 900 people while enrollment increased by more than 3,000.[15] Libby, Nichols, and Willard halls, the first dormitories on the Boulder campus erected with federal loans, were finished and occupied by 1955; Hallett Hall was completed and occupied by 1956.[16] By then, another ten units had been added to University Village, otherwise known as "Vetsville," providing accommodations for married students and their families.

The building programs of 1953–1956, although sizable by the standards of the time, made little headway in alleviating the pressure of rising enrollments on the Boulder campus facilities. Academic structures represented capital construction expenditures totaling about $2 million; new dormitories amounted to twice that amount. However, the pace of adding classroom and residential accommodations fell well behind the expanding student body.

In progress, in addition to the 1956 chemistry project, were new structures for the Law School and the Athens Court facility, and a married-student housing complex.

In 1955, Waldo Brockway, former business manager and then director of plant development from 1953 to 1959, was responsible for developing a program to acquire physical facilities for 13,000 students within ten years. The plan called for the expenditure of $22 million for academic structures, plus an additional $10 million for student housing.[17] To implement this scheme, Darley's administration sought the support of other public colleges and universities in Colorado for an appeal to the legislature for increased funds to promote capital improvements.

For nearly twenty years, construction of buildings (other than residential structures on the Boulder and Denver campuses) was funded principally from the proceeds of a state building mill levy. Although the University received $4 million from that source from 1946–1955, the future yield, if the levy were renewed in 1957 at the same rate, at best could finance about 3 percent of the construction projects required to keep up with the rising enrollment in the next ten years.[18]

Recognizing the need for expanded construction programs at all institutions of higher education in Colorado, in 1954 the State Planning Commission instructed all public colleges and universities to prepare estimates of building requirements for the next decade. Seven schools, acting through the Association of Presidents of the Institutions of Higher Learning in the State of Colorado, outlined projects aggregating $49.5 million.[19] The Fortieth General Assembly, at the request of Governor Edwin C. Johnson, authorized revised building mill levies designed to return $41.8 million to the schools over a ten-year period. Of that amount, the University of Colorado was assigned $19 million, one-third of which was for the Schools of Medicine and Nursing in Denver.[20]

The higher yield from the building mill levy enabled the University to carry on construction on a pay-as-you-go basis, while providing ample funds with which to match monies from outside Colorado for the building-expansion program. This was particularly important in the post-Sputnik era when the federal government, reacting to the Soviet Union's space successes among other concerns, made available grants with which to advance studies in languages, mathematics, and sciences.

The successful agitation for larger mill-levy revenues was but one aspect of the University's appeal for more support from the state because of rising enrollments. In order to meet that challenge, the school had to enlarge and upgrade its faculty and to establish new programs serving a broader segment of the college-age population.

Additional financial support also was required to recruit teachers and scholars when schools across the country similarly were attempting to expand their faculties. Low-level salaries endangered the quality of instruction, while the higher levels outside colleges and universities lured talented academicians from classrooms and laboratories to government and industry.[21]

However, the state was slow in responding to urgent pleas for additional money. In 1953, the legislature failed to appropriate funds commensurate with the rising costs prompted by the student population explosion. The University was forced into imposing a modest tuition increase while reducing teaching expenditures about 4 percent.[22] The following year, Governor Dan Thornton, recognizing the necessity of additional funding for higher education, asked the general assembly to initiate reforms permitting a more equitable distribution of available financial resources, most of which were, by law, earmarked for old-age pensions.[23] When, in 1956, the legislature ignored the University's request for $260,000 to improve faculty salaries on the Boulder campus, Darley asked the Regents to raise tuition "across-the-board" by $26. The additional revenue, he insisted, was needed to avert an exodus of the faculty and for a variety of improvement programs. The Board twice refused to act, but it did relent to the extent of allocating receipts from a larger-than-anticipated enrollment for faculty salaries.[24] This did not provide funds for expanding the overworked staff of the Extension Division, for purchasing classroom equipment, or for increasing physical-plant maintenance operations.[25]

In four fiscal years, from 1952–1956, the University's total income for the Boulder campus expanded more rapidly than did support derived from the state. Revenues from all sources jumped from $6.6 to $11.4 million, while legislative appropriations increased from $2.2 to $2.9 million.[26] Stated another way, income from all sources went up approximately 90 percent while monies derived from the state rose only 23 percent. In the same period, however, the yield from student tuitions and fees advanced slightly more than 40 percent, while the return from auxiliary enterprises and activities more than quadrupled.[27]

Additional funds from the state, other than appropriations for capital construction, were devoted largely to improving academic standards for lower division classes, and for new programs in upper division and graduate instruction. After having played a key role in advancing the status of the Medical School, through emphasis on research in the basic sciences, Darley, on assuming the presidency, encouraged similar activities throughout the University. In his view, Boulder had lagged too long behind the Denver campus in the conduct of research.[28]

The University, under Darley's leadership, accelerated the development of programs designed to stimulate investigations in the sciences. Following the pattern successfully employed in Denver, a conscious effort was made to attract outstanding scholars to Boulder. Wherever possible, they were assigned to well-equipped classrooms and laboratories, and were encouraged to work with able, motivated students (particularly at the graduate level), to create knowledge through research. Equivalent pursuits were fostered in the social sciences and humanities.

The sciences, however, were the focus of attention. Under W. F. Dyde, vice president and Dean of Faculties, established programs were quietly expanded in the Departments of Chemistry and Physics, as well as in the College of Engineering, while new activities were instituted as personnel, equipment, and facilities became available. With funds largely derived from the federal government, plans were initiated for a cyclotron and a computer center, and a study was inaugurated to determine the feasibility of erecting a nuclear reactor on the Boulder campus.[29]

The stress placed on research was partially responsible for the enrollment surge in the Graduate School. The number of students working for advanced degrees increased from 617 in the fall of 1953 to 859 three years later—a trend that continued for several years. By 1956, graduate programs having more than 45 students were those in business, chemistry, education, engineering, geology, physics, and psychology.[30] With the exception of the College of Education, which attracted large numbers of graduate students to the school's popular summer sessions, most of the growth in advanced studies was in the theoretical and applied sciences.

Indicative of the importance attached to the sciences was the formation of research agencies to promote studies of solar phenomena and the alpine environment peculiar to Colorado's Rocky Mountains. In the fifties, the High Altitude Observatory and the Institute for Arctic and Alpine Research were foremost in the University's drive for recognition as a science center.

The High Altitude Observatory of Harvard and the University of Colorado, formally organized in 1946, operated under the guidance of a Committee on Scientific Operations (Harlow Shapley, Donald Menzel, and Walter Orr Roberts—all astronomers).[31] The force behind the High Altitude Observatory was Roberts. His energy and persistence were largely responsible for the organization's success. He solicited funds to build a new observatory at Climax, including a sixteen-inch high resolution coronograph. He was also instrumental in negotiating contracts for a variety of scientific investigations with governmental agencies and the armed forces.[32]

The joint venture terminated in 1954. The decision to end the partnership came about, according to Harvard's Dean Bundy, because the High Altitude Observatory diverted Harvard's limited resources from more important projects. However, the reason appears to have been an irreconcilable conflict between Menzel and Roberts, arising, in part, from administrative reforms proposed by Roberts and supported by the University of Colorado. These changes would have eliminated, for all practical purposes, Harvard's control over the observatory's activities.[33] Rather than remain a junior member, Harvard withdrew and the High Altitude Observatory became a research affiliate of the University of Colorado.

Research in mountain ecology predated the founding of the solar observatory by more than 25 years. As early as 1908, Francis Ramaley, longtime head of the Biology Department, inaugurated summer classes at a mountain laboratory located at an altitude of 8,400 feet, near Toland in Gilpin County. The annual sessions continued until 1919. However, four years earlier, a number of faculty members began construction of what became known as "University Camp" on Forest Service land about 25 miles west of Boulder. That facility was relocated in 1921 to place it beyond Boulder's watershed. Renamed "Science Lodge," the site, located near the continental divide at an altitude of approximately 9,500 feet, became a center for the study of mountain geology, botany, and zoology.[34]

After conducting classes at Science Lodge from 1946 to 1950, John W. Marr (biology) took the lead in the latter year in organizing the Institute of Arctic and Alpine Research. Formally recognized by the Regents on April 20, 1951, with Marr as director, the institute conducted investigations in mountain biotics for the U.S. Army Quartermaster Research and Development Command. Subsequent grants from the Atomic Energy Commission and the National Science Foundation enabled the University to operate the only field station in the United States devoted to mountain research.[35]

Despite its preoccupation with growth, including the emergence of science-oriented programs, the Darley administration had to turn again and again to resolving frictions within the University and in its relations with the community. A persistent irritation during the years 1953–1956 arose from the recurring charges that communism was advocated by elements within the faculty and the student body. Allegations of subversion continued throughout Darley's tenure, but there was no repetition of the witch hunt that disrupted the closing years of Robert Stearns' administration.[36]

In the autumn of 1954, a new dimension was added to the controversies that centered about the University. Reverend Gladden William James, a retired missionary and chairman of the Boulder-based, nondenominational Foundation for the Authenticity of the Bible for Religious Liberty, Inc., publicly charged that professors at the state's leading university were openly contradicting the word of God by teaching that man was descended from lower animals. In subscribing to the theory of evolution, they were, according to James, utilizing the money of Christian taxpayers to promote fraud. Furthermore, by invading the field of religion, the teachers violated the federal Constitution, which provided for the separation of church and state in America.[37]

James, in time, carried the issue to the Board of Regents, as well as to the people of the state and to the legislature. The University's governing board, after listening to James' view that evolution as an expression of atheism should be banned from the campus, refused to take any action.[38] Undaunted, James sought a wider audience, using "Sounding Board," a discussion program aired by Denver's KLZ-TV to denounce the Regents for their lack of enlightenment.[39] In addition, James turned to the Colorado General Assembly seeking legal sanction for his anti-apeman crusade. He asked two Boulder County representatives to initiate legislation to safeguard the teachings of the Bible. Both men politely declined the honor, one insisting that the state had no business defining the curriculum of publicly supported schools.[40]

Rebuffed on all sides, Reverend James abandoned the effort to impose religious fundamentalism on public schools. The defunct crusade was quickly forgotten, and James received little notice two years later when he committed suicide.[41] By then, the question of man's origins were overshadowed by another dramatic issue, the perennial struggle to root out racial bias in student organizations on the Boulder campus.

Discrimination was the most troublesome problem faced by the Darley administration. Responding to concerns expressed by some students, faculty, and Regents, as well as to pressures outside the University, the president sought to bring an end to long-established restrictive practices in the selection of members for honorary, professional, and social organizations on the Boulder campus. Student groups, Darley insisted, had to exercise complete freedom in choosing initiates and to disregard regulations imposed by alumni or national fraternal societies.[42] His goal, at first, was self-determination. However, elements of the student body and the faculty sought much more; they hoped to eliminate racial bias, whatever its source.

The antidiscrimination campaign originated during the Great Depression when President Norlin appointed, on recommendation of the University Senate, an Ethnic Minorities Committee to investigate problems peculiar to minority students and to suggest corrective actions. Professors Robert L. Stearns (law), Earl Swisher and C. C. Eckhardt (history), the latter as chairman, were instrumental in gaining blacks the right to service in some of the shops in the Hill business district adjacent to the campus. The committee also attempted, without success, to persuade honorary and professional societies to cease discrimination in selecting members.[43]

The antibias crusade, suspended for the duration of World War II, was revived at its end. At the time, similar movements were under way elsewhere in the United States. Amherst College, Middlebury, Massachusetts Institute of Technology, Harvard, Connecticut, Brown, Massachusetts, Swarthmore, Chicago, Wisconsin, and the University of California were centers of agitation to impose antidiscrimination rules on many, if not all, student organizations.[44]

The movement on the Boulder campus was spearheaded by the Ethnic Minorities Committee with strong support from the administration and the Regents. The committee, composed at that time of Professors Clifford G. Houston (education), Omer Stewart (anthropology), and Edward C. King (law), the latter as chairman, acted in the summer of 1947 to block University recognition of an honorary society that openly practiced discrimination. The issue gained public attention earlier that year when the Committee on Student Organization and Social Life (SOSL), a subcommittee of the University Senate's Committee on Student Affairs, approved campus activities by Blue Key on condition that the local chapter seek removal of restrictive clauses from its national constitution or face, after three years, possible revocation of its charter.[45]

Blue Key, according to the preamble of its constitution, sought, among other things, to perpetuate faith in God, to support and defend the government of the United States, and to preserve the principles of good citizenship. Membership was limited, however, to Caucasian males.[46]

The Ethnic Minorities Committee asked President Stearns to reverse SOSL's action on the grounds that discrimination practiced by Blue Key was not only undemocratic and contrary to accepted standards of behavior, but also no organization had the right to call itself "national" if it excluded the sons of Colorado taxpayers because of race or color. Furthermore, recognition of the society exposed the University to the charge that it was both illiberal and reactionary.[47]

For these reasons, the committee asked that the Regents adopt rules to preclude racial bias at the University. Specifically, King, speaking for his colleagues, recommended that the school's governing board declare that no fraternity, sorority, or other organization be approved by the University if its charter, constitution, or bylaws sanctioned restrictions because of race, creed, or color. All honorary and professional fraternities and sororities already established on campus were to have five years in which to remove discriminatory clauses from their charters, constitutions, and bylaws. In addition, all social organizations were to be encouraged to discuss the question of ending discrimination with their national offices.[48]

In requesting the Regents to take action against honorary and professional societies, President Stearns, supporting the Ethnic Minorities Committee, insisted that the University should recognize only those groups which selected members on the basis of merit and achievement. The Board of Regents agreed. On November 21, 1947, it adopted a rule that no new charters were to be granted to organizations which practiced racial bias, and that within five years restrictive clauses had to be removed from the constitutions of honorary and professional groups on the Boulder campus. Failure to comply could lead to expulsion from the University.[49] Nothing was said at that time about seeking an end to discrimination by social organizations.

Within two years, the latter objective became the concern of the Associated Students of the University of Colorado (ASUC) and SOSL. Both groups insisted that organizations planning to establish new houses on the campus had to offer evidence that they did not discriminate in selecting members. The student government went even farther, insisting that existing Greek-letter houses which operated with restrictive clauses must submit annual reports indicating what steps were taken to remove objectionable provisions from their constitutions. The due date of October 15, 1951, was largely ignored by campus social groups.[50]

While the assault on racism in organized fraternity and sorority houses gained momentum, SOSL proceeded with the task of implementing the ban on discrimination by honorary and professional societies. Letters were circulated to each warning of the five-year grace period. In mid-1952, the committee's final notice brought responses indicating that all but one organization had complied with the Regents' rule. Eta Chapter of Alpha Chi Sigma, chemistry professional fraternity, was subsequently ordered to undergo deactivation. Appeals to the Senate Student Affairs Committee and Executive Committee were useless. However, on appeal, the Regents, by a 3 to 2 vote, ruled that Alpha Chi Sigma was, in fact, a social rather than a professional group, and did not violate the rule of November 21, 1947.[51]

The reinstatement of Eta Chapter had far-reaching consequences. It split the membership of the University's governing board and made the antibias crusade a partisan issue, with Democrats clearly favoring adoption of rules to preclude discrimination. The decision also focused attention on restrictive practices by social organizations and gave impetus to the movement to eliminate bias in University-sanctioned off-campus housing.

At the regular monthly meeting of the Regents on June 25, 1954, H. Vance Austin, supported by fellow-Democrat Kenneth Bundy, proposed (for action at the Board's next session) a motion calling for the elimination of discriminatory clauses in the constitutions of honorary, professional, and social organizations by September 1957. In addition, all students groups recognized by the University were to demonstrate—by their membership roll—a nondiscriminatory eligibility, admission, and membership policy by June 1958. If national Greek-letter fraternities and sororities failed to purge their constitutions of objectionable restrictions, Boulder chapters were to operate as purely local organizations.[52]

Little likelihood of winning additional support from members of the Board, many of whom thought the proposal too harsh, prompted Austin to modify his stand. During the meeting of October 1, he suggested that the Regents adopt a policy preventing any person from being "barred or discriminated against in any way, directly or indirectly, on account of race, creed or color in any facility or part of the University, including all fraternities and sororities, professional, honorary and/or social."[53]

That goal was to be achieved by refusing recognition to new organizations which displayed bias in the selection of members, and by requiring existing groups to make determined efforts to remove restrictive clauses in their constitutions prior to July 1, 1960. After that date, the University could withdraw recognition from organizations that practiced discrimination.[54]

Action on Austin's motion was delayed for two months while SOSL, at Darley's request, completed a study of appropriate remedies for the problem. The faculty committee eventually suggested that fraternities and sororities work toward the removal of restrictive clauses in their national constitutions, but without specific deadlines for completion of that action.[55] The University Senate endorsed SOSL's recommendations as more practicable than Austin's pending resolution.

The Regents, meeting on December 3, 1954, once again delayed action on the issue. The Austin and SOSL proposals were tabled for a year, ostensibly to allow the administration, students, and faculty an opportunity to review all aspects of the problem.[56] In fact, the Board wanted to give fraternities and sororities time to remove the offending restrictions from their constitutions, bylaws, and rituals without coercion from the University.

The issue was revived within less than a year, however, when campus sororities were publicly accused of widespread "behind-the-back" discrimination. A member of Kappa Delta resigned from the local chapter because it allegedly pledged only Caucasians. Furthermore, she insisted that all sororities on the Boulder campus, although they had removed legal provisions for discrimination in their constitutions, deliberately excluded minorities from membership.[57]

Reacting to the charge that the removal of legal sanctions did not end discrimination by sororities, on January 20, 1956, Darley circulated an open letter to the students and faculty outlining a plan for ending racial bias in off-campus housing. He proposed that each year all student social organizations were to certify to the University that considerations of race, creed, and color did not influence the selection of members.[58] Chapters unable to so certify were to be placed on probation and required, subject to the supervision of SOSL, to make progress in effectively eliminating discrimination. Any chapter on probation after April 30, 1960, was to lose the right to pledge and initiate members.

A decision on antidiscrimination measures was postponed again by the Regents during their regular meeting of January 22, 1956. Although Austin's motion was taken off the table, where it had been removed from consideration for more than a year, action on that proposal, as well as on Darley's more recent one, was deferred until March 19. On that day the Board was to hold public hearings prior to making a ruling on the matter.[59]

In the interim, Darley modified his antibias proposal. He suggested that a three-person faculty Committee on Student Organization Membership be empowered to police student organizations. Each year honorary, professional, and social groups were to submit reports to the panel indicating whether or not there were restrictions of any kind in the selection of members.[60] Organizations unable to certify free rights to membership were to be placed on probation. After April 30, 1962, offenders were to be denied opportunities to pledge and initiate members unless granted specific exemptions by the Regents.

The president's second proposal was criticized for delaying the enforcement of nondiscrimination. In addition, Austin and the Colorado branch of the American Civil Liberties Union denounced Darley's revised scheme because it seemingly invited social groups to discriminate with the approval of the University.[61]

The debate over discrimination gained momentum as the time approached for the hearings scheduled by the Regents. In addition to plans tendered by Austin and Darley, others were suggested by Regent Kenneth Bundy, the Associated Students of the University of Colorado, the Independent Student Association, and a group of 71 faculty members who acted apart from the University Senate, which had endorsed a proposal drafted by SOSL. All agreed on the need to end racial bias, but differed on methods and on the wisdom of imposing a deadline for compliance. Austin, Darley, Bundy, the University Senate, and the 71 faculty favored specific dates ranging from 1958 to 1962. ASUC and ISA opposed any time limit for remedial action.[62]

The climax came on March 19, as 63 people spoke for or against a ban on discrimination by social groups in a last-ditch attempt to influence the votes of the Regents. A standing-room-only crowd of at least 1,500 people filled the University Memorial Center ballroom. The evening session was moved to Macky Auditorium. A partisan crowd, generally formed by alumni and students from Greek-letter organizations, heard representatives of the Denver-based Fraternal Education Council, the Boulder campus Interfraternity Council, and the Panhellenic Association argue that the issue was not discrimination but freedom of choice, the right of societies to choose members without interference from the University.[63]

Proposals for an antidiscrimination rule came from the faculty, the Associated Students of the University of Colorado, the Independent Student Association, the Colorado Council of Churches, the National Association of Christians and Jews, the American Civil Liberties Union, and the Colorado State Industrial Union, AFL-CIO. All contended that discrimination by student social groups violated accepted principles of equality and democracy, and contradicted rationality—the ultimate goal of higher education in America.[64]

At 11:00 P.M., the Regents closed the hearings after 9½ hours and reconvened in President Darley's office, on the second floor of the building, to act on motions pending from previous sessions. The day filled with arguments for and against an antibias rule apparently had no impact on the Board. A party-line vote of 4 to 2, with Democrats in the majority, prohibited restrictions on memberships by student groups after September 1, 1962. Any organizations that limited participation because of race, creed, or color after that date were to be denied the right to engage in rushing, or to pledge and initiate new members. Regents Austin, Bundy, Elwood Brooks, and Tom Gilliam supported the motion, while Virginia Blue and Charles D. Bromley voiced disfavor.[65]

By the time the tumult and shouting subsided, it was apparent to many observers that the Regents had adopted an antidiscrimination policy which appealed to most students, faculty, and alumni. The rule of March 19, 1956, was reasonable and workable. Extremists on either side of the issue may have been displeased, but they were clearly in the minority. Student organizations had 6½ years in which to eliminate discriminatory provisions from their procedures. In the meantime, the University had an opportunity to turn its energies to a number of other problems which required attention. Most pressing of all was the selection of a new president.

Buffeted and battered by protracted controversies, Darley found himself, by the spring of 1956, to be in a position of reduced effectiveness as president of the University. For three years, he occupied a middle position between rival factions within the student body and the faculty, between the academic community and the larger arena of the city of Boulder and the state of Colorado, and between clashing personalities on the Board of Regents, which was divided not only philosophically on political grounds, but also on the fundamental question of what the institution should be. For example, the antibias crusade forced Darley to take positions which alienated first one and then another individual or group on which he depended for support. By the time the issue was resolved, his working relationships with the Regents, students, faculty, and the community had been eroded and were appreciably diminished.[66]

Furthermore, Darley had come to realize that the move from the Denver Medical Center to the Boulder campus was comparable to transferring from one institution to another, the latter being infinitely larger and more complex. His personal style of administration, particularly his reluctance to delegate authority to subordinates, placed a work load on the president that assumed staggering proportions, threatening not only to absorb Darley's private life but also to undermine his physical well-being.

Therefore, for a variety of reasons, when, in the spring of 1956, the Association of American Medical Colleges offered Darley the position of director, he eagerly responded. That decision, as Darley acknowledged, was prompted also by a desire to return to medical education to which he had a deep personal, as well as professional, commitment.[67]

During Darley's term of office, the University experienced some success in resolving problems arising from the student population explosion and from the necessity of developing new programs in an era of rapid advances in science and technology. The school erected several academic buildings and resident halls, and others, essential for future growth, were in the planning stage. At the same time, a science center emerged on the Boulder campus, indicated by the recognized quality of the chemistry and physics faculties, and the University was selected, in conjunction with the National Bureau of Standards, as a world data bank for the International Geophysical Year in 1957–58. Furthermore, preliminary steps were completed for the establishment of a cyclotron and computer center.[68]

By the time Darley left office, at the close of 1956, there was good reason to hope that his successor would have the administrative machinery with which to respond more effectively to rising enrollments, overloaded physical facilities, and the host of problems arising from a broadening curriculum. In 1955, a series of self-surveys conducted by committees of administrators and faculty revealed, among other things, serious deficiencies in the University's management. This prompted the Board of Regents, at Darley's suggestion, to authorize a comprehensive analysis of the institution's administrative organization and procedures.

After a thorough investigation of conditions on the Boulder and Denver campuses, the Public Administration Service of Chicago concluded that the school's achievement of educational goals was impeded by faulty administrative machinery. In the consulting firm's view this was paradoxical in that the administration of a university existed solely for the purpose of facilitating the educational process.[69]

The report revealed that the antiquated organization was incapable of providing effective executive leadership. The president, for example, functioned "in an administrative no-man's-land between the Regents, administrative officials, faculty and public, beset from each quarter by competing and oftentimes conflicting demands for his energies and loyalties." The president suffered from "unusual responsibility with an ill-defined authority and inadequate staff assistance."[70]

The school's second-ranking executive position was also the subject of pointed criticism. The vice president served in a dual capacity as Dean of Faculties, representing, in the view of the consultants, not only an illogical combination of administrative and academic duties and responsibilities, but also a work load too heavy for one person.[71] Further, there was no pattern to or logic for the implementation of academic programs on the Boulder campus. Colleges operated within colleges, departments within departments, some departments were larger than colleges, and some schools were in fact, if not in name, colleges. These and other anomalies produced organizational chaos.[72]

Concluding that the University's organization and administrative procedures had failed to develop along with teaching and research programs at Boulder and Denver, the Public Administration Service recommended several broad reforms. The Board of Regents, the consultants said, should refrain from involvement in administration, and function instead as a policy-making body. The office of the president should become the focal point for executive direction, fiscal planning, program development, integration, and interpretation for the University as a whole. Each of the two campuses should be given administrative freedom to conduct educational and service programs under presidential guidance, within the framework of the Regents' policies. Responsibility for administrative actions should be clearly located at several organizational levels, with decision-making delegated downward to the maximum extent consistent with the preservation of administrative unity. Finally, the faculty should clearly exercise responsibility for determining academic standards, policies, and programs.[73]

The task of implementing administrative reform fell to J. Quigg Newton, a vice president with the Ford Foundation at the time of his selection by the Regents as the eighth president of the University. A native of Denver and a descendant of a pioneer Colorado family, Newton graduated from Yale University and its Law School. He returned to Denver in 1938 to practice law, a career that was interrupted by World War II. After discharge from the U.S. Navy in 1946 with the rank of commander, Newton resumed his private law practice in the Mile High City.[74]

At the suggestion of Palmer Hoyt, editor of the *Denver Post*, and with encouragement from many friends, including U.S. Supreme Court Justice William O. Douglas, Newton decided to run for the office of mayor of the City of Denver in 1947. After a successful nonpartisan campaign as the symbol of change and progress against incumbent Benjamin F. Stapleton, Newton served two successive terms. As mayor, he carried out the thorough reorganization and modernization of an obsolete municipal apparatus.[75]

After eight years in city government, Newton sought a seat in the U.S. Senate. Declaring himself a Democrat, he ran unsuccessfully for the party's nomination against John H. Carroll. At the time, Newton was regarded by his social peers as a renegade for having repudiated the family tradition of Republicanism. Defeat prompted Newton to foresake politics. Following the close of his second mayoral term, he accepted a position with the Ford Foundation and moved his family to New York City. He remained there less than a year before returning to Colorado as president of the University.[76]

The majority Democrats on the Board of Regents, acting on a party-line vote, chose Newton because he had provided Denver with effective municipal government. The Board, already aware of the conclusions that were to appear in the Public Administration Service's report, realized that the University's management needed thoroughgoing reform. The initial step was the revitalization and expansion of the school's administrative structure. An enlarged staff, under the direction of a competent executive, could meet the ongoing challenges of growth.[77]

Many problems that plagued the Darley administration remained unresolved when Quigg Newton took office at the beginning of 1957. Enrollments continued to climb and construction continued to lag behind constantly rising demand. The goal of excellence, pursued until then with little fanfare, remained an elusive dream.

The size of the student body not only continued to grow, but also, on the Boulder campus, the clearly evident and recent shift in the direction of graduate study became distinctly more pronounced during Newton's presidency. Total enrollment rose from 9,844 in 1956 to 12,675 in 1963, an increase of nearly one-third, while the number of graduate students more than doubled, jumping from 859 to 2,211.[78] In the same period, the total of people served by the University in Boulder, on its medical campus, and through the statewide Extension Division increased from 20,415 to more than 42,300 annually.[79] Effective response to rising demand required a sizable expansion of the physical plant.

Several additions to the facilities provided accommodations for the student population explosion. In 1958, the Chemistry and Fleming Law buildings, on which work had started during the

Darley years, were completed on the Boulder campus. The Nuclear Physics Laboratory (cyclotron) and the Astro-Geophysics structure completed in 1960, the University Avenue Armory acquired from the state in 1961, and the Physical Science Research buildings opened on the east campus in 1961 and 1963 afforded space for science programs and contributed to Boulder's emergence as a research center.[80] Another building program was inaugurated on the medical campus and, in downtown Denver, the Extension Division, after having conducted classes in the city since 1912, acquired its first permanent home. For instructional purposes, the University purchased and remodeled the eight-story Tramway Building and adjoining car barn.[81]

Predictably, the challenge of growth compelled Quigg Newton to place top priority on administrative reorganization. The first round of personnel changes, announced in February 1957, filled four new positions. Eugene H. Wilson, director of libraries, became Associate Dean of Faculties, a move designed to lift some of the burden of academic administration from W. F. Dyde, who continued in the dual role of Dean of Faculties and Vice President of the University. John W. Bartram, formerly Darley's principal assistant, was named head of the Office of Budget and Planning, with primary responsibility for preparing annual requests for financial support from the state. James I. Doi, a consultant to the Association of State-Supported Institutions of Higher Learning in Colorado, was appointed Director of the Office of Institutional Research for the purpose of collecting and analyzing the data requisite for the effective utilization of the University's limited resources in a time of continuing expansion. Don F. Saunders, assistant dean of the Summer Session, was promoted to the post of Secretary of the Regents and the University, with the assignment of serving the Board and coordinating its activities with those of the administration.[82]

In naming Eugene Wilson to the second-highest academic position, Newton brought into the administration a man who in the next dozen years would serve in all of the top positions of leadership on the Boulder campus. In 1958, Wilson was named Dean of Faculties, and one year later also Vice President of the University at the time of Dyde's retirement. In 1959, he assumed the chairmanship of the long-range planning committee. Wilson also served as Acting Dean of Faculties for six months in 1963, and the following year moved into the vacant vice presidency for business affairs.[83]

The initial appointments of 1957, in which Wilson figured prominently, marked the beginning of comprehensive reorganization in the administration of academic, business, student, and medical affairs. The appointment of Oswald Tippo to the position of Provost, in 1960, placed academic matters on campuses under the direction of a single official. A former dean of the Graduate School at the University of Illinois, Tippo came to Colorado from Yale where he was Eaton Professor and chairman of the Department of Botany. A man of enormous energy and drive, Tippo sought to achieve Newton's goal of transforming the University of Colorado into one of the great institutions of higher learning in the United States. To that end, he worked to develop "a first-rate faculty with up-to-date facilities while teaching first-rate students."[84]

For a time, reorganization of business affairs was delayed pending the retirement of Business Manager Dillard Bray. In spring 1958 the vacancy was filled by the appointment of Leo Hill, a Colorado College graduate who had been the city manager of Columbia, Missouri, for six years. Hill absorbed the duties of treasurer in 1959, and four years later was designated vice president for business affairs. However, he resigned late in 1963 to accept the presidency of the First National Bank of Boulder.[85]

The reorganization of student affairs was also delayed. When Clifford Houston stepped down after ten years as Dean of Students to return to full-time teaching and research in the School of Education, his successor, in 1958, was Arthur H. Kiendl, Jr., a graduate of Columbia University Teachers College. At the time of his appointment to the position in Boulder, Kiendl was associate dean of Dartmouth College.[86]

Student activities administered by the University were consolidated, on Kiendl's recommendation, in a Division of Student Personnel Services. Discipline, housing, health facilities, recreation, and financial aid were placed under the jurisdiction of the Dean of Students, with supervision of requisite programs delegated to Pauline Parrish, Dean of Women; Harold E. Angelo, Dean of Men; and directors of several bureaus and departments.

As the Director of the University Memorial Center (UMC) and student activities, James E. Quigley supervised most nonacademic student functions, including an important segment of recreational programs. The five-story center, opened in September 1953, contained, in addition to offices and meeting rooms for student functions, a cafeteria and snack bar, ballroom, theater, bookstore, lounges, and a games area complete with bowling alleys, billiard and pool tables, and other facilities.[87]

The first indication that administrative reorganization could be controversial came in the summer of 1957 when Dr. Francis Manlove resigned as Director of the Medical Center. He had been appointed at the time Darley moved up to the presidency. Soon after Newton took office, Manlove, according to contemporary newspaper accounts, sought full implementation of the Public Administration Service's recommendation that the Denver campus be given autonomy. Newton initially refused, insisting that such action would create two universities in place of one. Mounting frustration prompted Manlove to turn from administration to teaching. Robert J. Glaser, who had come from Washington University (St. Louis) earlier that year to succeed Robert Lewis as Dean of the Medical School, assumed responsibility for business as well as academic affairs. Glaser's subsequent elevation to Vice President for Medical Affairs gained a large measure of independence from the Boulder campus for the center.[88]

The delay in administrative reorganization did not prevent the Medical Center from carrying forward the growth that characterized the Darley era. A ten-year plan, outlined in 1956, was completed during the Newton years and revealed that education, research, and service functions had outgrown existing facilities at the Medical Center. Expansion was planned in two phases, beginning with the construction of a new general hospital, clinical research building, and an out-patient office. This was to be followed by the remodeling of old structures to provide additional space for the Schools of Medicine and Nursing, enlargement of the Colorado Psychopathic Hospital, and construction of modern units for handling disturbed children.[89]

The facilities-expansion program was boosted by substantial private contributions. In 1960, the Eleanor Roosevelt Cancer Foundation announced a $750,000 grant for a research center as an integral part of the new hospital; the proceeds of the estate of Dr. Florence Sabin, totaling nearly $500,000, also were allocated. The enlarged facilities projected in the ten-year plan were designed to treat an estimated 20,000 in-patients and 200,000 out-patients annually.[90] Albert E. Humphreys, his children, and the Boettcher Foundation gave, in the memory of Ruth Boettcher Humphreys, the sum of $100,000 for a postgraduate center as part of the addition to Denison Library.

By 1963, enrollment at the Medical Center increased to approximately 1,000 students. Nearly three-fourths of this number were studying in the fifteen departments of the Medical School. The remainder were in related fields of nursing, medical and X-ray technology, and physical therapy. In addition, intensive refresher courses each year attracted as many as 3,000 practicing physicians to the Denver campus from the entire Rocky Mountain region.[91]

Medical campus income more than tripled in the decade 1953–1963, advancing from $5.2 to $7.7 million by 1956, and to $16.9 million seven years later. Money appropriated by the legislature increased from $2.3 to $6.2 million in ten years, the latter constituting 42 percent of receipts. Unlike the Boulder campus, tuition and fees made only a small contribution to the center's revenues, amounting to 3 percent of the total in 1963–64. Although four times larger, the yield from auxiliary enterprises and activities was also meager. However, sponsored research increased from less than $1 million to more than $3.75 million from 1956 to 1963, representing one-fifth of aggregrate income in the latter year.[92]

The Medical Center's growth aggravated the long-standing quarrel between the University and the Colorado Medical Society. For a time the debate over the faculty's insistence on the right to engage in private practice intensified before both sides finally agreed to sponsor legislation permitting Colorado General Hospital to accept nonindigent patients. Income from treatment was eventually used to augment salaries, enabling the school to attract and retain teachers who might not have been available without the extra financial inducement.[93]

A conflict between the University and the City of Denver was more troublesome. Mayor Richard Batterton announced on

April 30, 1960, that a thirteen-year relationship between the Medical Center and Denver General Hospital would end at the close of the next fiscal year. A contract providing for patient care at the municipal hospital, adopted in 1947 when Quigg Newton was mayor, was renegotiated ten years later. At that time, teaching and patient-care functions were separated, with the provision that administrators were to be responsible to the University for the former and to the Denver Board of Health and Hospitals for the latter. This plan was not fully implemented, however, because the two parties could not agree on the selection of department heads to supervise operations in the hospital. When the Medical School rejected candidates proposed by the Board of Health, that body, perhaps in part to free itself of influence by the academicians, insisted on terminating the agreement. The quarrel remained unresolved throughout the balance of Newton's years at the University of Colorado.[94]

Thoroughgoing administrative reform was a precondition for elevating the status of the University. In Newton's view when he assumed the presidency, it was a university with a reputation for social activities and intellectual requirements that were none too arduous. The potential was there for growth and development and, under the right kind of leadership, the University could become one of the outstanding institutions of higher learning in the United States.[95]

The decision to forge a prestige university in Colorado came at a time when many universities throughout the nation sought ways to enhance their standings among their competitors. All pursued that goal, following a variety of courses that might lead to greatness. Some publicized their age and long-established traditions. Others stressed newly won reputations for scholarship, the participation of graduates in public affairs, and the prowess of football or basketball teams. All professed excellence in teaching and research, and equated academic success with the number of recognized scholars and scientists on their faculties.

A poll conducted on the Boulder campus in 1956 indicated that academicians agreed, in a general way, on the method of pursuit as well as on the goal of greatness. When asked how to enhance the prestige of the University, most of those queried concluded that one way was through the dedication of the faculty and administration to the development and encouragement of research. Equally important were a "competent and distinguished faculty with freedom and security," and a "carefully selected student body." Other prerequisites for advanced status were academic freedom, well-equipped classrooms and laboratories, small classes, a first-class library, a wise and dynamic administration, and adequate salaries.[96]

Circumstances forced the Newton administration, on taking office in January 1957, immediately to seek higher levels of compensation for the faculty. Arguing that the quality of a university reflected the capacities of its teachers and scholars, the new president had to find a way to halt a threatened exodus of scientists from the Boulder campus. Three key men had already resigned to accept positions in industry, and there was every reason to believe that more would abandon academic pursuits unless salaries were quickly and substantially boosted.[97]

Faculty improvement, one of the essentials for greatness, required more than higher compensation. Teachers and scholars of wide reputation had to be attracted to the campus, while men and women already in professorial ranks had to be rewarded for achievements in classrooms, laboratories, and for scholarly publication. In addition, standards for reappointment, promotion, and tenure had to be raised to levels commensurate with the school's aspirations of greatness.

Public support was generated for the pursuit of excellence, including the upgrading of the faculty, largely because residents of Colorado—as Americans in general—in the fifties developed expectations that higher education could solve many problems that plagued society in the United States. However, the University's traditional organization, with sharp demarcations between disciplines, was not readily adaptable to contemporary problem-solving. The academic structure and curriculum had to undergo serious modification, with increasing stress on science programs and the development of research activities through interdisciplinary institutes and centers. These permitted more effective use of knowledge, personnel, and equipment, and proved to be highly effective in soliciting gifts and grants from foundations, industry, and government.

Interdisciplinary institutes, or the equivalent, took root on the Boulder campus after World War II. The High Altitude Observatory (HAO) was followed two years later by the Upper Air Laboratory, the predecessor of the Laboratory of Atmospheric and Space Physics (LASP), devoted to studies of scientific phenomena in the earth's upper atmosphere and beyond.[98] HAO and LASP, together with the Institute of Arctic and Alpine Research (INSTAAR), served as models for subsequent research.

The problem-solving role assumed by the University led to additional interdisciplinary programs. The Institute of Behavioral Sciences (IBS), formed in 1957, fostered investigations in the social sciences, working through the Behavior Research and Communications Research laboratories, research bureaus devoted to investigations in anthropological, economic, sociological, and political studies, and the Medical School's Preventive Medicine and Public Health Departments.[99] The Joint Institute of Laboratory Astrophysics (JILA), 1962, was a cooperative effort by the University and the National Bureau of Standards to promote research in the related fields of astronomy, aerodynamics, chemistry, physics, and mathematics, initially under the direction of Lewis M. Branscomb, assigned to the Boulder laboratories of NBS.[100] The Nuclear Physics Laboratory, or cyclotron, the only facility of its kind on a campus between St. Louis and the Pacific Coast, produced its initial hydrogen nuclei beam in 1962.[101] The Institute of Computing Science, 1962, provided instruction in the use of computers, including application for academic disciplines.[102] The Graduate School Computing Center, also opened in 1962, operated modern computer equipment for the use of all disciplines and institutes on the campus.[103]

Perhaps the best known research activity in the Boulder community, the National Center for Atmospheric Research (NCAR) was founded in 1960 by the University Corporation for Atmospheric Research. The latter, a nonprofit enterprise composed of several schools, later included the University of Colorado. The national center, with funds from the National Science Foundation and other sources, conducted studies related to all aspects of meteorology. The High Altitude Observatory was absorbed in 1961, serving as one of the center's four operating divisions. The director of NCAR, Walter Orr Roberts, played, along with Quigg Newton and Eugene Wilson, a major role in attracting the research facility to Colorado.[104]

The emergence of interdisciplinary programs committed to solving contemporary problems was one aspect of the University's pursuit of greatness. At the same time, the institution actively recruited distinguished teachers and scholars, encouraged the expansion of sponsored research, and attracted able graduate students with remunerative fellowships. In addition, the administration instituted a merit system to reward members of the faculty for outstanding contributions to advancements of knowledge.[105]

Many distinguished academicians who represented a wide range of disciplines and scholarly interests were attracted to the University of Colorado. Scientists included George Gamow (physics) and Bernhard Haurwitz (astro-geophysics), both Fellows of the National Academy of Sciences, Malcolm Correll (physics and general education), Lewis M. Branscomb (JILA), Edward L. King (chemistry), Meredith N. Runner (biology), and Ozzie G. Simmons (Institute of Behavioral Sciences). Other prominent appointments were William H. Miernyk (economics and Bureau of Business and Economic Research), Wallace Fowlie and Francois Jost (French), Donald F. Willis (Oriental languages), Harry T. Moore (English, a D. H. Lawrence specialist), Harold D. Kelling (English), and Andor Toth, Aksel Schiotz, and Jean Berger of the College of Music. These, and others, contributed to the University's reputation as a place of creativity.[106] This again raised the question whether research unduly detracted from or enriched and contributed to the teaching function—a debate that was not resolved.

The pursuit of excellence also affected the student body. New admission standards and increased emphasis on cultural and intellectual activities altered outlooks and pursuits. The "party school" that for a decade had attracted students from all parts of the country in search of opportunities for mountain recreation gradually changed as a new generation of students became caught in the intellectual ferment of the campus environment.[107] Interests in student traditions began to wane, and memberships in Greek-letter social organizations even declined. To some extent, national and international events displaced social functions and organized athletics as topics of concern. Reactions to the civil rights movement, especially the violence accompanying attempts to extend "sit-ins" and "freedom rides" throughout the South after 1960, signaled a growing sense of social awareness on the Boulder campus.[108]

The pursuit of greatness, although widely hailed on campus and off, was opposed by some members of the faculty, student body, alumni, and the community. The Newton administration was subjected to a barrage of criticism. In a large measure, this was an irrational reaction to rapid and far-reaching alterations taking place in the University's curriculum, organization, and size by people who, for a variety of reasons, hoped to preserve the status quo. Newton, as the symbol of change, was the target of much abuse. He was seen by some as the instigator of the institution's transformation and was accused of attempting to make Colorado's largest institution of higher learning the "Harvard of the West."[109]

In the opening months of the Newton administration, the outward calm of the Boulder campus was threatened by ominous rumblings from some of the faculty and alumni. At issue was the propriety of the new president's assertion that the University should be transformed into a prestige institution. The pursuit of greatness seemed to imply to many people that their Alma Mater was in some way deficient or inferior.[110] Faculty unrest was further aggravated by the appointment of distinguished scholars and ambitious administrators, many of whom attempted to reorganize departments, schools, and colleges without regard for tradition and established academic routines. Displeasure became outright discontent when large salaries were bestowed upon the newcomers for scholarly achievements. Unfortunately, some longtime staff members who had devoted their time and energies to teaching viewed such beneficence as favoritism toward "Democrats, liberals, and left-wingers."[111]

Unrest among the alumni reached crescendo proportions when the football coach was fired in the spring of 1962. Everett (Sonny) Grandelius, who had succeeded Dal Ward in 1959, was discharged three years later after the Buffaloes, under his direction, defeated the University of Oklahoma, captured the Big Eight title, and participated in the New Year's Day Orange Bowl classic. Following a thorough investigation of charges brought by the National Collegiate Athletic Association against the University of Colorado, Grandelius admitted having made—without the knowledge of the University's administration—illegal payments from a "slush fund" to football players. While Newton insisted that the University, in the interest of its integrity and respectability, could not condone cheating, many who actively supported the team believed that it was pointless to lose the services of a winning coach because of a few infractions of conference and NCAA rules.[112]

The 1962 football season was a nightmare for some of the alumni. The NCAA placed the University on probation for two years, excluding the football team from appearances in televised events or postseason bowl games. The Big Eight subsequently ruled ineligible twelve players who had admitted taking payments from the slush fund. Under the circumstances, interim head coach William E. (Bud) Davis, formerly Alumni Director, was fortunate to gain any victories that year. The team won its opening conference engagement with Kansas State and closed on an exhilarating note with a surprise victory over the Air Force Academy. Between those contests were humiliating losses, including stunning defeats at the hands of archrivals Oklahoma and Missouri.[113]

Some alumni were further alienated by the University's apparent determination to implement the Regents' ban of 1956 on discrimination by student organizations. That controversial rule was applied to approximately 270 honorary, professional, and social groups, including 15 sororities and 22 fraternities.[114] All but one fraternity, Phi Delta Theta, certified compliance by the deadline of September 1, 1962. The offender had the discrimination question on the agenda of its annual meeting which was scheduled for the final three days of August.

When the local chapter of Phi Delta Theta reported noncompliance, the University's administration imposed the probation required by the 1956 rule. Less than a week later, however, Dean Arthur Kiendl, following a telephone poll of accessible Regents, lifted the automatic prohibition on rushing, ostensibly because the fraternity had taken steps to remove the offending clause from its constitution.[115] Prior to the end of September, the Board of Regents formally endorsed Kiendl's action by setting aside the ban on participation in rushing, pledging, and initiation of members until September 1, 1964.[116] By that date, the chapter was in full compliance with the school's antibias rule.

The decision not to enforce the antidiscrimination rule may have reflected Newton's determination to avoid a confrontation with the Greek-letter alumni at a time when his administration was already under heavy attack. Members of the Regents ran for office under party labels—and owed their success in some measure to party support—which meant that their actions in governing the state's largest institution of higher education were influenced somewhat by political considerations. Elected the University's president by the majority of the Board who were Democrats over the opposition of two Republicans, Newton by 1961 had become the target of growing partisan criticism.

Opposition to the Newton administration, in time led by Regents and others who aspired to the presidency, coalesced as an expression of conservatism, a reaction against change. The president and his supporters on and off campus were portrayed by critics as proponents of liberalism and reform that was in fact "left-wingism," if not communism. This theme, exploited by the University's detractors for a decade and more, continued throughout the early years of Newton's tenure. Allegations of subversion did not become a partisan issue until the spring of 1961, when a Republican party official told a gathering of the faithful in Denver that there was too much left-wingism—he would not call it communism—at the Boulder school. The faculty, he continued, "expose our children to too much liberalism and there's got to be more balance."[117]

This view was widely circulated. One persistent critic, Esther C. Pickett, a Boulder realtor, had tried for years to rid the University of alleged subversion. Her crusade was intensified as part of a partisan offensive against the Newton administration. "Pickett's charge" was given credence when the campus newspaper published "Leftism at CU." That article, presented by the *Colorado Daily* as proof of its editorial independence, afforded Mrs. Pickett an opportunity to elaborate on her view that the University was a closed society. She opened her attack with the statement that a politically partisan administration sought "to march forward to 'greatness' behind a winning football team and flanked by a double standard of gold and silver." The latter were identified as the contributions of citizens and students to Newton's "extravaganza" in the form of higher taxes and increased tuitions. These monies were used to fashion "one of the nation's leading Meccas for liberal-leftist professors and administrators" and a "thoroughly hostile environment for faculty members and students holding opposite views."[118]

The University, Mrs. Pickett contended, resorted to budget "flimflam and public bamboozlement" to gain its ends. At large expense, it pursued "brainwashing and downright misrepresentation" in selling its goal of greatness to the people of Colorado at a time when the administration was pleading poverty. Inevitably, when the legislature's generosity fell short of the institution's self-proclaimed needs, tuitions were raised to fund pet projects, including the creation of "super-salary" professorships.[119]

Attempts to expose the University's wrongdoing, Mrs. Pickett continued, had been effectively blocked by partisan politics. The majority Democrats on the Board of Regents "did not care to see dirty linen washed in public." They were supported by Democrats who controlled the General Assembly, principally liberals from Denver, and by the state's largest daily newspaper, whose editorials were "uniformly uncritical, even worshipful, of the university."[120]

Similar criticism mounted until the University came under political siege in 1962, an election year for state government office seekers, including hopefuls for two seats on the Board of Regents. The assault intensified on January 26, when State Senator Earl A. Wolvington, a Republican from rural Sterling, suggested from the floor of the senate that the Newton administration contributed to a lowering of faculty morale and widespread immorality among students. He cited, for example, reports of cheating on examinations, shoplifting in the campus bookstore, drunkenness at parties, and "overnight" social functions.[121] The Regents responded by expressing confidence in the administration, faculty, and student body. Newton released a statement in which he emphatically denied the charges, concluding that the senator's rancor, whatever his motives, would not interrupt progress "toward the building of a truly great university for the State of Colorado."[122]

The University, however, remained an issue for the balance of the legislative session. Responding in the senate on February 13, George Brown, a Democrat from Denver, professed embarrassment for his colleague's remarks about the state's principal educational institution and suggested that greater service could have been performed in the public interest had matters of specific concern been referred to Newton and the Regents. Wolvington insisted that Brown lacked the character and background to attack him personally.[123] Furthermore, the senator from Sterling warned that he had previously discharged only pellets while he had enough ammunition "to fire a full load from both barrels."[124] The debate degenerated into a flurry of charges and countercharges, finally ending with a threat from Wolvington that the legislature would conduct a full investigation into the affairs of the University of Colorado.[125]

That spring the University was plunged deeper into the cauldron of state politics. Partisanship enveloped the Boulder campus following alleged discourtesies inflicted upon U.S. Senator Barry M. Goldwater. The chairman of the Senate Campaign Committee and spokesman for the conservative wing of the GOP, under the auspices of campus Young Republicans, on March 2 addressed a capacity audience in Macky Auditorium. This was one of five public appearances that week for the Republican, whose itinerary included convocations at the Air Force Academy and the University of Denver.[126]

In the days immediately following the political rally, spokesmen for various organizations publicly accused an element of the student body of having subjected Senator Goldwater to "abuse and vilification in violation of his constitutional rights and the dignity of his office." This was the position formally adopted by the Leyden-Chiles-Wickersham American Legion Post No. 1, Denver, in condemning the University's administration for failing to punish those guilty of wrongdoing. By taking no corrective action, the Legion's resolution stated, Newton and his staff condoned the behavior of students responsible for a disgraceful demonstration. The veteran's group also called for an investigation of subversive activities on the Boulder campus.[127]

The actions of the Young People's Socialist League were at issue. The group, one of nearly three hundred organizations on the campus, had 28 student members. They were accused of having heckled and otherwise interfered with Goldwater's presentation. Some critics questioned not only the organization's conduct at the political rally, but contended that it was un-American and subversive in that it was committed to the establishment of socialism in the United States.

Responding to the American Legion's resolution, Newton asked the faculty to conduct an investigation of the events of March 2. The University Senate's Committee on Student Affairs studied taped recordings of all proceedings in Macky Auditorium that day, and interviewed officers of campus political clubs and others who attended the political rally. A careful review of all evidence indicated that while the Young People's Socialist League may have been rude in some respects, Senator Goldwater was not subjected to abuse and vilification. "All things considered," the committee concluded in its report of April 18, "from the view of the YR's [it was] probably the most successful meeting ever held on the campus."[128]

After making the committee's report public, Newton called upon the American Legion to withdraw its charge that subversive activities were conducted on the campus of the University. He pledged once again to investigate any evidence of subversion by the faculty. However, in the absence of specific documentation he refused to interfere with the rights of teachers and students "to speak their minds honestly, whether what they say is popular or unpopular." The school, Newton continued, could not act on the basis of rumor, nor could it "in order to appease careless and poorly informed critics" destroy the very values that it was dedicated to perpetuate.[129]

Unsubstantiated allegations were exploited by some critics as an excuse to condemn the University and its president. One unsigned postal card, mailed from Durango on April 10, informed Newton that the American Legion's appraisal was indeed correct. "There are," the writer stated, "more *Pinks, Socialistic, Bolshe-*

vistic People on your campus than there are to be found at the University of Moscow!! (Russia not Idaho)." "Your office," the message continued, "as personified by *you* reeks with a *Pink Odor!!* C U is Pee You."[130]

Emotional outbursts could be ignored, but the alleged mistreatment of a U.S. senator continued to generate the controversy which swirled about the University of Colorado. On September 21, the *Colorado Daily* published an article by senior philosophy student Carl Mitcham, "Riding the Whale," in which the Arizona politician was allegedly libeled. Prodded by Newton, the campus Board of Publications, composed of equal numbers of students and faculty, placed editor Gary Althen on probation with the warning that he must refrain from printing controversial material. Two weeks later the newspaper published a letter from Mitcham, the content of which, according to critics, exceeded all bounds of propriety.[131]

Convinced that corrective action was required, Newton, after the Board of Publications failed to follow up its earlier warning to the editor of the *Colorado Daily*, fired Althen and appointed three administrators to the board, as authorized by recent action of the Regents. In this way, the president could hold the editor accountable for what appeared in the newspaper.[132] Newton also appointed a special committee, under the chairmanship of the dean of the School of Journalism, to investigate all University-sponsored publications and to recommend changes in policies regulating their activities on the campus.[133]

At the urging of ASUC, Newton explained his actions to the student body. Speaking to a capacity crowd in the UMC ballroom on October 23, he contended that irresponsible statements in the *Colorado Daily* had already harmed the University, and that the firing of Althen was to avoid the further risk of the additional damage which might have resulted from permitting Althen to remain as editor. The president insisted that this action did not contradict his earlier public statements that no attempt would be made to curb free expression on the campus. Rather, the school was fulfilling its "obligation to resist all threats to academic freedom, regardless of the direction from which they come." Those who published the newspaper had to be held accountable for their actions. Students cannot demand to be treated like adults, then excuse their conduct by insisting that they are "just a bunch of kids."[134]

Many of Newton's longtime supporters criticized his handling of the controversy. Senator Goldwater, they insisted, had not been injured by name-calling in the *Colorado Daily*. Politicians were frequently subjected to similar attacks in the press, and campus publications were among the chronic offenders.[135]

Although the Regents refused to act, and the faculty and student body supported the newspaper, Newton nevertheless had fired Althen. Some of the president's friends suggested that he had bowed to outside pressures. Rather than pursue a solution within the University, he had given in to demand for action against the *Colorado Daily* by people who viewed its editor as the symbol of all that was presumed wrong with the school. Althen was "proof" that radicalism flourished on the Boulder campus![136] When the University became the target of public wrath, Newton, in his attempt to prevent further irresponsible actions by students, muted the expression of unpopular views and, according to some, endangered academic freedom. That action split the liberals at the very time that conservatives intensified attacks on the University's leadership.

The controversy became a central issue in the state political campaign when Senator Goldwater rejected Newton's apology for Mitcham's attack upon his character and philosophy. On September 27, the president wrote the Arizonan that the words of the article published in the *Colorado Daily* were "obviously irresponsible and defamatory, and the University disavows them unqualifiedly."[137] Six days later, Goldwater responded that, after having made appearances at some 250 colleges and schools, only in Boulder had his presentation been interrupted by socialists, "or whatever you choose to call them." For this reason, it appeared that Newton either did not know what was going on or did not care. "To put it briefly," the letter concluded, "I doubt if you have the interest or concern to be in the position you hold."[138]

Angered by what appeared to be an attempt to influence the political campaign in Colorado, in a second letter Newton asserted that the senator's response was itself evidence that the behavior of a handful of students was not the issue. More pertinent was Goldwater's encouragement of an all-out assault on the

University by suppressive forces within the state. The Arizonan and those who supported him, the letter continued, believed that the function of higher learning was "to indoctrinate rather than educate; to control thought, rather than to stimulate it."[139]

In the statewide political campaign of that year, Republican office seekers generally condemned—and Democrats reluctantly defended—the University's administration. In the Regent's race, incumbents Charles D. (Jim) Bromley, a Denver lawyer and Republican, and Fred Betz, Jr., a Lamar journalist and Democrat, were joined by Dr. Dale Atkins, a Denver physician who hoped to increase the representation of the GOP on the Board. Bromley's vigorous canvass of the electorate played upon Newton as a central theme. It was his removal from the presidency that the candidate hoped to accomplish by winning reelection to a fourth term on the University's governing board.[140]

Although subjected to extreme provocation, Newton refused to engage in campaign controversy with his critic. In an appearance before officers of alumni clubs, the president reported numerous inquiries about his remaining silent during the growing attack on his leadership. The operation of the University, he observed, had always been nonpartisan, and that tradition had to be preserved. Since the chief executive officer was selected by and accountable to an elected body, he was precluded "from participating in the political campaign incident to the election of the Regents." Regardless of the outcome of the contest, the University would continue to function as it had in the past. Policies were made not by the president, or by one or two Regents, but by a majority of the Board.[141]

Republicans were swept into power on November 6. They captured the governor's office and the state legislature; Representative Peter Dominick defeated incumbent John Carroll in the race for a seat in the United States Senate. Bromley and Atkins scored easy victories, opening the way for a showdown on the question of the University's leadership. Less than one month following the election and four weeks before the new term for Regents, Newton announced that he was leaving office at the close of the academic year to accept the position of chief administrator of The Commonwealth Fund of New York.[142] That philanthropic foundation supported research and teaching in the fields of medicine, community health, and international education.

Ten days after the announcement of his resignation, Newton used a previously scheduled appearance before the Denver-area alumni to present his perspective on changes that had occurred in recent years. The University was, he said, the largest in the Rocky Mountain region, with by far the most comprehensive programs for graduate education and research. Organized along lines typical of state universities, the core was the College of Arts and Sciences, augmented by ten professional schools: architecture, business, education, engineering, journalism, law, medicine, music, nursing, and pharmacy. In addition, graduate instruction and research were conducted on both campuses in as many as 37 different fields. Statewide activities were carried on by the Extension Division, which maintained centers in Denver and Colorado Springs.[143]

The University also had changed internally. The teaching of undergraduates, once the school's primary concern, had given way to graduate education and research. In six years, for example, undergraduate enrollments increased 14 percent, while the number of graduate students more than doubled. This change came about not because of any deliberate decision by University officials, but rather as a response to the growing complexity of society and demands for advanced training in numerous occupations and professions.[144]

Influences mainly outside the University prompted its expansion and development to better serve the state, region, and nation. The University's vast resources were extended to many communities, and its capacity for problem-solving enhanced the well-being of the residents of the state. The school also played a larger role. It served as a major center for advanced study in the Rocky Mountain region, and was steadily evolving into one of the leading institutions of higher learning in the United States. As an emerging national center for education, the University strived to provide programs balanced between undergraduate and graduate studies, and between professional training and research.[145]

The pursuit of excellence had yielded a prestige institution dedicated to high standards of teaching and scholarship. The University acquired an outstanding faculty, a mature student body, enlarged library resources, and modern facilities for instruction and research. Despite the problems inherent in the recent period of rapid growth, the University, in Newton's opinion, was on its way to becoming one of America's most respected universities. That objective was attainable, however, only if the Regents, the general assembly, and the people wanted and supported the development of a superior institution of higher learning for Colorado.[146]

From the historian's perspective it is clear that the University, as an institution within which people engaged in intellectual pursuits, changed significantly during the years from 1953 to 1963. The evolutionary processes were by no means restricted to that period. However, it was a time when the University was transformed from a secluded cloister—an "ivory tower" existing apart from the mainstream of life in Colorado—into an arena for conflicting interests, subject to a sense of urgency for solving contemporary problems. Higher learning was now seen as a cure for socioeconomic ailments. The University accepted throngs of students, expanded existing programs, and created new ones as a means of serving a broader segment of society through teaching and research. Rapid growth provided opportunities for experimentation, but also raised another host of problems. The faculty tended to be less a community of scholars and more a corps of specialists. The student body became increasingly heterogeneous. More and more the University's function seemed to be one of job training and job placement. Inevitably, pressures exerted from within the institution as well as from the community, pushing and pulling in different directions, made the University conflict-prone.

Growth and aspirations of greatness provoked responses that thrust the institution into state politics. Widespread acceptance of charges leveled at the University and its leadership was reflected in the 1962 election returns. Popular support for higher education, at least for the University, had given way to disillusionment if not distrust. For the first time in more than a decade, the continued expansion of the state's largest institution of higher education was in doubt.

Six

DEVELOPING
A MULTI-CAMPUS
UNIVERSITY:
1960's to 1970's

I N SPITE OF the difficulties of the early sixties, in the decade after 1963 the University of Colorado experienced further substantial growth and change. The magnitude of the change is attested by those who knew the University as students early in the period and then returned for visits as well as by faculty and administrators who served continuously over these years. The kinds of change were diverse and, frequently, disturbing. The University more than doubled its student body and its faculty, developed new campuses in downtown Denver and in Colorado Springs, added considerably to the physical plant on the Boulder and medical campuses, and organized a multi-campus system of administration. Simultaneously the University experienced significant alterations in the Arts and Sciences curriculum, national recognition for several of its graduate programs, professional schools, and institutes, drastic shifts in the life-style of undergraduates, and some impressive athletic triumphs. There is no doubt that growth has brought evolution and achievement to the University, but it is also clear that the institution has some new problems. Faculty, students, and alumni raised many questions in 1975, among them: Has the University of Colorado become too large? Has the institution lost a sense of unity and purpose?

The University's development was linked to the continued rising demand for higher education in the United States in the 1960s. This demand had several components: because of the general population growth in the 1940s there was a much larger college-age group, eighteen to twenty-five years old; higher expectations for career advancement and an end to discrimination brought to college many who would not have been students in earlier generations; business and the government were increasingly dependent on trained professionals needing specialized education. Thus, the country embarked on a unique experiment—mass universal higher education. For a few years the federal government made every effort to support such an experiment with loans and scholarships; a period of economic growth provided further stimulus for funding.[1]

Between 1960 and 1970 the number of students enrolled nationally for degree credit more than doubled, from 3.2 million to 7.1 million.[2] In 1960, the student count on the Boulder campus of the University of Colorado was 11,054 and on the medical campus 687. Ten years later the figures were 20,658 for Boulder and 1,331 for the medical campus. In addition, in 1970 the student body on the downtown Denver campus was 6,987 and on the Colorado Springs campus 2,312.[3] Since 1970, however, enrollment growth has slowed, nationally and locally. The country's population growth has also slowed and the size of the college-age generation may, in fact, be in decline.[4]

Meanwhile the state of Colorado has changed. In 1975, the population at 2.4 million is almost 30 percent larger than in 1960. This is more rapid growth than in the country as a whole. Over 80 percent of these people are classified in the census as urban and virtually all of these reside along the eastern front range of the Rocky Mountains between Greeley and Fort Collins in the north and Pueblo in the south. The economy has evolved, grown stronger, but the state is not one of the dozen or so wealthiest in the nation. Mining and agriculture are no longer as important as they once were, though oil and gas production might have a significant future if the shale country west of the continental divide is developed. Government and companies in sales and services are the leading employers. Denver has regional offices of most of the important federal agencies. The Air Force and the Army dominate the Colorado Springs area and the Atomic Energy Commission has a large plant near Boulder. Manufacturing is now the leading income producer. The largest manufacturing employers in the state still include Martin Marietta (aerospace) and Colorado Fuel and Iron (steel) but are now joined by IBM (since 1965) and Kodak (since 1970). However, tourism has emerged as a major income source. In 1969, more than 5 million people visited the state's museums and scenic and historic sites. The next year 350,000 skiers came to Vail.[5] What does all this activity add up to in terms of the state's buying power? In 1970, personal income approximated $4,000 per capita while the state tax burden was $419 per capita; both figures are eighteenth nationally. Expenditures for education were at $283 per capita.[6] Higher education expenditures alone were $50.38 per capita and as high as fourth nationally.[7]

There are 19 public institutions of higher education in Colorado. The state obviously has a problem in defining institutional roles in order to distribute educational opportunity across the population centers. Before 1965, the Association of State Institutions of Higher Education and the general assembly's Legislative Committee for Education Beyond the High School tried to establish some principles for master planning. This cooperation was voluntary, not supervised by any state agency.[8] Beginning in 1963 Republican Governor John Love, concerned about the random growth and proliferation of colleges, worked for the creation of a policy body to advise the state government on meeting the student demand and the expenditures for higher education. In 1965, after much debate over recommendations from many sources, the general assembly voted to establish a Commission on Higher Education to develop long-range plans, review budget requests, and recommend priorities for funding. Since 1965, the commission, chaired for some time by Denver attorney Donald McKinlay with a staff under the direction of Frank Abbott, has furnished important leadership for the evolution of higher education in Colorado. The commission has supervised the growth of established institutions such as the University of Colorado, Colorado State University, Colorado School of Mines, and Colorado State College (now University of Northern Colorado, at Greeley), as well as the development of other state colleges and community colleges.[9]

The rise of the Commission on Higher Education parallels the erosion of the constitutional autonomy of the University of Colorado. In states where such autonomy exists it is commonly understood that the state constitution provides for the vesting of exclusive management and control of the institution in the governing board. This autonomy, however, has never been without limitations imposed by the legislative, executive, and judicial branches of state government, most importantly by the legislative power to appropriate. Concern in recent years in Colorado for efficiency in expenditures for higher education, one of the largest items in the state budget, coupled with questions raised in the press about educational goals and student activities on various campuses, have caused both the governor and the legislature to restrict, and even to stipulate, institutional expenditures. To this end, a state Department of Higher Education was organized in 1968, the director appointed by the Commission on Higher Education.

During 1969 the legislature took a hard look at the governance of higher education. Proposals for change included the creation of single boards for various combinations of universities and colleges. But the Committee on Organization of State Government determined, and the general assembly agreed in 1970, to retain the existing boards and to expand the functions and authority of the Commission on Higher Education. In 1971, a bill amending the constitution to amalgamate all boards into a single statewide board failed to get even a hearing.[10] The commission appeared to have the necessary backing to, in its own words,

> . . . help the Governor and the Legislature see the big issues in higher education and [thus] make well-considered decisions, whether in the establishment of new institutions, in the closing out of old programs, the funding of new buildings, or the establishment of support levels for regular operations.[11]

By 1975 the University of Colorado, however, lost some of its ability to exercise final judgment on the use not only of state funds but also those derived from other sources as well. The following areas were affected: tuition charges, expenditures in certain categories—for example, student aid, books for the library, nonacademic staff employment, and the purchasing of equipment and supplies. In 1970, the legislature began to appropriate on a line-item basis, directing the University's expenditures more precisely. Since 1971, if the University generates tuition above the budget, the state reduces its payments accordingly. The whole issue surfaced in 1972 when the voters were asked to approve an omnibus constitutional amendment which provided for an expanded Board of Regents, removing the president as a voting member of the Board, branch campuses and, when necessary, statutory regulation.

The possibility of statutory regulation suggested the eventual end of the University's constitutional autonomy. This may not be the case. In effect, the language of the amendment presented to the voters represented a compromise between legislative demand for the legality of its regulatory attempts in previous years and University requests for basic organizational changes. Apparently all participants in the negotiations agreed in principle and the voters, with the support of metropolitan Denver, narrowly passed the amendment.[12] Whether or not more intervention into the affairs of the University can be expected is difficult to forecast. The state does not now set salaries for faculty nor does it determine the qualifications for appointment and tenure. The opportunity is present but much will depend on future relations, say, between the University and the public, or the president and the Joint Budget Committee of the general assembly. The intervention trend is not peculiar to Colorado; the trend is part of a national picture and is much more evident in, for example, Michigan or California. However, it is comforting that when trust between the state university and state government is maintained, the educational functions of the university are unimpaired.[13]

Events during the Smiley administration, from July 1963 to June 1969, precipitated this erosion of the University's autonomy. Joseph R. Smiley, the ninth president, had a distinguished record of scholarship and academic administration. Born in Texas, he earned a Ph.D. in French literature at Columbia, was chairman of the French Department and dean of the College of Liberal Arts and Sciences at the University of Illinois, and came to Colorado from the presidency of the University of Texas at Austin, part of a multi-campus organization. Smiley brought not only experience that qualified him for the leadership of the University at this particular moment, he also possessed a warm, graceful style that helped calm the atmosphere after the turbulent final year of the Newton administration. And he could inspire students. In his first reported public talk he said, "One of the greatest challenges facing all education in this country today is to keep ever before our students the enormous responsibilities as well as the opportunities that are theirs because they are American and free."[14]

With enrollments climbing at the University and the state's concern for planning in higher education emerging, Smiley's presidency also followed a change in political control of the state. In the November 1962 elections, the Republicans gained control of both the legislature and the executive branch. Campaigning on a platform that the Democrats had overtaxed and overspent, the Republicans seemed to evoke a popular concern. They also had in John Love, a Colorado Springs attorney and a newcomer to politics, a most attractive leader. Except for the state House of Representatives in 1965 and 1966, the Republicans dominated the general assembly until 1975 as well as the governor's office. The Republicans' philosophy on taxation and public expenditures in the mid-sixties was more conservative than the Democrats' in the late fifties. Responsive to the increasing demands for public services, the Republicans in the decade 1963 to 1973 did push the state's expenditures from $424 million to $1.3 billion.[15] In part, the reapportionment of legislative districts, taking representation away from rural areas and adding it to urban ones under the principle of one man, one vote, coupled with the population increase, was responsible for this increase in spending. And inflation, at 5 percent a year, was a factor. Thus the Smiley administration not only had to deal with a state government that was less inclined to raise taxes and improve public services, but it was also in competition with more demands on the state tax dollar. The political composition of the Board of Regents changed too, but more slowly. Though Republican alumni Charles Bromley, a Denver attorney, and Dale Atkins, a Denver physician, were elected in 1962, the Democrats dominated the Board until 1964. In that year the resignation of a Democrat and the governor's appointment of a Republican brought a balance. The elections of 1964, however, returned two Democrats, Lamar publisher Fred Betz, Sr., and attorney Daniel Lynch. But in 1966 two Republicans were elected: Joseph Coors, an industrialist from Golden, and Harry Carlson, a former long-time Director of Athletics and Dean of Men at the University. Again in 1968 the Republicans won seats with alumnus Robert Gilbert, a Greeley banker, and Dr. Atkins. So after 1966 and for the remainder of Smiley's presidency the Republicans had a majority on the governing board of the University.[16]

Because of resignations in the last month of the Newton administration and the first months of his own, Smiley's main responsibility during 1963–64 was to organize a new administrative team. He was ably assisted during the transition by Eugene Wilson, vice president and former Dean of Faculties, and Ernest Wahlstrom, professor of geology, who both served in turn as Acting Dean of Faculties, and John Bartram, continuing as Director of the Budget. Smiley first appointed Glenn Barnett, Dean for Students at the University of Texas, as Vice President for Student Affairs. After reports from faculty-search committees and discussions with faculty, he secured from the Regents the appointments of John Conger, a psychologist on the medical faculty, as Vice President for Medical Affairs and Dean of Medicine, and Thurston Manning, a physicist and Provost at Oberlin, as Vice President for Academic Affairs and Dean of Faculties. A fourth vice presidency, for business affairs, went to Eugene Wilson. Further appointments included: William Baughn, from the University of Missouri, as Dean of Business; William Briggs, of the mathematics faculty, as Dean of Arts and Sciences; Harold Heim, of the Pharmacy faculty, as Dean of Pharmacy; John Reid, from the University of Michigan, as Dean of Law; and

James Brinton, from Stanford, as Dean of Journalism. Smiley also arranged for the appointment of Raphael Moses, a Boulder attorney, as the first employed legal counsel for the University. Final additions to the administration, in 1965, were the selection of James Archer, from the University of Wisconsin, as Dean of the Graduate School; and Katherine Smith, from the University of California, Los Angeles, as Dean of Nursing.[17]

As soon as Smiley arrived in Boulder he was confronted with a major policy debate. The University's role in higher education for Denver had been studied and discussed for three years. Unique among cities of its size, Denver had little in the way of public higher education. There were no community colleges and no state college; only the University's Extension Center. The presence of Denver University and the proximity of the University of Colorado largely explained this. Also, before reapportionment, rural interests were opposed to colleges in the Denver area. In this situation, the University had two substantive options: It could expand its operations in Denver into a branch campus or it could withdraw and allow the state to organize a new institution, perhaps another university. The second option seemed undesirable because of the prospect of competition for funds. But the first option had two considerable problems. As the state constitution prevented the University from establishing branches, an amendment, as in the case of the medical campus, would be necessary. However, the city's immediate need was for two-year community colleges which the University could not really provide.

The University had an opportunity after 1956, when it purchased property and buildings for its Extension Center, to develop a branch campus, but the Newton administration was more concerned about strengthening the quality of the Boulder campus and the Medical Center. In 1961 the general assembly actually asked the University to consider granting degrees for work done at its Denver center, and the administration responded with a lengthy report, prepared by Professor John Little (education), recommending associate and bachelor's degree programs.[18] The offer, essentially to undertake community-college academic instruction, did not fit the University's image and technical and vocational education was not covered in the University's response. So the initiative for promoting public higher education in Denver remained with the state.

The Legislative Committee on Education Beyond the High School had been pressing for state-supported community colleges, but a likely source of taxes was a problem.[19] A special task group forcefully recommended late in 1962 that a four-year state college with academic and technical programs replace the University's Extension Center. It, too, had no plans for vocational education.[20] Yet, in March 1963, the general assembly, concerned about projected student demand and uncertain of the University's capacity to meet it, enacted a statute authorizing a Metropolitan State College for Denver. The language of the statute allowed for planning only a lower division curriculum and specified coordination of course offerings with the University's Extension Center.[21]

During the 1963–64 academic year the University tried again to promote a solution for the capital city. President Smiley believed ". . . that the University's fate is crucially related to the decisions on meeting the needs for higher education in Denver."[22] By November, his administration had drawn another proposal which incorporated the earlier plan to convert the Extension Center into a degree-granting University Center with expanded graduate programs, except this one also included an offer to organize and manage a technical institute with two- or three-year programs. In addition, Denver's need for community colleges was stressed.[23] The Regents unanimously adopted the proposal and its policy implications. Regents Charles Bromley and Richard Bernick were particularly supportive, as was the president of the Associated Alumni. The Board went on to request from the legislature funds for an expanded University Center and placement on the 1964 election ballot of a constitutional amendment which authorized the University to establish degree-granting centers or branches. This was followed in March by the Regents' transferring the administration of the programs at the Denver center from the Extension Division to the various colleges and schools.[24] As the University, since 1962, allowed off-campus college-level instruction to earn credit toward degrees, the move from extension center to university center was logical.

The state, however, would not accept the University's direction. The general assembly ignored the request for funding for a university center and did not agree to present the constitutional amendment to the voters. Governor Love also refused to take action on the report of the Trustees of State Colleges for opening Metropolitan State College.[25] Instead, he was more sympathetic to recommendations of an out-of-state consultant on higher education. These recommendations, sharply critical of branch campuses, advocated community colleges and another university for Denver, as well as a higher education coordinating board for Colorado. In fact, the thrust of this advice was the need for a plan covering the entire state.[26] The governor, postponing a decision on Denver, in the spring of 1964 charged the Association of State Institutions of Higher Education with developing a master plan. This group published its report in December. In addition to advocating a coordinating council for higher education and a state-supported system of community colleges, over the University's objection it also called for a new four-year college in Denver.[27]

In March 1965, the general assembly at last made some important decisions for the future of higher education in Colorado and Denver. It authorized the organization of the Commission on Higher Education and it appropriated funds to open Metropolitan State College in the fall. As prospects for financing the community colleges in Denver were still not clear, Metropolitan State was to open with two-year programs. It could become either a community college or a four-year institution. This uncertainty, coupled with the University's independent action in converting its extension to a university center, furthered in the spring of 1965 by making admissions standards in Denver equivalent to Boulder, helped to preserve for the University an educational role in Denver.[28]

Meanwhile the Commission on Higher Education went to work. Late in 1966, after a year of study, it concluded that Colorado should have an articulated system of state-supported two-year community and technical colleges, general colleges, and universities. For Denver, the commission was prepared to recommend a community college, a four-year college, and a university center of the University of Colorado. Both the University and the commission came to an understanding, by restricting freshman admissions, that the University would emphasize upper-division and graduate study.[29] To settle the debate over the legality of the Denver center, the commission pressed the University to petition for an opinion from the attorney general. A carefully reasoned and documented presentation by the University's counsel, John Holloway, persuaded the attorney general that, because the University's programs in Denver were extensions of those in Boulder, the Denver center was not a branch campus in violation of the constitution.[30] With this matter settled, the general assembly went on in 1967 to authorize a three-campus community college for Denver and upper-division programs for Metropolitan State College. It also approved faculty and facility fund increments for the University's Denver center.[31]

On the surface the Smiley years were successful ones for financing the University. Total expenditures for 1963–64 were $46.8 million. Six years later the figure was $94.6 million, an increase of more than 100 percent. The net investment in land, buildings, and equipment, almost doubling, advanced from $72 million to $142 million. The main sources of income for operations developed as follows: state appropriations, from $16.8 to $28.5 million; tuition, from $6.7 to $13.7 million; sponsored research, from $7.1 to $17.7 million; and the hospitals, from $3.1 to $9.3 million. By 1969, student aid totaled $5.2 million and income from other activities and auxiliary enterprises, for example, conferences, housing, or athletics, exceeded $17 million. The expenditures for capital improvements were equally impressive. The state contributed $31.5 million and the federal government more than $9 million. Also noteworthy were the gifts in 1964 from the Williams Foundation of 60 acres of land in Boulder, 80 acres of land with buildings by the Cragmor Foundation in Colorado Springs, and the Fiske bequest of $1.5 million in 1968 which financed the planetarium.[32]

Yet, for the University's operating budget, the Smiley administration needed more money than appropriated by the general assembly. The requests for state support mounted from $21 million in 1964 to $36 million in 1969. For 1967–68 the University asked for $9 million more than was appropriated the year before. But each annual request was pared by at least $2 million and in two years, 1967–68 and 1968–69, by $5 and $7 million. Thus in 1969 the University only obtained what it regarded as necessary in 1967.[33]

Even his first budget was a disappointment for President Smiley. The appropriation for the Boulder campus was almost $300,000 less than the year before.[34] The second budget was no better. In presenting it to the Regents for approval in May 1965 Budget Director John Bartram stated ". . . that deficient appropriations will require curtailment in virtually all areas of University operations." Vice President Conger observed that there were insufficient funds for the operation of the Colorado General Hospital. It was necessary to go after a supplemental budget for the hospital.[35] For Smiley's third budget, Regent Lynch felt the University was not asking enough and he refused to approve it. When commenting on the appropriation for 1966–67 he concluded ". . . the University's path is definitely downward."[36]

For the 1967–68 budget, the University hoped to correct for the underfunding of previous years. Every effort was made to justify new faculty positions, higher salaries for faculty and staff, more books and periodicals for the libraries, additional support for research and public service. This budget was to be the first reviewed by the Commission on Higher Education. Calling it a "year of decision," Smiley wondered ". . . whether financial support from the state will enable it to move forward on many fronts. . . . The fact is that the University of Colorado is a good university; it is making gradual progress, but it is not yet ranked among the leading state institutions."[37] But negotiations with the commission, the Executive Budget Office, and the Joint Budget Committee proved to be relatively unsuccessful. More than $5 million was slashed from the request. The president concluded that the new budget for the Medical Center ". . . will permit continuation of present levels of service . . ." while those for Boulder and the centers ". . . meet only the most essential increase in the costs of current operations."[38]

Hopes were now pinned on the 1968–69 budget. In effect, Vice Presidents Manning and Conger resubmitted their requests for the previous year. Interestingly, during discussions within the Board, Regent Coors felt the University was asking for too much. He argued that ". . . the University budget request was unrealistic because [he] doubted the state could come up with the added tax dollars."[39] Sobered by the experience of two years, the last Smiley budget request was ". . . realistically modest." But, when analyzing the appropriation in May 1969, Vice President Manning concluded, ". . . the budget does not allow the University to keep even; and, in fact, the University will have to sink back in a great many places."[40]

The commission and the Joint Budget Committee did not believe the University was underbudgeted in this period. State expenditures for higher education almost doubled, going from $34.4 to $71.3 million. Analysis of the appropriations to all institutions of higher education does not reveal any discrimination toward the University. Budgets are based essentially on student enrollments with some provision for an institution's particular role. Enrollment advanced dramatically everywhere in the state. The University was not in a position to add any more students than it did. The state, although revenue after 1965 increased more rapidly than expected, also was not in a position to fund fully all the expenses of a multi-purpose university. Among legislators the expectation was that federal grants really made distinction among universities possible.[41] Again, this trend was not peculiar to Colorado. State support of higher education in the 1960s, when adjusted for enrollment and inflation, increased and shifted to newer forms of public institutions, community colleges specifically, which enroll the greatest number of students.[42]

Nevertheless, the impact of underbudgeting for the University's operating expenses was significant, especially in three areas: tuition, faculty-student ratios, and faculty salaries. For in-state students, the tuition on all campuses jumped 100 percent during this period. For out-of-state students, the principle of paying more than residents gave way to one of paying all of the costs, except at the Medical School.[43] The number of full-time faculty with the University advanced from 799 to 1,383, an increase of over 70 percent. As the student body grew by 30 percent, the consequence for the overall student-faculty ratio was to maintain it at approximately 20:1. Because of different teaching patterns across academic units, this ratio can only be a rough index for an institution. But the strongest universities seek a student faculty ratio of 15:1.[44] Faculty salaries slipped somewhat from medians in its comparison sample even though the University's average salary for faculty on the Boulder campus went from $10,000 to $13,000.[45]

In contrast, the University had reason to be more than satisfied with the state's funding of the construction, remodeling, and acquisition of new buildings. For the Medical Center, the basic planning decisions were made between 1955 and 1959; for Boulder, from 1959 to 1963.[46] So the mid-1960s were the implementation phase rather than the creative. The new buildings dramatically changed the appearance of the Medical Center and the scale of the Boulder Campus.

For the Medical Center, the most important physical changes, on or adjacent to the original property acquired in 1922, were the addition to Denison Library (1962), construction of a Children's Psychiatric Day Care Center (1962), remodeling of the Colorado Psychiatric Hospital (1962), the addition of a fourth floor to the Webb-Waring Institute for Medical Research (1964), construction of a new Colorado General Hospital with the Clinical Research Wing linking the hospital and the Medical School (1965), the remodeling of the School of Nursing (1966), and the construction of the J. F. Kennedy Child Development Center (1968).[47] In addition, the remodeling of the old hospital for use by the Medical School was started. Clearly, the completion of a new 450-bed hospital and research wing was a major achievement. Its total cost was more than $20 million, of which $17 million came from the state and $1,500,000 each from the federal government and private gifts.[48] The addition of the new hospital, a model of contemporary concrete and glass architecture, keynoted an ultramodern Medical Center while it overshadowed the former Georgian style of buildings.

At Boulder, the construction of new buildings on land beyond the original quadrangle shifted the focus of the campus from Old Main to the new administration building, Regent Hall, completed in 1965. The important new academic buildings were additions to Norlin Library (1964), the Physical Sciences Research Building Number 2 (1964), the Laboratory for Atmospheric and Space Physics (1965), the Life Sciences Research Building Number 1 (1965), the Engineering Center (1966), the Institute of Behavioral Genetics (1967), the Joint Institute for

Laboratory Astrophysics Tower (1967), and the Physical Sciences Research Building Number 3 (1969). Especially impressive and creative was the Engineering Center, combining laboratories, lecture halls, and office towers with colonnades and internal courts with plantings and fountains. Its total cost was $8.5 million, with $6 million coming from the state and $2.5 million from the federal government.[49] Buildings purchased for the University included the Behavioral Science buildings (1963, 1964) and the former Mt. Saint Gertrude's Academy building for Continuing Education (1969). Construction of attractive student residences also added to this long list: the Kittredge Village dormitories (1964), the East Campus Court apartments (1964), the Marine Court apartments (1964), and the Williams Village dormitories (1967). The Stearns and Darley Towers of the latter departed from standard dormitory construction, and changed the skyline of Boulder. Finally, an important addition for the University Memorial Center, the student union, was completed in 1965, and it helped to form a pleasant quadrangle with a fountain between Hellems and the Chemistry Building.[50]

The new buildings on the Boulder campus were much in keeping with the rural Italian style established by architect Charles Klauder in the 1920s. Even if some of the finer details were missing, the red tile roofs and light brown sandstone walls were maintained. Most important was the preservation of an overall continuity and harmony between old and new. Considering the eclecticism in architecture that has emerged on other university campuses since 1960, this is a rather special achievement. Much of the credit must go to the effective teamwork among University officials, faculty, and administration, and architects Hideo Sasaki and Pietro Belluschi. This cooperation not only brought the Boulder campus into the space age but also gave the University permanent visual distinction quite like that achieved at the University of Virginia or at Stanford.[51]

The Higher Education Facilities Act of 1963, channeling federal construction funds to colleges and universities, was a most important stimulus to the development of the University. But equally significant were the extraordinary federal grants for program improvements that came during the Smiley years. The policy decision of the National Science Foundation to promote new academic "centers of excellence" in science and engineering provided the opportunity. In 1959, science advisors to President Eisenhower recommended doubling, by 1970, the 15 to 20 existing first-rate centers of science. The benefits that would accrue for national defense and the economy were stressed. The final inspiration and, to some extent, the model for the NSF thrust was the contemporary Ford Foundation effort to encourage "peaks of excellence" in higher education throughout the country.[52] As Donald Hornig, science advisor to President Johnson, said in April 1964, "What we want is more good science, more widely distributed."[53] Later in the year, after prodding by the White House, Congress agreed to fund a science development program.

Previously the University had been one of a sample of institutions studied by NSF to assist in drawing up the guidelines for judging ". . . which have the greatest possibility of moving upward to a higher level of scientific quality and to have sound plans for maintaining this quality."[54] When NSF opened the competition, the University responded quickly. In April 1964, President Smiley charged a committee, chaired by Dean Max Peters of the College of Engineering, to design a proposal. After study of a number of recommendations from various science departments to expand their activities, a subcommittee of Professors Cristol (chemistry), MacIntyre (computer science), Prescott (biology), and Simmons (behavioral sciences) prepared a preliminary draft. This subcommittee agreed on a strategy for the proposal, ". . . which builds on present strengths but also gives substantial support to key areas that are vital to the University's overall scientific progress."[55] After thorough consultation within the University and with various state officials, including Governor Love, to secure approval and continuing support, the final proposal, prepared by Vice President Manning, was submitted early in 1965. In June, the NSF awarded a grant of $3.7 million, the largest the University ever received. Other recipients were Rice and Washington (St. Louis) Universities and the Universities of Arizona, Florida, Rochester, and Virginia.[56]

The expenditure of the grant was intended to last three years, but more time proved necessary to make faculty appointments and to complete the new physics building. More than two-thirds of the money went toward the addition of over 50 new faculty and the cost of their research support. The new faculty were added to physics, including astrophysics and astrogeophysics; chemistry; mathematics; psychology and the Institute of Behavioral Sciences; and three engineering departments, electrical, mechanical, and aerospace. More than $1 million of the grant was applied to the construction of the Duane Physics Building. The state matched this sum for the building and was expected to continue to support the new faculty appointed at a cost of more than $1 million a year.[57]

After obtaining the NSF grant for the physical and engineering sciences, the Smiley administration went to work to strengthen the life sciences. During the internal deliberations over the NSF proposal, the decision was to exclude biology from the application. The field was rapidly changing, especially with the rising prominence of cell biology, and it required special study. In the fall of 1965, Vice President Manning charged a committee of biological scientists under the chairmanship of Professor Kozloff of the Medical School to examine the possibilities for the life sciences at the University. After an extensive study, the Kozloff committee reported in June 1966 and forcefully recommended tripling the number of biologists, the organization of a new Department of Molecular and Cellular Biology, and additional development of the graduate program in the basic medical sciences.[58] With this direction, the administration applied for a Health Sciences Advancement Award from the National Institutes of Health and Dean Archer of the Graduate School drafted a preliminary proposal incorporating the Kozloff committee recommendations.[59] In December, the University passed the first review; it was one of 15 out of 127 invited to submit a full proposal. By the spring of 1967, the final proposal had gone out[60] and the Regents and the Commission on Higher Education approved a new Department of Molecular Biology.[61] In June, the University learned that it was one of 5 institutions, including Oregon, Purdue, Washington University (St. Louis), and Vanderbilt, to receive an NIH grant to accelerate teaching and research in the health sciences.

In 1966, the administration also approved the organization of two institutes, Developmental Biology and Behavioral Genetics, to involve the University with the new biology.[62] The NIH grant, totaling $2.7 million over a five-year period, put substantial federal support behind these efforts. The grant provided 10 new faculty members for the basic medical science departments and 11 for Molecular Biology in Boulder. More than $1 million was for equipment, including electron microscopes. A portion of the grant was especially marked for a closed-circuit television link between the Medical Center and Boulder to facilitate long-distance teaching and information exchange.[63]

The University's growing reputation undoubtedly helped win these federal grants—national rankings of academic departments seemed to confirm this. Two studies sponsored by the American Council on Education provided an external review of graduate programs in the humanities, the social sciences, the biological sciences, the physical sciences, and engineering. The first study, conducted in 1964 and published in 1966, surveyed 4,000 scholars from 29 academic disciplines in 106 institutions. This analysis of informed opinion focused on the quality of faculty and the effectiveness of graduate programs. For the quality of faculty, five ratings were used: distinguished, strong, good, adequate-plus, and marginal. The University placed four departments in the good category: psychology, astronomy, chemistry, and physics; and twelve departments in the adequate-plus: French, German, Spanish, history, bacteriology, biochemistry, physiology, zoology, geology, mathematics, civil engineering, and electrical engineering. In previous ratings, conducted in 1924, 1934, and 1937, the University did not appear.[64]

The second study, conducted in 1969 and published in 1970, polled 6,000 scholars from 36 disciplines in 130 institutions. This time the University placed four departments in the strong category: psychology, developmental biology, chemistry, and physics; eight departments in the good: anthropology, microbiology, molecular biology, pharmacology, astronomy, mathematics, civil engineering, and electrical engineering; and 15 other disciplines appeared as adequate-plus. Nationally, psychology was ranked fourteenth and developmental biology nineteenth. Between 1964 and 1969 the University not only had its best departments recognized, but also watched them advance in the evaluation order.[65]

Perhaps the most significant recognition the University gained in this period was its election to membership in the Association of American Universities in the spring of 1967. This group consists of those institutions in the United States generally considered to be preeminent in graduate study and research. The AAU was organized in 1900 by fourteen leading American universities. The University became the forty-third member and the only one in the Rocky Mountain region. After learning of the election President Smiley observed, "This honor represents the culmination of years of steady building by many individuals. . . ."[66] The University first sought membership in 1924.

Further evidence of the University's growing prestige was the appointment by the University in the 1960s of a number of outstanding faculty with established reputations in their fields. These scholars came from many universities including Columbia, Yale, Harvard, Chicago, Michigan, Illinois, and California. Any list of individuals would include Adolph Busemann (aerospace engineering), Edward Condon (physics), Lloyd Kozloff (microbiology), Robert Ayre (civil engineering), Stanislaw Ulam (mathematics), John Cobb (medicine), Petr Beckmann (electrical engineering), David Prescott (developmental biology), Stephen Fischer-Galati (history), Irwin Wilson (chemistry), John DeFries (behavioral genetics), Hugo Schmidt (German), Keith Porter (molecular biology), Gregory Kimble (psychology), Charles Slater (business), Kenneth Boulding (economics), and Gilbert White (geography).[67]

The growth of the size of the faculty during the Smiley years provided an opportunity for new appointments, but this growth also undermined the longstanding role of the Faculty Senate in the governance of the University. The meeting in a small university of the faculty as a deliberative body, along with the work of the Senate executive committee and its other special committees on budget, educational policy, personnel, etc., had provided effective communication between the faculty and the Regents through the administration. Responding to faculty concern over what many perceived to be an ineffective organization for a larger university, the Senate executive committee in February 1966 recommended that the president appoint an ad hoc committee to review the functions of the Senate and study faculty participation in governance at other universities.[68] Under the leadership of Professors Otis Lipstreu (business) and John

Loeffler (geography), 18 faculty conducted a thorough investigation lasting almost a year.

The ad hoc committee reported with a proposal to the Senate in May 1967. The general faculty had been polled on governance. The committee held meetings with many individuals, and more than 50 other University faculty organizations were examined. In addition, a draft of the proposal was circulated to all members of the Senate. The essential recommendation was for an elected representative body of approximately 50 faculty to be called the Faculty Council, to ". . . do the actual work of expressing the views of the faculty to the administration and the Regents."[69] The Senate would continue as a forum and ultimate source of faculty authority, but the council would meet regularly and take responsibility for the Senate committees. In this fashion, more than 130 faculty would be discussing with the administration basic policies for the University. The expectation was that these faculty would be in a position to express the views of their constituencies in the various colleges and schools. The report also attempted to clarify various roles in the governance of the University and concluded that it is the ". . . joint responsibility of a governing board, an administration, a faculty, and a student body."[70]

The Senate, concerned that it might be losing its authority, approved in principle the recommendation for a Faculty Council. It also charged another committee to revise the rules of the Senate to take account of a Faculty Council and to specify its rules and functions.[71] This committee, under the chairmanship of Professor Morris Garnsey (economics), made its report in October 1967. After careful provision for the Senate's final authority and the use of mail ballots where necessary, the main issue centered on whether representation to the Faculty Council should be by college or school or from the faculty as a whole. The issue was resolved for representation by college and school. Over the winter, first the Senate and then the Regents approved the new rules making way for the Faculty Council. The Senate charged its own Organization Committee with conducting elections for the council and the Senate committees.[72] The Faculty Council convened for its first meeting in September 1968 and elected Professor Courtland Peterson (law) its chairman. Such was the laborious process of Senate reform, but the outcome was to replace faculty town meetings with a representative assembly.[73]

Considering the pressures mounting on the University during 1967–68, this reorganization of the Senate, making possible more articulate communication between the faculty and the Regents, was timely. These pressures originated with a significant shift in the nation's mood. During the 1960's, demands for racial justice and economic opportunity in America, fused with a desire for world peace, shook earlier complacencies toward American society and convictions about the Cold War.[74] Naturally, the academic community became an important forum for the examination of these issues. But when debate turned to activism and campuses became either staging grounds for movements or places of confrontation, academic governance, structured for an earlier era, faced a difficult challenge. Faculty activism, student protests, and several disruptions at the University after 1966 brought sharp public reaction, including concern by the Board of Regents, and caused a number of distractions for the Smiley administration.

After 1965, the University had to deal with a reexamination of academic freedom. A fundamental concept for higher education is the freedom to teach and the freedom to learn. In an atmosphere charged with excitement over civil rights, this concept was susceptible to misinterpretation if not misuse. When the Supreme Court declared the teacher's loyalty oath in the state of Washington unconstitutional because of vagueness, debate over the 1921 Colorado Teacher's Loyalty Oath opened at the University. In March 1966, the faculty Senate resolved that the oath should be abolished. When the Regents were unable to get a court hearing, in February 1967 they approved a University oath for faculty and staff. Meanwhile the state oath was successfully challenged and the Federal District Court declared it unconstitutional. The Regents wanted to administer the University oath but further court decisions delayed them. The issue was resolved externally when, in the summer of 1969, the general assembly, governor, and federal court approved a new state oath act providing for a clear statement of loyalty to the state and of responsibility to the profession of education. Internally, during 1968–69, the issue was worked out in a compromise between the Faculty Council and the Regents over language in the Laws of the Regents on academic freedom. The new language defined academic freedom in a context of social and moral responsibility.[75]

The student unrest of the 1960s was a widespread and complex phenomenon. Its roots lay in existential philosophy encouraging modern man to equate personal involvement in great causes with fulfillment or salvation. Undoubtedly the writings of Mao Tse-tung and Che Guevara on contemporary revolution and Herbert Marcuse's critiques of democracy were important stimuli. But unrest on campus was definitively shaped by a series of events, in the country at large and at particular universities, which transformed the early idealism of the civil rights movement into disillusionment with the Vietnam War. This development was accompanied by a rising tide of irrationality and violence. The example of violence at home and in Southeast Asia helped turn protesters on campus from respecting the law to breaking it, and their activities escalated from disruption to terrorism. The violence, suggesting the need for change, attracted sympathy to radical causes on campuses from many liberals and even moderates. Finally, when segments of public opinion became sharply critical of students and higher education, this reaction itself undoubtedly fueled campus unrest at the decade's end.[76]

In the spring of 1963, as the civil rights leaders staged a dramatic nonviolent march on Washington, many students were involved and the prospects for social change seemed bright. This enthusiasm spread to projects for urban renewal with Vista and for aid to developing countries in the Peace Corps. The involvement of young people was considerable and the expectations were high. But the assassination of President Kennedy inaugurated a period of militancy and confrontation on the national scene. During the summer of 1964, after the passage of the Civil Rights Act, encounters in Mississippi between civil rights workers and local citizens resulted in bloodshed. The following summer, reacting to the poverty and hopelessness of the inner city, the Watts uprising occurred in Los Angeles. This sparked similar tragedies elsewhere, culminating in Newark and Detroit in 1967. Meanwhile President Johnson, in 1965, had turned to escalation in Vietnam, sending American troops to the south while bombing the north. The frustrations of the civil rights movement, the plight of the big cities, and the horrors of the war, all covered by television, had a profound effect on American youth, alienating many for the moment from traditional values and institutions. This alienation was reinforced by the assassinations of Martin Luther King and Robert Kennedy in the spring of 1968 and the behavior of the police with protesters during the Democratic presidential convention in Chicago that summer.[77]

Also as of 1963, most colleges and universities did not take sufficient account of the greater maturity of their students, many of whom had a more rigorous high school preparation, and certainly more experience and childhood freedom, than their predecessors. So protests were mounting over curriculum requirements and over rules for conduct and living arrangements. These protests, however, soon merged with disenchantment over national issues. As a result, unwillingness to respond to protests or intervention by campus administrations to bring demonstrations to an end could easily turn students against their own institutions.

The first of these situations occurred at Berkeley in the fall of 1964. There the Free Speech Movement, as it came to be called, after the administration suspended the use of university facilities for extramural political purposes, sought to establish the right of students to such political activity on campus. A series of incidents in turn set radical student leaders against the administration, brought a general student demand for the right to extramural political activity, university refusal of the demand, a sit-in with police intervention and arrests, and, finally, a strike in which students and faculty called off classes. There was no immediate resolution of the issue—only a promise to study a number of possible reforms: discipline procedures, governance, conditions of student life, rules for political activity, and curriculum. But the activists had introduced into campus protests new tactics that not only disrupted the university but also denied others their civil liberties. These tactics—blockading, harassing, sitting-in—gained publicity with the civil rights movement.[78]

As the media gave them extensive coverage, the events at Berkeley led to campus protest and disruptions elsewhere over the next few years. And slowly but surely the Vietnam War added its thrust. This was evident at Columbia in the spring of 1968. There the Students for a Democratic Society, which reorganized itself in Michigan during 1962, calling on students to work for a society where all men would more fully control their lives, decided with others to take over the university. SDS, in particular, intended to change Columbia into a political agency for putting an end to the war and to racism, as well as to the political system responsible for both. In April, SDS occupied five buildings, the administration finally called on the police to clear them out, and the following riot, arrests, and injuries produced a strike of students and faculty. Again, the disturbance called forth studies on possible reforms. But at Columbia the radicals sought more than a right to free speech or political activity; they attempted to seize the university and the resultant destruction of property, records, and papers ran to $250,000. In many ways the occurrence was a shock to the nation, even in a year of considerable violence and dismay.[79]

Unrest at the University's Boulder campus followed, sometimes quite closely, events elsewhere, but never reached the intensity of involvement achieved at Berkeley or Columbia. From 1963 to 1967, students, faculty, and visiting lecturers roundly criticized higher education, students protested undergraduate dormitory rules, students and faculty supported and participated in the civil rights movement, students joined the Peace Corps and Vista, and everyone debated national policies, including involvement in Vietnam. Perhaps the most newsworthy events were the appearance of students, professors, and a Regent in Selma, Alabama, in March 1965, and, with escalation evident, two teach-ins on Vietnam in May and July of that year. The teach-ins were criticized by the United States Senate's Internal Security Subcommittee, but charges of professors brainwashing students were never substantiated. That same year there was much interest in the events at Berkeley.[80]

During the next academic year, 1965–66, following the Watts tragedy, there were some large meetings. In October, 2,800 students convened to complain about University rules and a crowd of 2,000 students, faculty, and citizens attended a teach-in on civil rights. In November, more than 600 students observed a debate between professors on Vietnam. Then, in March, over 2,000 showed up for a symposium on contemporary religion.[81] Though a local chapter of SDS was organized in the spring of

1966, its public activities were confined to debates about the draft and the American Negro.[82]

The fall of 1966 was relatively quiet, but the following March an extremely heated debate over Vietnam occurred and a bomb threat to Hellems was reported.[83] For the next three years, until the fall of 1970, student protests and disturbances interfered with, even if they did not dominate, the life of the institution. Of the many occurrences, the most important were: A student blockade of the placement center to stop the Central Intelligence Agency from recruiting (October 1967); a march of 1,500 students, after the assassination of Martin Luther King, on Regent Hall to protest racism, end dormitory regulations, and promote student power (April 1968); the disruption of San Francisco State President Hayakawa's speech, titled "The SDS and Academic Freedom" (March 1969); the bombing of the Air Force ROTC office and a building of the Institute for Behavioral Science, resulting in minor damage (March 1970); the occupation of Regent Hall by 400 students (April 1970); and the student call for a strike to close the University after American intervention in Cambodia (May 1970).[84] After 1970, the unrest declined and disappeared, though not without some noteworthy off-campus disturbances in Boulder in the spring of 1971 and 1972. Taking account of what happened in this period at Chicago, Stanford, Wisconsin, Cornell, and Harvard—and the traditional exuberance of students with the onset of spring—unrest at the Boulder campus was noisy, at times unlawful, but never out of control.

The reaction of the University's administration to the events of 1967–68 was calm and constructive. After the CIA blockade, President Smiley stated publicly to students, "While the University of Colorado will continue vigorously to defend the right to dissent and to peaceful protest, it cannot and will not tolerate the interference by some with the rights of others."[85] Twenty-two students were brought before the University Discipline Committee and then were suspended. Students and faculty protested the harshness of this punishment but, after appeals, the president upheld the suspensions. Questions were raised, however, about discipline procedures, and a Senate committee, long at work on this very matter under the chairmanship of Professor Conrad

McBride (political science), went on to recommend new procedures to be administered by the faculty.[86]

In the meantime, Smiley had to deal with the demands of the march on Regent Hall. These demands, specifically, were for University condemnation of racism, abolition of women's curfews, self-determination in the dormitories on the length and frequency of visits, and student control of the University Memorial Center. The president moved quickly. He made an eloquent statement against racism, women's hours with parents' consent were abolished, and a committee was charged to study control of the UMC bookstore. Facing a divided Board of Regents on the perennial issue of dormitory visits, he settled for extending visiting hours under the existing rules.[87]

The reaction of the Board of Regents was not uniform, and reflected, as it should have, differences in public opinion. There was no discernible public consensus on dealing with campus unrest and the Board itself was equally divided with Republicans Atkins, Coors, and Gilbert reflecting conservative views and Republican Carlson, with Democrats Lynch and Betz, holding liberal views. Thus, at important moments, the decisions of the Board were decisively influenced by the views of the president of the University. This emerged in the summer of 1967 when the Regents singled out, for special discussion, the tenure cases of several faculty who had made radical statements or who had associated with radical groups. The occasion produced an important exchange between Regents Coors and Lynch over the role of the Board on personnel matters. Lynch maintained that personal beliefs were not germane to tenure decisions. Coors argued that patriotism was an essential quality. Smiley, however, had to break a tie vote of the Board on these cases and he supported the recommendations for tenure which came through the various levels of faculty and administrative review.[88]

The difficulties of such a situation were clear in 1968-69 in the controversy over the role of SDS on campus. In September, in keeping with the concept of the University as a "free market-place of ideas," Smiley broke a tie on the Board to allow the national council of SDS to meet in University facilities. When the meeting convened in October, the intention to keep it open to the press and public caused trouble. SDS determined to prohibit cameras and kept cameramen from entering. The president agreed to this and lost the confidence of the conservatives on the Board. At their October meeting, the Regents charged a faculty-student committee with examining the legitimacy of SDS. This committee's report, supporting SDS, along with considerable sympathy among students, was not influential with the Board which in November, with Smiley and Carlson absent because of the flu, voted to disaffiliate SDS and to ban it from the campus. After Regent Carlson called for a full meeting on the issue, the Board, in December, with Smiley breaking the tie, voted to reinstate SDS. This decision, popular on campus, was sharply criticized off campus. But the issue seemed settled until the chair-throwing and shouts which disrupted Hayakawa's speech, involving some SDS members, opened it again. The University then decided to expel two members of SDS; in May, the Regents banned the organization from campus. The next month, however, Smiley left the University, having resigned in February to take another presidency.[89]

The potential danger of SDS on the Boulder campus can never be determined. The example of the takeover at Columbia in the spring of 1968 and the state of siege at San Francisco State in the fall was certainly on the minds of the Regents during 1968–69. But the activity of SDS merged with a concern over the legitimacy of the Board's action in banning it from campus. Whatever the validity of the conservative position condemning radical student organizations, and there was much support for it throughout the state and the country, the liberal position coincided with the idea of a university as a place open to all ideas. Although student radicalism was never widespread at Boulder, much credit was due President Smiley and his administration for distinguishing between lawful protest and illegal disruption and their attempts to meet a wide range of student concerns. Further credit is due the leadership of the Faculty Council under Professor Peterson for carefully presenting faculty positions on academic freedom and student discipline to the Board during the year. And special recognition was earned by Regent Carlson, who spent his professional career working with students, for representing the idea of a university on the Board.

The appearance of SDS, a "fraternity" for social change,

symbolized a significant departure from the past for student culture. Not only were students more concerned about society and policies beyond campus, they also lost interest in many traditional campus activities. The attitude which stressed the importance of extracurricular participation as preparation for life, formulated in the 1920s and elaborated in the 1950s, simply lost its attractiveness. With so many more students than before there was much less opportunity to engage in athletics, work in student government or on the newspaper, or to participate in theater or various other clubs. At large public universities there was never enough housing for students on campus and, as new housing lagged behind the enrollment growth, the rise in numbers living off campus or commuting from home undercut interest in or time for the extracurricular. Students wished to establish their responsibility for their own social conduct: if they could live as adults there was no need for the rituals that were used to bring the young to maturity and to supervise the relations between sexes. And the affluence of the age, permitting many travel and the pursuit of experience or pleasure miles away from campus, made most campus activities seem boring—if not trivial.[90]

For the Boulder campus the concept *in loco parentis*, meaning the institution's assumption of the parents' responsibility for student conduct, was under challenge from the start of the decade. The intemperance of student publications, the circumventing of dormitory regulations, the destruction of University property, and student difficulties with the law off campus, among other matters, shook the basis for University discipline procedures.[91] The Smiley administration believed it must have full responsibility for academic dishonesty cases, but in 1966 it agreed to a review of discipline procedures. This review, conducted by the Faculty Senate Committee on Student Affairs, first under the chairmanship of Conrad McBride (political science) and then James Corbridge (law), was slowed by the disruptions from 1967 to 1969. But in 1969 the Regents approved not only a new procedure, but also a new discipline code. This code specified student rights and responsibilities and guaranteed independence for study and learning as long as there was no infringement of the rights of others, or violations of University rules or the laws of the community.[92] Since 1964, the University had been modifying its own rules for student life on campus; the most note-worthy examples were the new dormitory regulations. So, by 1969, students at the University were essentially in charge of themselves and free to make their own decisions about living, study, work, and play.

The changes in student life at Boulder in the 1960s were considerable. The established pattern of social activities broke up as football weekends became more clearly alumni affairs and formal parties and dances were no longer as frequent. Between 1963 and 1974, the number of social fraternities declined from 18 to 10 while the sororities dropped from 19 to 8. The opportunities for living in ultramodern townhouses or mountain cabins had more to offer. Many all-campus functions withered and disappeared—for example, the CU Days weekend in May and the elections of Homecoming Queens and Winter Carnival Kings. Informal parties and mass rock concerts became much more popular. With the shift to off-campus involvement, the University Memorial Center (UMC), the student union, became less of a social center and more a place for political activity. Quite in character was the founding, in 1965, of Clearing House, an organization designed to supply social service agencies in Boulder with part-time student volunteers. One institution to bridge successfully the changes in student interest was the Conference on World Affairs, originated in 1948 by Professor Howard Higman (sociology) to bring prominent speakers, such as Buckminster Fuller and Ralph Nader, to campus each spring to debate current issues.

This decline of the traditional extracurriculum naturally affected student government. Though elections for Associated Students of the University of Colorado (ASUC) leaders, the executive and the senate, promoted some rigorous discussions of platforms for change in the University and several large voter turnouts after 1966, the question of whether or not student government had any power persisted. By 1969, the ASUC essentially was over-shadowed by the demands of many different groups for an effective role in the governance of the University. Various student leaders now sought to speak directly to the Regents, to set fees for activities, and to participate in the selection of a president for the University. The campus newspaper, the *Colorado Daily*, however, strengthened its position. In 1971, after winning several national recognition awards for campus news coverage, the *Daily* obtained quasi-fiscal automony when it relinquished support from student fees and virtual editorial independence when the Regents ended their official sponsorship.[93]

In addition to new dormitory regulations and a new discipline code, the University's response to the changing student culture also included reforms for the joint boards which supervised a variety of student activities. These boards, composed of students and faculty, developed out of the Faculty Senate's traditional responsibility for student activities. In 1964, the Faculty Senate reaffirmed its responsibility for the joint boards but three years later agreed to share this responsibility with an ASUC Senate committee. During 1969–70, students secured a majority vote on the boards and the Faculty Senate turned its responsibility over to the University's vice president for student affairs. Between 1964 and 1969, several boards ceased to exist, one for Student Organizations and Social Life and another for Religious Programming, and new boards appeared: Recreation Services, Health Services, and Radio. The continuing boards were Student Finance, Publications, and for the UMC. Perhaps the most important ones were Finance and Publications, the former responsible for the level, allocation, and use of student fees, and the latter for the *Colorado Daily*. Efforts of the Joint Board on Publications helped to obtain autonomy for the *Daily*. But all of the boards made important contributions to the maintenance of a community based on decisions by consultation.[94]

A national survey of student opinion, conducted in the spring of 1969, determined that students were much more concerned about better teaching and curriculum reform than better dormitory conditions or even student power.[95] An ASUC-sponsored Day of Analysis at the University in May 1969 was critical of unimaginative teaching, negligible student-faculty contact, and too many large classes.[96] Committees in the College of Arts and Sciences, however, were at work studying reforms for degree requirements and the organizational structure of the college. The latter dominated the deliberations of the college faculty during the spring of 1969. Sparked by a continuing interest of the scientists to create smaller colleges for their own disciplines, i.e.

mathematical sciences or physical sciences or biological sciences, and student interest in smaller, more intimate learning situations, the college administration appointed a committee under the chairmanship of Professor Martin Cobin (communication and theater) to make a study. The committee made no single recommendation but did provide a list of options for the faculty to vote on. The essential choice, however, was between creating smaller colleges, clusters of disciplines with appropriate administrative and student advising components, or continuing with a single large college. Uncertain that change would bring desired or desirable results, the faculty voted to retain a single large college.[97]

The University as a whole was just getting down to considering a total response to the new times when Smiley resigned. In response to faculty concern, he had charged a committee in March 1968 to examine the academic community and ". . . to explore and recommend ways in which this community can be further strengthened." Entitled the Commission on the Academic Community, the committee's chairman was Professor Stanley Cristol (chemistry). After months of interviews and discussion, the commission reported in May 1969. Deciding to focus on the problem of University governance as central to all other problems, the report discussed the roles, perceived and actual, of students, faculty, administration, and the Regents in the decision-making process. Forceful recommendations emerged; for students more participation in policy-making, for faculty an initiative rather than a reactive posture for the Faculty Council, for the administration more decentralization and increased communication with students, faculty, and staff, and for the Regents more attention to fund-raising and publicity and less concern for the management of the institution. The report was clearly the most important self-study undertaken by the University in a decade and was in direct response to the troubled times. It was also, in many respects, an important planning document for the future. Unfortunately, the report became only one of many guides for a new administration.[98]

The Smiley administration did not come to an end all at once. Glenn Barnett resigned effective at the end of the 1967–68 academic year to take a post at another university. But Vice Presidents Manning and Conger continued their responsibilities for another year after Smiley's departure in June 1969. There was no exodus of deans; only James Archer (Graduate School) and John Reid (law) resigned in 1967–68. Lawson Crowe (philosophy) succeeded as Dean of the Graduate School and Don Sears of the law faculty followed Reid as law dean. Also with the retirement of Don Saunders, John Little, professor of education and associate Dean of Faculties, became Secretary of the Board of Regents. Meanwhile, the Regents made two new vice presidential appointments in 1968–69—Roland Rautenstraus for student affairs and university relations, and Joe Keen for the centers at Denver and Colorado Springs. Also that year, Ernest Wahlstrom returned as Dean of Faculties. Eugene Wilson, after years of experience in many posts with the University, became interim president for the summer of 1969.[99] Thus there was no such break in the continuity of administrative personnel as occurred with Newton's departure in 1963.

After six years, President Smiley and his colleagues registered a number of achievements and earned considerable recognition. They presided over a rapidly expanding institution and the origins of a multi-campus organization and advanced on the start made by the Newton administration on additions to the faculty, securing federal grants, and the construction of new facilities. Vice Presidents Manning at Boulder and Conger at the Medical Center provided skillful, respected leadership for each campus. However, Smiley had only started to deal with the changes necessitated by the student unrest. Without further opportunity to pursue its generally successful approaches to student needs and demands, the administration really left this responsibility as a major charge for its successor. This was also the case with problems resulting from the state's underbudgeting of the University. Though the request for state support is a continuing struggle and must always be a prime responsibility for university administrations, the slippage in faculty salaries between 1964 and 1969 in particular was an unfortunate legacy. On balance the Smiley years, while not as dynamic or as controversial as the Newton period, were ones of steady progress for the University.

In July 1969, after an extensive search by a faculty-student-alumni committee, the Regents appointed Frederick P. Thieme as the eleventh president of the University. An anthropologist,

Thieme earned the Ph.D. at Columbia and served on the faculty of the University of Michigan including a term as Chairman of the Department of Anthropology. For over a decade he was one of the top administrators at the University of Washington, first as Provost and then as Executive Vice President. In part responsible for the considerable progress at Washington during the 1960s, Thieme came with a reputation for dealing effectively with difficult situations and for excellent communication with the state legislature. The Regents believed he was the right man to take the leadership of the University in a time of student unrest and financial uncertainty.[100]

Thieme needed more than a year to organize his administrative team. With assistance from a faculty committee elected by the Faculty Council, the president selected Lawrence Silverman, an historian and vice chancellor from the University of Tennessee, as Provost and Vice President for Academic Affairs, and Dr. Robert Aldrich, a pediatrician from the medical faculty at the University of Washington, as Vice President for Health Affairs. Other appointments included Roland Rautenstraus as Vice President for University Relations, William Erskine, from the University of Washington, as Vice President for Business Affairs, and James Corbridge, of the University law faculty, as Vice President for Student Affairs. Thurston Manning remained for a short period as Vice President for Planning before accepting the presidency of another university and Eugene Wilson, after stepping down as interim president, returned for two years to the Vice Presidency for Business, before serving for a period as Secretary of the Board of Regents. Joe Keen continued as Vice President for the Denver and Colorado Springs centers as did John Bartram, serving his fourth successive administration, as Director of the Budget. Unfortunately, in the spring of 1971, Silverman had to resign as Provost for reasons of health. He was succeeded by Lawson Crowe, the Dean of the University's Graduate School. Another of President Thieme's appointments was that of J. Russell Nelson, a professor of finance at the University of Minnesota, who came in 1970 as associate Provost and was advanced to Vice President for Planning and Budgets in the fall of 1972.[101]

The Thieme administration was not destined to be a salutary one, either for himself or for the University, and his presidency came to an early end after only four and a half years. The causes of this unfortunate turn rest not only in the number of serious problems that emerged during the first two to three years, but also in his administration's difficulties in dealing with these problems and thus losing the confidence of the faculty and the Regents. It remains an open question, however, whether the problems were such that no administration could have faced them and remained in office.

In the background was a series of important changes in the makeup of the Board of Regents between 1970 and 1974. The elections of 1970 returned two Democrats, Betz for another term and University Professor of Economics Byron Johnson. Democrat Daniel Lynch chose not to run. With four Republicans and two Democrats, there was no change in the political composition of the Board until 1973. In the elections of 1972, historian Geraldine Bean, a Democrat, and banker Eric Schmidt, a Republican, were elected. With Regents Coors and Carlson no longer members—Coors had retired but the Republicans refused to renominate Carlson—the Board now had three from each party. But this balance was brief. In 1972, the voters approved a constitutional amendment to enlarge the Board to nine members. In July 1973, Governor Love appointed two attorneys, Democrat Raphael Moses and Republican Jack Anderson, and banker Thomas Moon, also a Republican, making five Republicans and four Democrats the composition of the Board. Thus, over a short span, President Thieme had to work with a constantly shifting membership on the Board and only two Regents, Dr. Atkins and publisher Betz, had long experience as members of the Board.[102]

The most pressing responsibility for the new president during his first three years was the continuing campus unrest. After three weeks in Boulder and several incidents, Thieme commented that "his honeymoon was over."[103] From September 1969 until June 1970, there were a series of protests, demonstrations, or marches over rents for off-campus housing, a moratorium in Vietnam, funds for the Educational Opportunity Programs, the presence of ROTC, and salaries for graduate students employed by the University, among other issues. In the late winter and early spring, the tempo of protest increased. The University police threatened to strike over their work conditions, and bomb-ings of the Air Force ROTC office and one of the Institute for Behavioral Science buildings occurred as did a bomb threat which emptied Norlin Library. In April, 400 students critical of the war in Vietnam staged a sit-in in Regent Hall which lasted for more than twelve hours and required the presence of faculty and more than 100 police to keep order. The month of May, the end of a difficult year, began with a disruption of an ROTC drill and proceeded to a student strike which interrupted the end of classes and the examination schedule.[104]

The strike had several sources. Throughout the year the Student Mobilization Committee (SMC) worked to end the war in Vietnam by advocating that the University abolish ROTC, cease defense-related research, and sell defense-related corporate stock. In April, the SMC was calling for a strike and its efforts produced the ROTC drill incident.[105] However, after the White House announced early in May that U.S. forces were in Cambodia, student leaders around the country called for a national strike against the war. Then, a consequence of student reaction, four students were killed in a clash with the National Guard at Kent State in Ohio. For the University, these events opened two weeks of debate on the war and on the possibilities and potentials of striking among students, faculty, and the administration. The SMC, the Student Senate, and a number of spokesmen at several large student meetings, wanted a strike "to end the business of the university as usual" in order to focus on the war, social issues, and educational problems.[106] The faculty, the Faculty Council, and the faculty Senate condemned the war, expressed sympathy for the student strike, recommended discussion groups for the war and other issues, and left to individual faculty how best to finish the academic year.[107] President Thieme determined to keep the University open; he made several impressive speeches to students and faculty expressing concern for both the war as a tragedy and the university as a useful institution.[108] When the dust settled, most students had taken their exams and gone home and the University had passed through the crisis without damage to its name or purpose.[109]

Although campus unrest persisted in various forms for another two years—including the bombing of Macky, shots fired at Regent Hall, bomb threats, and strike plans—after the fall of

1970 the frequency and intensity of these events in Boulder tapered off.[110] Also, the focus shifted from the war and came to settle on criticism of the University's Educational Opportunity Programs (EOP). These programs had started in the summer of 1968 to recruit students from minority cultures and to support their studies at the University with scholarships and tutorial assistance. By the 1969–70 academic year, approximately 800 students—Mexicans, blacks, and a few Indians—were receiving financial aid on the Boulder campus and at the Denver and Colorado Springs centers.[111] In February 1970, the Faculty Council, after a lengthy debate, approved a report from its Committee on Minority Programs.[112] This committee, under the chairmanship of Professor Richard Jessor (psychology), had made a thorough study, and advocated that the University take this important social responsibility seriously. The report recommended that the quota of minority students be 15 percent of the total student body, corresponding to the percentage of minorities in the population of the state. The report also suggested that if the legislature would not provide the funds for this number of minority students, then the University should reorder its own spending priorities to support the minority students.[113]

Beginning in the fall of 1970, and lasting over two years, much uncertainty and misunderstanding surrounded EOP. The Regents, uncertain of state support, held back on authorizing expansion.[114] Minority student leaders staged a series of protests culminating in an unpleasant scene in April 1972 when there was damage at the EOP office.[115] In addition to the question of financial support, the issues of administrative control of EOP and the organization of minority studies academic units emerged. In February 1972, the Faculty Committee on Minority Affairs made specific recommendations to place EOP under a supervisory board of faculty and EOP directors and to put overall responsibility for EOP, appointment of minority faculty, and the development of minority studies curricula under a vice president for minority affairs.[116] The Faculty Council enthusiastically approved these recommendations.[117] Yet a major problem underlay all this debate. Minority students were being admitted to the University—there were more than 1,000 registered during 1971–1972—but the dropout rate, no worse than for the University as a whole, was discouraging, considering the efforts to attract and hold these students.[118] Unfortunately, EOP objections and a tight University budget prohibited much progress in 1972 on the faculty recommendations for EOP.

On the national scene, campus unrest showed a marked decline after 1970 and, though protests continued, violence virtually disappeared. The phaseout of the war explains this but the vote for eighteen-year-olds, effective for elections in 1971, was important as another outlet for youthful energy. But new circumstances were shaping and adding to the skepticism among the public about higher education which the unrest had first stimulated. The job market for college graduates, except in certain specialized careers, declined seriously after 1969 and for Ph.D.s in the humanities almost disappeared. In addition, many academic institutions began to feel the effects of both inflation and a decline in financial support as soft spots appeared in the economy. There was a marked slowdown in the growth of federal grants, state tax support, and contributions from business. For 1972, public higher education expenditures in California and Illinois actually were reduced. Furthermore, public institutions not only faced austerity but also, for the first time, real accountability to their legislatures for the use of funds. Such accountability in practice meant reduced flexibility for the management of an institution. With this background lies the explanation for increasing tensions between faculty and administrations as the cost of living outpaced pay raises or tenure quotas influenced personnel decisions. A new interest in collective bargaining emerged among faculty, witnessed not only by the contract signed at the City University of New York in 1969 but also by the acceptance of bargaining in 1971 by the American Association of University Professors. This was a significant change for the oldest faculty professional organization which had always eschewed individual bargaining. All of these trends helped to place administrations in public institutions in difficult situations between faculties and legislatures.[119]

Before the full impact of these new trends hit the University in 1971–72, a routine review for the purposes of checking on accreditation by the North Central Association of Colleges and Secondary Schools uncovered some problems. The review in the spring of 1970 was conducted by a committee of academics from outside the University and chaired by Paul Dressel of Michigan State University, a scholar respected for his research on higher education. The committee's report, taking account of the magnitude and rapidity of the institution's growth since the last NCA visit in 1960, was sharply critical. Making judgments based on data provided by the University and campus interviews (in Boulder, Denver, and Colorado Springs, but not the Medical Center), the committee found fault with the University's academic planning, the small size of the central administration, the excessive autonomy of several departments and colleges or schools, low salaries of full professors, the lack of space and facilities for the nonscience departments, the dysfunctions of the centers in Denver and Colorado Springs, and the inadequate appropriations from the state.[120] Yet the committee found that "The faculty as a whole is impressive. . . . Certainly the potential is there, but only if a clear role is agreed upon for the University."[121] Thus, at the opening of a new decade, the University was told by outside experts that it needed more direction and more resources.

A similar message came from inside the University from a Long Range Goals study during 1970–71. This committee, proposed by Faculty Council Chairman Albert Bartlett (physics) and Provost Silverman, worked under the leadership of Professor Walter Simon (history). Though elected by the Faculty Council, the committee was insufficiently representative of faculty and not really in touch with planning in the various colleges and schools. However, the committee interviewed the representatives of many University constituencies, faculty, administration, students, alumni, Regents, and legislators, and it uncovered a number of issues, particularly for the Boulder campus. The more important were the need for planning, more consultation between the administration and the faculty, and a rededication to undergraduate teaching. During these interviews the committee became aware of the new national trends, the declining job market for graduates, the financial crunch for higher education, and faculty interest in collective bargaining. In the fall of 1971, the committee recommended boards for academic and physical planning, a reward structure to encourage both teaching and research, faculty elections for the key administrative posts in the University, including the president, from the ranks of the faculty, and the organization of small residential undergraduate colleges of 1,000 students and 50 faculty.[122] The report was not well received by the Faculty Council. The cost implications were considerable and the recommendations were viewed as anti-research and anti-administration. Also, the focus was really on the College of Arts and Sciences while the future of the medical campus and the centers in Denver and Colorado Springs was hardly touched. After lengthy debate, the Faculty Council shelved the report but approved new committees for planning.[123]

During the decade 1963–1973, academic planning occurred, steadily, at the level of the colleges and schools in the University. This planning resulted in a variety of curriculum or program changes. These changes were most dramatic in the College of Arts and Sciences. Here, reacting to the exponential growth in knowledge and the student desire for relevant course work, the accepted definition of a liberal education gave way. This definition emphasized competence in basic intellectual skills and familiarity with the major areas of knowledge. The new approach stressed the freedom to choose from and the opportunity to experiment with the array of knowledge. Changes in admission requirements for the college recognized that the high schools were providing more general education. Alterations in the graduation requirements for the degree virtually allowed students to study for a major and anything else of interest.[124] New programs emerged to facilitate the new freedom, especially the individually structured major and experimental studies in interdisciplinary fields or nontraditional subjects.[125] Associated pedagogical developments were, by comparison, less innovative. Responding to student complaints about the size of classes and the remoteness of professors, the college introduced a residential academic program for Sewall Hall and classes were taught by faculty in the residence hall.[126] Also, efforts were made to provide additional smaller classes in a number of disciplines.

The expansion of knowledge was of even more consequence for the Graduate School. New knowledge demanded not only more specialization of studies but also new specializations, including a renewed interest in interdisciplinary links. As the annual reports of the Dean of the Graduate School after 1963 show, the faculty developed many new courses, a number of new degrees (for example, computer science), and even several new institutes (for example, the Cooperative Institute for Research in the Environmental Sciences).[127] New rules provided for the registration of special students in credit courses without having to pursue a degree.[128] Although considerable debate occurred on the national scene over whether to provide teaching degrees alongside research degrees, that is, a Doctor of Arts in addition to the Doctor of Philosophy, few institutions made this change and the University hardly considered it. The issue of preparing scholars for college and university teaching was complex and reached to the heart of graduate education. The traditional role of graduate faculty, reinforced by grants from government, business, and foundations, lay in conducting research and training students to become researchers. But the increasing use in the 1960s of graduate students as teachers of undergraduates stimulated a demand for some training in teaching. The issue was resolved with the cutback in research funds and the decline of the market for college teachers. Now graduate faculty are expected to teach more undergraduates, and graduate students, in order to be even considered for positions, must have established their potential for research.[129]

All of the professional schools, at the undergraduate and graduate levels, responded to the rising concern in the public with social issues and problems with environment. Curriculum changes, especially in business, engineering, law, and architecture, reflected more interest in the social and behavioral sciences than before.[130] Architecture, in fact, changed its name to the College of Environmental Design. These schools also participated in the many curriculum changes taking place in their fields around the country. Business moved away from specific career training to the imparting of general management skills, including mathematical analysis, and Education added the study of the educational process to the responsibilities of teacher training and the preparation of administrators.[131] The School of Nursing, by incorporating liberal education with specific training, sought to graduate administrators and educators as well as practitioners.[132] Both Law and Medicine, while retaining basic introductory courses, permitted students to take more electives. A major reason for change in the medical curriculum was a new interest in training physicians for primary care of patients rather than specialized treatment, thus matching medical education and social needs.[133] At the graduate level, all of the professional schools developed more interest in and the capability for research and advancing knowledge.

Academic planning in this period was also responsible for the establishment of four new schools in the University: Journalism (1962), Architecture (1962), Dentistry (1967), and Public Affairs (1971). These schools, with the exception of Dentistry, were outgrowths of previous majors, departments, or institutes. All were responses to student interests or public demand for education and training in these fields; there was no existing dental school in the state. And the School of Public Affairs, dedicated to the preparation of men and women for professional work in the public sector in government or service agencies, was of special importance.[134]

Certainly one of the most responsive organizations within the University to the changes of the 1960s was the Extension Division. Responsible for credit and noncredit courses in various formats—classes, correspondence courses, and workshops, or conferences—the division provided a wide spectrum of educational services to the state. As interest in and recommendations for lifelong learning opportunities mounted, for career changes, for women, and for leisure, the division was in a position to meet them. In 1970, after a self-study, the administration changed the name from Extension to Continuing Education. By 1973, the division was providing instruction each year to more than 40,000 individuals. Noteworthy among the division's special programs have been the Real Estate Certification Program, Mini-College for Women, the Indian Education Program, the Community Design Center, Workshop for Directors of Volunteer Programs, the Spring Business Conference, and various conferences for personal growth and self-fulfillment.[135]

Over the period 1963–1973, the University's intercollegiate athletic program also brought recognition to the institution. Under the leadership of Eddie Crowder, the football team was rebuilt and again made a name for the University in the Big Eight Conference, generally regarded as the most powerful league in the country. Crowder's 1971 team ranked third in the nation behind Nebraska and Oklahoma, the leaders of the Big Eight. Crowder's teams at one time or another beat Alabama, Nebraska, Ohio State, Oklahoma, Louisiana State, and Penn State, and they played in five postseason bowl games. Basketball and skiing have been successful as well. Basketball Coach Russell "Sox" Walseth trained three Big Eight champions and skiing Coach Bill Marolt turned out four NCAA championship teams. College athletics, in financial straits in some institutions, had sound management at the University.[136]

Most of these activities were constrained to some extent by the level of funding for the University. The School of Public Affairs, for example, was started with an inadequate initial budget. The fiscal situation of the University in the period 1970–1974 did not improve over the years 1963–1969. The Thieme administration made a series of "go-ahead" budget requests to the legislature. For 1971–72, the University asked the state for $79 million to cover operations, 28 percent over the previous year's actual expenditures. It received only $68.7 million. The next year, after a request of $81 million, the University got $69.7 million.[137] Thus, while able to make modest improvements, the University could not take big steps forward. Between 1970 and 1974, total operating funds went up 45 percent from $109 to $161 million. Within these sums, state appropriations from the general fund rose 50 percent, from $32 to $49 million, 23 percent of which occurred between 1972–73 and 1973–74. Tuition income, however, almost doubled, going from $13.7 million to $24.7 million.[138] These were sizable increases but, with inflation at 5 percent a year on top of the budget base for the University at the end of the 1960s, the finances of the institution were very tight. The state increased its general fund expenditures over these four years by more than 70 percent, but the dollars going to higher education only advanced 25 percent. Yet among the higher education allocations, no other institution or group of institutions had as significant an increase in general fund support as the University.[139]

In this period, the state provided more than $12 million for capital construction. With additional support from federal and private sources, or revenue-earning activities, a number of new buildings appeared. On the Boulder campus, construction included buildings for the School of Business (1970), Physics

(1972), Molecular-Biology and Psychology (1973), Computer Science (1973), and additions for Law and Chemistry (1974). One of the largest private gifts ever received by the University, $500,000 from alumnus Ira Rothgerber, made the law additions possible. Also in Boulder a most impressive recreation center and a new family housing complex, Colorado Court, were completed. At the Medical Center, the ten-year program to rebuild virtually all of the facilities was completed in 1971 with final renovations for the Medical School. On the Colorado Springs campus, the first new building, a library-laboratory facility, opened in 1973. The building was named for Dr. George Dwire, the president of the Cragmor Foundation which donated the property for the campus to the University.[140]

Unsettling factors in the preparation of budget requests for the University during President Thieme's administration, and particularly during negotiations with the various state agencies, were the transformation to a multi-campus institution and the rise of the Auraria Higher Education Center in Denver. The University's movement toward a multi-campus organization was most uncertain. In 1970, the North Central Association accrediting report found considerable fault with the relationship between Boulder and the centers in Denver and Colorado Springs and recommended administrative autonomy.[141] But early in 1971 a consultant's report to the Commission on Higher Education advised that the University give up its Colorado Springs Center so that it could evolve as a four-year college on its own.[142] And, in the fall of 1971, the Committee on Organization of State Government in effect concluded that the University should not develop branch campuses in either downtown Denver or Colorado Springs.[143] With these matters to consider, the University could not be certain, even if the Regents decided to develop autonomy for the centers, whether or not the state would support a multi-campus University.

During 1972, however, the situation changed completely. The general assembly agreed in the spring to put on the ballot a constitutional amendment which would allow the University to organize branches.[144] Few were predicting voter approval, but University alumni groups, the Colorado Chamber of Commerce, and the Denver newspapers all gave their support. In November, the amendment passed by a narrow margin of 32,000 votes. Only 12 of 63 counties approved, but these included the Denver metropolitan area.[145] With this result, early in 1973 the Regents designated the former centers as campuses of the University and called for their autonomous development.[146] President Thieme started planning for a new administrative structure distinguishing between the central management of the University and the management of individual campuses.

The constitutional amendment was a start toward a brighter future for the Colorado Springs Center. The Extension Division established the center in 1952. Between 1962 and 1965, parallel with the University's decision to expand its programs in Denver, the Extension Center in Colorado Springs became a University Center for both undergraduate and graduate degree programs. The gift of the Cragmor property in 1965 really marked the opening of a new phase for the University in Colorado Springs. From 1965 to 1972, the number of students went from approximately 1,200 to more than 2,300. But both the University and the state had difficulty agreeing on satisfactory growth budgets for the center. As a result, few faculty were added and little in the way of facility improvement occurred. In the spring of 1971 it seemed as if the University might have to give up the center. The University also had difficulty in selecting a chief executive officer until the fall of 1971, when former Provost Lawrence Silverman became Vice President. One of Silverman's first decisions was to follow the North Central Association recommendation, and he organized an autonomous College of Arts and Sciences in 1972. Then he went on to be the first of campus executives to design a master plan and earn the approval of the Commission on Higher Education.[147] Though considerable problems remain, especially adequate budget support and relations with the state college in Pueblo, now a university, the Colorado Springs branch is a reality with expectations for a campus of 10,000 students.

For the Denver center, autonomy was involved with the development of the Auraria Higher Education Center. The origin of the Auraria idea, placing three institutions on one campus, came with the decision of the state to have a community college, a four-year college, and a university center in Denver and the consequent need to economize on capital construction costs. In

1968, after considerable study and discussion, the commission approved the Auraria location, the site of one of Denver's earliest settlements, as a campus for the three institutions.[148] Over the next four years, culminating in a $40 million capital construction appropriation by the general assembly in 1972, the financing, a package of federal, city, and state funds, was worked out to buy the property, clear it, and build the facilities. In the meantime, Governor Love appointed a board of directors to plan the campus, own the land, and manage the facilities.[149]

To this point, the University's interaction with Auraria planning was minimal. After pledging cooperation, the Regents became concerned about institutional control of their programs in Denver and about the competition between the institutions for capital construction funds. In 1970, they tried to clarify the role of the Denver center by referring to it as a "downtown University branch."[150] Almost 7,000 students were taking course work in many fields at both the undergraduate and graduate levels. Then, responding to the North Central Association criticism, the Vice President of the Denver center, Joe Keen, organized in the spring of 1971 an autonomous College of Arts and Sciences and the Regents and the commission approved.[151] But the existence of this college posed a problem of articulation with Metropolitan State College which also had degree programs in Arts and Sciences. The commission and other state agencies were concerned about overlap and duplication. President Thieme proposed an agreement with Metro State to phase down the Denver center's undergraduate program in Arts and Sciences.[152] But until the funding for Auraria was certain and the voters approved of branch campuses for the University, little real understanding on the University's role in Auraria could be reached.

The future of the Denver campus took shape during the winter and spring of 1973. The University, after the president and the Regents were persuaded by the faculty in Denver, determined to maintain a College of Arts and Sciences.[153] A meeting of the boards of all the Auraria institutions—Community College of Denver, Metropolitan State College, and the University—reaffirmed that Auraria would be a consortium with each institution controlling its own academic programs.[154] Final decisions were reached over the next year. In 1974, the general assembly passed a statute that clarified the role of the Auraria Board of Directors as essentially a landlord for the campus and specified which institutions would be responsible for common activities. For example, the University would manage the library. The commission also approved a master plan for the Denver campus which specified the University's role in undergraduate, graduate, and professional education for an eventual student population of 10,000.[155]

The uncertainty of the faculty on the Denver campus over Auraria planning merged with faculty criticism of the Thieme administration on the Boulder and medical campuses and resulted in April 1973 in a vote of no confidence in the president by faculty, staff, and students. Among the more important causes of the vote were the pressing of the legislature for more accountability for the use of funds, extremely tight budgets from 1971 to 1973, and a decline in federal funds. All of these matters restricted the flexibility of the administration and often put it in almost impossible situations. The budget for 1972–73 was difficult to manage. For Boulder it was broken into ten categories with a call for expenditure reports in these areas. Funds in other categories, such as library, staff salaries, and student aid, were allocated to various state agencies for redistribution to the University. Furthermore, with an enrollment cap of 20,000 students on the campus, there was insufficient extra tuition income to cover some $500,000 of salaries of faculty appointed under the NSF science development grant and which had to be absorbed by the University. Finally, the state reduced the funds for supporting personnel as well as for supplies and expenses. In order to absorb the salaries and the reductions, the University had to make its own cuts on the Boulder campus.[156] As a consequence, Faculty Council Chairman Professor Keith McLane (engineering) reported to the Regents in August 1972 that ". . . morale is exceedingly poor."[157]

On the medical campus, the year 1972–73 was especially difficult. As long ago as the 1950s, the University determined to open a School of Dentistry. Legislative support for planning, however, was only received in 1967. With the prospect of federal funds, planning for the school went on with the intention to open in the summer of 1973. But, in the fall of 1972, President Nixon vetoed the legislation containing the federal funds for the Dental

School. Considering the opposition of the commission to a dental school and the apparent unwillingness, early in the budget approval process, of the state to cover the loss of federal funds, President Thieme had to terminate the appointments of the dental faculty. At the same time, the University was asking the legislature for $3.7 million in a supplemental appropriation to cover the deficit in indigent-care revenues at the Colorado General Hospital on the medical campus. As there was much discussion in the press about the management practices at the Medical Center, it was not a propitious time to seek so much extra money. But, by the end of the spring, the legislature agreed to fund not only a dental school but also came up with a sizable appropriation to cover the deficit. In this process, however, nerves and relations were frayed between the University administration and faculty at the Medical Center and between the University and various state officials.[158]

During the winter of 1972–73, President Thieme's administration also faced difficulties with the staff on the Boulder campus. For several years, the salary levels of many whose contributions to the University were considerable had been slipping. For 1972–73, the legislature intended a 5.5 percent increase for staff, the same as for faculty, and appropriated the funds to the state controller for allocation to the University. Unfortunately, the appropriations were almost $700,000 short of the 5.5 percent increment and the difference had to be put into the supplemental request, holding up increases and causing consternation. Meanwhile, under a request from the state, the University employed a consultant to handle a staff job reclassification, a study that was rather insensitively conducted and not well received. Suggested, tentative titles and possible pay rates did not fit existing titles and pay. In the background was the growing possibility that the state itself would take over the University's staff and put it in the state personnel system. The supplemental funds were appropriated, and no statute was passed to put the University staff under the state. Yet again, the turmoil involved must be understood as background for the Boulder staff vote of no confidence in Thieme.[159]

Student activities in Boulder contributed something to the difficulties of the Thieme administration. By the end of the 1971–

72 academic year, protests over national issues almost disappeared. Student involvement in the Boulder City Council elections of 1971 was extensive but two years later student apathy toward city politics was evident.[160] Students, however, continued to be critical of the University. Thieme's effort to create a University Council to promote dialogue between representatives of students, faculty, and administration collapsed when the student representatives walked out in the winter of 1971 claiming that the council lacked authority. In the fall of 1972, the student government executive took the administration to task for allowing a group to use University facilities to organize another local chapter of SDS. Though a recent decision of the Supreme Court seemed to support the use intended, the Regents reaffirmed their 1969 ban on SDS. There were underlying currents of student discontent, particularly with the funding level for the Educational Opportunity Programs and salaries for graduate students. This last factor helps to explain the poll of graduate students in the spring of 1973 which, with a light return, expressed no confidence in the president of the University.[161]

Faculty restiveness, however, was a fundamental problem for Thieme. Salaries had slipped during the Smiley years, not drastically but comparatively, and, between 1970 and 1974, the annual increases made possible by the state averaged about 6 percent. In the spring of 1973, the median salary for all ranks on the Boulder campus was $16,343. During several of those years there was considerable criticism by faculty of the salary levels of the top administrators of the University, which were all above $35,000.[162] With inflation eating away at real income, faculty took some interest in the efforts of other faculties in collective bargaining around the country. Also, newer, younger members of the faculty were concerned about the decline in the availability of tenured positions as the size of the institution leveled off.[163] Over the winter of 1973–74, the local of the American Federation of Teachers pressed the Regents to recognize it as the bargaining agent for the faculty. Inspired by changes in the direction of its national organization, the American Association of University Professors went into competition with the AFT and sought to become the faculty agent. In March, the Faculty Council conducted an opinion poll on collective bargaining and of the 59 percent eligible who voted, 53 percent favored collective bargaining. With this poll in hand, the Faculty Senate immediately called for an election to select an agent. As the state's labor law did not cover public employees, the Regents postponed reaction to this development.[164]

The issue which really pitted the faculty, particularly on the Boulder campus, against President Thieme was whether the Reserve Officer Training Corps should offer courses for credit or become an extracurricular activity. This question was raised in the first year of his presidency and was not really resolved at its end, four years later. After a thorough study of ROTC, locally and nationally, a faculty committee recommended to the Faculty Council, in the spring of 1970, that ROTC make its course offerings more academic. The council voted instead to recommend extracurricular status and the faculty of the College of Arts and Sciences followed with its own recommendation to that effect. But a Faculty Council poll of the faculty, with half of those eligible responding, showed that 53 percent of these wanted to continue the existing policies for ROTC. As this discussion of ROTC took place during the intense antiwar feelings of April and May 1970, the administration sensed that quieter times were necessary for any resolution of the issue. Yet as ROTC contracts made clear, and the Defense Department continued to insist, ROTC could not stay on campus unless its courses received credit. The Regents also insisted that a state university should have ROTC programs. When Thieme was unable, after two years, to renegotiate the contracts and the Arts and Sciences faculty restated their position in the spring of 1972, the issue became less one of ROTC's role on campus and more of the right of faculty to determine graduation requirements. This right is carefully defined in the Laws of the Regents. Unfortunately, in February 1973, the administration, under some pressure to clear up the situation, told the faculty of Arts and Sciences that they were powerless to block credit for ROTC. Throughout this debate, student opinion was about equally divided over whether to keep ROTC as it was for the present or to reform it.[165]

The confrontation over ROTC, the difficulties with the new School of Dentistry, the misunderstandings with the staff, and the concerns of the Denver faculty all came to a head in the spring of

1973. The catalyst for the setting for the vote of no confidence in President Thieme was the call for a meeting in late March of the Senate of the University by the Denver faculty. The objective was to clarify the role of the Arts and Sciences college there and to secure the support of the faculty of the University. After a resolution to this effect was passed, a second motion, asking for a poll on Thieme's presidency, was approved.[166] The confidence-motion called for a mail ballot by the faculty. Over the next four weeks, those faculty endorsing the poll argued that President Thieme was not giving sufficient leadership to the institution, and the president countered that his administration was dealing, as best as possible, with intractable problems.[167] The outcome of the poll at the end of April was, with 61 percent of those eligible voting, that 76 percent of these—42 percent of the eligible—voted no confidence in Thieme. Similar no confidence votes were registered by the staff in Boulder and the Graduate Student Federation. Recognizing the difficulties with which President Thieme had to deal, the Regents at the next meeting of the Board voted 4 to 2 to support him.[168]

Unfortunately, this matter did not end in spring 1973. The staff continued to be uneasy and the attorney general, early in 1974, ruled that they must be incorporated into the state personnel system. The ROTC issue continued to divide the Regents and faculty members in Arts and Sciences; the faculty at the Medical Center, including the School of Medicine and the School of Nursing, had become quite critical of the administration of the center. The addition of the Dental School as a competitor for resources and debate over the future role of the basic sciences were largely responsible for the tensions at the center.[169] In the meantime, the size and structure of the Board of Regents changed. In July 1973, the size of the Board was increased to nine members and it elected its own chairman, banker Robert Gilbert. These developments, in a sense, demoted the president of the University, who in fact served as chairman, and isolated him from members of the Board.[170] Finally, throughout the fall, alumni displeasure with the leadership of football Coach Eddie Crowder developed and resulted in his resignation and replacement.[171] With all of these problems and a new sense of its authority, in April 1974 the Board decided on a vote of 7 to 2 to change the leadership of the University and to relieve Thieme as president.[172] The Board further resolved to appoint Executive Vice-President Roland Rautenstraus as president on an interim basis.

Nevertheless, President Thieme's stewardship was significant for the University. Ironically, his last budget, requested for 1974–75, marked a considerable improvement over the previous four years as state support jumped more than 20 percent.[173] During his term of office, the final organization of a multi-campus institution was achieved, the Educational Opportunity Programs expanded, and significant gains in private support occurred. In fact, private annual gifts to the University increased each year after 1969, reaching $1.6 million in 1973 and 1974.[174] Furthermore, Thieme made a number of important administrative appointments, individuals who would influence the University for many years. They were: Karl Openshaw, Dean of Education; John Lymberopoulos, Dean of Continuing Education; Duane Nuzum, Dean of the College of Environmental Design; Harry Ward, Dean of Medicine; Robert Wilcox, Dean of Public Affairs; Ellsworth Mason, Director of Libraries; Floyd Mann, Director of the Environmental Council; Milton Lipetz, Dean of the Graduate School; Harold Haak, Chancellor of the Denver campus; Virgil Erwin, Dean of Pharmacy; Mort Stern, Dean of Journalism; and Courtland Peterson, Dean of Law.[175] For the University, the years 1970–1974 were ones of strained development, especially tortuous for the administration. But as President Thieme commented, "Colorado has moved us steadily ahead in operating funds and salaries and wages since 1969, which was not the case for universities in many states."[176]

Epilogue

THE FUTURE
OF A
STATE UNIVERSITY

I N THE MID-1970s, the future for higher education in America
seems less certain than at any time since the 1930s. Enrollment
growth, after more than doubling in the 1960s, is slowing and
might reach a zero growth rate within a decade. Neither the federal government, business, nor philanthropy continue the level of
support or investment attained in the 1960s. The percentage of
GNP (Gross National Product) spent on higher education, not
including capital construction, doubled between 1960 and 1972,
from 1.1 to 2.2 percent. Since 1972 federal money for construction
has been cut by 90 percent and similar funds from state and private
sources have also declined. Inflation has dramatically increased
the cost of virtually all aspects of higher education since the late
1960s.[1]

The decline of enrollment growth has both demographic and
social components. U.S. Office of Education reports revealed in
1972 that the number of graduates from high school was leveling
off. Further reports showed that a declining birthrate would further reduce the size of the college-age generation. But changes in
individual aspirations and the demand of the labor market are also
important. For young students the connections between educa-

tion and work or between education and happiness, never very clear, now seem scarcely perceived; the interest is currently focused on life experience rather than formal education. And this feeling is reinforced by the difficulty many college graduates have had in finding suitable employment in recent years. Many parents now are also less coercive about the college attendance of their children. Older students, many of whom are already at work and have family responsibilities, are able to see the importance of education for careers, and even for leisure, in continuing their education. Further growth in higher education seems to depend on providing opportunity for adults of all ages for part-time study as their jobs or families permit.

Yet higher education in the United States remains a model for the rest of the world. We have a higher percentage of youth attending college, more of the GNP is spent on higher education and university-based research, and colleges are located within commuting distance of almost all Americans. These conditions should exist after the period of adjustment to the growth decline which is ahead. The future probably will be a period of stability for higher education, but at a high level of opportunity and activity in comparison to the country's past.[2]

Important questions, however, will persist. How can the higher educational process, once designed for the full-time, high-achieving student in a small institution, be adjusted for a much broader body of students with varying backgrounds and interests in large impersonal institutions? How can basic curriculum changes be achieved without significantly increasing the resources required? How can considerable variations in academic ability and learning speed be accommodated? How can colleges and universities build in the options needed by working students, women, and older students? Answers to these and other questions are central to providing sound educational experiences for near universal access to higher education in the United States. Clearly our national goal is to build a more meritocratic society while also making it more humane.[3]

Student activism, so much a part of the higher education scene between 1964 and 1971, has both abated and shifted its focus. With the diversity that exists among 11 million college students today, it is possible to maintain that students are apathetic. But it is also possible to show that students are lobbying, planning tuition strikes, marching, etc. And it is quite clear that many students are interested in issues that affect their lives—for example, grades, paying tuition, getting a job. Their organizing and demonstrating is often related to these concerns: tuition, financial aid, cuts in higher education funds, and the overall quality of their education. Then, too, there is no burning national issue today, such as the war in Vietnam, to arouse students' moral indignation and motivate their activism.[4]

At this time, the prospects for higher education in Colorado seem reasonably good. In November 1975, a Colorado Commission on Higher Education report stated that enrollment in all postsecondary public institutions was 7 percent over the previous year. Three institutions, the University at Boulder, Colorado State University, and the University of Northern Colorado, have more qualified applicants than budgeted spaces and have had to turn away prospective students. For the 1975–76 fiscal year, the legislature provided a record budget of $178 million for higher education. Faculty in public colleges and universities across the state received the highest salary raises in twenty years. Though the nation is experiencing an economic recession, the impact in Colorado is minimal. The state's revenue for 1975–76 may be somewhat behind projections, which will probably influence attitudes on spending for another year. For this year, the state decided to draw back some 2 percent of the budgets allocated and this has caused some strain. Nevertheless, construction goes forward on the Auraria campus in downtown Denver for Denver Community College, Metropolitan State College, and the University. This is a $70 million-plus project that will dominate higher education capital construction for the next five years.[5]

However, there are certain problems for the future. There are now surpluses of graduates in education, perhaps law, selected engineering fields, and in most of the liberal arts. There is underutilized capacity in the private sector of higher education and this poses the question of whether or not the state should provide tuition grants for use in private colleges and universities. In any case, some articulation between Metropolitan State College and Denver University seems necessary. The public institution has been developing engineering technician programs while the private institution has been losing engineering students and has been forced to close its engineering school. Yet Denver University has the only schools for library science and social work in the state; both fields have good employment opportunities. The rationale for many graduate programs, given the surpluses in some fields and the shifts in the economy, has become blurred. Whether the major public universities in Colorado can really shift resources into demand areas of training and research may become a dominant issue. As far as research and service are concerned, the state now sees the universities as repositories of ideas and expertise but the universities' capacity for the sort of applied research the state needs remains underdeveloped.[6]

For the University, the years 1974 to 1976 were those of adjustment. Riding a general tide in the state and nation, Democrats Louis Bein, a banker, Richard Bernick, and James Carrigan, both attorneys, were elected to the Board of Regents in November 1974. Their victories changed the Board's political makeup from a Republican majority to a Democratic one. Their first decision was to pick a new president. The nationwide search resulted in the choice of Roland Rautenstraus as the University's twelfth chief executive. Rautenstraus was serving as president on an interim basis, replacing President Thieme. He had long service with the University in the College of Engineering, where he was chairman of the Civil Engineering Department, and, most recently, in central administration as Vice President for University Relations. For a number of years, he was responsible for the negotiations with the state for the University's annual budgets. His skills and experience in these negotiations qualified him for the presidency, especially since the nature of the office has changed. With the development of autonomy for the four campuses of the University and the appointment of chancellors for each campus, the role of the president has shifted from direct management to general supervision, leaving more time for handling the University's public relations.

For President Rautenstraus, the main challenges have been the implementation of autonomy for the four campuses, the conversion of the University's staff to the state personnel system, the implementation of affirmative action principles in hiring more women and minorities for the faculty, and the launching of a "second-century" fund drive to raise $12 million for a variety of University projects, including endowed professorships.[7] All of these objectives will require a number of years for completion. Autonomy for the four campuses will probably necessitate some reallocation of resources and personnel but, more importantly, raises questions about the organization of the professional schools and the graduate school which were Boulder based, but now have programs on one or more of the other campuses. The alumni organization was restructured in 1975 to take account of the autonomous campuses and provide alumni support for the new campuses. And the Senate and Faculty Council will have to do the same.[8]

The most significant recent occurrence for the University was the faculty debate over collective bargaining and the close vote against selecting an agent in April 1975. The previous December, a referendum initiating a procedure approved by the Regents showed that the faculty in ten academic units favored collective bargaining. Law, business, engineering, medicine, chemistry and pharmacy did not. Then, in February 1975, an election monitored by the Colorado Department of Labor to select an agent occurred. Three groups competed for faculty support—the American Federation of Teachers (AFT), The American Association of University Professors (AAUP), and the Faculty for No Agent (FNA). No group received a majority so a second ballot was held in April. At that time, with over 77 percent of the eligible faculty voting, the FNA got 318 votes (39.3 percent), AFT had 297 (36.7 percent), the AAUP had 195 (24 percent). The campaign generated many leaflets, but attendance at public forums were disappointing. The AFT stressed that its chapter, with support from the national organization, could gain greater benefits for faculty from the University and the state. The AAUP, also an affiliate of a national professional organization, emphasized its local autonomy and its support of the present faculty governance structure. The FNA sought simply to strengthen the Faculty Council and its various committees. Important for the outcome of the vote, the AAUP refused an offer of the AFT during the campaign to join forces. Another important factor was the decision of the Regents to accept the original faculty and administration agreement that the vote for an agent be by the faculty as a whole rather than by campus or academic unit. Otherwise the Arts and Sciences faculties in Denver and Colorado Springs would have elected the AFT. These faculties, composed of younger men and women and generally lower paid, were much more convinced of the need for collective bargaining. In any case, the issue seems closed for the present.[9]

A kaleidoscope view of events in the University's chronicle for 1974 to 1976 would include the following: a new foundation-funded rheumatology laboratory at the Medical Center; the occupancy of Newton Court, an aesthetically designed new residence for married students on the location of the former Vetsville in Boulder; the start of construction for a building for the Dental School and two buildings for the Colorado Springs campus, one a library-classroom and the other a student center; the ranking of the School of Nursing among the top five in the country; the organization of a Denver campus Institute for Advanced Urban Studies; the inauguration of the Fiske Planetarium in Boulder; and the appointments of J. Russell Nelson, previously Vice President for Planning and Budgets, as Executive Vice President of the University, Mary Frances Berry, a professor of history from the University of Maryland, as Chancellor for the Boulder campus, and John Cowee, a professor of law and business administration from Marquette, as Chancellor for the Medical Center. All of these promise a bright future for the University.[10]

The main challenge ahead for the University consists of maintaining its role as the leader among public institutions of higher education in Colorado.[11] In part this will involve continual effort to improve the academic programs and the various services to the state and nation, but also necessary will be the capacity of the University to change functions as the needs of students and society change. On the agenda for the newer campuses in the University system, Denver and Colorado Springs, are the basic objectives of establishing themselves as places for university-level study and research. In Colorado Springs a physical plant must be constructed and the need for graduate education and training, especially in business and engineering, in El Paso county must be met. For Denver the future is linked to making the Auraria Higher Education Center operate as a consortium of three different institutions and meshing its academic programs with those at the Medical Center and in Boulder. At the Medical Center, planning now is concerned about more training for primary care of patients, ways to deliver more health services to rural areas, and more emphasis on preventive medicine. At Boulder—the centennial campus—many facilities will need renovation, but, equally crucial, more of a balance between the sciences, both natural and social sciences, and the humanities must be restored. The progress of the University since the 1950s has been measured largely in the strengthening of the sciences. A truly great university normally has strengths across the spectrum of academic programs. In sum, as the University begins its second century, the major goal will be to build to provide students—in as many fields as possible—the highest quality of educational experiences.

Appendix One

LECTURES
ON RESEARCH AND
CREATIVE WORK

Appointments to these lectureships are considered to be the highest honor the faculty can bestow on colleagues for outstanding scholarship.

1936 Dean Oliver C. Lester (Physics)
1937 Professor John B. Ekeley (Chemistry)
1938 Professor Theodore D. A. Cockerell (Biology)
1939 Professor Aubrey J. Kempner (Mathematics)
1940 Professor Francis Ramaley (Biology)
1941 Professor George F. Reynolds (English Literature)
1942 Professor Richard W. Whitehead (Physiology)
1943 Professor S. Harrison Thomson (History)
1944 Acting President Reuben G. Gustavson (Chemistry)
1945 Professor Karl F. Muenzinger (Psychology)
1946 Professor Alfred H. Washburn (Pediatrics)
1947 Professor Muriel Sibell Wolle (Art)
1948 Professor Earl H. Morris (Archaeology)
1949 Professor James W. Broxon (Physics)
1950 Professor Robert W. Pennak (Biology)
1951 Professor Earl C. Crockett (Economics)
1952 Dean Philip G. Worcester (Geology)

1953 Professor W. B. Pietenpol (Physics)
1954 Professor Colin B. Goodykoontz (History)
1955 Professor Cecil Effinger (Music)
1956 Professor Morris E. Garnsey (Economics)
1957 Professor Sarvadaman Chowla (Mathematics)
1958 Professor Edward D. Crabb (Biology)
1959 Professor Pierre C. Delattre (French)
1960 Professor Stanley J. Cristol (Chemistry)
1961 Professor Henry W. Ehrmann (Political Science)
1962 Professor Theodore T. Puck (Biophysics)
1963 Professor Hazel E. Barnes (Classics)
1964 Professor Kenneth R. Hammond (Psychology)
1965 Professor Frank S. Barnes (Electrical Engineering)
1966 Professor Lynn R. Wolfe (Fine Arts)
1967 Professor Margaret E. Altmann (Psychology)
1967 Professor David Hawkins (Philosophy)
1968 Professor Joseph D. Park (Chemistry)
1968 Professor C. Henry Kempe (Pediatrics)
1969 Professor George Gamow (Physics)
1969 Professor Homer H. Clark, Jr. (Law)
1970 Professor Edward U. Condon (Physics)
1970 Professor Thomas Starzl (Surgery)
1971 Professor Kenneth E. Boulding (Economics)
1971 Professor Stanislaw M. Ulam (Mathematics)
1972 Professor David Burge (Music)
1972 Professor David M. Prescott (Molecular, Cellular, and Developmental Biology)
1973 Professor Theodore R. Walker (Geological Sciences)
1973 Professor Bertram Morris (Philosophy)
1974 Professor Charles A. Barth (LASP, AstroGeophysics)
1974 Professor Stephen Fischer-Galati (History)
1975 Professor Keith R. Porter (Molecular Biology)
1975 Professor Gilbert F. White (Geography)
1976 Professor Irwin B. Wilson (Chemistry)

Appendix Two

CHAIRMEN
OF THE
FACULTY COUNCIL

The Faculty Council, organized in 1967, is an elected assembly which represents the voice of the faculty on major issues to the central administration and the Board of Regents.

Professor Courtland H. Peterson (Law)	1968–69
Professor Albert A. Bartlett (Physics)	1969–70
	1970–71
Professor Aaron Sayvetz (Integrated Studies)	1971–72
Professor Keith McLane (Engineering)	1972–73
Professor Dorothy R. Martin (Psychology)	1973–74
	1974–75
Professor John A. Tracy (Business)	1975–76

NOTES TO THE TEXT

Prologue

[1] Oscar Handlin and Mary F. Handlin, *The American College and American Culture* (1970), pp. 5, 19, 43, 84. Also Frederick Rudolph, *The American College and University: A History* (1962), *passim*.

[2] Walter P. Rodgers, *Andrew D. White and the Modern University* (1942), p. 47.

[3] Thomas W. Goodspeed, *A History of the University of Chicago Founded by John D. Rockefeller* (1916), p. 266.

[4] "Original Papers in Relation to a Course of Liberal Education," *The American Journal of Science and Arts* xv (1829), pp. 300, 312.

[5] Francis Wayland, *Report to the Corporation of Brown University on Changes in the System of Collegiate Education* (1850), pp. 12–13.

[6] Palmer C. Ricketts, *The History of Rensselaer Polytechnic Institute 1824–1914* (1934), p. 43.

[7] James B. Angell, *Selected Addresses* (1912), p. 42.

[8] Edward D. Eddy, Jr., *Colleges for Our Land and Time: The Land-Grant Idea in American Education* (1957), p. 27.

[9] *Ibid.*, p. 31.

[10] Michael McGiffert, *The Higher Learning in Colorado: An Historical Study 1860–1940* (1964), pp. 1–19.

[11] Allan Nevins, *The State Universities and Democracy* (1962), p. 25.

One

[1] Michael McGiffert, *The Higher Learning in Colorado: An Historical Study, 1860–1940* (1964), p. 44.

[2] *Denver Times*, October 26, 1878.

[3] McGiffert, p. 46. In 1889, when a uniform Normal School statute was passed in Colorado, it was patterned upon the systems then operating in Michigan and Pennsylvania.

[4] *Ibid.*

[5] *House Journal of the Legislative Assembly of the Territory of Colorado* (First Session, 1861), pp. 254, 281, 298–299. Hereafter cited as *House Journal*. See also James F. Willard, "Pioneers Overcame Many Obstacles to Secure University for Boulder," in *Boulder Daily Camera*, January 25, 1951. Hereafter cited as Willard, "Pioneers."

[6] *House Journal*, 1961, pp. 298–299.

[7] *General Laws, Joint Resolutions, Memorials, and Private Acts, Passed at the First Session of the Legislative Assembly of the Territory of Colorado* (1861), p. 144.

[8] F. O. Repplier, *As a Town Grows: The Schools of Boulder, Colorado, in the Pageant of the Years 1860–1959* (1959), pp. 7–8.

[9] For a good discussion of the economic revival of the 1870s see Percy S. Fritz, *Colorado, the Centennial State* (1941), pp. 214–220, 227–232. See also Leroy R. Hafen, *Colorado: The Story of a Western Commonwealth* (1933), pp. 175–187.

[10] The premature efforts came in 1864, 1865–66, and in 1867. See Fritz, *Colorado*, pp. 233–234.

[11] As quoted in Repplier, p. 2.

[12] Amos Bixby, "History of Boulder County" in *History of Clear Creek and Boulder Valleys, Colorado* (1880), p. 401. See also Lynn J. Perrigo, "A Municipal History of Boulder, Colorado" (unpublished ms., 1946), p. 4.

[13] Perrigo, pp. 6–8; Repplier, pp. 10–12. During the decade 1860–70, Boulder's population grew from 325 persons to 343, not a notable increase for a ten-year period. U.S. Department of the Interior, *Population of the U.S. in 1860* (1864), p. 559; *The Statistics of the Population of the U.S., 1870* (1872), p. 95.

[14] The Erie-Boulder section of the Denver and Boulder Valley Railroad was financed by a bond issue subscribed by the people of Boulder. Bixby, pp. 403–404.

[15] Perrigo, pp. 14–17; Bixby, p. 403. See also *U.S. Census, 1880*, p. 112.

[16] McGiffert, pp. 3–4.

[17] *House Journal, 1870*, pp. 27–28.

[18] *Boulder County News*, January 18, 1870.

[19] *House Journal, 1870*, pp. 51–52, 55.

[20] *Council Journal of the Legislative Assembly of the Territory of Colorado, 1870*, pp. 139–140. Hereafter cited as *Council Journal*.

[21] Willard, "Pioneers"; *Boulder County News*, January 18, 1870.

[22] Minutes of the Board of Trustees of the University of Colorado, January 29, 1870, University Archives, University of Colorado, p. 3. Hereafter cited as Minutes of the Trustees.

[23] Minutes of the Trustees, April 4, 1870, pp. 7–9.

[24] Willard, "Pioneers."

[25] Minutes of the Trustees, January 4, 1872, p. 11; *House Journal, 1872*, pp. 104, 108, 172, 176–177.

[26] Minutes of the Trustees, January 5, 1872, p. 31. Reorganization was necessitated because two Trustees died and two others left Colorado. The reorganized Board contained two more Boulderites: Nathan Thompson,

minister of the First Congregational Church, and George C. Corning, a Boulder banker. Minutes of the Trustees, January 1, 1872, p. 11.

27 Minutes of the Trustees, January 2, 1872, p. 28; January 4, 1872, pp. 29–30, 31–33; January 6, 1872, p. 34.

28 Willard, "Pioneers."

29 *Boulder County News*, July 4, 1873.

30 Minutes of the Trustees, January 6, 1874, p. 44.

31 Minutes of the Trustees, January 13, 1874, p. 46; *House Journal, 1874*, p. 3.

32 *Denver Daily Times*, February 2, 1874. For accounts of the council debate see the *Denver Tribune*, February 5, 1874, pp. 161–163. The *Rocky Mountain News*, February 6, 1874, notes only that an attempt to delay the bill failed, but does not mention the debate.

33 *Council Journal, 1864*, p. 191.

34 *House Journal, 1874*, p. 9.

35 It is significant that the accounts of this ride date mostly from a period more than thirty years removed from the time when it was supposed to have taken place. In reporting on the legislative proceedings, the *Boulder County News* makes no mention of it, nor do any of the Denver newspapers which followed the legislative news. A fairly extensive account of the history of events leading up to the opening of the University in the *Boulder County News*, September 7, 1877, does not say anything about a ride, and Willard's "Pioneers," an excellent short history, does not mention a ride either. It is probable that if such a dramatic event occurred, it would have been reported. This is not to say positively the ride did not take place but simply to note the weight of evidence is against it.

36 *Council Journal, 1874*, p. 163.

37 February 13, 1874.

38 May 8, 1874.

39 Minutes of the Trustees, February 13, 1874, p. 47.

40 Minutes of the Trustees, July 18, 1874, p. 52.

41 Minutes of the Trustees, July 28, 1874, p. 54; August 1, 1874, p. 56.

42 Auditor L. C. Charles' letter was printed in the *Boulder County News*, October 2, 1874.

43 *Boulder County News*, October 2, October 9, 1874; Minutes of the Trustees, October 13, 1874, p. 63; April 12, 1875, p. 68; May 1, 1875, p. 69.

44 Minutes of the Trustees, May 1, 1875, p. 69.

45 Willard, "Pioneers"; Minutes of the Trustees, June 21, 1875, p. 75; June 22, 1875, p. 76; July 22, 1875, p. 80. Altogether there were 35 bids, ranging from $28,700 to $42,000. The Trustees accepted the low bid.

46 Willard, "Pioneers." There is a detailed account of the day's events in the *Boulder County News*, September 24, 1875.

47 *Boulder County News*, September 24, 1875.

48 Willard, "Pioneers"; *Boulder County News*, January 21, 1876.

49 *House Journal, 1876*, pp. 79, 87, 154, 259. The house's appropriation was $7,500; it was doubled by the council.

50 Minutes of the Trustees, April 18, 1876, p. 98.

[51] Hafen, p. 196.

[52] Fritz, pp. 234–235.

[53] *Proceedings of the Constitutional Convention Held in Denver, December 20, 1875, to Frame a Constitution for the State of Colorado* (1907), p. 12.

[54] Minutes of the Trustees, October 30, 1876, p. 108. Only five members were present.

[55] Minutes of the Board of Regents, December 23, 1876, Office of the Secretary of the Regents, University of Colorado, p. 1. Hereafter cited as Minutes of the Regents.

[56] Minutes of the Regents, March 27, 1877, pp. 4–5; March 28, 1877, p. 5.

[57] *Boulder County News*, January 14, 1876.

[58] *Denver Tribune*, January 24, 1876.

[59] Colorado, *General Laws of the State of Colorado* (1877), pp. 923–924. Hereafter cited as General Laws.

[60] The Regents were required under the Law of March 1877 to include in the University "Classical, Philosophical, Normal, Scientific, Law and such other departments, with such courses of instruction and elective studies as the Board of Regents may determine." *General Laws*, 1877, pp. 921–922.

[61] At least some members of his family were not impressed by their new home. Jane, one of Sewall's daughters, remembered the loneliness of the huge building set above and apart from the town, and with no trees nearby. Jane Sewall, *Jane, Dear Child* (1957), p. 41.

[62] A good account of the opening ceremonies is in Willard, "Pioneers." Also in the *Boulder County News*, September 7, 1877.

[63] This number evidently fluctuated during the term. In early January 1878, the University reported its enrollment as 65 students. *Boulder County News*, January 4, 1878.

[64] McGiffert, p. 31.

[65] *Boulder County News*, October 26, 1877.

[66] "Quarto-Centennial Celebration, University of Colorado, November 13, 14, and 15, 1902," *University of Colorado Bulletin* II (December 1902), p. 103.

[67] Colorado, Fifth General Assembly, *Session Laws*, 1885, p. 59.

[68] The University lands situation was discussed in some detail by Governor James Grant in his message to the 1885 legislature. See the *Boulder County Herald*, January 21, 1885.

[69] The 1877 law contained an optimistic clause stating that any moneys left over from the levy after University requirements for the year were met were to be placed in a fund for use by the University for special projects. *General Laws*, 1877, p. 926.

[70] Minutes of the Regents, April 7, 1885, p. 82.

[71] Minutes of the Regents, May 30, 1887, p. 128. In addition to the general fund, there was a special fund, primarily from donations. This fund usually varied between $1,000 and $3,000 for many years.

[72] Minutes of the Regents, May 28, 1888, p. 150; January 9, 1889, p. 164; May 27, 1889, p. 171; April 2, 1890, p. 193. A good summary of the Uni-

versity's financial situation up to 1910 is the *Eighteenth Biennial Report of the Board of Regents of the University of Colorado* (1911).

73 Hafen, Chapter XIII, *passim*; pp. 247–249.

74 Colorado, Second General Assembly, *Session Laws*, 1879, p. 15.

75 Colorado, Fourth General Assembly, *Session Laws*, 1883, pp. 18, 29, 288.

76 Between 1880 and 1890 Boulder's population increased from 3,000 to about 3,300, while in the state as a whole, population more than doubled. *U.S. Census, 1890*, Part I, p. 77.

77 *University Catalogue, 1878–1879*, pp. 9–14.

78 There were only two public high schools in 1877. Repplier, p. 22. See also McGiffert, pp. 30–31.

79 *General Laws*, 1887, p. 22. For details of these programs see *University Catalogue, 1878–1879*, pp. 7–9, 15–16.

80 Repplier, p. 26.

81 Repplier, pp. 26–28; McGiffert, p. 34.

82 The *Boulder News and Courier*, June 23, 1882, stressed the contribution the University's graduates would make to the state, repaying the state many times over for the costs of their education. For an account of the Commencement Exercises in 1882, see the issue of June 16, 1882. See also the account in the *Colorado Alumnus*, November 1927, p. 18; and the reminiscence by Henry Drumm, "The First Commencement," *Colorado Alumnus*, July 1934, p. 9.

83 *University Catalogue, 1887–1888*, p. 72.

84 Minutes of the Regents, March 28, 1877, p. 7.

85 Minutes of the Regents, June 29, 1878, p. 14.

86 Minutes of the Regents, June 7, 1879, p. 21; May 21, 1881, p. 38; June 13, 1883, p. 54; June 2, 1885, p. 90. Mary Rippon was consistently at the low end of the salary scale until her retirement, a clear case of sexual discrimination typical of the times. When professors' salaries were fixed at $1,800 in 1885, Mary Rippon's was $1,400.

87 Minutes of the Regents, January 16, 1885, pp. 67–73. Also *Boulder County Herald*, January 21, 1885.

88 McGiffert, p. 34.

89 According to McGiffert, p. 31, cowboys in the 1870s could earn as much as $100 a month—a good wage in those days.

90 *Boulder County Herald*, issues of December 1880, February 1881. Hanus evidently did not prosper, for he returned to his former position at the University early in 1882.

91 Jane Sewall, pp. 94–96.

92 Minutes of the Regents, May 5, 1883, p. 53; November 3, 1883, p. 57.

93 "Disappearance of Cottage 2 Recalls Many Events," *Colorado Alumnus*, November 1927, p. 18.

94 Minutes of the Regents, April 4, 1883, p. 50; June 11, 1883, p. 60.

95 *University Catalogue, 1883–1884*, p. 17; *1888–1889*, p. 6.

96 Judith Hannemann, "A Medical School Is Born—1883," *Quarterly* (University of Colorado School of Medicine), XIII No. 3 (1971), p. 5.

97 Old Main was formally referred to as the "University Building" until about 1899, when enough other classroom buildings on campus made it expedient to designate it the "Main Building." Although commonly used well before World War I, the name "Old Main" was not officially used until about 1920. Campus maps in the University catalogues show this development in nomenclature.

98 Minutes of the Regents, June 2, 1885, pp. 89–90. Richard W. Whitehead and Robert L. Perkin, "Medical Education in Colorado, 1881–1971," *Rocky Mountain Medical Journal* 68 (June 1971): 150. William E. Davis, *Glory Colorado! A History of the University of Colorado, 1858–1963* (1965), p. 50.

99 Davis, pp. 59–60.

100 Minutes of the Regents, April 7, 1885, p. 82.

101 Minutes of the Regents, April 7, 1886, p. 103; *Boulder County Herald*, April 14, 1886. In defense of Sewall, the *Herald* in an earlier issue, February 24, noted the University was the only state institution of higher learning with no debt.

102 Minutes of the Regents, June 1, 1886, p. 111. Later he served as acting president until his successor took office on July 1, 1887.

103 *Boulder County Herald*, June 9, 1886. See also the *Denver Republican*, June 7, 1886.

104 *Boulder County Herald*, March 16, 1887.

105 *Boulder County Herald*, January 19, 1887.

106 The *Herald* answered the governor's claims on where student enrollment ought to be by noting that average college attendance in the nation was 167 students, with only ten colleges having enrollments greater than 500.

107 As reported in the *Boulder County Herald*, July 20, 1887.

108 The Regents voted $200 to help pay expenses of faculty who made tours on behalf of the University. Minutes of the Regents, June 1, 1886, p. 111.

109 *Boulder County Herald*, July 27, 1887; August 31, 1887; Minutes of the Regents, October 4, 1887, pp. 136–139; Davis, p. 61.

110 *Boulder County Herald*, November 23, 1887.

111 *University Catalogue, 1891–1892*, p. 78.

112 University catalogues in these years show the roster of full- and part-time professors as 16 in 1887 and 30 in 1892, an approximate doubling of faculty during the Hale years.

113 As reported in the *Boulder County Herald*, February 13, 1889.

114 *The University Portfolio*, December 1879.

115 *Ibid.*, April 1883.

116 *Ibid.*, April 1881; October 1882.

117 Davis, pp. 67–69; *Boulder County Herald*, October 21 and 28, 1891.

118 *Boulder County Herald*, September 25, 1889.

119 *Boulder County Herald*, January 15, July 23, 1890; Minutes of the Regents, May 27, 1889, p. 174; October 2, 1889, p. 181; January 9, 1890,

p. 187. At the same time they authorized the construction of Woodbury, the Regents also approved additions to the women's cottage.

120 Colorado General Assembly, *Session Laws, 1891*, p. 400; *Boulder County Herald*, May 27, 1891.

121 *Boulder County Herald*, May 27, 1891. The presence of women students, and their role in University life, was important from the beginning. The first woman to get a University degree was Helen Florence Tyler ('86).

122 The *Herald* noted on September 9, 1891, that the new Normal School at Greeley had just raised the salary of its president to $5,000, exactly double Hale's.

Two

1 Davis, pp. 76–77.

2 Minutes of the Regents, December 9, 1891, p. 233.

3 *University of Colorado Bulletin* 14:1 (January 1914): 34.

4 Minutes of the Regents, January 13, 1892, p. 237; *ibid.*, January 23, 1892, pp. 241–243.

5 "Proceedings at the Inauguration of James H. Baker" (1892), pp. 17, 33.

6 In 1892 the University was guaranteed only about $40,000 annually from mill tax revenues. Between 1891 and 1896 special appropriations averaged $21,000 annually. "Some Notes on University Statistics," January 20, 1897, reprinted in "Statement of Needs of the University of Colorado for the Biennial Period 1898–1900" (1897), pp. 3, 9.

7 For a good general discussion of the development of the state's economy, see Carl Ubbelohde, Maxine Benson, and Duane Smith, *A Colorado History*, 3rd ed. (1972), pp. 151–162, 193–223.

8 Hafen, pp. 270–274.

9 "The Law School—Past and Present," *University of Colorado Alumnus* 19 (December 1929): 4–5, 16; Homer C. Washburn, "Recent Developments Within the College of Pharmacy," 41 (February 1941): 8–9; Hazen W. Kendrick, "Growth of the School of Business, 1906–1941" 41:4–5.

10 For specific criticisms, see C. A. Briggs, "Report on University of Colorado Architecture to Office of Planning" (mimeographed, 1962), pp. 1–2.

11 Colorado, Eighteenth General Assembly, *Session Laws*, 1911, pp. 161–162; see also Minutes of the Regents, August 6 and 7, 1909, pp. 357–359.

12 James H. Baker, "University Administrative Problems Outside of Teaching," National Education Association, *Journal of Proceedings and Addresses* (1910), p. 538; "Appreciation of the Services of James H. Baker, President of the University of Colorado, January 1, 1892, to January 1, 1914," *University of Colorado Bulletin* 14:1 (January 1914): 9.

13 *Colorado Alumnus* 16:2 (February 1926): 3, 9.

14 *Report of James H. Baker to the State Superintendent of Public Schools* (1892), p. 6.

[15] Davis, pp. 91–92; 149–150.

[16] *Fifteenth Biennial Report of the Board of Regents of the University of Colorado, October 1, 1906* (1906), p. 12.

[17] Two of Baker's curriculum reforms which failed were the School of Theology and a School of Social and Home Services.

[18] *Silver and Gold*, September 12, 1895.

[19] *Boulder Daily Camera*, June 2, 1893.

[20] Repplier, p. 50.

[21] *Eighth Biennial Report of the Superintendent of Public Instruction of the State of Colorado, December, 1892* (1892), pp. 801–804.

[22] *Silver and Gold*, February 26, 1912.

[23] Whitehead and Perkin, pp. 135–179.

[24] Minutes of the Regents, April 6, 1892. Under the new arrangement, only the first year of the three-year medical course remained in Boulder.

[25] McGiffert, p. 136.

[26] *University Catalogue, 1892–1893*, p. 37.

[27] Whitehead and Perkin, p. 157.

[28] Abraham Flexner, *Medical Education in the United States and Canada, Bulletin No. 4* (New York: 1910).

[29] *Ibid.*, pp. 197–199.

[30] Whitehead and Perkin, p. 146.

[31] McGiffert, p. 36.

[32] Baker himself was most profoundly influenced by the politically active role assumed by the University of Wisconsin in the early twentieth century under President Charles R. Van Hise. Rudolph, pp. 363–364.

[33] Baker, *Educational Aims and Needs* (1913), pp. 131, 161.

[34] McGiffert, p. 70.

[35] These figures include only those institutions offering full undergraduate programs; they omit more specialized institutions.

[36] The details of these and other intercollegiate conflicts are explained in greater detail in McGiffert, *passim.*

[37] *Rocky Mountain News*, March 2, 1911.

[38] *Fifteenth Biennial Report of the Board of Regents of the University of Colorado, October 1, 1916*, p. 12; see also James H. Baker to Governor John F. Shafroth, May 30, 1911, and Baker to Shafroth, May 31, 1911, Shafroth Papers, State Archives, Denver.

[39] For descriptions of the development of colonial colleges, see Rudolph. For a particularly colorful account of this trend in nineteenth-century frontier areas, see Daniel J. Boorstin, *The Americans: The National Experience* (1965), pp. 152–161.

[40] National Education Association, *Journal of Proceedings and Addresses* (1897), p. 315.

[41] *Boulder Daily Camera*, May 14, 1898.

[42] Henry S. Pritchett to Governor John F. Shafroth, April 20, 1910, Shafroth Papers.

[43] See the discussion of college admissions in Chapter III.

[44] McGiffert, p. 38.

[45] Baker, *Of Himself and Other Things* (1922), pp. 90–91.
[46] Don C. Sowers, "The Tax Problem in Colorado" (1928), p. 35.
[47] *Denver Republican*, January 29, 1899; *ibid.*, June 7, 1899.
[48] Baker, *Of Himself and Other Things*, p. 90.
[49] Colorado, Ninth General Assembly, *Session Laws*, 1893, p. 475.
[50] *Ibid.*, pp. 474–475; Colorado, Tenth General Assembly, *Session Laws*, 1895, p. 113; Colorado, Eleventh General Assembly, *Session Laws*, 1897, p. 93; Minutes of the Regents, June 27, 1899.
[51] "Some Notes on University Statistics," January 20, 1897, pp. 3, 9.
[52] *Boulder Daily Camera*, April 8, 1897.
[53] *Twelfth Biennial Report of the Board of Regents, University of Colorado*, 1900, p. 11.
[54] Colorado, Tenth General Assembly, *Session Laws*, 1895, pp. 237–238.
[55] Minutes of the Regents, April 13, 1898.
[56] *Ibid.*, July 31, 1899.
[57] Governor Charles S. Thomas issued a proclamation on November 17, 1899, authorizing the $70,000 debt. Minutes of the Regents, January 10, 1900.
[58] *Boulder Daily Camera*, July 14, 1899.
[59] Minutes of the Regents, January 21, 1900.
[60] See, for example, Colorado, Thirteenth General Assembly, *Session Laws*, 1901, p. 73; Colorado, Fourteenth General Assembly, *Session Laws*, 1903, p. 466; and Colorado, Fifteenth General Assembly, *Session Laws*, 1905, pp. 109–110.
[61] Minutes of the Regents, April 15, 1903.
[62] *Rocky Mountain News*, January 22, 1913.
[63] *University of Colorado Bulletin* 14:1 (January 1914): 13–14.
[64] Davis, pp. 88–90.
[65] Antoinette Bigelow, "The University in 1910," *Colorado Alumnus* 24 (May 1934), p. 10.
[66] *Silver and Gold*, September 29, 1910; *ibid.*, October 6, 1910; *ibid.*, November 29, 1911.
[67] *Boulder Daily Camera*, October 24–26, 1910.
[68] Baker, "University Reminiscences," *Colorado Alumnus* 14 (February 1924): 23.
[69] Davis, pp. 209–210.
[70] "Fifty Years Sees Traditions Fixed on Colorado Campus," *Colorado Alumnus* 17 (November 1927): 21.
[71] Davis, p. 142.
[72] Minutes of the Regents, January 15, 1904; *ibid.*, April 22, 1914.
[73] Minutes of the Regents, May 30, 1898. Three decades later, there were still no rules regarding tenure. Dr. Jacob Van Ek, former Dean of Arts and Sciences, recalls that as late as the 1930s, he and department chairpersons decided who would be retained. Their discussions were informal, and no dismissals were ever challenged. Oral interview with Jacob Van Ek by Mark Foster, July 18, 1975. Professor J. D. A. Ogilvie, for several years chairman of the Department of English and a member of the faculty from

1930 until 1971, recalls that there were no formal rules for tenure until after Walters F. Dyde became Dean of the Faculty in 1943. Oral interview with J. D. A. Ogilvie by Mark Foster, July 21, 1975.

74 The University Senate Minute Book, February 7, 1908–June 1, 1917, pp. 3–7, 125.

75 Davis, pp. 227–228.

76 *Boulder Daily Camera*, June 1, 1914.

77 *Ibid.*, June 17, 1915.

78 *Denver Post*, July 7, 1915; *Rocky Mountain News*, July 7, 1915.

79 "Report of the Committee of Inquiry Concerning Charges of Violation of Academic Freedom at the University of Colorado, Submitted January 1916," *Bulletin of the American Association of University Professors* (April 1916): 3–70.

80 High as these figures seem, they are small when contrasted to figures for other schools. For example, Harvard lost 40 percent of its students, Yale 35 percent, and Wisconsin 30 percent. Robert L. Kelly, "The American College and the Great War," *Scribner's Magazine* 68 (January 1918): 81.

81 Least of all Norlin himself. See George Norlin to Livingston Farrand, February 9, 1919. Transfiles, President's Office, University of Colorado. Hereafter cited as Transfiles, President's office.

82 *Boulder Daily Camera*, April 10, 1917.

83 *Silver and Gold*, April 24, 1917.

84 Irene P. McKeehan and George Norlin, "The University of Colorado and the War," *Colorado Alumnus* 8 (April 1918): 6.

85 Thomas M. Marshall, "The University of Colorado in Wartime," *University of Colorado Bulletin* 18:10 (October 1918): 4, 8, 9; "Military History of the University of Colorado," *Coloradoan* (1919): 110–111; *Silver and Gold*, December 14, 1917; *Boulder Daily Camera*, May 15, 1918; *ibid.*, September 25, 1918.

86 George Norlin to Wendell Stephens (secretary to the governor), December 17, 1917, Julius C. Gunter Papers, Correspondence 1917, State Archives, Denver.

87 Minutes of the Regents, April 18, 1918; *ibid.*, June 3, 1918.

88 For comparison, see McGiffert, pp. 118–124; Rudolph, pp. 412–416.

89 *Boulder Daily Camera*, September 23, 1918.

90 "Military History of the University," pp. 110–112.

91 *Silver and Gold*, January 31, 1919.

Three

1 *Colorado Alumnus* XXIX (June 1939): 2. The University's growth in enrollments between 1920 and 1940 mirrored the growth in college enrollments nationally. Enrollments grew from just under 600,000 in 1920 to nearly 1,500,000 in 1940. *Yearbook on Higher Education, 1973–74* (1974), p. 490.

[2] George Norlin, "Hitlerism: Why and Whither" (address in Denver, October 1933), in *Things in the Saddle* (1940), pp. 104–123; see also *Fascism and Citizenship* (1940), *passim.*

[3] Dixon Wecter, "A President in Action: George Norlin," *Atlantic Monthly* (June 1939), p. 787.

[4] Norlin had served as Dean of the Graduate School and as acting president for a brief period in 1914 between the administrations of Baker and Farrand.

[5] Norlin to Farrand, February 19, 1919. Transfiles, President's Office.

[6] *Silver and Gold*, February 28, 1919.

[7] Wecter, p. 785.

[8] According to Dr. Jacob Van Ek, longtime intimate of Norlin's, the president refused to set foot on the floor of the legislative chamber. Rather, he would visit Denver, take a room at the University Club, and receive those legislators who desired to make an appointment with him. Interview with Jacob Van Ek by Mark Foster, January 9, 1975. Hereafter cited as Van Ek Interview.

[9] Ralph L. Crosman, "Report on Constitutional Amendment Campaign for the Benefit of Colorado State Supported Institutions of Higher Learning Conducted Immediately Preceding the Election," November 4, 1920 (mimeographed). Transfiles, President's Office.

[10] Dean Van Ek recalled that during their nearly twenty-year intimate working relationship, they were never on a first name basis. Even Mrs. Norlin referred to her husband as Dr. Norlin, at least in the presence of others. Van Ek Interview.

[11] Norlin, "Integrity in Education," address to Colorado Education Association, Denver, November 5, 1925, *Colorado Alumnus* XVI (January 1926): 7–9.

[12] This does not suggest that the University ignored its natural and physical science departments or its professional schools during the Norlin years.

[13] *Colorado Alumnus*, November 1938, p. 5.

[14] "The Campus Beautiful," *Colorado Alumnus*, October 1937, p. 6.

[15] More detailed accounts of the emergence of the Colorado style may be found in "The Campus Beautiful," *Colorado Alumnus*, October 1937, pp. 6–7; and "Architectural Development on the Campus at Boulder" (address by Norlin, June 9, 1940). Transfiles, President's Office.

[16] Minutes of the Regents, April 9, 1918.

[17] *Silver and Gold*, July 13, 1920.

[18] Minutes of the Regents, February 15, 1947.

[19] For an account of the specifications of the Ku Klux Klan against the University, see George Norlin to J. S. Boggs, February 4, 1939, Ralph L. Carr Papers, State Archives, Denver. The mill levy was restored following a ten-year interruption in 1937.

[20] The University of Colorado's share of the mill tax levy had been roughly 40 percent of the funds collected between 1917 and 1926.

[21] *Silver and Gold*, February 11, 1927.

22 *Ibid.*

23 Norlin, "Statement on the Condition and of the Necessities of the University of Colorado," to governor and Twenty-eighth General Assembly, 1930. Transfiles, President's Office.

24 George Norlin to Owen Nelson, May 24, 1920. Transfiles, President's Office.

25 The University's Medical School officials realized that the University's and the state's interests would best be served by moving all instruction and clinical work to Denver. The reasons are too complex to be discussed in detail, but are in Maurice H. Rees, "Report to the President and Board of Regents," 1919. Transfiles, President's Office.

26 Livingston Farrand to George Norlin, February 28, 1919. Transfiles, President's Office.

27 Abraham Flexner, Secretary of General Education Board, Rockefeller Foundation, to George Norlin, November 8, 1920. Transfiles, President's Office.

28 George Norlin to Governor Oliver H. Shoup, January 14, 1921, Shoup Papers, State Archives, Denver; Minutes of the Regents, February 15, 1921.

29 Some $500,000 had to be raised from sources other than those already cited. Most of the remainder came from individual donors. The Carnegie Foundation contributed $100,000; Mrs. Mary Reed gave $120,000; Fred Bonfils' gift of land was appraised at $31,000, etc. Davis, p. 275.

30 *Ibid.*

31 Maurice H. Rees to George Norlin, December 10, 1926. Transfiles, President's Office.

32 The annual grant of $50,000 for maintenance from the Rockefeller Foundation would expire after three years.

33 George Norlin to Governor William E. Sweet, December 18, 1922. Transfiles, President's Office.

34 The legislature generally covered the Medical School and Colorado General Hospital deficits by special appropriations. Interview with Robert Winslow, Budget Director, Colorado General Hospital, by Mark Foster, May 8, 1975. In all likelihood, the necessity of regularly covering Medical School deficits made legislators less friendly toward funding other special needs of the University.

35 Such conflicting ideas are further developed in McGiffert, pp. 173–223.

36 Alfred H. Lloyd to George Norlin, November 4, 1924. Transfiles, President's Office.

37 George Norlin to Alfred H. Lloyd, November 7, 1924. Transfiles, President's Office.

38 "Information Concerning the University of Colorado for the Association of American Universities" (unpublished ms., 1923). Transfiles, President's Office. Report of the Graduate School for the Period 1921–1922, p. 21. Transfiles, President's Office.

39 *Colorado Alumnus*, May 1924, p. 25.

NOTES TO THE TEXT

[40] Davis, p. 404.

[41] Jacob Van Ek to Fred Rost, November 4, 1929, College of Arts and Sciences Files, Hellems Hall, University of Colorado. Hereafter cited as Arts and Sciences Files.

[42] George Norlin to David H. Stevens, March 8, 1937. Transfiles, President's Office.

[43] Davis, pp. 305, 423.

[44] Rudolph, pp. 452–461. For a more extensive analysis of the emergence of honors programs across the country and also at Colorado, see Joseph W. Cohen and Walter D. Weir, "Honors at the University of Colorado" (1957); and Joseph W. Cohen (ed.), *The Superior Student in American Higher Education* (1966).

[45] Van Ek, "The Honors Plan" (undated ms.). Arts and Sciences Files.

[46] *Silver and Gold*, May 2, 1932.

[47] Cohen (ed.), *The Superior Student*, p. 21.

[48] History Department memo to Dr. James F. Willard, Honors Committee, April 5, 1930. Arts and Sciences Files.

[49] George R. Waggoner, "Departmental Honors at the University of Kansas," in Cohen (ed.), *The Superior Student*, p. 142.

[50] Cohen and Weir, "A Brief Account of Honors at Colorado" (mimeographed report, 1956), p. 44, in possession of Van Ek.

[51] Van Ek (untitled ms., ca. 1938). Arts and Sciences Files.

[52] For example, see *Denver Post*, January 4 and 7, 1922; *Rocky Mountain News*, April 11, 1924.

[53] Davis, pp. 328–330.

[54] *Ibid.*, pp. 324–331.

[55] *Silver and Gold*, May 22, 1928.

[56] *Ibid.*, December 6, 1927.

[57] *Ibid.*, October 19, 1920.

[58] *Ibid.*, December 12, 1930.

[59] *Ibid.*, February 14, 1933; February 27, 1934.

[60] *Ibid.*, October 16, 1931.

[61] *Ibid.*, September 18, 1934.

[62] Interview with Harry Carlson by Mark Foster, October 11, 1974, hereafter cited as Carlson Interview; *Silver and Gold*, March 11, 1932.

[63] Carlson Interview.

[64] *Silver and Gold*, June 2, 1931. The administration did not believe students mature enough to run their own affairs again until 1937.

[65] *Rocky Mountain News*, February 22, 1939; Minutes of the Regents, March 3, 1939.

[66] *Silver and Gold*, November 15, 1932.

[67] For a longer discussion of these incidents, see Davis, pp. 414–417.

[68] Theodore D. A. Cockerell to George Norlin, quoted in *University of Colorado Studies: Series in Bibliography #1* (1965), p. 5.

[69] Minutes of the Regents, March 9, 1920.

[70] Several hundred "position description" forms for 1938 are located in the Teller Ammons Papers, Colorado State Archives, Denver.

[71] Francis Wolle, "Position Description," 1938; and Edna Romig, "Position Description," 1938. Ammons Papers.

[72] Wecter, p. 787.

[73] Etta M. Gibson to Jacob Van Ek, July 9, 1937. Arts and Sciences Files.

[74] Charles N. Meador to George Norlin, August 31, 1917. Transfiles, President's Office.

[75] Many letters to Norlin demonstrated this fact. See, for example, Dr. Walter C. Toepelman to George Norlin, July 5, 1920; Dr. F. G. Emerson to Frederick B. R. Hellems, June 26, 1920. Transfiles, President's Office.

[76] McGiffert, p. 163.

[77] Norlin to Shoup, September 23, 1919. Transfiles, President's Office.

[78] Minutes of the Regents, November 21, 1919.

[79] Norlin to Sweet, October 8, 1924, Sweet Papers, State Archives, Denver.

[80] It would have been unrealistic to expect Colorado to compete with top professional salaries at such prestigious and "established" universities as Chicago, Harvard, Columbia, and Michigan, all of which had a top salary of $8,000. The study did, however, point out such extreme differentials. Cynical state legislators may have been less than fully persuaded by Colorado's study, which compared university salaries only with those of a number of top private universities and those of 26 carefully *selected* state universities (see "Statistics of State Universities, 1921," mimeographed. Transfiles, President's Office).

[81] Minutes of the Regents, December 17, 1926.

[82] Van Ek Interview; Wecter, p. 787.

[83] Donald M. Bennett to Oliver C. Lester, March 21, 1922; and Bennett to George Norlin, July 29, 1922. Transfiles, President's Office.

[84] Colin B. Goodykoontz, faculty personnel records (inactive file, reel 14), Regent Hall; Van Ek, faculty personnel records (inactive file, reels 3-7), Regent Hall.

[85] *Colorado Alumnus,* March 1935, p. 12.

[86] Wecter, p. 798.

[87] Van Ek Interview.

[88] *Colorado Yearbook, 1939-1940,* p. 10.

[89] Ubbelohde, Benson, and Smith, pp. 301-302.

[90] *Colorado Yearbook, 1941-1942,* p. 91. For an analysis of Colorado's economy during the 1930s, see James F. Wickens, "Colorado in the Great Depression: A Study in New Deal Politics" (Ph.D. dissertation, University of Denver, 1964).

[91] *Thirty-first Biennial Report of the Board of Regents, 1936-1938,* p. 5. Of all major areas of state expenditures, public education was the *only* area showing an actual decline in dollar expenditure between 1930 and 1939. State funding for all educational institutions declined from $4,040,000 to $3,861,000 during the 1930s.

[92] *Colorado Yearbook, 1939-1940,* p. 143.

[93] Minutes of the Regents, April 19, 1929; May 25, 1934; and April 29, 1938.

[94] Norlin recalled, some years later, that Morley promised the University what it wanted in the way of funding "provided the University would dismiss from its staff all Catholics and all Jews." The University "preferred to do without that support." George Norlin to J. S. Boggs, February 4, 1939. Transfiles, President's Office.

[95] *Silver and Gold*, August 10, 1920, and February 11, 1938.

[96] Norlin, "The American Public and Education" (mimeographed), address to Boulder Chamber of Commerce, January 5, 1932, Norlin Papers, University Archives, Norlin Library, University of Colorado.

[97] *Colorado Alumnus*, May 1933, p. 8.

[98] *Silver and Gold*, February 11, 1938.

[99] Lester W. Cole to George Norlin, April 3, 1927. Transfiles, President's Office.

[100] *Silver and Gold*, January 22, 1937.

[101] George Norlin to J. P. McKelvie, State Budget and Efficiency Commission, August 24, 1936, Edwin C. Johnson Papers, State Archives, Denver.

[102] Rees to Norlin, January 4, 1939. Transfiles, President's Office.

[103] Ralph Ellsworth to Regents, May 4, 1939. Transfiles, President's Office.

[104] Ellsworth to Robert L. Stearns, September 14, 1939. Transfiles, President's Office.

[105] In November 1933, the Regents considered closing the school, since it was producing a budget deficit of $150,000. Minutes of the Regents, November 17, 1933.

[106] Alan Gregg, Director of General Education Board, Rockefeller Foundation, to Maurice H. Rees, January 20, 1936. Transfiles, President's Office.

[107] Rees to Norlin, January 6, 1938. Transfiles, President's Office.

[108] *Silver and Gold*, March 3, 1939.

[109] By the end of January, the state treasurer had temporarily impounded all funds intended for the University, and Norlin admitted that unless they were released the University would have to close on March 1. Although the funds were released eventually, the University came within a matter of days of being forced to close.

[110] *Silver and Gold*, January 13, 1939.

[111] "Statement Showing Cost and Source of Funds for New Buildings Constructed and Under Construction from 1933 to Date," June 1939 (mimeographed). Transfiles, President's Office.

[112] Edward D. Foster, Denver Director, Colorado State Planning Commission, to Waldo E. Brockway, December 2, 1938. Transfiles, President's Office.

[113] "Statement Showing Cost and Source of Funds for New Buildings." Transfiles, President's Office.

[114] *Ibid.*

[115] For a good survey of the development of interuniversity relations in Colorado between 1860 and 1940, see McGiffert, *passim.*

[116] *Ibid.,* pp. x–xii, Tables I and II.

[117] Minutes of the Regents, February 15, 1921; see also *Colorado Alumnus,* February 1921, pp. 1–2.

[118] Frederick B. R. Hellems, H. M. Barrett, and Don C. Sowers, "A Formal Statement from the University Committee on Junior Colleges," February 1927. Arts and Sciences Files.

[119] *Colorado Alumnus,* December 1927, p. 9.

[120] Norlin, "Education and the Economic Crisis" (mimeographed, radio address presented over KOA Radio, May 5, 1932), Norlin Papers.

[121] For a colorful, though biased, account of the old-age pension plan's history, see O. Otto Moore, *Mile High Harbor* (1947).

[122] *Denver Post,* November 1, 1936.

[123] Farnsworth Crowder, "Who Pays the Pension?," *Survey Geographic,* July 1938, p. 378.

[124] Minutes of the Regents, February 18, 1938.

[125] For example, see "Campaign Handbook," Federation for Workable Old-Age Pensions, Inc., in Rudolph Johnson Papers, Box 6, Western History Collection, University of Colorado.

[126] See *The Bulletin* of the National Annuity League (NAL), May 12, 1938; also *Bulletin,* June 23, July 7, July 14, July 21, and July 28, 1838.

[127] *The Bulletin,* June 23, 1938.

[128] As evidence of the NAL's strength, when the old-age pension amendment repeal vote was counted in November 1938, the pensioners won by an even larger margin than in 1936—in spite of the combined opposition of most influential newspapers, the Colorado and Denver Chambers of Commerce, etc.

[129] Jacob Van Ek to Jesse H. Newton, January 3, 1923. Arts and Sciences Files.

[130] John C. Unger, Superintendent of Schools, Hugo, Colorado, to Jacob Van Ek, February 23, 1933. Arts and Sciences Files.

[131] *Silver and Gold,* November 29, 1932.

[132] Unger to Van Ek, February 23, 1933. Arts and Sciences Files.

[133] *Rocky Mountain News,* June 1–4, 11, 1939.

[134] Minutes of the Regents, May 2, 1939.

[135] Norlin to Stearns, May 26, 1940. Transfiles, President's Office.

[136] *Twenty-second Biennial Report of the Board of Regents, 1918–1920,* p. 45. *Thirty-second Biennial Report of the Board of Regents, 1938–1940,* p. 23.

Four

[1] Speeches File, Robert L. Stearns Papers, University Archives, University of Colorado.

[2] *Denver Post,* September 8, 1939. Also *Colorado Alumnus,* October

1939; *Rocky Mountain News,* September 9, 1939; and the Oral History Interview with Robert L. Stearns by John A. Brennan, March 28, 1969, Stearns Papers. Hereafter cited as Stearns Interview.

[3] Minutes of the Regents, December 8, 1939; also January 19, February 16, May 23, and October 4, 1940. Also *Denver Post,* December 8, 1939, and January 19, 1940; *Rocky Mountain News,* December 8 and 9, 1939.

[4] *Denver Post,* November 25 and 26, 1940.

[5] *Ibid.,* November 2, 1940. The agreement is in the Minutes of the Regents, November 1, 1941.

[6] Report of the University of Colorado Coordinating Committee on National Defense, December 20, 1940, World War II File. Transfiles, President's Office. For a discussion of the "History in the Making" series, see the Oral History Interview with Jacob Van Ek by Philip I. Mitterling, December 1974, Oral History Collection, University Archives. Hereafter cited as Van Ek Interview. Also *Silver and Gold,* September 24 and October 8, 1940.

[7] *Silver and Gold,* May 22, 1940. Also October 18, 1940.

[8] *Ibid.,* October 7, 1941. Also the Report of the Committee on Education and National Defense, 1942, World War II File. Transfiles, President's Office.

[9] *Ibid.,* December 9 and 12, 1941.

[10] *Ibid.,* April 3 and March 24, 1942; Minutes of the Regents, January 16, February 26, March 10, and March 20, 1942. On Japanese-American relocation see Jacobus ten Broeck, Edward N. Barnhart, and Floyd W. Matson, *Prejudice, War and the Constitution* (1954), and Roger Daniels, *Concentration Camps USA: Japanese Americans and World War II* (1972).

[11] Stearns Interview; and the Oral History Interview with Morris Judd by Philip I. Mitterling, November 1974, Oral History Collection, University Archives. Hereafter cited as Judd Interview. Also W. F. Dyde to Robert L. Stearns, July 23, 1943, and Dyde to Stearns, May 20, 1943, in the Stearns-Dyde Correspondence, 1942 and 1943, Stearns Papers. Additional reminiscences concerning the Japanese Language School are in the Oral History Interview with Morris Garnsey by Philip I. Mitterling, September 1974, Oral History Collection, University Archives. Hereafter cited as Garnsey Interview.

[12] Davis, p. 457. Also *Silver and Gold,* January 12 and July 1, 1943; and Robert L. Stearns' Letter to Friends, Students and Prospective Students of the University of Colorado, July 28, 1943, World War II File. Transfiles, President's Office.

[13] Robert L. Stearns to W. F. Dyde, October 5, 1942, in the World War II File. Transfiles, President's Office. E. Ray Campbell to Stearns, January 8, 1944; Brigadier General Byron Gates to the Secretary of the Board of Regents, August 12, 1943; Stearns to Lt. Col. W. B. Leach, August 18, 1943; Brigadier General Lauris Norstad to the Board of Regents, February 12, 1945, all in the Stearns File. Transfiles, President's Office; and the Stearns Interview.

[14] *Rocky Mountain News,* March 15, 1944. Also *Silver and Gold,* March

17, 1944; *Denver Post,* March 15, 1944; *Boulder Daily Camera,* March 15, 1944.

[15] See *Silver and Gold,* March 17, 1944; *Denver Post,* March 18 and 19, 1944; *Rocky Mountain News,* March 18, 1944; and *Boulder Daily Camera,* March 17, 1944.

[16] Minutes of the Regents, March 17, 1944. Also *Denver Post,* March 17, 1944; *Boulder Daily Camera,* March 17, 1944.

[17] *Silver and Gold,* March 24 and 28, 1944; and Report of the Committee on Convocations and Lectures of the University Senate to the President of the University of Colorado, Convocations File. Transfiles, President's Office.

[18] Minutes of the Regents, April 22, 1944; *Silver and Gold,* April 25, 1944.

[19] Reuben G. Gustavson to Dean Jacob Van Ek, June 14, 1945, Files of Jacob Van Ek, University of Colorado. Hereafter cited as Van Ek Files. Also the Minutes of the Regents, May 25, 1945.

[20] Reuben G. Gustavson to Robert L. Stearns, May 29, 1945; and Merritt H. Perkins to Stearns, May 28, 1945, Stearns File. Transfiles, President's Office; and the Garnsey Interview. Also Perkins to Gustavson, July 5, 1945, Van Ek Files.

[21] Reuben G. Gustavson to Robert L. Stearns, May 29, 1945, Stearns File. Transfiles, President's Office. And Minutes of the Regents, May 25, 1945.

[22] W. E. Brockway to Robert L. Stearns, June 1, 1945; and draft of the letter from Stearns to Merritt Perkins, June 1, 1945, Stearns File. Transfiles, President's Office. See also Reuben G. Gustavson to Dean Jacob Van Ek, June 14, 1945, Van Ek Files; Warren Raeder, Norman A. Parker, and Carl W. Borgmann to Robert L. Stearns, June 4, 1945, Minutes of the Regents, July 20, 1945; *Rocky Mountain News,* July 7, 1945; *Silver and Gold,* July 13, 1945.

[23] Minutes of the Regents, July 20, 1945.

[24] *Ibid.,* July 27, 1945; *Silver and Gold,* July 31, 1945.

[25] See Report of the Committee of Five; Report to the President from the Committee appointed to make recommendations for the deanship of the Graduate School, May 1946, both in the Van Ek Files; Minutes of the Regents, May 31, 1946.

[26] Minutes of the Regents, June 7, 1946; statement of the Regents Sub-Committee to the Committee of Five, n.d., Van Ek Files; AAUP Chapter Minutes, May 19, 1945, American Association of University Professors Papers, University Archives. See the Oral History Interview with Carl Borgmann by Philip I. Mitterling, December 1974, Oral History Collection, University Archives. Also the Oral History Interview with John W. Bartram by Philip I. Mitterling, November 1974, *ibid.* Hereafter cited as Bartram Interview.

[27] Maurice H. Rees to Robert L. Stearns, May 20, 1943; Medical School Files. Transfiles, President's Office. See also Ward Darley to the Executive Faculty, University of Colorado School of Medicine, November 6, 1944,

Reports, vol. 2, 1940–46, Archives, Denison Library, Medical Center, University of Colorado. Hereafter cited as Darley Report.

[28] Rees to Stearns, May 20, 1943; and the Officers of the Sophomore Class to R. G. Gustavson, June 11, 1944, Medical School Files. Transfiles, President's Office.

[29] Public Policy Committee of the Colorado Medical Society, et al., to R. G. Gustavson, August 14, 1943, *House of Delegates Confidential Handbook, Seventy-fourth Annual Session, Colorado State Medical Society, September 27, 28, and 29, 1944*, in Reports, vol. 2, 1940–46 (hereafter cited as *Handbook*); Minutes of the Regents, October 15, November 19, and December 17, 1943, January 21, March 17, and May 23, 1944. Also Maurice H. Rees to Reuben G. Gustavson, November 22, 1943; Gustavson to Charles B. Sinclair, December 3, 1943; F. E. Wilson to Gustavson, December 13, 1943; Gustavson to Dr. Lyman Mason, November 30, 1943; Gustavson to Deane W. Malott, January 11, 1944; and Gustavson to Rees, February 28, 1944, all in the Medical School Files. Transfiles, President's Office.

[30] See Maurice H. Rees to Reuben G. Gustavson, n.d.; Rees to Gustavson, May 25, 1944; Rees to Gustavson, June 19, 1944; Gustavson to Rees, June 29, 1944, Medical School Files. Transfiles, President's Office; Minutes of the Regents, July 28 and August 18, 1944; and Gustavson to Dr. Bradford Murphey, August 4, 1944, in the *Handbook, 1944*. Also Rees to Murphey, August 7, 1944, *ibid.*

[31] Public Policy Committee of the Colorado State Medical Society, et al., to Dr. Reuben G. Gustavson, August 30, 1944, *Handbook*, 1944. Also Darley Report.

[32] Robert C. Lewis, et al., to Maurice H. Rees, August 16, 1944, Minutes of the Regents, September 15, 1944; *ibid.*, August 18, 1944, January 19, and February 16, 1945; Reuben Gustavson to Bernard B. Longwell, et al., December 11, 1944; and Report of the Special Committee on Private Practice and Consultation Work on the Part of Full-Time Members of the School of Medicine Faculty, to be presented at the Regular Meetings of the Executive Faculty on January 16 and February 6, 1945, both in Reports, vol. 2, 1940–46; Gustavson to Rees, May 17, 1945; and Robert L. Stearns to Dr. E. R. Mugrage, August 10, 1945, Medical School Files. Transfiles, President's Office. Also the *House of Delegates Confidential Handbook, Seventy-fifth Annual Session, Colorado State Medical Society, September 19, 20, and 21, 1945*, in Reports, vol. 2, 1940–46.

[33] Ward Darley to Robert L. Stearns, August 13, 1946, in Minutes of the Regents, August 23, 1946; *ibid.*, December 20, 1947. Also the Oral History Interview with Ward Darley by Philip I. Mitterling, July 1974, Ward Darley Collection, University Archives, University of Colorado. Hereafter cited as Darley Interview.

[34] Darley Report; Committee Report, Post-Graduate Medical Training, at the University of Colorado School of Medicine and Hospitals, December 4, 1944; Report of the Health Representative Post-War Advisory Committee, February 16, 1945, both in Reports, vol. 2, 1940–46. Also Ward Dar-

ley to the Boettcher Foundation, March 3, 1948, Medical School Files. Transfiles, President's Office.

[35] Darley Report; Report of the Health Representative Post-War Advisory Committee, February 16, 1945, Reports, vol. 2, 1940–46. Also Report of the Special Committee for the Study of Problems of the School of Medicine, February 6, 1945, *ibid.*

[36] Henry Swan (ed.), "Medical Education: Undergraduate Curriculum, University of Colorado, School of Medicine, October 15, 1949," Curriculum, School of Medicine, Archives, Denison Library; and "Medical Education in Colorado, University of Colorado School of Medicine, Progress Report, January 1942–January 1947," Reports, vol. 2, 1940–46, *ibid.*

[37] *Ibid.* Also Harriet Hunter, "Psychiatric Liaison Work: A Twelve-Year Survey," *ibid.*

[38] *Ibid.* Also Annual Report of the Director to the Board of Control of the Child Research Council, October 1946, Reports, vol. 2, 1940–46, *ibid.*

[39] Contract with the City and County of Denver, Medical School Files. Transfiles, President's Office; Ward Darley, "Medical Education in Colorado, July 1947–June 1949," Reports, 1947–49. Hereafter cited as Darley, "Medical Education." See also Report of the President and Staff to the Directors of the Commonwealth Fund, n.d.; Medical Education, University of Colorado, Medical Center and Denver Bureau of Health and Hospitals—Demonstration and Teaching Comprehensive Medical Care, January 1951, Medical School Files. Transfiles, President's Office; and "A Program for the Medical Care of the Indigent of Denver, Colorado, 1951," City of Denver, University of Colorado, Amalgamation of Hospital and Other Services, Archives, Denison Library.

[40] Darley, "Medical Education"; Darley to Emory W. Morris, November 5, 1946, Reports, vol. 2, 1940–46; Benjamin G. Horning to Darley, January 23, 1947; Darley to Horning, February 1, 1947; Frode Jensen to P. G. Worcester, November 1, 1948; Worcester, et al., to Robert L. Stearns, November 23, 1948; and Darley to Stearns, May 5, 1949, all in the Medical School Files. Transfiles, President's Office.

[41] All of these activities are outlined in Darley, "Medical Education." See also Darley to Robert L. Stearns, August 22 and 27, 1947, Medical School Files. Transfiles, President's Office; H. Mason Morfit, "Historical Notes on the Development of Bonfils Tumor Clinic," *Department of Surgery Newsletter*, vol. 2 (July 10, 1957); and Darley Interview.

[42] Ward Darley to the Boettcher Foundation, March 3, 1948, Medical School Files. Transfiles, President's Office.

[43] Darley, "Medical Education." Also Theodore T. Puck to Ward Darley, January 21, 1950, Medical School Files. Transfiles, President's Office.

[44] Darley, "Medical Education"; An Explanation of the Financial Needs of the School of Medicine of the University of Colorado for the 1947–49 Biennial Period; Report to the Executive Faculty by the Committee on the Budget and Fiscal Policy, January 18, 1949; Robert C. Lewis to Robert L. Stearns, May 22, 1950; Budget and Fiscal Policy Committee to the Executive Faculty, May 14, 1952; and Ward Darley, "A Proposal that the Principle of

Merit Salary Increases Be Established at the University of Colorado School of Medicine," n.d., all in the Medical School Files. Transfiles, President's Office. Also the Legislative Bulletin to all members of the faculty and staff, January 7, 1947, Legislature File, *ibid.*

45 Correspondence and other documents concerning these plans are in the Medical School Files. Transfiles, President's Office. See Ward Darley to Robert L. Stearns, April 30, 1949; Darley to Stearns, May 3, 1949; Summary of Conference on Regional Cooperation in Medical Education, November 2, 1949; Darley to Senator Eugene Milliken, August 3, 1951; Darley to Dean Joseph C. Hinsey, September 24, 1951; and Stearns to George D. Humphrey, October 23, 1952.

46 Minutes of the Regents, July 9, 1947; Robert L. Stearns to Lee Knous, June 30, 1949, *ibid.*, June 29, 1949; John W. Bartram to President Stearns, October 16, 1952, Medical School Files. Transfiles, President's Office. Also Darley, "Medical Education."

47 John W. Metzger to Homer F. Bedford, et al., May 3, 1949; Robert L. Stearns, "A few observations on the subject of our relationships with other state departments," July 20, 1949; Harold A. Thomson to John W. Bartram, August 26, 1949; Charles D. Bromley to Robert L. Stearns, January 10, 1953, all in the Legal-Civil Service File. Transfiles, President's Office. Also Bartram Interview; *Denver Post*, July 19, 1949; *Silver and Gold*, June 23, July 1, August 2, October 6, October 13, 1949, and January 6, 1950.

48 Legislative Bulletin to all members of the faculty and staffs, January 7, 1947, Legislature File. Transfiles, President's Office; and "So *You're* Having Troubles, Mr. Legislator? Well . . . We're Having Ours, Too!," University Bulletin, 1946, Reports, vol. 2, 1940–46.

49 Legislative Bulletin to all members of the faculty and staffs, January 7, 1947; Robert L. Stearns to Alumni and Friends of the University of Colorado, January 31, 1947; Legislative Bulletin No. II (Confidential), March 6, 1947; and the Memorandum Concerning the Income Tax Fight in the Thirty-sixth General Assembly, March 26, 1947, all in the Legislature File. Transfiles, President's Office. Also *Silver and Gold*, January 31, February 7, and April 18, 1947.

50 See the W. F. Dyde and S. M. Hill Memorandum to President Stearns, September 14, 1950; S. M. Hill Memorandum to President Stearns, August 2, 1950; W. F. Dyde Memorandum to President Stearns, September 13, 1950; W. F. Dyde Memorandum to President Stearns, January 25, 1951; W. F. Dyde Memorandum to President Stearns, December 13, 1951, in the Legislature File. Transfiles, President's Office; *Silver and Gold*, January 6, 1950, March 29, November 15, 1951, and February 12, 1952. Also Minutes of the Regents, January 21, 1949.

51 See *Silver and Gold*, September 25, 1945, January 4, and March 15, 1946. Also Robert L. Stearns to Joseph P. Tufts, September 12, 1945; the Statement Concerning University of Colorado Veteran Student Trailer-Housing Project, October 1, 1945; W. E. Brockway to Marshall W. Amis, December 27, 1945; and Leo W. Rector to Stearns, November 24, 1945, in the Housing File. Transfiles, President's Office; and Davis, pp. 520–523.

52 *Silver and Gold,* March 22, 1946, and July 9, 1948; Minutes of the Regents, January 17, 1947. See also W. E. Brockway to Trautwein & Howard, November 25, 1945; and the draft of a letter to the People of the State of Colorado, n.d., Housing File. Transfiles, President's Office; Davis, pp. 520–523.

53 See *Silver and Gold,* October 28 and 31, 1947; Minutes of the Regents, September 4, September 22, and November 21, 1947, March 16, 1948; Davis, pp. 526–527.

54 See the report of the King Committee in Minutes of the Regents, August 23, 1946; Oral History Interview with Wesley Brittin by Philip I. Mitterling, November 1974, Oral History Collection, University Archives. Hereafter cited as Brittin Interview. See also Davis, pp. 523–525.

55 Robert L. Stearns to W. C. Duvall, et al., June 21, 1947, Research File. Transfiles, President's Office. Also W. F. Dyde to Paul Dean, October 30, 1947. Chemistry File. *Ibid.*; Oral History Interview with Stanley Cristol by Philip I. Mitterling, October 1974, Oral History Collection, University Archives. Hereafter cited as Cristol Interview.

56 See C. P. Malick to W. F. Dyde, May 7, 1945; P. G. Worcester to Robert L. Stearns, July 26, 1945, Graduate School File. Transfiles, President's Office; Minutes of the Regents, March 16, 1951; Oral History Interview with Eugene Wilson by Philip I. Mitterling, November 1974, Oral History Collection, University Archives.

57 See the Graduate School Report, September 12, 1952; P. G. Worcester to W. F. Dyde, February 2, 1948; and Graduate School Report, 1949, all in the Graduate School File. Transfiles, President's Office.

58 Cristol Interview; Atomic Energy Research Project in the Chemistry Department of the University of Colorado, n.d., Atomic Energy Commission File. Transfiles, President's Office.

59 Brittin Interview.

60 See "The High Altitude Observatory of Harvard University and the University of Colorado," n.d.; Donald H. Menzel, "The High Altitude Observatory of Harvard University and the University of Colorado," n.d.; Harlow Shapley to R. G. Gustavson, February 3, 1945, all in the High Altitude Observatory File. Transfiles, President's Office. Also Shapley to Robert L. Stearns, August 7, 1945, Minutes of the Regents, August 21, 1945.

61 Reuben G. Gustavson to Robert L. Stearns, February 19, 1945; Stearns to Harlow Shapley, August 22, 1945; J. Churchill Owen and Peter H. Holme to Stearns, September 17, 1945; Donald H. Menzel to Stearns, February 5, 1947; Menzel to Stearns, June 25, 1947; Stearns to Menzel, January 10, 1948; High Altitude Observatory, summary of ideas developed in conference at the Denver Club, August 29, 1950; and Walter Orr Roberts to W. F. Dyde, May 2, 1951, all in the High Altitude Observatory File. Transfiles, President's Office.

62 *Silver and Gold,* March 4 and 7, 1947. See also *Denver Post,* March 3, 1947; and Minutes of the Regents, February 3, 1948. Davis has detailed the University's record in the Big Six in *Glory Colorado!* pp. 565–574.

63 For details of the AYD controversy see *Silver and Gold,* November

22 and 26, 1946; January 10, February 11, February 14, and February 18, 1947. Also Minutes of the Regents, March 21, 1947.

64 *Silver and Gold*, March 28, 1947.

65 Senate Committee on Faculty Privilege and Tenure, Transcript of Hearings in the Matter of Professor David Hawkins, University of Colorado, March–April, 1951, Privilege and Tenure Committee Files, President's Office. Hereafter cited as Hawkins Hearing. See also Eighty-first Congress, Second Session, *Hearings Before the Committee on Un-American Activities of the House of Representatives*, December 20, 21, and 22, 1950; *Denver Post*, January 28, 1951; Carey McWilliams, "The Case of David Hawkins," *The Nation* 172 (March 10, 1951): 228; Oral History Interview with David Hawkins by Philip I. Mitterling, November 1974, Oral History Collection, University Archives. Hereafter cited as Hawkins Interview.

66 *Denver Post*, January 29, 1951. Also *Silver and Gold*, January 30, 1951.

67 *Denver Post*, January 30, 1951; *Rocky Mountain News*, February 1, 1951.

68 Minutes of the Regents, February 2, 1951; *Boulder Daily Camera*, February 6, 1951; *Silver and Gold*, February 2 and March 8, 1951. Also George R. Stewart, *The Year of the Oath: The Fight for Academic Freedom at the University of California* (1950).

69 Minutes of the Regents, February 2, 1951; *Boulder Daily Camera*, February 7, 1951; *Rocky Mountain News*, February 1, 1951; *Silver and Gold*, February 8, 1951; Robert M. MacIver, *Academic Freedom In Our Time* (1955), p. 299; Report of a Conference of Six with President Stearns, February 13, 1951, AAUP, President's File, 1948–1959, Correspondence, University Archives.

70 Minutes of the Regents, February 16, 1951. Also *Denver Post*, February 1, 1951; MacIver, pp. 290–295.

71 See the Memorandum for the General Secretary of the American Association of University Professors on the investigation at the University of Colorado. Prepared by Professor Calvin Grieder, president of the University of Colorado Chapter, AAUP, February 23, 1951, AAUP File, University Archives; *Rocky Mountain News*, February 3, 1951; *Denver Post*, February 15, 1951; and MacIver, p. 292.

72 Hawkins Hearing. See the committee's report as it was published in the *Denver Post*, April 22, 1951. Also Hawkins Interview.

73 *Denver Post*, April 22, 1951.

74 Transcript of Final Hearing in the Matter of Professor David Hawkins, May 11, 1951, Privilege and Tenure Committee Files, President's Office. See also *Denver Post*, May 11 and 13, 1951; *Silver and Gold*, May 15, 1951; and *Rocky Mountain News*, May 12, 1951.

75 Paul Dean to Irving Goodman, February 7, 1951; Robert L. Stearns to Captain R. O. Myers, September 11, 1947; and Dean to Goodman, March 14, 1951, all in the Files, President's Office.

76 RLS, Confidential Memorandum, April 26, 1951, *ibid*. Also Jacob Van Ek to Stearns, August 8, 1951, Van Ek Files.

[77] Irving Goodman to Paul Dean, May 2, 1951; Goodman to Robert L. Stearns and Jacob Van Ek (telegram), May 22, 1951; Goodman to Stearns, May 25, 1951; and Stearns to Goodman, June 2, 1951, Files, President's Office.

[78] Summary of Hutchinson-Hafer Report according to the Regents of the University of Colorado by Robert L. Stearns, president, June 29, 1951, *ibid*. Also Minutes of the Regents, June 29, 1951; *Silver and Gold*, July 3, 1951; *Denver Post*, June 29, 1951.

[79] *Boulder Daily Camera*, July 29, 1951.

[80] Jacob Van Ek to Robert L. Stearns, August 8, 1951, Van Ek Files; and Dudley Wynn to Stearns, July 28, 1951, Files of Morris Judd, Greeley, Colorado. Hereafter cited as Judd Files. See also Dudley Wynn to Leo Koutouzos, Albuquerque, February 22, 1954, Joseph Cohen Papers, Western History Collection, University of Colorado.

[81] *Silver and Gold*, December 11, 1951. Also Judd Interview; review of the Judd case in Cohen Papers.

[82] See the chronology of the Judd case; Robert L. Stearns to the Privilege and Tenure Committee, April 22, 1952, in the Judd Files.

[83] Minutes of the Regents, August 10, 1951.

[84] W. F. Dyde to Morris A. Judd, August 11, 1951, Judd Files; Edward J. Machle to Robert L. Stearns, November 27, 1951, Cohen Papers; Machle to Stearns, December 17, 1951, Minority Report, Privilege and Tenure Committee, May 20, 1952, Privilege and Tenure Committee Files. Faculty Council, University Archives.

[85] Morris A. Judd to the University Senate Committee on Academic Privilege and Tenure, January 11, 1952; Henry W. Ehrmann to Morris A. Judd, January 11, 1952; Robert L. Stearns to the Committee on Privilege and Tenure, April 22, 1952, all in the Judd Files. Also Garnsey Interview; MacIver, pp. 296–297.

[86] Robert L. Stearns to the Committee on Privilege and Tenure, March 12, 1952, Judd Files. Also Ralph Himstead to Henry W. Ehrmann, February 18, 1952, *ibid*.

[87] Minutes of the Senate, April 2, 1952, Judd Files; also Minutes of the Regents, June 3, 1953.

[88] Robert L. Stearns to the Committee on Privilege and Tenure, April 22, 1952, Judd Files; Archibald Buchanan, et al., to Robert L. Stearns, May 19, 1952, Privilege and Tenure Committee Files. Faculty Council, University Archives; Minority Report, Privilege and Tenure Committee.

[89] Minutes of the Regents, May 16, 1952; *Silver and Gold*, May 20 and 23, 1952; Burton L. Jones to Robert L. Stearns, May 23, 1952, AAUP, President's File, Correspondence, 1948–1959, University Archives; *Boulder Daily Camera*, June 3, 1952.

[90] Ralph Himstead to Eugene H. Wilson, July 28 and 29, 1952; Wilson to Himstead, August 7, 1952, in the files of Eugene Wilson, Boulder. Also the *AAUP Bulletin* 42 (Spring 1956): 69.

[91] Robert L. Stearns to the Board of Regents, September 2, 1952, Minutes of the Regents, September 2, 1952.

[92] *Denver Post,* February 15 and March 11, 1953; *Colorado Daily,* February 17 and March 11, 1953; *Rocky Mountain News,* March 10 and 11, 1953; and *Boulder Daily Camera,* March 11, 1953. Also the letter from Robert W. Albright in the Senate Committee on Faculty Personnel, Committee Document, n.d., Privilege and Tenure Committee Files. Faculty Council, University Archives.

[93] *Denver Post,* March 13, 14, 15, and 16, 1953; *Rocky Mountain News,* March 14 and 15, 1953; *Colorado Daily,* March 12, 1953. The limerick was recalled by Professor Byron Johnson.

[94] *Denver Post,* March 20, 1953; *Rocky Mountain News,* March 20, 1953; *Colorado Daily,* March 19, 1953; Minutes of the Regents, March 20, 1953.

[95] H. Vance Austin to Philip I. Mitterling, January 21, 1975, author's personal files; and Eugene Milliken to Robert L. Stearns, April 28, 1953, Files, President's Office.

Five

[1] Colorado State Planning Division, *Colorado Year Book, 1962–1964* (1964), pp. 373–379, 855. Also John G. Wells, "Behind Colorado's Growth," *Colorado Quarterly* 10 (Spring 1962): 347–364.

[2] Colorado State Planning Division, *Colorado Year Book, 1956–1958* (1958), 589–590, 711; *Colorado Year Book, 1962–1964,* pp. 620–623.

[3] Colorado State Planning Division, *Colorado Year Book, 1962–1964,* pp. 900–901. Also William H. Miernyk, Ernest R. Bonner, John H. Chapman, Jr., and Kenneth Shellhammer, "The Impact of Space and Space-Related Activities on a Local Economy: A Case Study of Boulder, Colorado," Part I, "The Input-Output Analysis" (1965), pp. 6–7; City of Boulder, "Public Facilities Plan and Capital Improvements Program, 1963–1985," (1963), pp. 1–9, 34–36.

[4] Miernyk, Bonner, Chapman, and Shellhammer, pp. 6–7.

[5] Colorado State Planning Division, *Colorado Year Book, 1962–1964,* p. 418. These figures for the Boulder campus differ slightly from those in the University of Colorado, Office of Admissions, "Enrollment Statistics, 1950–1965." Furthermore, the State Planning Division does not consider the impact of changing enrollments at the Denver medical campus, or the extension centers in Denver and Colorado Springs.

[6] Curriculum Vitae, Ward Darley Papers, Western History Collection, Minutes of the Regents, September 2, 1952, pp. 1–2, and February 28, 1953, p. 1. Also *Colorado Daily,* March 3, 1953; December 17, 1956.

[7] *Colorado Daily,* August 8, 1953.

[8] University of Colorado, Office of Admissions, "Enrollment Statistics, 1953–1956." These figures are fall semester head counts for respective years. See also Association of Presidents of the Institutions of Higher Learning in the State of Colorado, *The Rising Tide: A Forecast of the Probable Enrollments in Colorado's Seven State-Supported Colleges in the Next Fifteen Years* (1954), *passim; Colorado Daily,* November 29, 1954.

[9] *Colorado Daily*, September 23, 1954.

[10] *Ibid.*, October 23, 24, 1953; June 23, 1954.

[11] *Ibid.*, August 18, 1953; September 23, 1954.

[12] *Ibid.*, October 23, 1953; June 23, September 23, 1954.

[13] *Ibid.*, May 18, 1955, January 9, 1957. Also Thomas R. Mason, "Building for the Boom," *Colorado Alumnus* 45 (July–August 1955): 2–4.

[14] *Colorado Daily*, June 29, 1956; February 4, 1959.

[15] *Ibid.*, August 18, 1953.

[16] *Ibid.*, September 23, 1954; November 28, 1955; Physical Plant Department, *Capital Projects Costs for 1955–1966* (1967), pp. 14–73.

[17] *Colorado Daily*, May 18, 1955.

[18] Colorado State Planning Division, *Colorado Year Book, 1951–1955* (1955), pp. 675–677; *Colorado Year Book, 1956–1958*, pp. 397–398.

[19] *Ibid.*, *Colorado Year Book, 1951–1955*, p. 676; *Colorado Year Book, 1956–1958*, p. 398.

[20] *Ibid.*, *Colorado Year Book, 1956–1958*, p. 399.

[21] Carl McGuire and Otis Lipstreau, "In Education—You Get What You Pay For," *Colorado Alumnus* 44 (May 1954):4. See also *Colorado Daily*, January 8, May 19, 1954; November 7, 13, 1956.

[22] *Colorado Daily*, January 7, 1954.

[23] *Ibid.*, January 7, 8, 1954.

[24] *Ibid.*, February 20, 27, 28; April 18, 23, 1956.

[25] *Ibid.*, February 20, 28, 1956.

[26] Total income was derived from state appropriations, student tuitions and fees, endowments, sales and services from education departments, athletics, health services, and auxiliary enterprises. See University of Colorado, *Financial Reports, 1952–1956* (1952–1956), *passim*.

[27] Auxiliary enterprises that generated income on the Boulder campus were residence halls, housing for married students and the faculty, the bookstore, University Memorial Center, and rental properties. *Ibid.*

[28] Oral history interview with John W. Bartram by Lee Scamehorn, January 20, 1974, Oral History Collection, University Archives, University of Colorado.

[29] Max Schaible, "Science Center," *Colorado Alumnus* 48 (February 1957): 6–7.

[30] Dayton D. McKean, "Graduate Work at the University of Colorado, 1959" (typescript), Graduate School File, University Archives, University of Colorado. See also *Graduate School Items* 4 (January 1957), *passim*.

[31] "High Altitude Observatory (HAO)," summary of conference at Denver Club, August 20, 1950, copy in HAO Files. Transfiles, President's Office. In the same file are correspondence and documents pertinent to the Harvard-University of Colorado partnership. See Robert L. Stearns to Reuben G. Gustavson, November 30, 1944; Harlow Shapley to Gustavson, February 3, 1945; Shapley to Stearns, January 1, and August 7, 1945; and Stearns to Shapley, May 7, 1946. Hereafter cited as HAO Files.

[32] Kenneth Bundy to Robert L. Stearns, May 12, 1954; R. I. Hislop to Ward Darley, May 19, 1954, in HAO Files.

[33] Tom Knowles to Ward Darley, May 4, 1954; Stearns to Bundy, May 19, 1954, in HAO Files.

[34] The origin and evolution of the University's mountain ecology research program is delineated in Markely Paddock, "History of University Camp and Science Lodge, 1914–1964" (typescript), Institute of Arctic and Alpine Research File. University Archives, University of Colorado.

[35] *Ibid.*

[36] The recurring theme of communism and subversion is reported in *Colorado Daily*, February 12, 13, December 2, 7, 1953; June 23, 1954; April 29, May 3, 4, 5, 10, 1955; April 23, 1956.

[37] *Ibid.*, November 29, 30, December 1, 1954; January 19, 1955.

[38] *Ibid.*, December 6, 1954.

[39] *Ibid.*, December 7, 1954.

[40] *Ibid.*, January 19, 24, 1955.

[41] *Ibid.*, April 30, 1957.

[42] Interview with John W. Bartram, January 20, 1975. See also Ward Darley, "An Open Letter to the Faculty and Students," January 20, 1956, in Discrimination–Minorities File. Transfiles, President's Office. Hereafter cited as Discrimination File.

[43] Darley to H. Vance Austin, February 10, 1956, *ibid.*

[44] Edward C. King to Robert L. Stearns, July 24, 1947, *ibid.* See also *Colorado Daily*, March 19, 1954.

[45] King to Stearns, July 24, 1947.

[46] *Ibid.*

[47] *Ibid.*

[48] *Ibid.*

[49] *Colorado Daily*, March 19, 1954; February 27, 1959.

[50] *Ibid.*, October 6, 1954; February 27, 1959. See also Walter B. Lovelace, "Our Double Standard," *Colorado Alumnus* 45 (September 1954):3.

[51] "Appeal of Alpha Chi Sigma: Chronology," in Discrimination File. Also Minutes of the Regents, March 19, 1954, p. 1; Lovelace, pp. 3–4.

[52] Minutes of the Regents, August 27, 1954, p. 2.

[53] *Ibid.*, October 1, 1954, pp. 15–16.

[54] *Ibid.*

[55] *Colorado Daily*, October 6, 7, 22, 25, 1954.

[56] Minutes of the Regents, December 3, 1954, p. 1. Also *Colorado Daily*, December 6, 1954.

[57] *Colorado Daily*, January 13, 19, 20, 1956; February 27, 1959.

[58] Darley, "An Open Letter to the Faculty and Students," January 20, 1956.

[59] Minutes of the Regents, January 20, 1956, pp. 1–3. Also *Colorado Daily*, January 23, 1956.

[60] *Colorado Daily*, February 20, 23, 29, 1956.

[61] *Ibid.*, February 20, 21, 27, 1956.

[62] *Ibid.*, February 28, 29, 1956.

[63] William H. E. Holmes, Jr., "Democracy–University of Colorado

Style," pp. 9–10 (reprint); Discrimination File. Also *Denver Post*, March 19, 20, 1956; *Rocky Mountain News*, March 20, 1956.

[64] Holmes, p. 9. Also *Denver Post*, March 19, 20, 1956; *Rocky Mountain News*, March 20, 1956.

[65] Oral History Interview with H. Vance Austin by Lee Scamehorn, June 6, 1975, Oral History Collection. See also *Denver Post*, March 20, 1956.

[66] Interview with John W. Bartram, January 20, 1975.

[67] Oral History Interview with Ward Darley by John W. Brennan, November 21, 1973, Ward Darley Papers, Western History Collection. Hereafter cited as Darley Interview by Brennan.

[68] Public Administration Service, *The Administration of the University of Colorado: A Survey Report* (1956), p. 1.

[69] *Ibid.*

[70] *Ibid.*, p. 18.

[71] *Ibid.*, p. 22.

[72] *Ibid.*, p. 23.

[73] *Ibid.*, p. 14.

[74] Oral History Interview with Quigg Newton by Lee Scamehorn, January 6, 1975, Oral History Collection.

[75] *Ibid.*

[76] *Ibid.*

[77] Interview with H. Vance Austin, June 6, 1975.

[78] Statistics are for the fall semester. University of Colorado, Office of Admissions, "Enrollment Statistics, 1956–1963."

[79] *Ibid.*, University of Colorado, "Catalogue, 1963–1964," *Bulletin* 63 (April 23, 1963): 1.

[80] Physical Plant Department, *Capital Projects Costs, 1955–1966*, pp. 14–73.

[81] University of Colorado Committee for the Study of University Extension, Interim Report on the Denver Extension Center (1960) (copy), Extension Division File. Transfiles, President's Office. See also Timothy Grieder, "College Off the Campus," *Colorado Alumnus* 48 (September–October 1958): 4–5.

[82] Oral history interviews by Lee Scamehorn with John W. Bartram, January 20, 1975, Don F. Saunders, March 27, 1975, and Eugene H. Wilson, November 4, 1974, Oral History Collection. Also *Colorado Daily*, February 20, 21, September 19, 1957.

[83] Interview with Eugene H. Wilson, November 4, 1974; *Colorado Daily*, April 26, September 29, 1957; May 26, 1958; February 28, 1959; "Four Staffers Take New Posts," *Colorado Alumnus* 54 (January 1954): 1; "Eugene H. Wilson Named President for Interim," *Colorado Alumnus* 59 (June 1969): 1.

[84] "Provost Working to Meet President Newton's Goals," *Colorado Alumnus* 51 (December 1960): 6.

[85] "Leo Hill Given Promotion to University Vice Presidency," *ibid.*, 54 (October 1963): 4. Also *Colorado Daily*, June 24, 1958.

86 "Division of Student Personnel Services," *Colorado Alumnus* 52 (January 1962): 5. Also *Colorado Daily*, May 9, 1957; September 22, 1958.

87 "Division of Student Personnel Services," pp. 5–6. Also "Miss Parrish New Dean of Women After July 1," *Colorado Alumnus* 50 (April 1960): 1; "Davis Named Dean of Men," *Colorado Alumnus* 53 (March 1963): 1; "Faculty Staffers Accept Higher University Duties," *Colorado Alumnus* 55 (October 1964): 3; *Colorado Daily*, June 18, September 28, 1953; February 29, 1960; February 26, 1963. Parrish succeeded Mary Ethel Ball, who retired in 1960. Angelo succeeded Harry Carlson, who remained Professor of Physical Education and Director of Athletics. Angelo resigned in 1962 to enter private business and was succeeded by William E. (Bud) Davis. Quigley succeeded Davis in 1964.

88 Whitehead and Perkin, "Medical Education in Colorado, 1881–1971," *Rocky Mountain Medical Journal* 68 (June 1971): 173. See also "Glaser Named CU Vice President," *Colorado Alumnus* 50 (September 1959): 3; *Colorado Daily*, July 14, October 1, 1953; November 12, 1956; August 13, 16, 1958.

89 Whitehead and Perkin, pp. 174–175; Robert J. Glaser, "Continued Growth of the Medical Campus Is Assured by $17.5 Million Medical Building Program," *Colorado Alumnus* 49 (January–February 1959): 2–3. See also *Colorado Daily*, October 24, 1956; October 21, 1957; February 27, 1958; April 22, 1959; March 13, 1963.

90 Whitehead and Perkin, p. 174. Also "Medical Expansion Given Boost," *Colorado Alumnus* 51 (November 1960): 1; "Cancer Research Center Set for Medical School," *Colorado Alumnus* 51 (April 1961): 1; *Colorado Daily*, October 10, 1960; March 6, September 15, 20, 1961; April 23, 1962; March 13, 1963.

91 School of Medicine Catalogue, *University of Colorado Bulletin* 64 (January 2, 1964): 7; 65 (March 4, 1965): 7.

92 University of Colorado, *Financial Reports, 1953–1963, passim.*

93 *Colorado Daily*, February 4, March 1, 1955; February 20, 1956; February 4, 1959.

94 *Ibid.*, May 2, June 29, September 15, 1960; March 21, 1961; November 16, December 11, 1962; January 10, 1963; Whitehead and Perkin, p. 175.

95 Interview with Quigg Newton, January 6, 1975.

96 "What Makes a Great University?" *Colorado Alumnus* 46 (January–February 1956): 2.

97 *Colorado Daily*, December 20, 21, 1956.

98 "Instruments Being Constructed at CU Will Collect Data from Earth Satellite," *Colorado Alumnus* 50 (January 1960): 1; "LASP Celebrates Birthday," *Colorado Alumnus* 56 (November 1965): 8; "Observatory Studies Planets, Sun from Space Platform," *Colorado Alumnus* 57 (April 1967): 6–7.

99 "Behavioral Science Research Center Straddles Disciplines," *ibid.*, 54 (April 1964): 7. Also *Colorado Daily*, October 9, 1957; January 6, 1959; July 7, 1961.

100 *Colorado Daily*, April 17, 1962.

[101] *Ibid.*, December 11, 1959; "Several Years of Scientific Labors Rewarded with Cyclotron Operation," *Colorado Alumnus* 52 (May 1962): 5.

[102] "Computer Institute Gets Regent Nod," *Colorado Alumnus* 53 (November 1962): 1, 3.

[103] *Ibid.; Colorado Daily*, May 17, 1962; November 2, 1962.

[104] The University of Colorado was formally admitted to the UCAR in 1964. The successful effort to bring NCAR to Boulder, and the merger of HAO with the Center, is discussed in W. O. Roberts to Quigg Newton, June 11, 1958; Thomas F. Malone to Quigg Newton, December 29, 1958; Newton to Malone, December 29, 1958; Roberts to University Science Council, March 23, 1959; W. G. Worcester to Newton, April 10, 1959; Robert J. Low to Newton, March 2, 1961; and Roberts to "Friends of the High Altitude Observatory," November 28, 1961.

[105] "Memorandum of Progress, University of Colorado, 1956–1962," (typescript), Quigg Newton File, President's Office, pp. 1–3, 6–7, 11–12.

[106] *Ibid.*, pp. 2–3.

[107] Lawrence G. Weiss, "Goldwater and Colorado U.," *The Nation* 195 (December 8, 1962): 402.

[108] *Colorado Daily*, April 1, 1960; July 3, September 15, 1961. See also "Dean Quigley Depicts Today's Students," *Colorado Alumnus* 58 (March 1968): 3.

[109] Warren H. Carroll, "Counterattack at Colorado," *National Review* 14 (June 18, 1963): 494.

[110] Interview with Quigg Newton, January 6, 1975. Also Weiss, p. 402.

[111] Weiss, p. 402.

[112] Initial charges of wrongdoing were contained in a letter from Arthur J. Bergstrom, Secretary, NCAA Committee on Infractions, to Newton, November 14, 1961. A special committee, composed of Don W. Sears (chairman), Storm Bull, Edward C. King, Don Saunders, and Warren O. Thompson, submitted their report to Newton on February 14, 1962. All documents pertinent to charges, investigations, and actions against coaches and players are in special files under control of the Secretary to the Board of Regents. See also "Regents Fire Grandelius for Violations, Untruths," *Colorado Alumnus* 52 (April 1962): 1, 7; Bill Furlong, "Anatomy of a College Recruiting Scandal," *Sport* 34 (November 1962): 14–17, 88–92.

[113] "Buffs Annihilate Air Force," *Colorado Alumnus* 53 (December 1962): 12.

[114] In 1956 there were 16 sororities and 23 fraternities. In the next six years, two of each left the campus for financial and other reasons, and one each of new chapters located in Boulder. See University of Colorado News Service, "Background of the University of Colorado Anti-Discrimination Policy," August 31, 1962.

[115] *Denver Post*, September 1, 5, 1962; "Regents Reaffirm Discrimination Rule," *Colorado Alumnus* 53 (October 1962): 9.

[116] Minutes of the Regents, September 28, 1962, pp. 30–38. Also *Colorado Daily*, October 1, 1962.

[117] *Colorado Daily*, April 24, 1961.

118 *Ibid.*, "Gadfly," December 1, 1961.

119 *Ibid.*

120 *Ibid.*

121 *Boulder Daily Camera*, January 26, 1962; *Rocky Mountain News*, January 27, 1962; *Denver Post*, January 27, 1962.

122 *Denver Post*, January 28, 1962.

123 *Rocky Mountain News*, February 14, 1962.

124 *Ibid.*

125 *Ibid.*, May 30, 1962.

126 *Ibid.*, March 2, 3, 1962; *Denver Post*, March 3, 1962.

127 Resolution, March 13, 1962.

128 Committee on Student Affairs, Report, April 18, 1962.

129 Quigg Newton to Marshall Reddish, May 4, 1962 (copy), Goldwater File. Transfiles, President's Office.

130 Postal card in *ibid.*, received April 12, 1962.

131 Notes prepared by Quigg Newton for remarks to University Senate, October 16, 1962, in Goldwater File. Transfiles, President's Office. Also *Colorado Daily*, September 21, October 3, 1962.

132 Notes prepared by Quigg Newton for remarks to University Senate, October 16, 1962. Also "President Newton Fires Daily Editor," *Colorado Alumnus* 53 (November 1962): 1, 4; "Newton Discusses Position on Firing Daily Editor," *Colorado Alumnus* 53 (December 1962): 5.

133 "Student Newspaper's Role Gets Study," *Colorado Alumnus* 53 (November 1962): 2; "Colorado Daily Status Reviewed," *Colorado Alumnus* 53 (April 1963): 1, 4. The full range of University-sanctioned publications is identified in "CU Has Many Student Publications with Costs Carried by the Students," *Colorado Alumnus* 50 (December 1959): 3.

134 University of Colorado News Service, releases, October 2, 3, 1962.

135 Weiss, p. 404.

136 *Ibid.*

137 Quigg Newton to Senator Goldwater, September 27, 1962, in Minutes of the Regents, September 28, 1962, pp. 23–24.

138 Senator Goldwater to Quigg Newton, October 2, 1962, in Goldwater File.

139 Newton to Goldwater, October 3, 1962, *ibid.*

140 Topics discussed by Bromley during the campaign are outlined in "An Inventory of Recent Attacks on the University" (November 1962), and "Charges Against the University by Regent Charles D. Bromley and Rebuttals" (December 1962), (typescripts), Charles D. Bromley File. Transfiles, President's Office.

141 University News Service, release, September 29, 1962.

142 *Ibid.*, December 5, 1962.

143 Typescript of speech to Denver Alumni, December 15, 1962, in Quigg Newton File. Transfiles, President's Office.

144 *Ibid.*

145 *Ibid.*

146 *Ibid.* See also letter of resignation, Quigg Newton to Board of Regents, December 5, 1962, Minutes of the Regents, December 15, 1962, pp. 9–10.

Six

1 For perceptive, and detailed, analyses of higher education in the 1960s see Christopher Jenks and David Riesman, *The Academic Revolution* (1968), pp. 90–97, and Paul Woodring, *The Higher Learning in America: A Reassessment* (1968), pp. 55–67.

2 *The Chronicle of Higher Education,* August 19, 1974.

3 University of Colorado, Office of Institutional Research, *Historical Summary of Student and Faculty Data* (1974), p. 1. Hereafter cited as *Student and Faculty Data.*

4 See Neal R. Peirce, *The Mountain States of America* (1972), pp. 29–66.

5 The University of Colorado, College of Business and Administration, and the Colorado Division of Commerce and Development, *Business-Economic Outlook Forum, 1970* (1969), *passim; ibid., 1975* (1974), *passim.*

6 Roger A. Walton, *Colorado: Government and Politics* (1973), pp. 145–148.

7 *The Chronicle of Higher Education,* October 12, 1970.

8 See Association of State Institutions of Higher Education in Colorado, *Program for the General Differentiation and Coordination of Functions Among the State-Supported Institutions of Higher Education 1963–1970* (1962), pp. 1–6; and *A Program for the Development and Coordination of Higher Education in Colorado 1964–1970* (1964), pp. 1–7.

9 See Colorado Commission on Higher Education, *Strengthening Higher Education in Colorado* (1967), pp. 1–14, hereafter cited as *Strengthening Higher Education;* and *Planning for the '70s: Higher Education in Colorado* (1971), pp. iv–viii, hereafter cited as *Planning for the '70s.*

10 *Denver Post,* February 16, 1971.

11 *Planning for the '70s,* p. 43.

12 *Silver and Gold,* October 8, 15, December 3, 1974. *Boulder Daily Camera,* November 22, 1974. These particular events have major consequences for the future of the University, and the roles of individuals in the preparation of the language of the amendment, as well as the voting response of various groups, need more thorough study than they have received.

13 Lyman A. Glenny and Thomas K. Dalglish, *Public Universities, State Agencies and the Law—Constitutional Autonomy in Decline* (1973), pp. 1–4, 143–153.

14 *Denver Post,* July 26, 1963.

15 Colorado, Forty-fourth General Assembly, *Appropriations Report, 1963–1964* (1964), pp. 11–12; Forty-ninth General Assembly, *Appropriations Report, 1973–1974* (1974), pp. 11–12.

16 For an excellent outline history of the Board of Regents in this period

see Clifford G. Houston, Homer P. Rainey, and Eugene H. Wilson, *The University of Colorado 1963-1973: A Review* (1973), Part III, Appendix B.
17 Minutes of the Regents, 1963-1965, *passim*. It is just not possible to list all of the officers of the university or to note the many changes of personnel that frequently occur.
18 University of Colorado, *Report on the Study of the Denver and Colorado Springs Extension Centers* (1961), pp. i–iii.
19 The Legislative Committee for Education Beyond the High School, *Report to the Colorado General Assembly, Study No. 2* (1961), pp. 5–8.
20 Task Group on Post High School Education in the Denver Metropolitan Area, *Individual Opportunity and Economic Growth in the Denver Metropolitan Area* (1963).
21 Colorado, Forty-fourth General Assembly, *Session Laws* (1963), pp. 879–881.
22 Joseph R. Smiley to Jeremiah Allen, June 12, 1963, Metropolitan State College Files. Transfiles, President's Office.
23 University of Colorado, *Proposal to Meet the Needs of Public Higher Education in the Denver Metropolitan Area* (1963), pp. 1–9. Also University of Colorado, Office of Institutional Research, *Models of Higher Education Programs in Metropolitan Denver* (1964), pp. 1–10.
24 Minutes of the Regents, November 18, 1963, pp. 101–102; March 21, 1964, pp. 198–200.
25 *Denver Post*, January 22, 1964.
26 See Higher Education Plan Suggested by John Dale Russell, July 2, 1963, Metropolitan State College File. Transfiles, President's Office.
27 Association of State Institutions of Higher Education in Colorado, *A Program for the Development and Coordination of Higher Education in Colorado, 1964-1970* (1964), pp. 1–7, 163–166.
28 Colorado, Forty-fifth General Assembly, *Session Laws* (1965), pp. 346–347. Minutes of the Regents, May 29, 1965, pp. 30–32.
29 *Strengthening Higher Education*, pp. 1, 15–19.
30 John P. Holloway, *Memorandum of Authorities in Support of the Right of the Regents of the University of Colorado to Maintain Branches or Centers of the University at Locations Other than Boulder* (1966), pp. 9–20. Also Joseph R. Smiley to Duke W. Dunbar, November 30, 1966, and Dunbar to Smiley, December 21, 1966, Metropolitan State College File. Transfiles, President's Office.
31 Colorado, Forty-sixth General Assembly, *Session Laws* (1967), pp. 448–449, and *Appropriations Report 1966-1967, passim*.
32 University of Colorado, *Financial Report 1963-1964, 1968-1969, passim*.
33 University of Colorado, Office of Institutional Research, Ten-Year Budget Analysis: Boulder Campus (1971), *passim*, and Budget Papers, Files. Vice President in Academic Affairs Office.
34 Minutes of the Regents, April 24, 1964, pp. 24–32.
35 *Ibid.*, May 29, 1965, pp. 241–243.
36 *Ibid.*, October 15, 1965, pp. 68–78; May 25, 1966, p. 280.

[37] *Ibid.*, October 17, 1966, pp. 81–89.

[38] *Ibid.*, May 19, 1967, pp. 4–5.

[39] *Ibid.*, August 14, 1967, pp. 11–18.

[40] *Ibid.*, August 16, 1968, pp. 11–18; May 23, 1969, pp. 513–536.

[41] Colorado, Forty-fourth General Assembly, *Appropriations Report, 1963–1964, passim;* Forty-seventh General Assembly, *Appropriations Report, 1968–1969, passim.*

[42] Lyman A. Glenny, James R. Kidder, *State Tax Support of Higher Education: Revenue Appropriation Trends and Patterns, 1963–1973* (1973), pp. 9–13, 28–29.

[43] University of Colorado, Office of Institutional Research, Tuition and Fees from 1960–1975, *passim.*

[44] University of Colorado, Office of Institutional Research, Student and Faculty Data, *passim.*

[45] University of Colorado, Office of Institutional Research, Ten-Year Record of Faculty-Student Ratios (1967), *passim.*

[46] University of Colorado, *The Medical Center: Master Planning to Meet Immediate and Long-Range Program Requirements* (1959), pp. 19–22. Also University of Colorado, Planning Office, *Reference Notebook on Campus Development—Boulder* (1965), Sections V, VI.

[47] University of Colorado, *Financial Report: 1969–1970* (1970), p. 79.

[48] Whitehead and Perkin, p. 174.

[49] Sigfried Mandel and Margaret Shipley, *Proud Past, Bright Future—A History of the College of Engineering at the University of Colorado, 1893–1966* (1966), pp. 305–310.

[50] University of Colorado, *Financial Report: 1969–1970* (1970), pp. 76–78.

[51] John Morris Dixon, "Colorado U: Respect for a Robust Environment," *Architectural Forum* (October 1966), pp. 54–65.

[52] John Walsh, "Centers for Excellence: New NSF Science Development Program," *Science* (December 1964), pp. 1563–1566.

[53] Dr. Donald F. Hornig, address before the American Physical Society, Shoreham Hotel, Washington, D.C., April 29, 1964.

[54] National Science Foundation, *Science Development Program for Colleges and Universities, 1964 and 1965* (1964), p. 1, Science Development Grant File. Vice President for Academic Affairs Office.

[55] *Ad Hoc* Committee for NSF Science Development Proposal, *Application for National Science Foundation Grant* (July 1964), p. 8, Science Development Grant File. Vice President for Academic Affairs Office.

[56] *Boulder Daily Camera*, July 2, 1965.

[57] Memorandum Science Development Program, June 5, 1967, Science Development Grant File. Vice President for Academic Affairs Office.

[58] The All-University Life Sciences Committee, *Life Sciences at the University of Colorado* (1966), pp. 41–45.

[59] University of Colorado, *Programs for Advancement of Basic Medical and Biological Sciences* (1966), *passim.* Health Sciences Grant File. Vice

President for Academic Affairs Office.

60 University of Colorado, *Programs for Advancing the Health Sciences* (1967), *passim*, Health Sciences Grant File, Vice President for Academic Affairs Office.

61 Minutes of the Regents, April 14, 1967, p. 294.

62 *Ibid.*, November 23, 1965, p. 121; January 25, 1967, pp. 203–204.

63 *Boulder Daily Camera*, July 30, 1967.

64 Allan M. Carter, *An Assessment of Quality in Graduate Education* (1966), *passim*.

65 Kenneth D. Roose, Charles J. Anderson, *A Rating of Graduate Programs* (1970), *passim*.

66 *Denver Post*, May 21, 1967.

67 Minutes of the Regents, 1963–1969, *passim*.

68 Minutes of the Executive Committee, Faculty Senate, February 14, 1966, University Archives, University of Colorado. Hereafter cited as Minutes of the Executive Committee, or Faculty Senate, or Minutes of the Faculty Senate.

69 Ad Hoc Committee on Senate Organization, *A Report on a Proposed Organization of the Senate*, February 1967, p. i.

70 *Ibid.*, p. 2.

71 Minutes of the Faculty Senate, May 16, 1967.

72 Drafting Committee on Senate Rules, *Proposed Rules of the Senate*, October 1967, *passim*. Minutes of the Regents, February 24, 1968, pp. 250–251; May 20, 1968, p. 398, Exhibit A.

73 Archie R. Dykes, *Faculty Participation in Academic Decision-Making* (1968), pp. 37–43. T. R. McConnell, Kenneth P. Mortimer, *The Faculty in University Governance* (1971), pp. 166–189.

74 See William L. O'Neill, ed., *American Society since 1945* (1969), pp. 3–30, and Lawrence S. Wittmer, *Cold War America* (1974), pp. 302–333.

75 Minutes of the Regents, April 14, 1966, pp. 13–14; February 17, 1967, pp. 247–248; December 15, 1967, pp. 172–183; June 28, 1968, pp. 455–458; February 15, 1969, pp. 395–399.

76 See generally Irwin Unger, *The Movement: A History of the American New Left 1959–1972* (1974), especially pp. 82–117; Joseph A. Califano, Jr., *The Student Revolution: A Global Confrontation* (1970), especially pp. 15–17; Alan Adelson, *SDS—A Profile* (1972), especially pp. ix–xii.

77 The President's Commission on Campus Unrest, *Chronicle of Higher Education*, October 5, 1970, pp. 4–11.

78 Verne Stadtman, *The University of California 1868–1968* (1970), pp. 443–487.

79 See Report of Fact-Finding Commission, *Crisis at Columbia* (1968), pp. 189–199, and Roger Kahn, *The Battle for Morningside Heights* (1970), *passim*.

80 *Colorado Daily*, March 15, May 7, July 28, October 28, 1965.

81 *Ibid.*, October 7, October 29, November 19, 1965; March 10, 1966.

82 *Ibid.*, February 8, 1966.

83 *Ibid.*, March 2, March 16, 1967.

[84] *Ibid.*, October 26, 1967; April 12, 1968; March 4, 1969; March 2, April 14, May 4–May 8, May 11, May 14, 1970.

[85] Joseph R. Smiley to Students of the University of Colorado, November 6, 1967, Students' File. Transfiles, President's Office.

[86] Minutes of the Faculty Senate, January 10, 16, March 19, April 23, May 21, 1968.

[87] *Colorado Daily*, April 22, 23, 24, 1968.

[88] Minutes of the Regents, June 23, 1967, pp. 399–401; August 14, 1967, pp. 17–26.

[89] *Ibid.*, September 20, 1968, pp. 101–104; October 25, 1968, pp. 156–161; November 22, 1968, pp. 202–220, 232–243 (Report of Joint Board on Student Organizations and Social Life); December 13, 1968, pp. 281–283, Exhibit C; May 23, 1969, pp. 519–522, Exhibit B.

[90] See Seymour M. Lipset, *Rebellion in the University* (1971), pp. 178–196, and with Gerald M. Schaflander, *Passion and Politics: Student Activism in America* (1971), pp. 267–280.

[91] For a range of examples, see *Colorado Daily*, February 21, May 19, 1964; April 21, August 4, 1965; February 11, May 25, May 27, 1966; October 6, May 22, 1967.

[92] Faculty Senate, Committee on Student Affairs, *A Report on Discipline Procedures and Policy*, May 1968. Minutes of the Faculty Senate, May 21, 1968. Minutes of the Regents, August 16, 1968, pp. 28–36; March 15, 1969, pp. 441–448.

[93] Contrast the yearbook, *The Coloradan*, 1963, with the 1974 edition. Student Organizations at the University of Colorado, Report of a Special Committee to the Board of Regents (January 1968), *passim*. Also Interview with Dean for Student Affairs James E. Quigley by Frederick S. Allen, September 17, 1974. *Colorado Daily*, April 11, 1966; May 18, 1967. Minutes of the Regents, April 30, 1971, pp. 560–565, 614–615.

[94] Faculty Senate, Committee on Student Affairs, *A Report on the Reorganization of Student Government*, April 1964. Minutes of the Faculty Senate, April 28, 1964. Faculty Senate, Committee on Student Affairs, *Uniform Bylaws for the Joint Boards* (revision), February 1967, and *Report to the Regents on the Joint Boards*, May 1970. Minutes of the Faculty Council, May 14, 1970. Minutes of the Regents, May 26, 1970, pp. 448–450, Appendix A.

[95] *The Chronicle of Higher Education*, October 19, 1969.

[96] *Colorado Daily*, May 8, 1969.

[97] Ernest E. Wahlstrom to the Faculty, December 26, 1968, January 10, 1969; Martin Cobin to Vice President Manning and Dean Wahlstrom, May 16, 1969; University Reorganization File, Vice President for Academic Affairs Office. Minutes of the Faculty of the College of Arts and Sciences, May 15, 1969.

[98] The Commission on the Academic Community, *Report to the President of the University of Colorado*, May 1969, *passim*.

[99] Minutes of the Regents, 1967–1969, *passim*.

[100] *Colorado Daily*, August 11, 1969.

101 Minutes of the Regents, 1970–1972, *passim.*
102 Houston, Rainey, Wilson, Part III, Appendix B.
103 Minutes of the Faculty Council, September 18, 1969, and as reported in the *Colorado Daily,* September 19, 1969.
104 *Colorado Daily,* September 4, 10, 17, October 1, 6, 16, 29, November 14, 26, 1969; February 2, 27, March 2, 4, 26, April 13, 14, 15, 1970.
105 *Ibid.,* March 26, April 6, 10, 16, May 1.
106 *Ibid.,* May 4, 5, 6.
107 Minutes of the Faculty Council, May 7, 1970; *Colorado Daily,* May 11, 1970.
108 *Colorado Daily,* May 6, 7, 8, 11, 15.
109 *Ibid.,* May 12, 13, 14. Summaries of Deans' Reports for Period of "Strike" Week, Student Strike File, Vice President for Academic Affairs Office.
110 For illustration of the declining unrest see *Colorado Daily,* September 17, October 12, November 4, 1970; April 29, June 18, June 23, October 14, 1971; March 8, April 21, 25, 28, May 2, 10, June 12, 1972.
111 Data in EOP Memorandum, Educational Opportunity Programs File, Provost's Office.
112 Minutes of the Faculty Council, February 12, 1970.
113 The Faculty Council Committee on Minority Programs, *Equality of Educational Opportunity and the University of Colorado: A Report to the Faculty Council* (1970), pp. 17–18.
114 Minutes of the Regents, October 16, 1970, pp. 219–228; November 13, 1970, pp. 277–290, 328–331; March 22, 1972, pp. 121–123.
115 *Colorado Daily,* October 16, November 2, 16, 1970; November 22, December 10, 1971; February 18, March 20, 21, April 3, 7, 18, 25, 26, 1972.
116 The University Committee on Minority Affairs, Recommendations for Reorganizing the Administrative Structure of the Educational Opportunity Programs on the Boulder Campus (1972), *passim.*
117 Minutes of the Faculty Council, March 12, 1972.
118 Educational Opportunity Programs Boulder Campus, Status Report, Fall 1971, Educational Opportunity Programs File, Provost's Office. *Silver and Gold,* April 13, 1972.
119 *The Chronicle of Higher Education,* December 7, 14, 1970; January 4, February 8, March 1, 8, April 19, June 7, July 5, September 27, October 4, November 22, 1971; February 14, March 6, 27, April 3, 10, 17, May 15, 22, 1972.
120 Visiting Committees for the Commission on Institutions of Higher Education of the North Central Association of Colleges and Secondary Schools, *Report of a Visit to the University of Colorado* (1970), *passim.* Hereafter cited as North Central Association, *Report.*
121 *Ibid.,* p. 6, 15.
122 The Faculty Council Committee on Long Range Goals, *Report* (1971), *passim.*
123 Minutes of the Faculty Council, November 9, December 9, 1971; January 20, 1972.

[124] See College of Arts and Sciences, *Annual Report, 1966–1967*, p. 4, and *Annual Report, 1968–1969*, pp. 5–8.

[125] *Ibid., Annual Report, 1969–1970*, pp. 6–7.

[126] See Residential Academic Program Proposal (1969), Residential Academic Proposal File, Vice President for Academic Affairs Office, and Office of Research and Program Development, Division of Student Affairs, *Inside Sewall Hall—A Second-Year Look at the Residential Academic Program, 1971–1972* (1972), *passim*.

[127] See Graduate School, *Annual Report, 1967–1968*, pp. 2–4.

[128] *Ibid., Annual Report, 1969–1970*, pp. 3–5.

[129] *Ibid.*, pp. 29–30, Graduate School Colloquia.

[130] See School (College) of Business and Administration, *Annual Report, 1967–1968*, p. 2, and *Annual Report, 1971–1972*, p. 2; College of Engineering, *Annual Report, 1969–1970*, pp. 9–15, also Report of the Committee on Goals of the College of Engineering (1971), Part II, pp. 10–11, 61–62, 68, 100; Law School, *Annual Report, 1968–1969*, p. 1; School of Architecture, *Annual Report, 1969–1970*, p. 7.

[131] College (School) of Business and Administration, *Annual Report, 1971–1972*, pp. 2–4, and School of Education, *Ten Years of Progress, 1959–1969* (1969), pp. 7, 11–15, 45, and *Annual Report, 1971–1972*, pp. 1–2, 16–17.

[132] School of Nursing, *Annual Reports, 1965–1966, 1966–1967*, pp. 17–29, and *Annual Report, 1972–1973*, pp. 25–27.

[133] Law School, *Annual Report, 1970–1971*, pp. 1–3, and Law School Plan (1971), *passim*; The Curriculum Committee for the First and Second Years, *Report to the Medical Faculty* (1968), *passim*, and Ad Hoc Committee for Curriculum Revision, *Report to the Medical Faculty* (1973), *passim*.

[134] Minutes of the Regents, 1962–1971, *passim*.

[135] The Extension Division Staff Committee, Summary Report (1969), *passim*, and Division of Continuing Education, *Annual Report, 1971–1972*, *passim*, and *Annual Report, 1972–1973*, *passim*.

[136] University of Colorado, Department of Intercollegiate Athletic News Files, courtesy of Mike Moran.

[137] For request budgets, see Minutes of the Regents, either August or September meetings, 1971–1974. For operating budgets, see Minutes of the Regents, either May or June meetings, 1971–1972.

[138] For appropriations, see University of Colorado, *Financial Report 1970–1971* (1971), pp. 14–15, and *Financial Report 1973–1975* (1974), p. 1.

[139] For state expenditures, see Colorado Forty-ninth General Assembly, *Appropriations Report, 1973–1974*, p. 12.

[140] University of Colorado, *Financial Report 1973–1974* (1974).

[141] North Central Association, *Report*.

[142] Baxter, McDonald and Company, *Post-Secondary Educational Alternatives in El Paso and Pueblo Counties* (1971), pp. 1–4.

[143] Colorado, Forty-eighth General Assembly, Minutes of the Committee on Organization of State Government, October 8, November 2, 1971; and *Report* (1971), pp. 5–9.

¹⁴⁴ Colorado, Forty-eighth General Assembly, *Session Laws* (1972), pp. 644–646.
¹⁴⁵ University of Colorado, Office of Institutional Research, Results by County for Amendment 4.
¹⁴⁶ Minutes of the Regents, January 23, 1973, p. 4.
¹⁴⁷ University of Colorado at Colorado Springs, *Master Plan* (1973), pp. 1–6; and interview with Helen Foster by Frederick S. Allen, May 1975.
¹⁴⁸ Colorado Commission on Higher Education, *Higher Education in the Metropolitan Denver Area* (1970), pp. 34–45.
¹⁴⁹ Colorado, Forty-eighth General Assembly, *Session Laws* (1972), pp. 52–120, and Board of Directors, *The Auraria Higher Education Center* (1975), pp. 13–14.
¹⁵⁰ Minutes of the Regents, August 15, 1970, pp. 87–89.
¹⁵¹ *Ibid.*, May 26, 1971, pp. 646–647.
¹⁵² *Ibid.*, February 23, 1972, pp. 454–457.
¹⁵³ *Ibid.*, March 21, 1973, pp. 642–658.
¹⁵⁴ Memorandum UCD-Auraria Progress Report, August 7, 1973, *passim*, University of Colorado at Denver File, Provost's Office.
¹⁵⁵ Colorado, Forty-ninth General Assembly, *Session Laws* (1974), pp. 390–395, and University of Colorado at Denver, *Master Plan* (1974), pp. 2–10.
¹⁵⁶ *Silver and Gold*, June 8, 15, July 13, 1972.
¹⁵⁷ Minutes of the Regents, August 23, 1972, pp. 3–4.
¹⁵⁸ *Silver and Gold*, February 22, March 8, April 12, 1973. Minutes of the Regents, October 27, 1972, pp. 255–256; December 20, 1972, pp. 380–381; February 28, 1973, pp. 530–531, Exhibit J. Minutes of the Executive Faculty, School of Medicine, February 7, March 16, 29, 1973.
¹⁵⁹ *Silver and Gold*, October 26, 1972; January 26, February 15, March 1, 8, 1973.
¹⁶⁰ *Colorado Daily*, November 3, 1971; November 7, 1974.
¹⁶¹ *Ibid.*, September 30, November 6, 24, 1970; January 21, 27, September 23, 1971; September 25, 1972; February 7, April 12, 24, June 11, 25, July 10, August 7, 1973; February 12, 28, May 8, 1974.
¹⁶² For salary comparisons, see University of Colorado, Personnel Roster and Departmental Budgets (1972–1973), *passim.*
¹⁶³ For a study of faculty morale, see Ralph Henard, "Assessment of the University Environment: Perceptions of the Faculty, Students, Administrators, and Selected Subgroups" (unpublished Ph.D. dissertation, University of Colorado, 1973), pp. 366–368.
¹⁶⁴ *Silver and Gold*, January 29, March 12, April 2, 9, 1974.
¹⁶⁵ Office of the Chancellor, *Report to the Board of Regents on the Status of ROTC Programs on the Boulder Campus* (1975), pp. 1–3.
¹⁶⁶ Minutes of the Faculty Council, March 8, 1973, and Minutes of the Faculty Senate, March 22, 1973.
¹⁶⁷ *Silver and Gold*, April 5, 12, 1973.
¹⁶⁸ Minutes of the Regents, April 25, 1973, pp. 721–730.
¹⁶⁹ *Silver and Gold*, September 11, 25, October 9, 1973; January 22,

February 5, 1974. Minutes of the Executive Faculty, School of Medicine, September 13, October 25, December 13, 1973, February 14, 1974.

[170] *Silver and Gold,* November 27, 1973, January 22, 1974. *Colorado Daily,* January 21, 1974.

[171] Minutes of the Regents, April 25, 1974, pp. 1333–1354.

[172] University of Colorado, Operating Budgets and Estimates, 1974–1975.

[173] University of Colorado Foundation, Inc., *The 1970 Report on Annual Giving* (1970), p. 12; *ibid.* (1974), p. 15.

[174] Minutes of the Regents, 1970–1974, *passim.*

[175] Frederick P. Thieme, State of the University Address, Boulder, Colorado, September 23, 1973.

Epilogue

[1] The Carnegie Foundation for the Advancement of Teaching, *More Than Survival* (1975), pp. 1–8.

[2] *The Chronicle of Higher Education,* March 24, 31, April 7, 28, May 12, October 6, November 10, 17, 1975.

[3] Clark Kerr, address, the University of Colorado, June 19, 1974, *Colorado Daily,* June 20, 1974. Fund for the Improvement of Postsecondary Education, Department of Health, Education, and Welfare, *Fiscal Year 1976 Program Information* (1975), p. 10.

[4] The *Chronicle of Higher Education,* April 26, 1976.

[5] *Denver Post,* November 2, 3, 7, 1975.

[6] Colorado Commission on Higher Education, *Task Forces—Preliminary Reports* (1975), *passim.*

[7] *Silver and Gold,* January 28, April 1, 22, May 6, June 10, August 5, 12, 1975.

[8] *Colorado Alumnus,* April 1975; *Silver and Gold,* July 22, October 7, 21, 1975.

[9] *Silver and Gold,* December 10, 1974, April 8, 1975.

[10] Edwin Banks, "Significant Events at the University of Colorado," (President's Office, University of Colorado, 1974–76) *passim.*

[11] As the legislature has cut drastically the budget for the Colorado Commission on Higher Education in 1976–1977 and thus limited its role in budget recommendations, the University must reckon in the future with an as yet unknown budget review process.

INDEX

Abbott, Frank, 207
Academic Community, Commission
  of the, 235
Academic freedom: Brewster case,
  78–79; under Newton, 200;
  post–World War II, 124–29;
  reexamined (1960s), 225–26;
  SDS issue and, 230–31; during
  World War II, 80–81. *See also*
  Anti-Communism
Academic planning, 243–45
Accreditation review, results
  of 1970, 241–42
Administrative reforms in
  Newton years, 184, 186–88, 190
Admissions standards, 67;
  1950s, 166; 1963–1973, 243;
  under Newton, 193; under
  Norlin, 113–14
Albright, Robert, 163
Aldrich, Robert, 237
Allegiance, oath of (loyalty
  oath), 151–52, 156, 158, 163, 225
Allen, James, 121
Allin, Arthur, 75
Althen, Gary, 200

American Association of
  University Professors (AAUP),
  78, 128, 129, 160, 162, 223, 240, 260
American colleges and
  universities, evolution of, 3–13
American Council of Education,
  222
American Federation of
  Teachers (AFT), 128, 252, 260
American Youth for Democracy,
  149
Ammons, Elias, 78, 80
Anderson, Jack, 238
Andrews, George A., 23
Angell, James, 5, 11, 56
Angelo, Harold E., 187
Anti-Communism: 1944, 124–25;
  in Newton years, 196–200;
  post–World War II, 148–65
Archer, James, 212, 221, 236
Architecture, School of, 245
Architecture and Architectural
  Engineering, Department of, 169
Arnett, Anthony, 23
Arthur, Rex P., 119–20

Arts and Sciences, College of,
36, 203; autonomy of, 248, 249;
changes in (1963–1973), 243;
1886 enrollment in, 38; Honors
program in, 95–96; new construction projects for (1921;
1938), 89, 109; in 1950s, 169;
under Norlin, 95–98
Associated Students of the
University of Colorado (ASUC),
98, 128, 177, 180–81, 200, 233
Association of American Medical
Colleges, 182
Association of American
Universities, 93
Association of Presidents of
Higher Learning, 170
Association of State-Supported
Institutions of Higher Learning,
186
Association of State Institutions
of Higher Education, 207, 214
Athletics: under Baker, 73–74;
in Depression years, 99;
evolution of, 9; in 1920s, 98;
in 1960s, 194; during World
War I, 81. See also Football
Atkins, Dale, 202, 211, 230, 238
Auraria Higher Education Center,
248–50, 258, 261
Austin, H. Vance, 161, 178–81
Autonomy: call for administrative,
247–48, 259–60; eroding of, 207–10
Aydelotte, Frank, 95
Ayre, Robert, 223

Baker, James Hutchins, 15, 37,
50, 52–77, 79, 82
Balluschi, Pietro, 219
Barnett, Glenn, 211, 235
Bartlett, Albert, 242
Bartram, John W., 186, 211,
216, 237
Batterton, Richard, 189
Baughn, William, 211
Bean, Geraldine, 238
Beattie, Wayne, 153

Beckmann, Petr, 223
Bein, Louis, 259
Berger, Jean, 193
Berkley, Junius, 22, 29, 32
Bernick, Richard, 213, 259
Berry, Mary Frances, 261
Betz, Fred, Jr., 202
Betz, Fred, Sr., 211, 230, 238
Big Eight Athletic conference
(earlier Big Six Athletic con-
ference), 148, 194–95, 245–46
Bigelow, Antoinette, 72
Biophysics, Department of, 137, 145
Blue, Virginia, 181
Board of Regents. See Regents,
Board of
Board of Trustees, 21–29
Boettcher, Ruth, 189
Borgmann, Carl, 127–29
Boulding, Kenneth, 223
Brackett, J. Raymond, 38, 57
Bramhall, Frederick, 121, 128
Branscomb, Lewis M., 193
Bray, Dillard, 187
Brewster, James H., 78–79
Bridges, Harry, 124–26, 128
Briggs, William, 211
Brinton, James, 212
Brockway, Waldo E., 109, 110,
119, 123, 170
Bromley, Charles D. (Jim), 119,
211; discrimination and, 181;
Hawkins affair and, 155; in
McCarthy era, 163; Newton and,
202; in Smiley years, 213
Brooks, Elwood, 181
Brown, George, 198
Broxon, James, 146, 149
Buchanan, Archibald, 161
Building and construction: under
Baker, 55–56; under Darley, 168–
71; under Farrand, 79; under
Newton, 185, 188; 1975–1976, 258;
under Norlin, 83, 88–91, 108–11,
116; under Smiley, 218–22; starting
construction of University, 27–

28; under Stearns, 117, 143–44;
under Thieme, 246–47
Bundy, Kenneth, 178, 181
Bundy, McGeorge, 173
Busemann, Lloyd, 223
Business Administration, School
of, 94

Campus life: under Baker, 71,
73–75; in Depression era, 99;
1960s–1970s, 233
Carlson, Harry, 99, 148, 211,
231, 238
Carr, Ralph, 109
Carrigan, James, 259
Carroll, John H., 185, 202
Cass, Lewis, 16
Castleman, Frank R., 74
Censorship, threat of (1944), 125.
See also Academic freedom
Chapman, Roy, 126
Chemistry and Physics, Department
of, 120, 172
Civil rights movement, 194,
226–27
Civil War (1861–1865), 17
Class boycotts, 1930s, 101
Cobb, John, 223
Cobin, Martin, 235
Cockerell, Theodore D. A., 76, 101
Cohen, Joseph, 126–28
Cold War, 117, 225; McCarthyism
following, 148–65
Cole, Lawrence, 114, 115, 125
Collective bargaining, 241, 252–53,
260–61
Colorado Federation of Teachers,
162
Colorado General Hospital, 109,
134, 135, 139, 189–90, 216;
constructed, 90–92
Colorado Psychopathic Hospital,
139, 188
Colorado Springs Center, 247–48
Colorado, University of: evaluated
(1964; 1969), 222; future of,
261–62; legislation establishing,

16–17, 20–21; opening of
(1877), 32
Community college issue, 212–15
Condon, Edward, 223
Conger, John, 211, 216, 235, 236
Construction. See Building and
construction
Convocations Committee, 124–26
Coordinating Committee on
National Defense, 120
Coors, Joseph, 211, 216, 230, 238
Copland, Aaron, 164
Corbridge, James, 232, 237
Cornell, Ezra, 5
Corning, George, 26
Correll, Malcolm, 193
Counseling (and guidance) under
Norlin, 101, 102
Courses. See Curriculum
Cowee, John, 261
Cristol, Stanley, 146, 220, 235
Crockett, Earl, 121, 140–41
Crosman, Ralph, 128
Crowder, Eddie, 245, 254
Crowe, Lawson, 236, 237
Curriculum: under Baker, 56–59,
61–64, 66–67; changes in
(19th century), 7; classical,
6, 36, 66; EOP, 240–41, 255;
high school, affected by
changes in university curriculum,
114; Honors program as part
of, 95–96; medieval, 5; under
Newton, 191–94; 1956, 183;
1963–1973, 205, 243–44; under
Norlin, 84, 95; post–World War
II Medical School, 134–35;
pragmatic character of (1870s),
30; under Sewall, 32, 36–38;
student concern over (1960s),
227, 234; women's college, 9;
in World War I, 81

Darley, Ward, 133–35, 138–39, 166,
168–82, 185–86, 188
Davis, Jefferson, 16
Davis, William E. (Bud), xi, 195

Dean, Paul, 153, 155
Debate teams, 1920s, 98
DeFries, John, 223
Denison, Mrs. Charles, 61
Dennett, Isaac C., 38
Dentistry, School of, 245, 250–51,
253, 254
Depression era (1930s), 98, 104–9
DeSouchet, William, 161
Dimick, L. C., 27
Discipline: under Baker, 73–74;
following student unrest
(1960s), 229; new code of
(1969), 232–34. See also
Dismissals; Expulsions;
Suspensions
Discipline Committee, 229
Discrimination. See Racism
Dismissals: Goodman, 156–58;
Hawkins, 152–53
Dittmer, Karl, 146
Doi, James I., 186
Dolloff, Levi, 29
Dominick, Peter, 202
Donner, Robert, 155
Dormitories: under Baker, 71–72;
under Darley, 169; under Hale,
50; new regulations for (1969),
232–34; under Sewall, 39–41;
under Stearns, 117, 143
Douglas, William O., 184
Douglass, Hail, 163
Dow, Justin E., 32, 38–39
Dressel, Paul, 242
Drumm, Henry A., 38
Dunbar, Duke, 140, 151
Dwire, George, 247
Dyde, W. F., 120, 123, 124, 127,
172, 186

Eaton, Benjamin H., 46
Eckhardt, C. C., 176
Education, College of, 58–59,
169, 173
Educational Opportunity
Programs (EOP), 240–41, 255

Ehrmann, Henry, 160
Eisenhower, Dwight D., 220
Elbert, Samuel H., 25
Electives under Sewall, 37
Ellsworth, Ralph, 108
Engineering, Department of
(later College of Engineering),
42, 43, 172
Enlistment in World War I, 79–80
Enrollment: under Baker, 61, 67;
College of Arts and Sciences
(1886), 38; College of Education
(1911), 59; dorms built to increase
(1884), 40–41; 1877, 32; 1887, 46;
1892, 47, 54; 1893–1900, 55, 62;
EOP, 240; 1930s, 106,
141; 1940s, 140, 142; 1951–1963,
158, 167–68, 185; 1960s–1970s,
206, 210, 217, 250; Extension
Division (1914), 60; Graduate
School (1919–39; 1956), 92–93,
172–73; under Hale, 51; Law
School (1902), 57; in Medical
Department (1883), 42; Medical
School (World War I; 1963), 90,
189; national (1870; 1970; 1972),
4, 250; under Norlin, 83;
Preparatory Department (1886,
1892; 1893), 37, 38, 54; under
Sewall, 39; in Summer School
(1904; 1920), 95; in World War
II, 117
Erskine, William, 237
Erwin, Virgil, 255
Ethnic Minorities Committee,
175–77
Expulsions, 1904, 72
Extension Division, 60, 184, 186,
212–13, 245, 248
Extracurricular activities:
appearance of, 9; decline of
(1960s–1970s), 233; in
Depression years, 99; under
Hale, 49; under Sewall, 48.
See also Debate teams; Football;
Fraternities; Sororities

Faculty: in assault against
racism, 181; in Baker years,
75–76; and collective bargaining,
241, 252–53, 260–61; contemplated
dismissal of Jewish and Catholic
(1927), 90; in Hale years, 48;
Hawkins affair and, 152, 153;
Japanese-American, 122; of
Medical Department (1885),
43; Medical School (1920s),
92–93; medieval, 5–6; in
Newton years, 194, 200–1, 203;
in Norlin years, 104; in
Sewall years, 38–40; in
Smiley years, 217, 223–24;
in Stearns years, 117; student
unrest (1960s) and, 229; under
Thieme, 252–53; in World War
I, 80; in World War II, 122.
See also Research; Salaries
Faculty Council: administrative
autonomy issue and, 260;
banning SDS from campus and,
231; Cambodian invasion and,
239; collective bargaining
and, 252–53; EOP and, 240;
formed, 224; Long Range Goals
study and, 243; new role for,
235
Faculty Group for Study of
Academic Freedom, 157, 158
Faculty for No Agent (FNA), 260
Faculty Personnel, Committee
on, 160
Farrand, Livingston, 52, 77–79
81, 85, 91
Federal funds, 84; for Medical
Center, 138; in 1950s, 167, 169,
170–71; 1960s–1970s, 206; under
Norlin, 108–10, 116; under
Smiley, 215; under Thieme, 246,
250, 251, 254–55
Fischer-Galati, Stephen, 223
Fisher, Valentine, 115–16
Fitzgerald, F. Scott, 97
Five, Committee of, 128, 129

Fleming, John D., 78
Flexner, Abraham, 61–62
Folsom, Fred G., 74
Folsom, Mrs. Fred G., 40
Football: in Depression years,
99–100; first intercollegiate
game of (1869), 9; under Hale,
49; importance of (1920s), 97;
under Newton, 194–95; 1960s–
1970s, 233, 245–46
Fowlie, Wallace, 193
Franklin, Benjamin, 7
Franklin, Walter, 149
Fraternal Education Council, 181
Fraternities: under Baker, 75;
decline of (1960s–1970s), 233;
in Depression years, 99–100;
discrimination in, 177–81, 195;
under Newton, 193; in World
War I, 81
Free tuition: attempts to increase
enrollment with, 46; under
Sewall, 39
Free Speech Movement, 277
Freedom of speech. *See* Academic
freedom
Fuller, Buckminster, 233
Fulton, Henry, 58, 71
Funds. *See* Federal funds;
Private grants; State funds;
Tuition

Gamow, George, 193
Garfield, James, 49
Garnsey, Morris, 126–28, 161,
163, 224
General Surgery, Department of,
136
Gilbert, Robert, 211, 230
Gilliam, Tom, 181
Gilman, Daniel, 13
Gilpin, William, 17
Glaser, Robert J., 188
Goldwater, Barry M., 198–201
Goodman, Irving, 146, 155–58,
162–63

Goodykoontz, Colin B., 104
Grading: abolition of, favored,
49; by letters (1934), 96
Graduate School, 52, 57-58;
changes in (1963-1973), 243-44;
enrollment in (1919-1939; 1956),
92-93, 172-73; under Newton,
203; under Norlin, 93-94; in
Stearns years, 144-46
Graduate Student Federation, 254
Graduating classes: 1882, 38; 1891,
51; 1928, 97; 1938, 158
Graduation requirements, 1963-
1973, 243, 244
Graham, Thomas W., 21, 22
Grandelius, Everett (Sonny),
194-95
Grant, Ulysses S., 29, 57
Grants. See Private grants
Grievance Committee, 161
Gross National Product (GNP),
percentage of, spent on higher
education (1960-1972), 256
Guevara, Che, 226
Gustavson, Reuben G., 123-27,
130-31

Haak, Harold, 255
Hafer, Harold, 152, 156, 159,
162, 164
Hale, Horace Morrison, 37,
45-51, 59, 67, 74
Hallett, Moses, 57, 70, 74, 76
Hanus, Paul H., 38, 40
Harper, William Rainey, 5
Harvard, John, 4
Harvard-CU Corporation, 147-48,
173
Hasson, Lt. W. F. C., 43
Haurwitz, Bernard, 193
Hawkins, David, 149-55, 162
Hayakawa (president of San
Francisco State University), 231
Heim, Harold, 211
Hellems, Fred B. R., 70
Hewett, A. W. (Woody), 151, 154

Higher education: evolution of,
3-13; future of, 256-58
Higher Education, Commission
on (Colo.), 207-8, 216, 221, 247,
258
Higher Education, Department of,
208
Hill, Leo, 187
Hilliard, Benjamin C., 124
Himstead, Ralph, 162
Hingman, Howard, 233
Hitler, Adolf, 85
Holloway, John, 215
Holly, Charles F., 17
Honors program, 95-96
Hoover, J. Edgar, 150
Hornig, Donald, 220
Houston, Clifford G., 176, 187
Hoyt, Palmer, 184
Human Growth, Department of,
135
Humphreys, Albert E., 189
Hutchinson, Dudley, 152, 156,
159, 162, 164

Independent Student Association
(ISA), 180, 181
Interdisciplinary programs under
Newton, 191-93
Inter-Fraternity Council, 81
Investment scandal, 114-15, 119-20

Jackson, Andrew, 8
James, Gladden William, 174-75
Jefferson, Thomas, 4-5
Jensen, Frode, 136
Jessor, Richard, 240
Job market, shrinking (1969-
1970s), 241, 256-57
Johnson, Byron, 238
Johnson, Edwin C., 170
Johnson, Lyndon B., 220, 226
Jones, Howard Mumford, 151
Jost, François, 193
Journalism, School of, 245
Judd, Morris, 158-63

Kauvar, Solomon, 135
Keen, Joe, 236, 237, 249
Kelling, Harold D., 193
Kempner, Aubrey, 153
Kennedy, John F., 226
Kennedy, Robert F., 227
Ketchum, Milo, 58
Kiendl, Arthur H., Jr., 187,
    195–96
Kimble, Gregory, 223
King, Edward C., 144, 149, 176, 193
King, Martin Luther, Jr., 227, 229
Klauder, Charles, 88–89, 219
Knous, Lee, 139
Kozloff, Lloyd, 221, 223

Lacher, John, 145, 146
Law School, 57
Legislative Committee for
    Education Beyond the High
    School, 207, 213
Legislation establishing
    University of Colorado,
    16–17, 20–21
Lester, Oliver C., 76, 93, 106
Lewis, Fulton, Jr., 155
Lewis, Robert, 188
Liberal Arts, College of, 54.
    See also Arts and Sciences,
    College of
Liberalism, attacked, 196–202
Library: in Depression years,
    107–8; new (1939), 109
Lincoln, Abraham, 16
Lipetz, Milton, 255
Lipstreu, Otis, 223
Little, John, 212, 236
Livingston, John, 164
Loeffler, John, 223–24
Long, Huey, 119
Longwell, Bernard, 153
Lory, Charles, 110–11
Love, John, 207, 210, 214, 230,
    238, 249
Loyalty oath (oath of
    allegiance), 151–52, 156, 158,
    163, 225

Lymberopoulos, John, 255
Lynch, Daniel, 211, 216, 230, 238

McBride, Conrad, 229–30, 232
McCarthy, Joe, 162
McCarthy era, 117, 148–65
McCook, Edward, 21
McDowell, William F., 61
McGiffert, Michael, xi
McGuire, Carl, 149
Machle, Edward, 159
MacIntyre, 220
McKinlay, Donald, 207
Macky, Andrew J., 56
McLane, Keith, 250
Malick, Clay, 126–28, 153, 154
Manlove, Francis, 188
Mann, Floyd, 255
Manning, Thurston, 211, 216–17,
    220, 221, 235–37
Mao Tse-tung, 226
Marcuse, Herbert, 226
Marr, John W., 174
Marxist Study Group, 154
Mason, Ellsworth, 255
Maxwell, James P., 22, 24–25
Meador, Charles N., 102
Mechanical Engineering,
    Department of, 58, 120
Medical Center, 135–38, 165, 190,
    212; expansion of (1953–1963),
    188–89; failure of, 262; 1974–
    1976, 261; under Smiley, 216, 218,
    222; under Thieme, 251, 254
Medical Department, 41–46, 54
Medical School: under Baker,
    60–61; controversy involving,
    129–33; under Darley, 172; in
    Depression years, 107–9; enroll-
    ment in World War I; 1963),
    90, 189; under Norlin, 79, 84,
    90–92, 110–11, 116; post–World
    War II, 133–40, 155; under
    Smiley, 217, 218; ten-year plan
    to expand, 188; under Thieme
    254; in World War II, 121
Meek, John, 146

Mencken, H. L., 97
Menzel, Donald, 148, 173
Merrick, Allen E., 101
Metzger, John W., 139
Miernyk, William H., 193
Military training in World
    War II, 123
Milliken, Eugene, 164
Minority group students:
    EOP for, 240–41, 255. *See also*
    Racism
Mitcham, Carl, 200, 201
Molecular and Cellular Biology,
    Department of, 221
Moon, Thomas, 238
Moore, Harry T., 193
Morley, Clarence J., 106
Morrill, Justin, 11
Moses, Raphael, 212, 238
Music Department (Conservatory
    of Music), 41, 42, 48

Nader, Ralph, 233
National Collegiate Athletic
    Association, 195
Nelson, J. Russell, 237, 261
Newcomb, 9
Newton, Quigg, ix, 166, 168, 184–
    203, 211, 212, 236
Nichols, Capt. David M., 25
Nixon, Richard M., 250
Norlin, George, 76, 77, 79–116, 125
Normal Department, 37–38, 42, 49
North Central Association of
    Colleges and Secondary Schools,
    240–41, 248, 249
Novak, Leo, 161
Nursing, School of, 188, 244,
    254, 261
Nuzum, Duane, 255

Oakes, Bernard (Bunny), 99
Old-age pension issue, 111–14
Oles, Mrs. George, 57
Oncology, Division of, 136
Openshaw, Karl, 255
Oppenheimer, J. Robert, 150

Pacifism: in 1930s, 100–1; in
    World War II, 121
Palmer, C. S., 38
Panhellenic Council, 181
Park, Joseph, 146
Parker, Norman, 127
Parrish, Pauline, 187
Perkins, Merritt, 126
Peters, Max, 220
Petersen, Elmore, 128, 162
Peterson, Courtland, 224, 255
Pharmacy, School of, 42, 60
Philosophy and Pedagogy,
    Department of, 58, 159–60
Pickett, Esther C., 196–97
Porter, Keith, 223
Preparatory Department, 37–38,
    42, 49, 53–54, 59–60
Prescott, David, 220, 223
Private grants, 57, 70; for
    affiliation with Harvard, 148;
    to build Medical School hospital,
    91; from Mrs. Denison, 61; in
    Depression years, 106; from
    National Cancer Institute, 137;
    from National Foundation for
    Infantile Paralysis, 136; from
    National Institutes of Health,
    221–22; from National Science
    Foundation, 220–21; 1973 and
    1974, 255; research, 146, 174;
    from Rockefeller Foundation,
    79, 91, 94, 108, 110; from
    Rothberger, 247; in Smiley years,
    215; for ten-year plan, 188–89;
    from W. I. Kellogg Foundation,
    136
Privilege and Tenure Committee,
    130, 153–55, 160–62
Proctoring under Norlin, 102
Psychiatry, Department of, 136
Psychology, Department of, 107,
    169
Psychosomatic Medicine,
    Department of, 136
Public Administration Service,
    183–85, 188

Public Affairs, School of, 245, 246
Puck, Theodore, 137

Quigg, Mayor J., 135
Quigley, James E., 188

Racism: assault on, 175–81, 195–96;
civil rights movement and, 194,
226–27; students' protests and
(1960s), 228
Raeder, Warren, 127
Ramaley, Francis, 76, 173
Rautenstraus, Roland, 236, 237,
255, 259
Rees, Maurice H., 92, 107, 108,
129–31
Regents, Board of, 139, 174; academic freedom and, 125–29; affiliation with Harvard and, 147;
and autonomy of university
(1970s), 209; Baker administration
and, 53, 58–60, 69–72, 76, 77; collective bargaining and, 260;
created, 29; Darley administration
and, 171, 182; EOP and, 240;
Faculty Council and, 224–25; Hale
administration and, 46, 50, 51; in
McCarthy era, 152–64; new code
of discipline and, 232; Newton
administration and, 184–86, 196–
98, 200–3; 1960s–1970s changes
and, 233–34; Norlin administration and, 85, 88–89, 100, 101, 112,
114–15; political makeup of (1974–
1976), 259; racial discrimination
and, 176–81, 195–96; and religious
fundamentalism issue, 175; and
Sewall administration, 32–34, 37,
39–45; School of Medicine-Medical
Society controversy and, 131–32;
under Smiley, 211, 213, 216, 221,
223; Stearns administration and,
119, 142; student participation
and, 235; student unrest and
(1968), 230–31; and Thieme administration, 236–38, 247–49; in

World War I, 81, 82; in World
War II, 122, 123
Reid, John, 211, 236
Rense, William, 146
Research, 64; under Darley, 172–
74; in German universities, 7;
medical, 137–38; under Newton,
189, 192–93; under Norlin, 101;
under Smiley, 215; in Stearns
years, 144–48, 173
Reserve Officer Training Corps
(ROTC), 238–39; under Thieme,
253, 254; in World War I, 80, 82;
in World War II, 120
Rippon, Mary, 36, 38, 39, 70
Roberts, Walter Orr, 148, 173, 192
Rockefeller, John D., 5
Roosevelt, Franklin D., 125
Rothberger, Ira, 247
Routt, John L., 27
Runner, Meredith N., 193
Russell, James E., 66

Sabin, Florence, 135, 189
Salaries: under Baker, 75, 76; free-
dom of speech and denied in-
creases in (1940s), 126–28; under
Hale, 47–48; Medical School, 130–
32; under Newton, 191; under
Norlin, 102–4; paid by research
grants, 146; received by Baker, 53;
School of Medicine (post–World
War II), 138; under Sewall, 38–
39; under Smiley, 217–18, 251–52
Sasaki, Hideo, 219
Saunders, Don, 236
Schiotz, Aksel, 193
Schmidt, Eric, 238
Schmidt, Hugo, 223
Scientific Operations, Committee on,
173
Sears, Don, 236
Sewall, Joseph, 29, 31, 32–46, 48–49,
51
Shapley, Harlow, 147, 173
Sheridan, Gen. Philip, 71
Shorey, Paul, 85

Shoup, Oliver, 91, 103
Silverman, Lawrence, 237, 242, 248
Simmons, Ozzie G., 193, 220
Slater, Charles, 223
Sloane, William, 150, 155
Smiley, Joseph R., 209–36
Smith, Katherine, 212
Smith, Marinus, 23
Snyder, Zachariah X., 65
Social unrest, 1960s, 226–29, 238–39, 258
Sommers, Mrs. William, 148
Sororities: decline of (1960s–1970s), 233; in Depression years, 99–100; discrimination in, 177–81
Sowers, Don C., 112
Spanish Civil War (1936–1939), 101
Sports. See Athletics; Football
Spurlock, Benjamin, 161
Stapleton, Benjamin F., 184
State elections, 1962, 201–2
State funds, 43–44, 46; early 1900s, 71; in 1870s, 21, 22, 24–28, 31, 33–35; in 1890s, 67–69; in 1911, 57; in 1917, 65; 1950s, 167, 170–72; 1960s–1970s, 207–9, 213–18, 258; for Colorado General Hospital, 139–40; under Farrand, 79; under Hale, 50; legislation establishing (1877), 30–31; under Newton, 189; under Norlin, 84, 86, 90, 91, 103–6, 108–12, 116; under Stearns, 138, 140–42; under Thieme, 246, 250–51
State universities, evolution of, 10–13
Stearns, Robert L., 115, 117–29, 140–65, 174, 176–77
Stern, Mort, 255
Stewart, Omer, 176
Storke, Frederick, 153
Strikes: labor, 78; 1910, 73; 1971, 239; peace (1936), 100–1
Student Affairs, Committee on, 199, 232
Student Army Training Corps (SATC), 80

Student housing: under Sewall, 39–40; in Stearns years, 142–43. See also Dormitories
Student Mobilization Committee (SMC), 239
Student Organization Membership, Committee on, 180
Student Organization and Social Life, Committee on (SOSL), 176, 177, 179, 180–81
Student participation: 1969–1970, 234–35; under Sewall, 49
Student unrest: in 1904, 72; in 1930s, 101; in 1960s, 225–31, 238–41; in 1970s, 251–52, 257–58
Students: in assault against racism, 175–81; Communist (1946–1950), 156; in Depression years, 98–100; under Hale, 50; Hawkins affair and, 153; medieval, 6; minority group, 240–41, 255 (see also Racism); under Newton, 203–4; in 1920s, characterized, 97–98; under Sewall, 39–40, 49; in World War I, 79–80; in World War II, 121–23
Students for a Democratic Society (SDS), 227–28, 230–31, 252
Summer School, 59, 94–95
Suspensions following student unrest (1960s), 229–30
Sweeting, Orville, 146
Swisher, Earl, 176

Technology, School of (Applied Science, School of), 58
Thieme, Frederick P., 236–54
Thomas, Trevor P., 124
Thornton, Dan, 153, 163, 164, 171
Tippo, Oswald, 187
Toth, Andor, 193
Trustees, Board of, 21–29. See also Regents, Board of
Tuition: increasing (1930s; 1956), 106–7, 171; Medical School (post–World War II), 138–39; under Smiley, 217; under Stearns, 141,

142; under Thieme, 246. *See also* Free tuition

Ulam, Stanislaw, 223

Van Ek, Jacob, 94–96, 102, 104, 120–21; academic freedom and, 128, 129; admissions policy and, 113, 114; in McCarthy era, 156–58, 164
Van Rensselaer, Stephen, 7
Vassar, Matthew, 9
Vietnam War, 226–29, 238–39, 258

Wahlstrom, Ernest, 211, 236
Walker, Edwin, 126, 127, 128
Walne, Florence, 122
Walseth, Russell (Sox), 246
Ward, Harry, 255
Walz, Frank, 146
Washington, George, 3
Wayland, Francis, 7
Webster, Daniel, 10
Wells, John H., 21
Western Interstate Commission of Higher Education, 138
Whicher, George F., 126
White, Andrew, 5

White, Byron (Whizzer), 100
White, Gilbert, 223
Whitehead, W. R., 42, 43
Whiteley, Richard H., 38
Whitham, Myron, 97
Widner, Amos, 21, 22
Wilcox, Robert, 255
Wilhite, E. S., 16
Willard, James F., 76
Willis, Donald F., 193
Wilson, Eugene H., 193; as Dean of Faculties, 186–87; in McCarthy era, 153, 162; as Vice President, 211, 236, 237
Wilson, Irwin, 223
Wolcott, Frank H., 114, 119, 120
Wolvington, Earl A., 197–98
Worcester, Philip G., 129, 145
World War I (1914–1918), 79–81
World War II (1939–1945), 117, 120–22
Wyatt, Morton, 163–64

Youth Committee against the War, 121
Young Communist League, 149
Young People's Socialist League, 199
Young Republicans, 198